A Collector's Guide to

Spoons
Around the World

A Collector's Guide to Spoons Around the World

by
Dorothy T. Rainwater
and
Donna H. Felger

PHOTOGRAPHS BY H IVAN RAINWATER

Everybodys Press, Inc.
and
Thomas Nelson Inc., Publishers

Library of Congress Catalog Card Number: 76-46719
ISBN 0-8407-4328-9

Prepared and Produced by Everybodys Press, Inc.
Printed in the United States of America
Design by Frank Smith

This Edition Prepared for Distribution by
THOMAS NELSON INC., PUBLISHERS

CONTENTS

INTRODUCTION A note about the marks vii
ACKNOWLEDGMENTS viii
PICTURE CREDITS x
I.   HISTORY OF THE SPOON 1
II.   SAINTS AND SINNERS 27
III. SPECIAL TYPES OF SPOONS 67
        Caddy spoons 67
        Bonbon spoons 83
        Monkey spoons 86
        Salt spoons 91
        Snuff spoons 91
        Mustache spoons 93
        Pap or caudle spoons 95
        Infant feeding spoons 95
        Medicine spoons 98
IV.   THE OLD WORLD 102
        Europe 102
        Asia 258
        Africa 270
V.   THE NEW WORLD 301
        North America 301
        South America 341
VI.   PEOPLE OF THE WORLD 350
VII. THE PACIFIC WORLD 364
VIII. PAGES FROM CATALOGS 385
BIBLIOGRAPHY 396
INDEX 401

INTRODUCTION

Many volumes have aleady been written about spoons. So, why one more? The writers have been contacted by collectors and dealers who have all expressed the need for a book dealing with spoons that are collectible today. With but few exceptions, the spoons in this volume fall into that category. Only a few are "museum specimens." Even those, in most cases, were once discovered by enthusiastic collectors who sought them out in shops all over the world. Kaahumanu's silver spoons, now in Bernice P. Bishop Museum, Honolulu, were discovered only a few years ago by a Maui doctor during a visit to New York. His knowledge of Hawaiian history enabled him to recognize their significance. Two Victorian spoons, once the gift of Queen Victoria herself, were purchased at a Parke-Bernet auction only a year ago. Other treasures are waiting to be found by knowledgeable collectors.

A Note About the Marks

Determination of the country of origin and dating of spoons would have been made easier for the collector had all countries adopted a marking system as logical and as rigidly enforced as the British. Unfotunately, none have.

There are many spoons that bear confusing marks. Rampant lions, for instance, abound in several countries, and a vast menagerie of other animals confront those who seek to identify marks. Sometimes, because of space limitations, marks are poorly stamped, or none at all are used. To add to the confusion, there are quantities of spoons of nineteenth century manufacture whose marks were made deliberately confusing. Bernard Muller, as well as other makers in Germany and the Netherlands who specialized in the reproduction of antique pieces, were allowed by law to punch articles with period hallmarks, provided that (a) the articles were sold for export and (b) in addition to the marks used for one town they struck additional marks which would not normally be found in combination, thus the article would not be passed off as a genuine period piece. These articles may or may not also bear English import marks and the initials "BM", "JC&S", "LS" or others. Muller used many other combinations of initials apart from his own.

Designs and ideas flowed freely from one country to another so it is often impossible now to determine just where a particular idea began. Among the nineteenth century Apostle spoons, for instance, there are several sets of spoons with figures modeled "in the round," which are so nearly identical that they appear to have come from the same molds. (See Saints & Sinners) They bear the following marks: Francis Higgins, London, 1850-51; H.H., London, 1874-75; R.S., London, 1887-88; Whiting Mfg. Co. and Gorham Mfg. Co. trademarks, 1887 and later: and the Moscow city mark used from 1891-96. Related to these, but with figures more flattened rather than being completely "in the round," are Apostle figures bearing the following: nineteenth century Nürnburg hallmarks; R. K. & Sons, Inc.; Joseph Mayer & Sons, 1897; and a very large set with German marks accompanied by English import marks for Sheffield, dated 1899. These figures are all so similar that one can only conclude that they were modeled after the same set of statues, or that the designers in the various companies copied one another. The figures are large, making comparisons relatively easy. Similar comparisons could be made between Continental sets.

Most of the American spoons made primarily for the collector bear a trademark or a tradename which can be traced.

Many spoons of Continental origin bear no marks at all; some have only numerals indicating the quality of the metal. Sometimes the country of origin may be determined by the spelling of place names or of persons being commemorated. For example, a large set of Apostle spoons bears no marks at all, but the spelling of Ss. Andreas, Jakobus, Johannes, etc., reveals their German origin.

Other spoons bear cryptic symbols and not one word to aid in the identification of the person, place or thing being commemorated. Even the country of origin may sometimes not be determined with certainty. Many thousands of miles have been traveled and many more thousands of pages in hundreds of books have been turned in an effort to identify these. This pursuit has focused attention on aspects of history previously ignored. Aside from being a painless way to learn history, the writers have found the contacts made with others all over the world to be most rewarding of all.

ACKNOWLEDGMENTS

The title of this volume could very properly be "Friends Around the World" because without the help of friends—old and new—it would not have been possible. Far too many of them must remain nameless and are recorded only in the memory of their cheerful and smiling assistance as they somehow fathomed the meaning of our faltering Italian or scrambled German when we were trying to find our way through the halls of unfamiliar museums.

The response of collectors and friends who lent their spoons to be photographed has been overwhelming. No mere word of thanks can express our appreciation to the airline captain who, between flights, brought along and opened up a tremendous bag of spoons and patiently helped with the photography. Nor are mere words sufficient to express the gratitude to those collectors all across the country who have opened their homes and their collections to us for study.

Special acknowledgment is made to Beulah D. Hodgson, Editor of the Magazine *Silver*, for her assistance and encouragement and for permission to reprint certain materials from that publication.

We feel a special attachment to and gratitude for the personal attention given to our work by R. Champlin Sheridan, Jr., President of Everybodys Press and to A. Christian Revi, Editor of *Spinning Wheel* Magazine and to Richard M. Robey.

We wish to express our gratitude to the individuals and institutions mentioned below for their generosity in loaning spoons to be photographed, for photographs, for information and other assistance.

Anne Ainot, Massachusetts
Albany Institute
  Mrs. Elizabeth Dennis
Mr. and Mrs. Carl R. Almgren, California
Walter Angst, Maryland
Arab Information Center, Washington, D.C.
  Nawal Qawar
Belgian Embassy, Washington, D.C.
  Ernest Staes
Talbot Bielefeldt, Maryland
Bowie Library, Maryland
  Bohdan Kohutiak
British Embassy, Washington, D.C.
British Information Services, New York
Buck Lodge Junior High School Library, Maryland
  Mrs. Emily Beall
Museo de Capodimonte, Naples, Italy
  Prof. Raffaele Causa
Chicago Historical Society

Art Institute of Chicago
  Vivian J. Scheidemantel
Frank Cooper, Maryland
Danish Embassy, Washington, D.C.
  Knud Damgaard
Danmarks Guldsmedeforening, Copenhagen,
  Denmark
Mrs. Frank DeVos, Washington
Cmdr. Frederick F. Duggan, Jr., Maryland
Rosemary Elmo, Maryland
Kimberly B. Felger, Maryland
Embassy of Finland, Washington, D.C.
  Per-Erik Lönnfors
Mrs. Olin M. Fisk, Massachusetts
Ambassade de France, New York
  Mrs. Monique Polgar
Prof. Alfonso de Franciscis, Naples, Italy
The Franklin Mint
German Embassy, Washington, D.C.
  Marie-Louise Roessler
Gorham Company, Rhode Island
  Brendon J. Murphy
Royal Greek Embassy
Mrs. J. A. Greeley, Connecticut
Ray Greenfield, Hawaii
Mrs. Pearl Gunnerson, Florida
Peggy Gunnerson, Florida
Mr. and Mrs. Zera Hair, Delaware
Mrs. Niels S. Hoegsberg, California
Mrs. Charles T. Hughes, New York
International Silver Company
  E. P. Hogan, Historical Library
  Richard Croteau, Photographer
Embassy of Japan, Washington, D.C.
Leonard Jones, Ltd., Circencester, Glos.,
  England
  David Wilkins
Michael P. Kieltyka, Washington
Mrs. Karl Laden, Maryland
Mrs. Frank J. Lewis, Michigan
Mrs. J Guy Lewis, Michigan
Lunt Silversmiths, Massachusetts
Lt. Col. (Ret.) and Mrs. David Marshall,
  Maryland
Karl Miller, Maryland
Mrs. J. C. Mitchell, Florida

Multnomah County Library, Oregon
Royal Netherlands Embassy, Washington, D.C.
  J. B. Braaksma
University of the State of New York
  William M. Pillsbury
  John S. Still
New Zealand Embassy, Washington, D.C.
Richard L. Nix, Texas
Norsk Folkemuseum, Oslo, Norway
  Jorunn Fossberg
Royal Norwegian Embassy, Washington, D.C.
  Harold Svanøe Midttun
Reed & Barton Silversmiths, Massachusetts
  Roger Hallowell, President
Schweiz. Landesmuseum, Zurich, Switzerland
  Alain Ch. Gruber
Mrs. O'Darien Schaefer, North Carolina
Edwin Selkregg, Pennsylvania
The Magazine *Silver*
  Beulah D. Hodgson, Editor
Smithsonian Institution Museum of History
  and Technology
  V. Clain-Stefanelli
Mrs. Margaret F. Stark, California
Mrs. R. P. Sullivan, California
Mrs. Aubrey Swanson
Royal Swedish Embassy, Washington, D.C.
  Birgitta Moberg
E. J. Towle Company, Washington
  Paul W. Happold
Cathy Tozzi, New York
Mrs. F. Gregory Troyer, Hawaii
Turkish Embassy, Washington, D.C.
  Tuluy Tanc
Victoria & Albert Museum, London, England
  Michael Snowden
Barbara Vitale, New York
National Library of Wales, Aberystwyth, Wales
  Gwyneth Lewis
Mrs. Douglas Warner, Maryland
Mrs. J. H. Willett, Maryland
Edward G. Wilson, Antiques, Pennsylvania
  Herbert Wilson
Winchester College, Winchester, England
  J. M. G. Blakiston
  Peter J. Gwyn

PICTURE CREDITS

The photographs for this book were taken by H Ivan Rainwater with the exceptions noted below.

I HISTORY OF THE SPOON

1-3 Meyer's *Handbook of Ornament.*
4-7 National Museum of Antiquities, Edinburgh, Scotland.
8 Drawing
9-10 Leonard Jones, Ltd., Circencester, Glos., England.
16-18 Drawings
23-24 Drawings
25-30 Leonard Jones, Ltd., Circencester, Glos, England.
37 Drawing
43 Leonard Jones, Ltd., Circencester, Glos., England.
47-55 Leonard Jones, Ltd., Circencester, Glos., England.
56-57 Carl R. Almgren, California.
81 By permission of the Magazine *Antiques* (May 1970); photographs by H Ivan Rainwater.
82 By permission of the Magazine *Antiques* (February 1971); photograph by Raymond Sato, Honolulu Academy of Arts.
99 Carl R. Almgren, California.
116 Carl R. Almgren, California.

II SAINTS AND SINNERS

143 (a to m) Art Institute of Chicago.
282-284 Mrs. Niels S. Hoegsberg, California.
296 *The Art Journal Illustrated Catalogue of the Industry of All Nations.*
300 Gorham Company catalog, 1888.
301 (a to m) The Gorham Company.
315 (a to l) Joseph Mayer & Bros., catalog, 1915(?). Courtesy Beulah D. Hodgson.
316 (a to l) E. J. Towle Company.
320-321 Carl R. Almgren, California.
322 (a to m) The Franklin Mint

III SPECIAL TYPES OF SPOONS

356-357 Leonard Jones, Ltd., Circencester, Glos., England.
523a Washington Post.

523b Reed & Barton Silversmiths.
528-529 Reed & Barton Silversmiths.
533a C. Rogers & Bros., catalog 1885. Courtesy E. P. Hogan, International Silver Company.
534-537 United States Patent Office.

IV THE OLD WORLD

566 Mrs. Niels S. Hoegsberg, California.
594 Norsk, New York.
622-628 Mrs. Niels S. Hoegsberg, California.
1249-1250 Carl R. Almgren, California.
1316-1319 Carl B. Felger, Maryland.
1332 Carl B. Felger, Maryland.
1344 Carl B. Felger, Maryland.
1477 *Harper's Monthly,* June-November 1883.
1489 Drawings by Beulah D. Hodgson.

V THE NEW WORLD

1582 Edwin Selkregg, Pennsylvania.
1602 Carl B. Felger, Maryland
1614 Shreve, Crump & Low, Boston.
1623-1625 Edwin Selkregg, Pennsylvania.
1649-1670 Richard Nix; photographer, Wade H. Knight, Texas.
1744-1745 Carl R. Almgren, California.
1749-1750 Carl R. Almgren, California.

VI PEOPLE OF THE WORLD

1783 Mrs. Niels S. Hoegsberg; Henderson Photographers, Oakland, California.
1788 Mrs. Niels S. Hoegsberg, California.
1794 Lunt Silversmiths
1820 Mrs. Niels S. Hoegsberg, California.

VII THE PACIFIC WORLD

1867-1872 Carl R. Almgren, California.
1884 Carl R. Almgren, California.

VIII PAGES FROM OLD CATALOGS

1910-1913 International Silver Company, photographer, Richard Croteau.
1914-1920 E. J. Towle Company, Seattle, Washington.
1921 Chicago Historical Society.

1

2

I
History of the Spoon

Among the earliest inventions of man, the first spoons may have been shells picked up along the beach or chips of wood from the forest floor.

Prehistoric peoples concentrated along the borders of the seas and other bodies of water. These shores provided shells which served as natural spoons.

The Greek word for spoon was *kochliarion* (χοχλίαϱιον), and the Latin was *cochlear*, both having been derived from *cochlea* (χοχλίας) meaning a snail-

---

1 **Egyptian,** Lotus blossom motif.
2 **Egyptian,** Papyrus motif.
3 **Egyptian,** antique bronze patera with lip.
4 **Roman** spoon from Traprain Law. Rho Chi symbol in the bowl. The back of the bowl is modeled after a scallop shell. 8¼" (210 mm.)
5 & 6 **Roman** spoons from Traprain Law as they appeared on excavation.

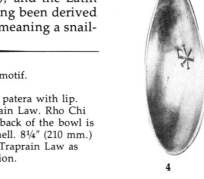

4

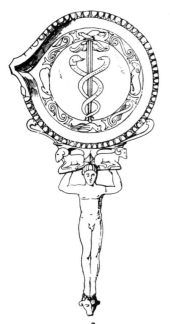

3

5

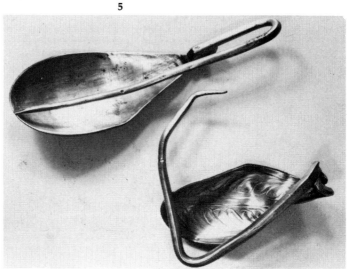

6

shell of spiral shape, suggesting that a shell was the common spoon of Southern Europe. The French *cuillère* (spoon) is a survival.

The Anglo-Saxon *spon*, meaning a chip or splinter of wood, is the source of our English word "spoon." However, *cochlear* was retained in medieval wills and inventories.

It is useless to speculate now on which material provided the first spoons. Neither wood nor shell survive for long periods of time in exposed situations so it is of other materials that the earliest specimens are now known. Silver and

10

7 **Dolphin** spoon from Traprain Law. 5″ (127 mm.)

8 **Spoon From Sutton Hoo.** Two silver spoons were found, inscribed with the names Paul and Saul. 10″ (254 mm.) Now in the British Museum.

9 **Corinium Spoon Reproduction.** Corinium, the Roman town, is the modern Cirencester and was in Roman times the second largest town in Britain. Such spoons were used for the opening and eating of shell-fish, for piercing eggshells so that evil spirits could not use them as boats, and for the eating of snails. Similar spoons of bronze have been excavated from old Roman sites and may be seen in many English museums. Made by Francis Howard, Ltd., Sheffield, for Leonard Jones, Cirencester.

10 **Corinium Christening Spoon.** A replica of a Roman spoon used two thousand years ago as a christening gift. After the adoption of Christianity in 312 A.D., the Chi Rho symbol was engraved in the bowl to indicate that the child had been baptized. (Chi Rho are the first two letters of the Greek word "*Christos*" meaning "Christ." Made by Francis Howard, Ltd., Sheffield, for Leonard Jones, Cirencestor.

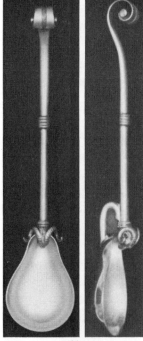

11

8

9

7

14

gold were used but spoons were also made of ivory, bronze, latten (a mixture of brass and tin), flint, bone, horn, pewter, copper, rock crystal, slate and iron.

Spoons of gold are mentioned in the Pentateuch (Exodus XXV, 29: Numbers VII, 84, 86) when Moses is commanded to make dishes and spoons of pure gold for the Tabernacle. The presentation of spoons as gifts is also rooted in ancient history as these twelve spoons of gold filled with incense were among the offerings of princes at the dedication of the altar of the Tabernacle (Numbers VII, 14–80). The maker of the spoons was Bezaleel (Exodus XXXI, 1–5) and while none of them have survived, we may assume that they were similar in appearance to those found in tombs of the pharaohs erected more than four thousand years ago.

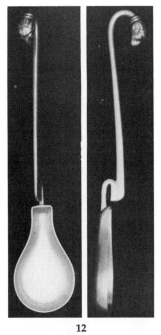

12

Egyptian spoons were generally made of wood, ivory, bronze, flint and slate. They were often richly decorated with symbols related to Egyptian religious beliefs (Fig. 1–3). In form, many resembled paterae, or covered vessels, the cover rotating around a pin.

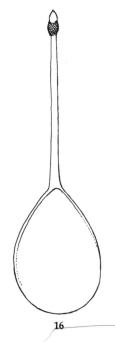

15

Greek, Roman and early Christian spoons were made mostly of bronze or silver, though Roman spoons of bone were fairly common; gold was used for ceremonial spoons. The stems of these spoons are usually pointed spikes which were used for opening shellfish and extracting the edible parts. Bowls are round, egg-shaped, fig-shaped, pointed ovals and other shapes but most have in common the "keel and disk" arrangement in which the union of the bowl and stem is offset with the bowl being lower than the handle.

In 1919 archaeologists unearthed a

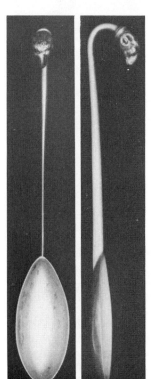

13

11-13 **Roman Reproduction Spoons.** No marks.
14 **Iranian Folding Spoon,** excavated at Amlash, Iran. 6th-8th century. No marks.
15 **Pottery Spoon,** excavated at El Chanel, Colima, Mexico. Circa 500-700 A.D.
16 **Acorn Knop,** London, early 15th century.

16

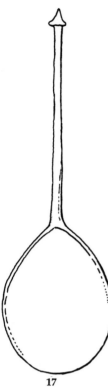

17

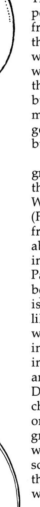

18

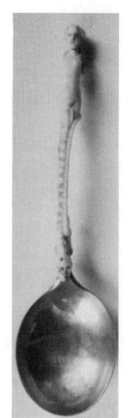

19

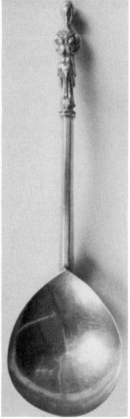

20

vast hoard of fourth century Roman silver and other relics on the hill of Dumpelder (or Dumpender), now popularly known as Traprain Law, in the county of East Lothian, Scotland. According to legend, this hill was the residence of King Loth, hero of Lothian. The discovery was the most extensive of its kind in the British Isles up to that time. The relics included silver, bronze, iron, pottery and coins indicating occupation from the latter Stone Age to sometime in the fifth century. Typical Roman spoons were found, and also a most unusual one with a dolphin handle (Fig. 4–7). Most of the silver was in deplorable condition; but in the 1920s reproductions were made by Brook & Son, manufacturing goldsmiths and silversmiths in Edinburgh.

Two silver spoons were found in the great Saxon ship burial at Sutton Hoo, on the north bank of the Deben River near Woodbridge, Suffolk, England, in 1939 (Fig. 8). They are of a well-known type from the eastern Mediterranean region about the sixth century A.D. They have inscribed on them in Greek the names Paul and Saul. Thought by some to have been for liturgical purposes, this theory is doubted by others who feel it is unlikely that his pre-apostolic name Saul would have been so used. (St. Paul, originally named Saul, repudiated the teachings of Jesus but after being struck blind and having a vision while on the road to Damascus, he accepted Christianity. He changed his name to Paul and became one of Jesus' disciples.) The crude engraving of the name Saul, in comparison with the carefully done, symmetrical inscription of Paul, leads to the theory that the engraver or copier was unfamiliar with the name and started to put his

---

17 **Diamond Point,** London early 15th century.
18 **Maidenhead,** London, 1578.
19 **Ivory Figure,** silver-gilt bowl. No marks. Italian (?), 18th century.
20 **Maidenhead,** silver-gilt. No marks.

4

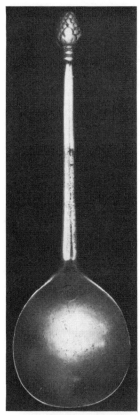

21

22

letters vertically before he realized his mistake and the first letter ⊓ , for P, has been incised ⊏ , making it an S. Other errors are evident in the engraving of the name Saul.

Because of the Roman occupation of Britain from 43 to 410 A.D., numerous Roman spoons have been found in many locations. The earliest English spoons were probably modeled after these. The old Roman spoons are models today for current reproductions (Fig. 9–13). After the fall of the Roman Empire and the withdrawal of Roman troops the uncultured people who then dominated nearly the whole of Europe for almost two centuries most likely used spoons of whatever material was most easily obtainable and could be shaped with the least expenditure of labor. The word "*spon*" or chip of wood, points to wood as the material used by our Teutonic ancestors. Horn and bone were also doubtless used during what is known as the Anglo-Saxon period. Few spoons of metals, or precious metals at least, from this period have been found. Those few cannot be considered ordinary domestic spoons.

Spoons have long been one of man's most portable possessions as shown by a folding one from the sixth to the eighth century, excavated at Amlash, Iran, a village in Gilan province situated in the high valleys east of the Sefid Rud (river) which empties into the Caspian Sea near Resht, north and west of the capital, Teheran (Fig. 14).

Pre-Columbian artifacts found in the New World include spoons made of wood, pottery, bone, horn, shell, ivory and stone. Some were elaborately decorated (See Northwest Coast Indian

---

21 **Strawberry Knop,** latten, 17th century. Mark in bowl illegible.
22 **Pine Cone Knop Reproduction.** Marked: STERLING 65
23 **Slip-End** spoon, France, circa 1400.
24 **Slip-End,** London, 1637.

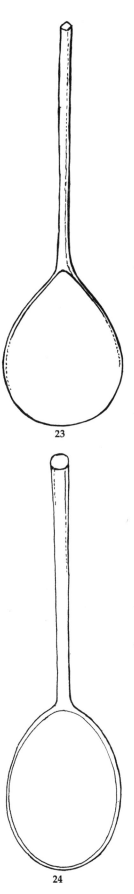

23

24

27

28

spoons) while others were simple in form and had no decoration (Fig. 15).

During the Middle Ages (fifth century to 1550) domestic spoons appear to have been made of wood or horn. Bone, ivory, serpentine, rock crystal and glass were used occasionally. The use of gold for spoons seems to have been confined to royalty; silver spoons were found only in the homes of the wealthy. Beginning in the fourteenth century, and possibly a little earlier, spoons of brass, pewter, and tinned iron were common. Few of these were marked so it is to the silver spoons that we must turn for the purpose of accurate dating of style changes.

The marking of silver and gold is of ancient origin, beginning at least as early as Roman and Byzantine times. Most countries of Europe have had some system of control since medieval times. While intended primarily as guarantees

25

29

25 **Pudsey Spoon Reproduction.** The original belonging to the Pudsey family of Bolton Hall, is now in the Myers Museum, Liverpool. One of the earliest seal top spoons, it has a five-petaled flower on the top. According to tradition it was given to Sir Ralph Pudsey by King Henry VI after the Battle of Hexham. The tradition is shattered by the fact that stamped in the bowl of the original spoon is the leopard *crowned* and on the back of the stem is the Lombardic letter "h", the London marks for the year 1525-26— fifty-four years after Henry VI was deposed in favor of Edward, the son of Richard Plantagenet, 3rd Duke of York, who became king as Edward IV in 1461.

26 **Owl Knop Reproduction.** The original set of six bearing the London hallmark of 1506 is now in Corpus Christi College, Oxford.

27 **Lion Séjant Reproduction.** The original is dated 1570.

28 **Writhen Knop Reproduction.** The original was made in London in 1500. Writhen knop spoons appear in the Inventory of the Merchant Taylors Company for 1487.

29 **Seal Top Reproduction** of a 16th century spoon.

30 **Pine Cone Knop Reproduction.** The original was made in London in 1538. 25 - 30. Maker: Francis Howard Ltd., Sheffield.

26

30

of quality, some systems have also provided additional information valuable to the collector. The best of these is the English system. From the year 1300 it has been compulsory in England to have an official mark impressed upon silverware before offering it for sale. Beginning with the year 1363 every master goldsmith (the terms goldsmith and silversmith are interchangeable in this usage) in England was required to have his own mark. City marks, standard marks, date letters, duty marks and others were added, all of which help the collector.

In the fourteenth century spoon handles were mainly hexagonal and the bowls were fig-shaped, but different styles of knops or ends of spoon handles developed. These were in the form of acorns and diamond points (Fig. 16, 17).

Maidenhead spoons appear to have come next (Fig. 18). On these, the knop is a head, bust, or in some instances, a half-figure. Thought to have received their name from representations of the Virgin, they were made from the latter part of the fourteenth century until the reign of Elizabeth I (1558) when they naturally fell into disfavor. An approximate date may be assigned to old specimens as the hair arrangements and headdresses conformed to current styles. Spoons have continued through the centuries to be decorated with

32

---

31 **Cherub-Head,** Denmark. A type common in the 17th century. This example was inscribed for presentation as a christening gift in 1774, and, presumably, any marks it may have borne were effaced. Translation of the inscriptions inside the bowl are "Anno 1774/ God [is] my Hope/Congratulations/Best of Everything/Happy/Satisfied/Greetings and Food." On the back of the bowl are inscriptions which in translation read: "Oh, if the World shall long exist, I some food will need, but how can I obtain it when I have no money"; and, "The Lord did help—He is helping me yet."

32 **Seal Top,** Maker: Isaac Callard, London, 1730-31.

33 **Seal Top,** Lincoln guildmark.

31

33

7

34

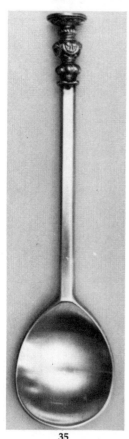

35

female figures, usually of a more secular nature (Fig. 19, 20).

The first known mention of English silver spoons occurred in a will of 1259. They were referred to only as a dozen silver spoons with no description. Later wills and inventories were more explicit. It was in a will of 1440 that we find the first mention of spoons whose knops represented "de fradelett," or spoons with fruitlet knops. Some of these fruitlet knops have been identified as bunches of grapes. Spoons of this type were made on the Continent where, in France, mulberries were often used; strawberries and blackberries were used in Germany. The stem and bowl remained unchanged from earlier spoons (Fig. 21–22).

"Slip-end" or "slipped-in-the-stalk" spoons were a simple type introduced in the fifteenth century and which lasted well into Restoration days (1660). These spoons have no knops but appear to have been simply sliced off at an angle. The stems are hexagonal and the bowls pear-shaped (Fig. 23, 24).

Writhen or twisted knop spoons appeared about 1487. The bulb-shaped knops were formed of several twisted strands of wire, thick in the middle and smaller at the ends. This style lasted for about twenty-five years and disappeared completely.

Birds, and infrequently animals, formed the finials on spoons beginning with the sixteenth century. The lion séjant (Fig. 27), dove and owl were used in England; the dove and falcon in France, and the stork and eagle in Germany and the Low Countries.

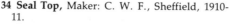

34 **Seal Top,** Maker: C. W. F., Sheffield, 1910-11.
35 **Seal Top Reproduction,** made for *Horizon Magazine* in 1967 by the Gorham Company. The original was made in 1593 and is in Christ's College, Cambridge.
36 **Baluster Top,** Continental, no marks.
37 **Puritan,** London, 1665-66.

36

37

Also introduced in the sixteenth century were the pine cone (Fig. 30), seal tops (Fig. 25, 32–35), ribbed and fluted balls (Fig. 28), spear point and scallop shell knops.

Saints, or other important persons of the Church, were also represented on spoons. These figures may be distinguished one from another by the symbols they bear. When the personage rep-

---

38 Trifid End, pair. Maker: "S over W" within a shield, London. The maker's name has not been traced but has been found on similar spoons bearing London date letters for 1685-95. The back view shows the channeled rattails and marks.

39 Folding Trifid End, no marks. Circa 1700-10.

40 Pewter Trifid End, mark illegible.

41 Latten Trifid End, facsimile of a latten spoon found in excavations at Wakefield, Virginia. The original was brought from England in 1657 by John Washington. Maker: Gebelein, Boston.

39

41

40

38

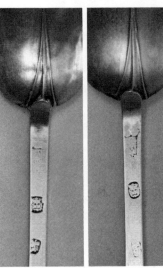

back   back

42

resented is accompanied by an apostolic emblem, the spoon is known as an Apostle spoon. Introduced from the Continent about 1450 they continued in popularity for about two hundred years. (See Saints & Sinners) Closely related to Apostle spoons are those whose finials are saints, angels or cherubim heads (Fig. 31).

Contemporary with the Apostle spoon, but much rarer, is the lion séjant spoon, the finial of which is an heraldic seated lion (Fig. 27). The scarcity of English lion séjant spoons is puzzling because the lion has from early times been the crest or ensign of the kings of England. The seated lion with a shield between the front paws was used in France in the middle of the sixteenth century as the finial. This motif has been adopted in other countries and used on into the twentieth century (Fig. 24).

Seal-top spoons were a rarity before

44

42 **Copeland Spoon,** an unusual trifid end variant. Reproduction of the oldest known dated piece of American pewter. Its maker was Joseph Copeland who lived at the time the mold was made (1675) thirty miles southeast of Jamestown, Virginia in the small town of Chuckatuck. Only the handle was found intact when discovered by archaeologists in 1930, but the bowl is the same shape as other examples that were found in Jamestown. Copeland's mark which makes the spoon unique, is found on the end of the handle. This type of spoon was a general purpose tablespoon, used for eating and serving. Reproduction in pewter by the Stieff Company, Baltimore.

43 **Trifid End Reproduction.** Between 1680-90 trifid end spoons were often elaborately decorated with floral scrolls in relief. Maker: Francis Howard Ltd., Sheffield.

44 **Trifid End Reproduction** of a William & Mary (1690) "scratch engraved" spoon with foliate motif; channeled rat-tail. Maker: G. F., London, 1876-77.

45 **Trifid End Reproduction** with engraving typical of 1650-90. The maker of this reproduction, C. G. Hallberg, was one of the leaders in l'Art Nouveau movement. Marked: C. G. Hallberg/Swedish state mark/date letter (U6) for 1898.

43

45

46

48

47

49

the late 1550s but from about 1560 until about 1670 they were made more constantly than any other type. The name is somewhat misleading as it does not seem that this type of knop was ever intended to be used as a seal. The gradual change in the shape of the spoon bowl from a fig-shape to one more nearly oval is well-illustrated by a comparison of seal-top spoons (Fig. 32–35).

About 1560 a new type of spoon, the baluster top, was introduced. The earliest examples have hexagonal stems and circular balusters; later ones have circular stems (Fig. 36). Baluster top spoons were made in pewter in the sixteenth century. Those of latten belong to the second half of the seventeenth century and are considered rare.

Many fifteenth, sixteenth and seventeenth century spoons of Continental origin were made with stems that are four-sided. These include Apostles, lion séjants, cherub heads, ball knops and others.

It was about the middle of the seventeenth century that the spoon stem was changed from the hexagonal to a flat handle and knops all but disappeared (Fig. 38–46). The flat handle had been used in the Near East in the Middle Ages and was known during the Renaissance on the Continent. While it was used in Scotland as early as 1565 it did not reach its height of popularity in England until about 1640-75. The shape of the bowl continued to change from the rounded fig-shape to elliptical with the wider part of the bowl being next to the stem. This egg-shape continued to be fashionable, gradually becoming even smaller at the extremity until about 1760 when it as-

---

46 Wavy End Reproduction, marked: H·F NS
47-55 18th Century Emblematic or "Fancy Back" Spoon reproductions. Among the designs used were the (48) "Fleur-de-Lis," an old English device much used in heraldry; the (49) "Milkmaid" in period dress, with a

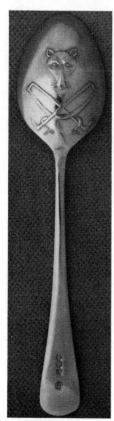

50

51

sumed the shape familiar in modern spoons.

Spoons with flat stems became fashionable on the Continent about the middle of the seventeenth century and only a few years later simultaneously in England, Ireland and Scotland. The severely plain style suited the puritanical taste of that period. The stems were at first simply squared off on the end. Most were without any type of decoration but occasionally examples are found with engraved designs, mainly on the back of the handle and that part of the bowl nearest the handle. Early ones have a short "rat-tail" marking the attachment of the bowl and handle.

The rat-tail is a continuation of the stem on the back of the spoon bowl and is reminiscent of the days when spoons had bowls of a different material from the handle. Rat-tails became a general feature of spoons of the baroque period, possibly the result of English influence. Rat-tails survived until the eighteenth century and disappeared completely with the rococo style. During the last years of the vogue they were merely indicated by converging engraved lines on the back of the spoon bowl. A modification of the rat-tail was the double-drop used around 1735-62.

By the 1660s a few of the flat-stemmed spoons called trifid-ends appeared with small notches in the ends (Fig. 38–39). The earliest ones have very small cuts at the extreme edges with a large lobe in the middle. Trifid-ends assumed several shapes, some larger or smaller and some being more deeply notched and others on which the little side lobes curved outward. Trifid-end spoons were made

yoke holding two wooden pails; the (50) "Fox and Crop"; the (51) "Stag": the (52) "Ship" design probably commemorating the raids of French shipping by Bristol privateers (c. 1759); the (53) "Birdcage" a political commentary commemorating the release of John Wilkes from unjust imprisonment (I

52

53

54

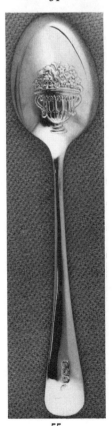

55

in great quantities in pewter and latten (Fig. 40–42). Some trifid-end spoons were elaborately engraved or decorated in relief both back and front (Fig. 43–45).

About 1700 the trifid-end style was replaced by the wavy-end with the middle lobe being sometimes rather pointed and upturned slightly at the end as had been the trifid-ends (Fig. 46).

The next development was that the stem instead of being flat for its entire length, was rounded in cross-section for about one-half to two-thirds its length from the bowl upwards. The wavy-end was replaced by a rounded one and the end of the stem made much thicker than formerly. The end was still turned up and was marked by a transverse ridge or midrib, on each side of which a concavity sloped to each edge. This style reached this country about 1720 but it was made in England by 1705. The midrib style lasted until around 1770. The rat-tail was still present but by about 1730 was replaced by a rounded drop or a double-drop. Other types of rococo ornamentation were also used from about the middle of the eighteenth century and consisted of shells and scrolls and other "fancy backs" (Fig. 47–51).

Before 1750 there was also introduced a style in which the end of the spoon handle was turned back in an Ionic volute, the upper edges of the volute being sculptured in deeply-cut grooves which converge slightly above the mid-point of the handle. This style, commonly called "Onslow," was followed by a general down-turning of handles. (See III, Fig. 437) These turned back spoon handles

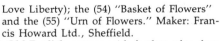

Love Liberty); the (54) "Basket of Flowers" and the (55) "Urn of Flowers." Maker: Francis Howard Ltd., Sheffield.

56 **Old English** pattern with feather edge decoration. Maker: Hester Bateman, London, 1783-84.

57 **Old English** pattern with engraved and embossed decoration; fluted bowl. Makers: Peter, Ann & William Bateman, London, 1801-02.

56

57

58

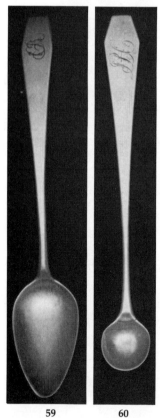

59   60

61

62

were frequently decorated with bright-cut designs, feather-edge or beaded borders; others were plain. They are known by the generic term "Old English" (Fig. 56–58).

A modification of the Old English pattern, used especially in Scotland and Ireland from about 1730 to 1800, has a slightly pointed rather than rounded end. Another modification, which seems to be peculiarly American, is the coffin-end spoon. The handle is turned back as in the Old English but the end is shaped like the old-fashioned coffin (Fig. 59–60). This style first appeared about 1795 and lasted until about 1810.

Fiddle handles appeared on the Continent during the latter half of the eighteenth century, about 1800 in England and about 1805 in this country. Fiddle handles were first made with straight or "finless" stems but the shouldered stems appeared within a few years and were made in a variety of shapes (Fig. 61–67). Some handles curved up and others down, many were plain and others were decorated with a thread design, die-embossed shell, sheaf-of-wheat or basket-of-flowers. Handles of some were broad and spatulate while others had a definite waist (Fig. 65–67).

From about 1840 spoon bowls became more pointed. Handle designs which reflected every taste from the severely plain to the most ornate were adapted from Continental styles which had been in use from seventy-five to one hundred years (Fig. 68–71).

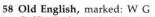

58 **Old English,** marked: W G
59 **Coffin End,** marked: BASSETT
60 **Coffin End,** marked: [Barton] (Joseph Barton, Utica, N. Y., adv. 1804-11)
61 **Finless Fiddle Back,** marked: W. G. Forbes (in script) (William Graham Forbes, New York City, directory, 1796-1809)
62 **Fiddle Back,** marked: M·DEYOUNG with Baltimore Assay Office marks for 1822. (Michael DeYoung, Baltimore, w. c. 1816-36)

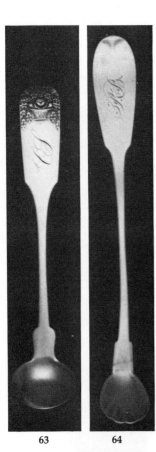

63   64

Changes through the years have affected not only the shapes of bowls and handles but also their relative proportions. The ancient Romans liked an oval bowl and a long narrow stem. By the Middle Ages the bowl had become more rounded; in the thirteenth and fourteenth centuries the stem was short. It was lengthened in the early part of the fifteenth century and then became short again. Bowls were proportionately large until about the beginning of the eighteenth century when the flattened spoon stem was replaced by one that is rounded in cross-section for about one-half to two-thirds its length.

Teaspoons were not made until after the introduction of tea about 1660 and the small size of teacups of that period called for spoons in proportion. They were approximately the size of our after-dinner coffee spoons. Until about 1775 spoons were of three sizes; the teaspoon, already mentioned; the porringer spoon, a little smaller than our present dessert spoon; and the tablespoon, with a handle somewhat shorter than those of today.

Many spoon types had their beginnings on the Continent. Included among them was the folding spoon which could be carried in the pocket. Those that have

66

———— •·• ————

63 **Fiddle Back with Basket Of Flowers** design, marked: DeRIEMER & MEAD (C. B. De-Riemer & E. Mead, Ithaca, N. Y., adv. 1830-31)

64 **Fiddle Back,** Marked: H. I. SAWYER (New York City, w. c. 1840)

65 **Fiddle Back,** marked: BRINSMAID & HILDRETH (William Bliss Brinsmaid & Chester Hildreth, Burlington, Vermont, first advertised 1854)

66 **Fiddle Back,** marked: BRINSMAID'S/B/ "Honey bee"/D (James E., William Bliss and Sedgwick Swift Brinsmaid, brothers) They advertised (*Free Press* 12/28/1845) that this mark would be used on all their spoons.

67 **Fiddle Back,** marked: J.B.&S.M. Knowles (trademark)/COIN (J. B. & S. M. Knowles, Providence, Rhode Island) Firm organized 1852.

65   67

68

69

detail

70

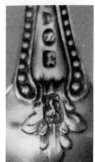

detail

71

survived are mostly of French or German origin and are usually pewter, latten or copper with only a few made of the precious metals.

Though there is some evidence that forks were used by the Romans, their use was not universal until they were introduced from Italy about the first quarter of the seventeenth century. They did not come into general use until about 1660; until that time individuals carried their own. These were often combined with a detachable spoon bowl and a toothpick which screwed into the end of the handle. The fork tines were fitted into loops on the back of the spoon bowl and the handle was made to fold so that the whole could be carried in the pocket. A sliding sleeve kept the handle rigid when in use. Early examples of these are rare but some were made as late as the early twentieth century (Fig. 72–74).

Another type of spoon, the original use of which is still debated, is the mote spoon (Fig. 75–76). The handles are long and slender, tapering to a barbed and pointed end. They rarely bear a full set of marks. Early types are simply pierced with holes and are thought to date from about 1690. Later ones are perforated with elaborate geometric designs. They have been described as olive spoons, strawberry spoons and tea strainers. Some hold that the barbed end was for spearing fruit from hot punch. Others believe that their most probable use was

68 **Double-Die Embossed,** the first flatware design patent in the United States. Design Patent #26, by Michael Gibney, New York, December 4. 1844.

69 **Engraved Design**

70 **Beaded Design,** double-die embossed, maker: George B. Sharp, Philadelphia, c. 1848-71.

71 **Engraved Design,** marked: WARNER 11. (A. E. Warner, Baltimore, w. 1805-70) The figure "11" denotes 11 oz. pure silver to the pound troy (12 oz.)

72

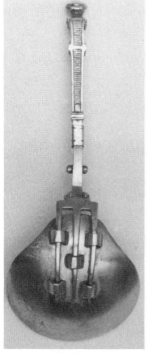

back

73

74

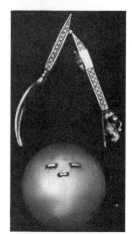

for clearing the spouts of teapots. They have been found in three sizes and the date letters on some late examples (1781–82) indicate that they were made after a fixed strainer had been placed in the union of the spout with the pot doing away with the necessity of a separate strainer. Also, many of the teapots of this period were made with S-shaped spouts, through which it would have been impossible to have thrust a straight spiked stem. Mote spoons were sometimes accompanied by a set of teaspoons giving credence to the belief that they were to be used as tea strainers or to skim the floating tea-leaves (motes) from the surface of the tea in the cup. Separate tea-strainers came into use about 1790. American-made examples of mote spoons are extremely rare.

The marrow spoon was developed about 1690 from the ordinary spoon on which the handle was simply made concave for use in extracting marrow from bones (Fig. 77–80). Later, in the eighteenth century examples, the bowl was omitted and a wide scoop made one end and a narrow one on the other. Marrow is no longer thought to be an epicurean dish in most countries though it is still highly regarded in some Continental areas. So, one often finds marrow spoons which have been converted into lobster picks by filing a V-shape in the smaller end to produce a small two-tined fork.

72 **Combination Folding Fork and Spoon.**
Front and back views showing the method of attaching spoon bowl to the fork. The handle folds for ease in carrying and has a sliding sleeve to keep it rigid while in use. Rotterdam 1922.

73 **Combination Folding Fork and Spoon,** unmarked, but the style of workmanship and the Florentine emblem suggest an Italian origin.

74 **Combination Folding Fork and Spoon.** The symbol in the bowl is the coat-of-arms of the city of Enkhuizen, the Netherlands. Marks indicate it was made in Amsterdam.

75

76

back

77   78

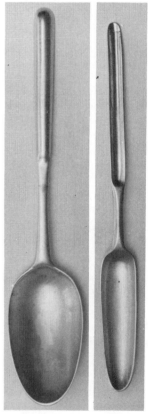

79   80

Caddy spoons and salt spoons were introduced toward the end of the seventeenth century and snuff spoons in the eighteenth. (See Chapter III)

Spoons of the precious metals have long been regarded as valuable articles to be handed down in wills at least as early as the middle of the thirteenth century. Wills and inventories also reveal that they were often given as gifts. The Inventory of the King's Jewelhouse (Henry VIII) lists 431 spoons, 12 of which were given to him. The presentation of spoons as gifts is a custom that has continued through the years (Fig. 81–83).

In the creation of spoons man's artistic nature has found full expression and the figures, faces, and places found on them seem almost endless. The figures of the Apostles on spoons are already well-known; less well-known are the "worthies"—kings, queens, cavaliers (Fig. 84), birds (Fig. 90), and animals—even the whimsical portrayal of hooves of the latter (Fig. 85–88). This whimsy extends to the representation of such things as "My Broom," (Fig. 89) which forms the entire spoon, made in London in 1856. A whistle is an integral part of a spoon made in Edinburgh in 1866. It is beautifully engraved in a Scottish thistle design (Fig. 91)*. Victorian English silver

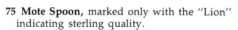

75 **Mote Spoon,** marked only with the "Lion" indicating sterling quality.
76 **Mote Spoon,** only the maker's mark "W·P"
77 **Marrow Scoop,** maker: Richard Crossley (?), London, 1796-97.
78 **Marrow Scoop,** maker: Pillar & Co., Calcutta.
79 **Marrow Spoon,** maker: Elias Cachart, London, 1757-58.
80 **Marrow Scoop,** maker: James Douglas, Dublin, 1732-33.

* According to Madeleine Bingham in her *Scotland Under Mary Stuart*, "ramhorn spoons were carried everywhere, often in the bonnet of the owner. One end was formed into a whistle, from which came the old saying: 'Better the supping end no the whistle end!' " This silver spoon may be a direct descendant of this whistle-spoon custom.

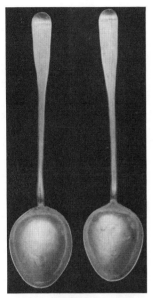

81

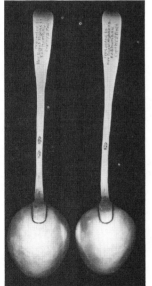

back

detail

catalogs illustrate numerous marmalade spoons on whose handles can be found a bust of a Roman gladiator (Fig. 92).

Other spoons were used for ceremon-

—◆·◆·◆—

81 **Kaahumanu's Silver Spoons,** a pair of spoons given to Her Royal Highness, Queen Kaahumanu, by Captain W. C. B. Finch of the U.S. sloop of war *Vincennes* during a diplomatic visit to Hawaii in 1829. They were a personal gift to the Queen. Maker: J·E, name not traced.

82 **Kamehameha IV's Silver.** A spoon from the silver service given to King Kamehameha IV by Emperor Napoleon III in 1858. Three hundred and fifty-two pieces are in use at Washington Place Honolulu, Hawaii (the Governor's Mansion) while 158 are in the Archives of Hawaii. The service was made by Martial Bernard of Paris, who specialized in the fabrication of jewelry and presentation silver for use by French Ambassadors.

83 **Victorian Spoons,** said to have been among the presents from Queen Victoria to Prince Belosselsky-Belozersky in 1853 on the occasion of his marriage to a German bride. Maker: John S. Hunt, London 1849-50.

82

83

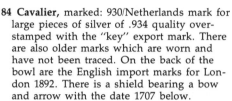

84 **Cavalier,** marked: 930/Netherlands mark for large pieces of silver of .934 quality over-stamped with the "key" export mark. There are also older marks which are worn and have not been traced. On the back of the bowl are the English import marks for London 1892. There is a shield bearing a bow and arrow with the date 1707 below.

85 **Chamonix Hoof,** marked: "3 hound's heads,"/LJ "Buda-Pesth" engraved on the back.

86 **Chamonix Hoof,** marked: "Crescent & crown"/800 "Berne 1888" engraved in bowl.

87 **Chamonix Hoof,** marked: "Crescent & crown"/800/"eagle"

88 **Horse's Hoof** which has been identified as the hoof of George II's horse. Maker: Martin Hall & Co., Ltd., Sheffield, 1870-71.

89 **"My Broom"** in the form of a spoon. "MY BROOM" on handle back. Maker: Charles T. and George Fox, London 1856-57.

90 **Owl,** English registry marks for 1879.

90

84

85   86   87   88   89

91

96

---

91 **Scottish Whistle Spoon,** maker: I & W___, Edinburgh 1866-67.

92 **Victorian Serving Spoon,** electroplate. Marked:___D & S. On the back of the lower part of the handle is the symbol ⚑ a variation of the sign of Hermes. Apparently adapted from housemarks of the Middle Ages. It closely resembles the housemark of the Welser family, wealthy banking family of Augsburg, Germany.

93 **German Wedding Spoon.** The inscription on the handle (in German) may be translated "Let God's Wisdom Give You Ambition."

94 **Ceremonial Spoon.** The motif of the pelican piercing her breast in order to feed her young is derived from an ancient Christian symbol signifying atonement and piety. Marked: 830.

95 **Ceremonial Spoon.** The marks have been deliberately obliterated.

96 **Ceremonial Spoon,** marked: N in a circle/ other marks illegible.

92

93

94

front   95   back

front   97   back

97 & 98 Ceremonial Spoons, no marks.
99 Welsh Love Spoon
     A quintuple love spoon carved of
wood with the Wheel of Fortune in the
center. Above, mounted riders are clasping
swans.
100 Love Spoon, probably Scandinavian. The
carving of a pair of chained love spoons
meant that the carver began with a block of
wood slightly longer than the total finished
article, in this case 37 inches.
101 Modern Love Spoon
102 Philippine Wooden Spoon. The carving of
wood figures in the Phillippines is a long-
established tradition. The human form is
usually simplified, even cubistic, but not dis-
torted. In this simplification, arms and legs
are represented but often without hands or
feet. Philippine carvings were not as highly
stylized as those from Nukuoro (southeast
Caroline Islands) on which faces were completely eliminated and heads are smooth and
egg-shaped.
103 Treen or Wooden Spoon. The country of

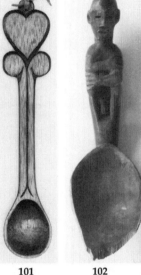

101   102

98

99

100

103

104

105 front   106 front

105 back   106 back

107

108   109

110   111

ial purposes. They often bear inscriptions, "words of wisdom" or advice for the newly married, or by their engraved symbols carry a message (Fig. 93–98).

The carved wooden, or "treen," love-spoon is thought of today as being peculiarly Welsh although the practice of making and giving them was known to a lesser extent in many European countries (Fig. 99–101). The young man carved one of these treasures for presentation to the young lady of his choice—the one with whom he wished to "spoon." Her acceptance of this love token indicated that she had consented to his formal offer of marriage. The love-spoon was then prominently displayed above the cottage fireplace and eventually became a family heirloom.

Love-spoons, carved from one piece of wood, became a custom by 1760, each being carved with only the aid of a pocket knife. Various woods were used, most of them being such fruit woods as were available. Each of the motifs is symbolic of an individual expression of sentiment. Early love-spoons were carved only by the individual young man but by the early nineteenth century were being sold at fairs. While love-spoons are still carved and sold in certain areas, these commercial articles show none of the craftsmanship of old ones, nor do they convey the same tender sentiments.

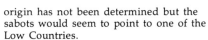

origin has not been determined but the sabots would seem to point to one of the Low Countries.

104 Horn Spoon with Silver Mount, possibly Scandinavian.

105 & 106 Carved Ivory "Harvest" Figures, bowls and handles silvergilt. Marked: Augsburg city mark/Crowned GR/13

107 Emerald (synthetic) Birthstone. Marked: S & Co., 1969

108 Garnet, Belgium, no mark.

109 Opal, Australia, marked: SILVER

110 Basket of Flowers, "caged" semi-precious stones, marked: 800

111 Basket of Flowers, "caged" semi-precious stones, marked: 800

Wooden spoons are known from all over the world, some being crudely carved while others exhibit much imagination as well as great skill in carving (Fig. 102–103).

Horn, wood, ivory and other materials have often been combined with gold or silver to create spoons of unusual interest (Fig. 104–106).

Precious and semi-precious stones are often set into spoons, a custom which goes back at least to Anglo-Saxon times (Fig. 107–111).

Spoons of crystal, porcelain, those with plique-à-jour and some of the ones decorated with various colored enamels were designed more as articles of beauty than for utility (Fig. 112–142).

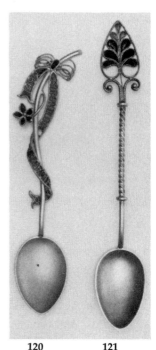

front   112   back

112 **Enameled Spoons,** The scenes are typical of the 18th century pastoral
114 of the 18th century pastoral delights immortalized on canvas by Boucher and in Gobelin tapestries. No. marks.
115 **Faceted Crystal.** When suspended by a cord and tapped, this spoon rings like a bell.
116 **Baccarat Spoon,** France.
117 & 118 **Floral Porcelain Spoons,** no marks.

120   121

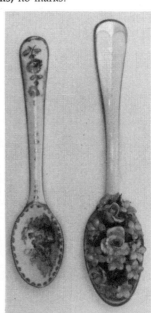

113   114   115   116   117   118   119

122

129

130

The flowers in the one on the right are separately modeled and set into the bowl as in a basket. No marks.

119 to 133 Plique-À-Jour, a technique in which translucent enamel without a metal backing is enclosed within filigree fretworks outlining the design and creating a stained glass or jewel-like effect. Plique-à-jour is frequently combined with transparent enamel work which is applied over silver or gold. Designs are often fanciful and the finished products are not intended for practical use as they are extremely fragile.

119 Marked: B & F STERLING
120 No marks
121 Marked: STERLING
122 No marks
123 Marked: 925 S Maker: Theodor Olsen, Bergen, Norway
124 Marked: MH 930S
125 Marked: MH 930S
126 Marked: H RTZ [Hertz]
127 Marked: J. L. 830
128 Marked: STERLING
129 Marks worn
130 Marked: G·A·S

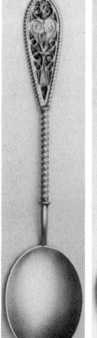

123

124

125

126

127

128

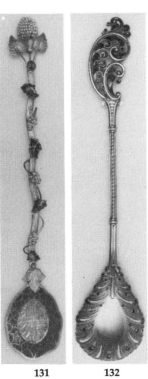

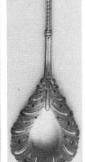

131 No mark
132 No mark
133 Marked: 925 S JGK
134 to 138 Afternoon Tea Spoons. Transparent enamel in rainbow colors is applied over engine-turning to create some of the beautiful and quite usable spoons for which the Scandinavian countries are noted.
134 Marked: MADE IN SWEDEN GAB/ "crown"/S 09
135 Marked: NORWAY STERLING Maker: DA (David Anderson, Oslo) 925S "scales"
136 Marked: "Crown"/STERLING
137 Marked: STERLING MADE IN NORWAY
138 No marks
139 Rose of Hildebrand, marked: JVH/800
140 ENAMELED FRUIT SPOON, marked: 924/Copenhagen city mark/Peter Hertz
141 MOSIAC SPOON, marked: ITALY
142 FILIGREE, marked: MADE IN FRANCE

142

131   132

135   136

133   134   137   138   139   140   141

26

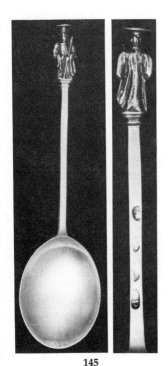

144

146

II
SAINTS AND
SINNERS

Of all the types of spoons none are more interesting than Apostle spoons and those bearing figures and symbols representing the saints. These spoons were probably the most popular types made during the Tudor period in England where they had been introduced from the Continent about 1450. In England they retained their popularity for about two hundred years when the Protestant prejudice against images caused them to fall into temporary disfavor.

Apostle spoons have been most eagerly sought by collectors and are held by many to be the first souvenir or commemorative spoons since they were given to godchildren as baptismal gifts. About the middle of the nineteenth century there was a great revival of interest in them and thousands were made in England and on the Continent. Many were sold near cathedrals. Most of the Apostle spoons found in antique shops today are of this Victorian vintage, or later.

Apostle spoons were made in England in great numbers until Commonwealth times (1654). Examples of the old types were made as late as the reign of William and Mary (1689) and even very early Georgian specimens—possibly

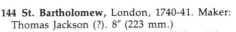

144 **St. Bartholomew,** London, 1740-41. Maker: Thomas Jackson (?). 8" (223 mm.)
145 **St. Thomas,** Dublin, 1749-50. Maker: John Pittar 7⅜" (187 mm)
146 **St. Peter,** London, Maker: B.C. Probably Ben Cooper whose mark was registered in London February 27, 1748. 6 15/16" (178 mm.)
147 **St. Michael,** Edinburgh, 1761-62. Maker: James Ker & William Dempster. 7⅝" (193 mm.)

145

147

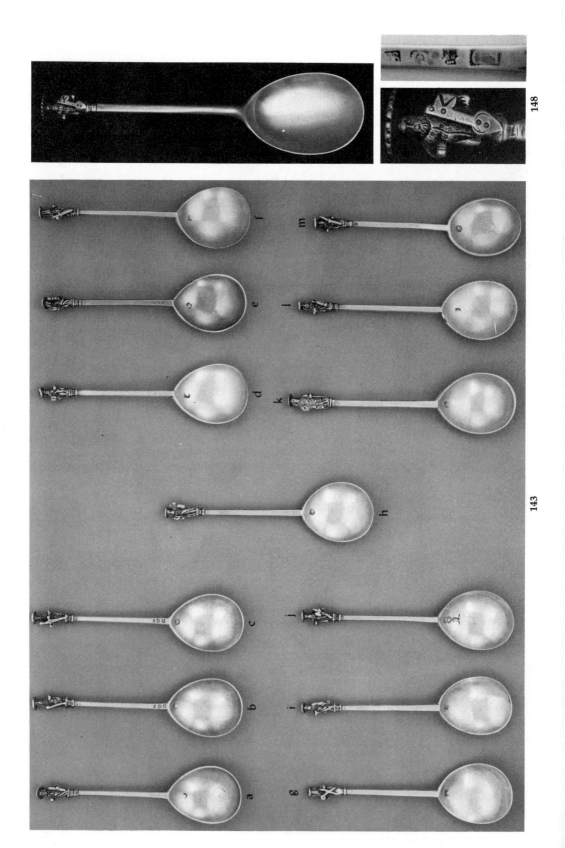

143

148

149

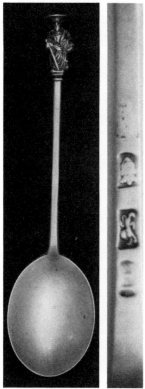

150   detail

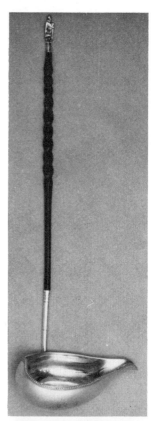

143 (a) St. Jude (St. Thomas ?), London, 1530-31. Marks: a fringed S, leopard's head crowned and date letter Gothic N. 7⅜" (188 mm.) **(b) St. James The Greater,** London, 1599-1600. Marks: T, lion passant, leopard's head crowned, Gothic B. 7 3/16" (183) mm.) **(c) St. Phillip (St. Paul ?),** London, 1599-1600. Marks: T, lion passant, leopard's head crowned, Gothic B. Initials DGF stamped on stems of (b) and (c). 7 7/16" (189 mm.) **(d) St. Matthew,** London, 1602-03. Marks: Crescent encircling a W, lion passant, leopard's head crowned, Gothic E. 7⅜" (188 mm.) **(e) St. John,** London, 1609-10. Marks: Crescent encircling a W, lion passant, leopard's head crowned, Gothic M. 7⅛" (181 mm.) **(f) St. Bartholomew,** London 1618-19. Marks: Crescent encircling a mullet, lion passant, leopard's head crowned, Gothic a. 7⅜" (188 mm.) **(g) St. Andrew,** London, 1626-27. Marks: Crescent encircling a mullet, lion passant, leopard's head crowned, Gothic i. 7" (178 mm.) **(h) Master,** London, 1628-29. Marks: R I, mullet below, leopard's head crowned, lion passang, Gothic l. 7 3/16" (183 mm.) **(i) St. Peter,** London 1628-29. Marks: R I, mullet below, leopard's head crowned, lion passant, Gothic l. 7¼" (185 mm.) **(j) St. Matthias (St. Jude ?),** London, 1636-37. Marks: RC, three pellets above, mullet and two pellets below, leopard's head crowned, lion passant, "t". Later crest engraved in bowl. Inscribed on back of bowl: GC/SC/1646. 7 5/16" (186 mm.) **(k) St. Simon Zelotes,** London, 1637-38. Marks: TP in shaped shield, lion passant, leopard's head crowned, Gothic v. Engraved on back: MS/IB/1665. 7 13/16" (198 mm.) **(l) St. James The Less,** London, 1640-41. Marks: RC, three pellets above and mullet below, lion passant, leopard's head crowned and Inscribed: MP/EB/1643 on back. 7 9/16" (192 mm.) **(m) St. Thomas (St. Matthias ?),** London, 1647-48. Marks: W, three pellets above, mullet below, lion passant, leopard's head crowned, 7 3/32" (180 mm.)

148 St. Peter, Edinburgh, 1761-62. Maker: James Ker & William Dempster. 7 9/16" (192 mm.)

149 St. Peter, London, 1774-75. Maker: William Fearne. 6 15/16" (177 mm.)

150 St. Paul, London. The date letter is too worn to read but John Lamb was known to be working 1783-84. The King's head, not used on this spoon, but would have been required by 1785, so the spoon had to have been made earlier. 7 7/16" (189 mm.)

157 Apostle, London, 1790-91. (See drawing for maker's mark.) Handle is twisted whalebone. 14" (356 mm.)

    157

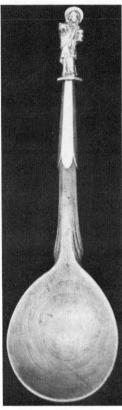

made to complete a set—are encountered.

The earliest written record of Apostle spoons was in the year 1494-95 when "xiii cocliaria cum Apostolis super corum fines" are mentioned in a Will in the York Registry.

For many years no English Apostle spoons made prior to 1490 were known but two came to light whose style of workmanship and treatment of the fig-

---

151-156 Apostles and Saints, Left to right: Ss. Peter; Cecelia, Alfred or David; Paul, James the Less or Jude; James Major or Thomas; Bartholomew. An elaborate floral design is engraved on the back of the bowl of each. No marks. The style is that of 17th century Swiss spoons. Average length 6" (153 mm.)

158 St. Matthias (or possibly St. Jude), 17th century. (See drawing for marks.) The handle is hollow. 6 9/16" (166 mm.)

159 St. John, No marks. Half of the handle and the bowl are made of wood.

158

159

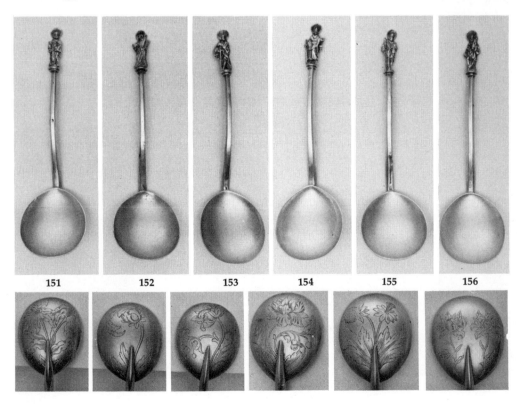

151   152   153   154   155   156

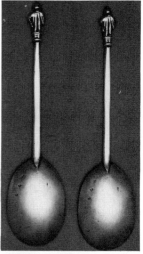

back   166   back

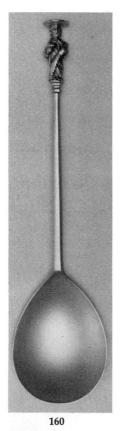

160

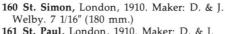

160 **St. Simon,** London, 1910. Maker: D. & J. Welby. 7 1/16" (180 mm.)

161 **St. Paul,** London, 1910. Maker: D. & J. Welby. 7" (178 mm.)

162 **St. Philip** (or Paul), London, 1910. Maker: S. G. 7½" (191 mm.)

163 **St. James The Less,** Sheffield, 1908-09. Maker: Thomas Bradbury & Sons. 5⅜" (132 mm.)

164 **St. Bartholomew,** Sheffield, 1908-09. Maker: Thomas Bradbury & Sons. 3⅞" (99 mm.)

165 **St. James The Less,** London, 1911-12. Maker: L. A. Crichton. Reproduction of an early English Apostle spoon. An excellent example of a well-made reproduction, clearly marked with modern marks and with no intent to deceive. 7 1/16" (179 mm.)

166 **St. Matthew.** A pair of spoons cast from an old one. Note that the marks are placed in identical spots on the backs of both spoons. Also, the same small blemishes are identical on both spoons. The fact that the marks and blemishes are identical proves that they are recastings. 7⅜" (188 mm.)

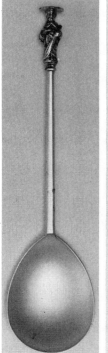

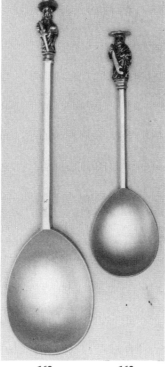

161   162   163   164   165   detail

31

167

168

ures places them between 1460-75. Being made before 1478 they do not bear the London hallmarks which were established by law that year.

Apostle spoons received their name because each is surmounted by a small figure of one of the Apostles bearing the symbol associated with him. A complete set consists of thirteen spoons—that is, twelve Apostles and a Master spoon bearing the figure of Christ.

A favorite christening gift in Tudor and early Stuart times, a set of thirteen would be given by wealthy sponsors while those of lesser means gave four, representing the Evangelists. Still

169

167 **St. Peter,** Chester, 1950-51. Maker: GH.
168 **St. Matthew,** Chester, 1950-51. Maker: GH.
169 **St. Philip,** Chester, 1950-51. Maker: GH.
  Average length of 25-27 9" (230 mm.)
170-176 **Left to right: SS. Philip, John, Matthias, The Master, Matthew, Simon, Peter.** The enlarged view of THE MASTER shows the CVB marks which appears to be in imitation of a mark used by the New York silversmith, Cornelius Vander Burch (1653-1699). No Apostle spoons have been recorded by New York makers. Average length 3⅞" (198 mm.)

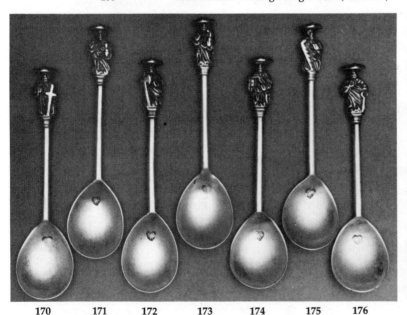

170   171   172   173   174   175   176

Enlarged view 173

177

178

179

poorer people gave a single spoon, representing the Apostle after whom the child was to be named, or possibly the patron saint of the sponsor.

Apostle spoons were treasured and handed down from one generation to another. They are listed frequently in American inventories of the seventeenth century, supposedly having been brought by early settlers as treasured possessions, or perhaps sent as a christening gift. While spoons are the most numerous of early American silversmiths' creations, none are known to have made Apostle spoons.

Early English Apostle spoons have straight, hexagonal stems and fig-shaped bowls, and, except for the terminal figures look much like other spoons of that period. The shape of the bowl changed gradually to an oval and the stem became flattened. The figures on most early English Apostle spoons are surmounted by a nimbus. On spoons of 1490 the nimbus is attached almost vertically and flat to the back of the head of the figure. On spoons dated 1492 the nimbus is tilted forward and upward until it declines almost diagonally over the back of the head. Until about 1510-15 this angle underwent no perceptible change but by 1550 it became somewhat more pronounced. In the reign of Elizabeth I (1558-1603) this change was continued until about the close of her reign the nimbus had reached a horizontal position, being placed on the head of the Apostle at right angles to the stem, similar to the

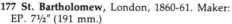

177 **St. Bartholomew**, London, 1860-61. Maker: EP. 7½" (191 mm.)

178 **St. Paul**, London, no date letter. 7 13/16" (198 mm.)

179 **Apostle**, London, 1868-69. Maker: HL/HL 6" (152 mm.)

180 **The Master**, London, 1869-70. Maker: EB 7 5/16" (185 mm.) The lower part of the handle depicts David holding the head of Goliath.

181 **St. Paul**. Edinburgh, 1867-68. Maker: Mackay & Chisholm. 7" (178 mm.)

180

181

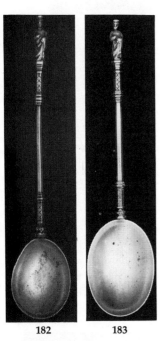

position of the seal on seal-top spoons. This position was retained until Apostle spoons temporarily declined in fashion. The nimbus on later spoons was often pierced for the light to pass through, as if representing the rays of glory. (Rays of light were an ancient emblem of divine power.) On others of

---

182 Apostle, no marks. 8″ (203 mm.)
183 Apostle, Sheffield, 1876-77. Maker: J. E. B. 8½″ (216 mm.)
184 Apostle, Sheffield, date letter S. Maker: W. W. Harrison & Co. (Electroplate) 8⅞″ (225 mm.)
185 Apostle, Sheffield, 1889-90. Maker: H H.
186 Apostle, electroplate, no marks.
187 Apostle, London, 1877-78. Maker: H H. 7⅜″ (188 mm.)
188 St. Paul, London, 1901-02. Maker: Ss & H LD 7 1/16″ (179 mm.)
189 St. Paul, London, 1901-02. Maker: Wm. Hutton & Sons. 6½″ (165 mm.)

182   183

189

184   185   186   187   188

190   191

192

the seventeenth century the nimbus was frequently ornamented with the figure of a dove in low relief, symbolizing the Holy Spirit. The nimbus may also be plain or have floral decorations.

On English spoons the Apostle stands upright while on a few Continental spoons seated Apostles are to be found.

Very early figures were well-modeled; regrettably, the workmanship on later figures deteriorated, many later ones being roughly cast and roughly finished. Continental Apostle spoons

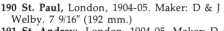

190 **St. Paul,** London, 1904-05. Maker: D & J Welby. 7 9/16" (192 mm.)
191 **St. Andrew,** London, 1904-05. Maker: D & J Welby. 7 9/16" (192 mm.)
192 **St. Peter,** London, 1891-92. Maker: L. Hancock. 8 5/16" (211 mm.)
193 **St. Barnabas (?),** Birmingham, 1887-88. Maker: JMB. 7" (178 mm.)
194 **St. Peter,** London, 1874-75. Maker: H. H. 6¼" (159 mm.)
195 **Apostle,** Utrecht (?). See drawing for marks.
196-199 **Apostle,** Sheffield. Maker: Sanson & Creswick. Electroplate. 8¾" (222 mm.)
200-205 **Apostles,** marked: "Star/Crown/Fleur-de-lis"

200   201

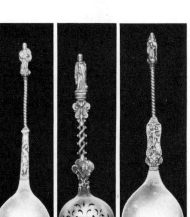

193   194   195

196   197   198   199

202   203

were generally smaller, and, as a rule, better modeled than English ones.

The Apostles are most often represented as full, standing figures, each bearing his emblem, usually in the right hand. Sometimes a book is carried in the left. The emblem was at times cast solid with the figure; on others it was cast separately and soldered on; consequently, some have been broken off and lost. Most figures were gilded, and sometimes the entire spoon.

A complete set of Apostle spoons often included a Master spoon bearing the image of the Saviour. The latter may

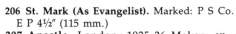

206 **St. Mark (As Evangelist).** Marked: P S Co. E P 4½″ (115 mm.)
207 **Apostle,** London, 1925-26 Maker: HL 4 1/16″ (112 mm.)
208 **St. Paul,** Amsterdam city mark. 3½″ (89 mm.)
209 **St. Simon (?).** Marked: ZZ "Key" export mark for the Netherlands.
210 **Apostle,** no marks. Probably the Netherlands. S in bowl. 6⅞″ (175 mm.)

210

204   205   206   207   208   209

211   212

be identified by the "Orb and Cross" held in the left hand while the right hand is usually raised in benediction. The Orb and Cross are symbolic of the world and man's redemption and were

211 St. John, London, 1891-92. Maker: JGM. 4¼" (109 mm.)

212 St. James the Greater (?), Birmingham, 1890-01. Maker: JMB. 5" (127 mm.)

213 St. James The Greater (?), marked: HJC & Co Ltd 4 1/16" (103 mm.)

214 Apostle, marked: C C Other marks illegible. 5⅛" (130 mm.)

215-216 Apostles, Hoorn guildmark, N2 and dagger standard mark. St. Michael in both bowls. 4¾" (120 mm.)

217 Apostle, no marks. 6¾" (172 mm.)

218 Apostle, Marked: STERLING. The cock symbolizes St. Peter's denial of Christ. 5¼" (134 mm.)

219 St. Thomas (?), marked: the small dagger used in the Netherlands on objects .934-.833 standard; used 1814-1953. 6 3/16" (157 mm.)

220 Apostles. The center figure is St. Luke as Evangelist; right, St. Bartholomew; left, St. Thomas; top center, Mary and Child. Marked: N/Fleur-de-lis/IS. 9 1/16" (232 mm.) The cherubs found on so many Apostle spoons are said to symbolize immortality.

220

213   214

215   216   217   back   218   219

221

probably derived from the Crux Ansata (See IV, Fig. 1363–1364).

The Apostles in sacred art, though always twelve in number (Matthew 10:1-4, Mark 3:14-19, Luke 6:13-16, John 1:40-49), are not always the same personages. Ss. Peter, Andrew, James the Elder, John, Philip, Bartholomew, Thomas, Matthew, James the Less, Jude and Simon are those of the original twelve found on Apostle spoons. Judas

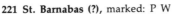

221 **St. Barnabas (?)**, marked: P W
222 **St. Barnabas (?)**, marked: D "key" (export mark for the Netherlands) and another illegible mark. 6⅛" (155 mm.)
223 **St. Andrew**, marks illegible. 4⅞" (125 mm.)
224 **Apostle**, (See drawing for marks) 7½" (190 mm.)
225 **Apostle**, no marks. 7⅛" (188 mm.)
226 **Apostle**, the Netherlands, 17th century. (The cross was used as the emblem for SS. Andrew, Philip and Jude.)
227 **St. Matthew or St. Matthias**, marks illegible. 7⅞" (200 mm.)
228 **St. Matthew**, French "weevil" mark for foreign plate.

228

222

223

224

225

226

227

229

Iscariot, always listed last because of his treachery, is never represented on Apostle spoons. After his betrayal of Christ, he had no place among the Twelve. His place was taken by St. Matthias (Acts 1:15-26). St. Paul sometimes replaces St. Jude.

The use of symbols or emblems originated far back in history when artists found it necessary to identify subjects in the minds of people who were

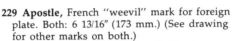

229 Apostle, French "weevil" mark for foreign plate. Both: 6 13/16" (173 mm.) (See drawing for other marks on both.)

230 St. John, Sheffield. Maker: J. Harrison. Electroplate. 8 5/16" (211 mm.)

231 St. Thomas, Sheffield. Maker: J. Harrison. Electroplate. 8 3/16" (208 mm.)

232 St. James, Sheffield. Maker: AT & W, Electroplate. 8 3/16" (208 mm.)

233 St. James The Greater, no marks. 8¼" (252 mm.)

234 St. Thomas, Sheffield, date letter a. Maker: W. W. Harrison. 7 13/16" (198 mm.)

234

230

231

232

233

235

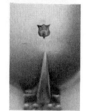

back

unable to read. The giving of symbols in early days was not left to the artists but was dictated by long usage and the sanction of the Church. The Emperor Constantine laid down stern laws concerning the pictorial treatment of sacred subjects when he presided over the Nicene Conference in 325 A.D.

The attributes or symbols by which the individual Apostles are identified

---

235 St. Peter, marked: F. W. S. (Frank Wood ? Sheffield) 7⅜″ (183 mm.)
236 St. Thomas, marked: 800. 7 1/16″ (181 mm.)
237 St. James The Less, Chester, 1908-09. Maker: J. M. B. 6 13/16″ (173 mm.)
238 The Master, London, 1895-96. Maker: CB. 7½″ (190 mm.)
239 The Master, maker: JW HJL 7 13/16″ (198 mm.)
240 The Master, London, 1881-82. Maker: JA JS 8″ (204 mm.)
241 The Master, London, 1882-83. Maker: WJB 7¾″ (197 mm.)

241

236   **237**   **238**   **239**   **240**

were connected with their lives, the many legends associated with them, or were the instruments of their martyrdom. (All are said to have met violent death except St. John, who died at Ephesus at nearly one hundred years of age.)

Other symbols were derived from pagan mythology. The palm leaf, a pagan symbol of victory, is sometimes identified with a martyr's triumph over death, or a spiritual victory.

The Apostles and the emblems most often found on spoons are: St. Peter, a

242-247 **Apostles,** left to right: SS. PAUL, PETER, THOMAS or JAMES MAJOR, MATTHEW, BARNABAS (?) THE MASTER. (See drawing for marks.) Average length 6 15/16″ (177 mm.)

248 **St. Philip 5¼″** (133 mm.)

249 **St. Simon,** 5 5/16″ (135 mm.) Marks on 248 and 249 similar to set of six below.

248   249

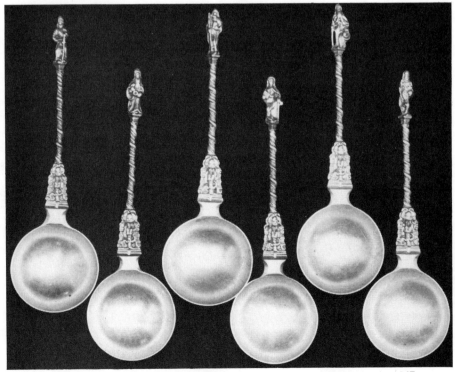

242   243   244   245   246   247

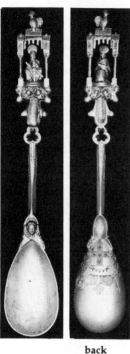

back

key; St. Andrew, a saltire cross; St. James the Greater, a pilgrim's staff; St. John, the Cup of Sorrow in the left hand, while the right hand is uplifted (because of the uplifted hand, in case an emblem is lost, St. John and the Master spoon may be confused); St. Philip, a staff with a cross on the end; St. Barth-

250 **St. Andrea (St. Andrew)** Italian. (See drawing for marks.)

251 **St. Lucas (St. Luke)** as Evangelist. Nuremberg. Apostle knives are rare. 7⅜" (189 mm.)

252 **Apostle,** marks illegible. 7 7/16" (188 mm.)

253 **St. Andrew,** Lübeck, Germany, early 18th (?) century. 7 3/16" (188 mm.)

254 **St. Barnabas (?),** Lübeck, Germany, early 18th (?) century. 7 3/16" (183 mm.)

255 **St. Bartholomew,** marks similar to II-242 to 247. 5" (127 mm.)

256 **St. Andrew,** marks illegible. The peacock symbolizes eternal life, resurrection, and immortality. 7" (178 mm.)

260 **St. Matthias or St Jude,** no marks. 8¼" (210 mm.)

D 250

260

251   252   253   254   255   256

42

261

olomew, a flaying or butcher knife; St. Thomas, a carpenter's square or a spear; St. Matthew, a purse or money bag; St. James the Less, a fuller's bat; St. Jude, a halberd or a cross; St. Simon, a long saw; St. Matthias, a spear or an axe; and St. Paul, a sword.

Because more than one symbol can represent any particular Apostle it is almost impossible to be certain of the identification of a single specimen. Because of this difficulty, the meanings of the various symbols and some addi-

---

257-259 Apostles, marked: 800 GERMANY "Crescent & crown" n (Old German letter).
261 St. Thomas, no marks. 7⅞" (200 mm.)
262 St. Bartholomew, Augsburg, Germany. 7⅝" (194 mm.)
263 St. Petrus (St. Peter), Augsburg, Germany. "1690" engraved on the back. 6 13/16" (173 mm.)
267 St. Peter, Liegnitz, Germany, early 17th century. 6⅞" (175 mm.)

267

257 258 259

262

263

back

tional ones associated with the Apostles are given here. While early silversmiths almost always restricted their representations to the emblems already mentioned, additional symbols can be found on late spoons as supplementary means of identification.

264 Apostle, Lübeck (?), Germany. 7 5/16″ (186 mm.)
265 St. Simon, marked: "Fish" (for silver less than .833 standard), another worn mark on back.
266 St. Luke as Evangelist, marked: A in a shield with a crown, "Fish" standard mark, "1655" and a shield enclosing a fleur-de-lis engraved on back of bowl. 7⅞″ (200 mm.)
268 The Master, marked: Amsterdam date letter for 1850. 7 1/16″ (180 mm.)
269 St. Simon, marks: "Fish" standard mark. 7¼″ (184 mm.)
270 St. Thomas, marks: .833 standard mark, date letter for 1902. 6¾″ (171 mm.)
271 Apostle, "Amsterdam April 1888" engraved in bowl.

268   271

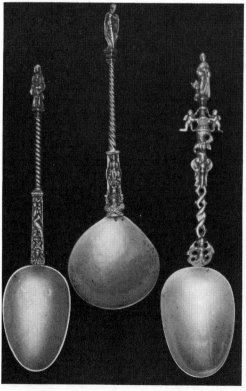

264   265   266   269   270

272

273

274

275

Simon, also called Peter, heads the list of the disciples as he was the spokesman for the group. The name "Peter" which is the Greek for "rock" was given to him by Jesus (Matthew 16:18).

St. Peter is usually represented in sacred art by a key or crossed keys of gold and silver. These are a reminder of Jesus' words to him, "I will give you the keys of the kingdom of heaven." (Matthew 16:19). Early painters often used a fish to represent St. Peter, a reference to his vocation, but it was of broader significance and was later applied to all the Apostles. He is also often accompanied by a cock as it was Peter who three times denied that he knew Jesus "before the cock crows" (Matthew 26:34, 74-75; Mark 14:72; Luke 22:34; 22:61). Because Peter felt unworthy to die in the manner as had Christ, he requested that his cross be inverted so that he might look heavenward as he was crucified. This tradition of his humility has been handed down but the actual manner of his death, probably as a martyr in Rome at the close of Nero's reign, is uncertain.

St. Andrew is most often represented by a saltire cross (X-shaped). Two fishes may be placed in his hands or two fishes crossed to form an X may also be used. Andrew was Peter's younger brother. He shared Peter's home in Bathsaida and was also a fisherman (Matthew 4:18). Andrew is said to have preached in Scythia (Russia), Cappadocia, and Bithynia. He was put to death by crucifixion in Greece in 69

272 **St. Paul or St. Thomas**
273 **St. John** (See drawing for marks on 272 and 273) Both also have London import marks for foreign plate, 1894-95 and initials "L. L." 7¾" (197 mm.)
274 **St. Philip**
275 **St. Matthias or St. Jude** (See drawing for marks on 274 and 275). Both have London import marks for foreign plate, 1893-94 and initials "L. L." 7⅝" (194 mm.)

45

A.D., being bound, rather than nailed, to the cross in order to prolong his suffering.

According to tradition, a monk carrying some of the relics of St. Andrew was shipwrecked off the coast of Scotland, since which time a diagonal cross, white on a blue field has formed the Scottish emblem. This St. Andrew's cross appears as the diagonal "X" in the British Union Jack, representing Scotland.

St. James the Elder (or Greater) is symbolized by a staff with a scallop shell, or sometimes by three gold shells on a blue field, referring to the long pil-

276-281 Apostles, marked: MG M. Other marks illegible. Average length 7¾" (192 mm.)

282-284 St. John, St. Simon, St. Thomas. All Swiss.

285 Engraved St. Marcus: this is in error. The figure could be St. Alfred, champion of England and Christianity, (849-899 A.D.), or St. Cecilia, a Roman woman who wrote hymns and sang beautifully, patroness of music; martyred about 200 A.D. It could also be David, who was symbolized by a harp.

282

283

284

285

276   277   278   279   280   281

286

287

288

grimages he made to establish the Christian faith in Spain. Other symbols used are the pilgrim's staff, a pilgrim's cloak with a hat or cap, and rarely, a wallet. The cap, if used, is always supplementary, never replacing his distinctive emblem of a staff. James was one of the two sets of brothers who were fishermen—James and John, surnamed Boanerges, meaning "The Sons of Thunder" (Mark 3:17) and Peter and Andrew. James was the first of the Twelve to die. After working fourteen years in the church in Jerusalem, Herod Agrippa (Herod the Younger) ordered his death by decapitation in 44 A.D. (Acts 12:1-2).

St. James the Elder is the patron saint of Spain and of pilgrims.

St. John, "The Beloved Apostle," is represented in sacred art by a gold cup or chalice with a silver serpent on a blue field. Early writers say that John was ordered by the Emperor Domitian to drink a cup of poisoned wine and when he took up the cup to drink, the poison departed in the form of a snake. Others feel that the basis of the cup as a symbol of John is in reference that John and James should drink of His cup (Mark 10:38-39). John is constantly referred to as the disciple whom Jesus loved (John 13:23; 21:7; 21:20). It was he who Jesus chose to care for His own mother, Mary (John 19:26-27).

---

286 St. John
287 Engraved St. Bartholomeo; another error. The attribute of St. Bartholmew is the butcher or flaying knife. The figure is more likely that of St. Valentine. He was a priest who was active in assisting martyrs in time of persecution. He was himself martyred 269 A.D All the above (285-287) average 7½" (190 mm.) Probably made in Nuremberg c. 1800. The small figures within the arches are Cherabim, holding books. They represent Divine Wisdom.
288 St. Paulus, no marks. 4⅜" (112 mm.)
289-290 Apostles, Marten Pewter, Plymouth, Massachusetts. Pewter. 289 is 3 7/16" (87 mm.) 290 is 3 5/16" (84 mm.)

289

290

291

292

293

detail

294

295

John preached in Asia Minor, especially in the city of Ephesus. He was banished to the Isle of Patmos in 95 A.D., and sentenced to hard labor in a quarry. He is believed to be the only one of the Twelve to die a natural death, supposedly at Ephesus at a very advanced age.

John has also been symbolized by an eagle rising from a large cauldron or kettle, referring to his miraculous deliverance without injury when the Emperor Domitian tried to put him to death by placing him in burning oil. A book or scroll is sometimes added to the eagle because of the version of the Gospel he wrote, for the three Epistles, and the Revelation which bears his name.

St. Philip is represented by a gold staff surmounted by a cross and often with two loaves of bread (sometimes shown as silver roundels), one on each side of the cross on a red field. He is sometimes shown with a small cross in his hand. The staff and cross are symbolic of his successful missionary journeys and especially the miracle at Heliopolis where, aided by the cross, he caused a serpent idol to disappear.

Philip is not often mentioned in the Gospel narratives. He is associated chiefly with the account of the miracle of Feeding the Five Thousand (Matthew 7:14-21; Mark 6:35-44; Luke 9:10-17; John 6:5-14), and as being present at the gathering of the disciples in

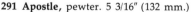

291 **Apostle,** pewter. 5 3/16" (132 mm.)

292 **Apostle,** latten, 18th century. 7 5/16" (186 mm.)

293 **Virgin Mary,** holding St. John and Infant Christ. Brass.

294 **"Chinese Apostle,"** marked: L-W, and Chinese characters. Attributed to the firm of Luen Wo. Listed as "jewelers" at 42 Nanking Road, Shanghai, in 1909. 8¼" (210 mm.)

295 **St. John,** London, 1894-95. Maker: W. Hutton & Sons, Ltd. 8" (203 mm.) The similarity between the two spoons is remarkable.
The Chinese "Apostle" is a late manifestation of China Trade silver.

48

296

297

298

Jerusalem after the Ascension (Acts 1:13).

Although there is no conclusive evidence that he was martyred, Philip is said to have been crucified at Heliopolis head downwards when the priests of the serpent idol were enraged by the overthrow of their god.

St. Bartholomew is represented by three, or more often only one, flaying knives with silver blades and gold handles on a red field. He is also represented with a book (the Gospel according to Matthew) in one hand, or with an open Bible and a flaying knife. Bartholomew and Nathanael (Nathaniel) are held to be names for the same person, with Bartholomew being the surname for the Apostle who John calls Nathanael. He joined the Twelve at the invitation of his friend Philip. He came from Cana (where Jesus performed his first miracle), a town about three miles from Nazareth. Bartholomew is said to have preached in Armenia, Cicilia, and as far away as India. It was in Armenia that it is supposed that he died by being flayed.

St. Thomas, the seventh Apostle (Matthew 10:3), was also known by the name of Didymus (John 20:24), meaning "twin." He is known as "The Doubter" because he refused to believe in the Resurrection of Christ until convinced by sight and touch (John 20:25-27). His usual emblems are a spear or arrow with a silver head and tawny handle

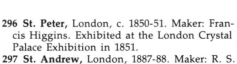

296 **St. Peter,** London, c. 1850-51. Maker: Francis Higgins. Exhibited at the London Crystal Palace Exhibition in 1851.

297 **St. Andrew,** London, 1887-88. Maker: R. S. 7 11/16" (196 mm.)

298 **St. Paul,** marked twice with Moscow city mark used between 1891-96; another imperfectly stamped mark that is illegible. 6⅜" (160 mm.)

299 **St. Paul,** Whiting Mfg. Co., trademark, STERLING. 6⅜" (160 mm.) These two are so nearly identical that they must have come from the same molds.

299

302

303

behind a carpenter's square with a silver blade, gold handle, all on a red field, showing his trade as a builder and the instrument of his death. The square also refers to the legend of the palace, real and spiritual, built for the king of Indies, Gondoforus (Gondophorus).

Thomas also doubted the Assumption of the Virgin until she appeared to him in glory and lowered her girdle to him from Heaven. Her girdle is sometimes used as his symbol.

St. Matthew the Publican or tax collector (Matthew 9:9) of the Roman Empire is symbolized by three silver purses or money bags, or a purse, a chest, or money box on a red field; sometimes, a battle-axe. Matthew, whose original name was Levi, was a tax collector (Luke 5:27) for Herod at Capernaum. He taxed people and goods crossing the Sea of Galilee or those who passed along the Damascus Road which ran along the shore.

Matthew is most often represented by the symbols of his profession. The battle-axe, when used, refers to his martyrdom, which is said to have taken place in Ethiopia where he was crucified on a Tau cross and decapitated. He is also sometimes shown with a book or pen as writer of the Gospel. Sometimes an angel holds his inkhorn.

St. James the Less, also called The Little because of his small stature, is often referred to as The Minor. This was to distinguish him from the other James who was taller and bigger. According to legend, he was a relative of Jesus' and was the first bishop of Jerusalem. His

---

302-313 Marked: N in a square; crowned A; 930. Also, S.B.L. in rectangle; F (for foreign silver); Sheffield city mark and the date letter g for the year 1899.
302 **St. Paul**
303 **St. Simon**
304 **St. Bartholomew**
305 **St. Matthew**

304

305

306

307

usual attribute is a fuller's bat which refers to the tradition that he was cast down from a pinnacle of the temple in Jerusalem, beaten with a club, stoned, and then dismembered. Three stones are sometimes used as symbols, while more often he is shown leaning on a fuller's bat or club. A saw with handle uppermost, is also used. In paintings, the saw has a silver blade and gold handle on a red field.

St. Jude was also referred to as Thaddaeus, Labbaeus, Judas, or Judas Lebbaeus. Matthew calls him "Labbaeus, whose surname was Thaddaeus" (Matthew 10:3). According to tradition, he was the brother of St. James the Less, and they are thought to have been relatives of the Virgin Mary. After the death of Christ, Jude is said to have traveled through Syria and Asia Minor with St. Simon Zelotes, preaching the gospel. In Persia, both were martyred for their faith, St. Jude being transfixed with a lance or beheaded with a halberd. For this reason, his attribute in art is the lance or the halberd. Sometimes the lance is combined with a club and an inverted cross. These are the only symbols for him recorded on old spoons. In pictorial art, however, St. Jude is frequently symbolized by a gold ship with silver sails on a red field. This symbol of a sailboat with a mast in the shape of a cross, or a long staff with a cross at the end, refers to his missionary journeys. The ship, of course, also represents the Church.

St. Simon Zelotes (the Zealot) was a member of the Zealots (Luke 6:15), an organization of Jewish patriots who were opposed to the Romans ruling their land.

Traditions concerning his martyrdom vary. According to one legend, St.

---

306 St. Jude
307 St. Peter
308 St. James Major
309 St. Thomas

308

309

Simon was crucified; another says that he was sawed asunder. A large saw is his usual attribute.

Simon and his co-worker, Jude, traveled together in Mesopotamia. Sometimes one or two oars appear on a shield with a battle-axe or a saw to represent him. In paintings, a gold book with page edges of white with a silver fish resting on top of it, and all on a red field, symbolize Simon as a fisher of men through the power of the Gospel.

Judas Iscariot is always listed last as his treachery earned him this place among the Twelve. Judas was the only one of the Twelve who was not from Galilee. "Iscariot" means "man of Kerioth," a town in southern Judea. He was treasurer of the group. He is best known as the betrayer of Jesus. When he is symbolized, a blank yellow shield, a money bag and thirty pieces of silver, or a rope around his neck are shown. The rope, of course, refers to his suicide. The thirty pieces of silver (Matthew 27:4) and a straw-colored rope coiled to make the letter "J" are sometimes shown on a black field. Judas Iscariot is never represented on Apostle spoons.

St. Matthias was chosen by lot to take the place of Judas Iscariot (Acts 1:15-26). He served as a missionary in Judea where he is said to have been stoned and beheaded. His emblems are a sword, battle or woodman's axe, or a lance. The double-edged axe in conjunction with a stone or the open Bible, is his most common symbol. In paintings, the axe has a silver head, and tawny handle, a white open book with the inscription "super Mathiam" in black except the upper case "M" of red, all on a red field, are used. St. Matthias is the patron saint of carpenters.

St. Paul as one of the Twelve Apostles is sometimes symbolized instead of St. Jude. He is usually represented with one or two swords, the instrument of his death. He is sometimes symbolized by an open Bible with a sword behind it. The Bible bears the inscription "Spiritus Gladius," meaning "Sword of the Spirit." St. Paul is also represented by two crossed swords, one referring to the good fight of faith that he fought, and the other to his martrydom by the sword. Occasionally, a book and serpent are used to signify his escape from death by the bite of one. A phoenix and palm are used in allusion to his teaching of the resurrection.

St. Barnabas is included among the Apostles, although like St. Paul, he was not one of the Twelve. According to tradition, he was especially successful as a preacher, hence the Gospel (book) is his symbol.

While the early painters occasionally used several emblems for some of the Apostles, careful study indicates that silversmiths always gave the same symbol to each with the exceptions of SS. Thomas, Matthias, Matthew and Jude. For these, two sets of symbols were used and are usually designated as Italian and German, as they follow in general the early paintings of those countries. Under the Italian system, St. Thomas was given a square, St. Matthias a spear, and St. Jude a halberd. Under the German system, St. Thomas was given a spear, St. Matthias an axe and St. Jude a cross.

Paintings and sculpture were often the inspiration for early silversmiths' representations of the Apostles but later silversmiths, not sufficiently versed in legendary art to interpret the works of old masters and identify the representations of the Apostles, often invented or borrowed symbols for their Apostle spoons.

Apostle spoons of the late fifteenth to mid-seventeenth centuries are rarely to be found except in museums and a few private collections. They are scarcely within the means of the average collector even when the rare specimen is found. Nineteenth-century ones with

their elaborate handles and often beautifully modeled figures are not to be compared with the early ones for rarity, but for those collectors who are not content to see only those things which are safely behind glass in museums, a collection and study of nineteenth-century Apostle spoons can be rewarding. They were made in great numbers and sold at or near cathedrals throughout Europe.

Eighteenth-century English Apostle spoons are more apt to follow the older styles. They can be found though their numbers are not overwhelming.

---

300 Apostles, Gorham Company, c. 1888. Their size varies from 6½″ to 6⅝″ (165-167 mm.)
310 St. James Minor
311 St. John

310

311

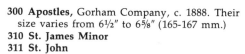

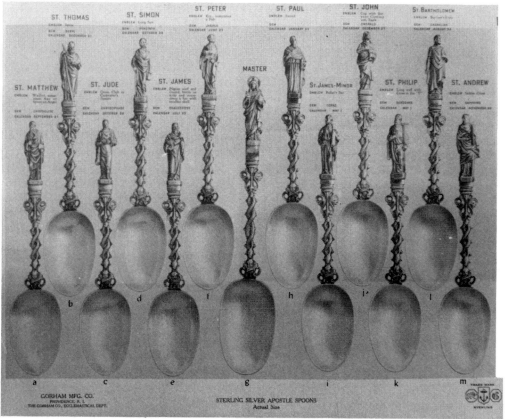

300

Determination of the age of Continental Apostle spoons presents a problem because marking requirements were not as rigid and dating devices not precise. Some of the more florid styles originated on the Continent quite early but have been continued over a long period of time.

While it is extremely difficult to date the Apostle spoons made on the Continent, those made in England present no such problem because of the rigid hallmarking regulations in force for more than six and one-half centuries. Comparison of these with Continental ones will often provide a clue to dating the latter.

A radical departure in style from the old English Apostle spoons is illustrated by a set made by Francis Higgins & Son (London), silversmiths established in 1789 and known principally as spoon and fork makers. This set was exhibited at the London Great Exhibition of the Industry of All Nations 1851 (Crystal Palace). St. Peter of this set is shown in the *Art Journal Illustrated Catalogue* of the Exhibition. (Fig. 296) St. Peter, of a set made by the Gorham Company in 1888, exhibits the same tilt of the head, the key held in the same position and spoon handles that are virtually identical but for a small variation in the cherub-head decoration near the bowl (Fig. 300f). Only the bowls show any substantial difference. These figures are all modeled completely "in the round."

Also virtually identical to the Francis Higgins set and the Gorham set, is another one by a London silversmith whose initials are "R.S." (Fig. 297) This set bears the date letters for 1887-88. There are minor variations in the handle and the bowl is a shell form rather than the usual egg-shape.

Still another set is so nearly identical to the Gorham spoons that close examination shows that the figures and handles might have come from the same molds. The surprising note about the one spoon available for close examination (St. Paul) is marked twice with the Moscow city mark used from 1891-96, (Fig. 298) and another imperfectly stamped mark that has not been deciphered.

An Apostle from a set made in Nuremberg, Germany, appears identical in pose, in the emblem he carries and even to the folds of his garments, to St. Jude of the Gorham set (Fig. 314f) St. Jude from still another set, marked "JLC" in an oval, 9, STERLING, is closely related. (Fig. 319)

Eleven spoons from another German set—St. James the Greater is missing—are almost identical to a set made by the Joseph Mayer Company of Seattle, Washington (now the E. J. Towle Company) about 1904. Still another similar set, marked "R. K. & Sons, Inc. STERLING," is represented here by St. Matthew and accompanied by St. Matthew of the Mayer set. (Fig. 317-318)

The figures on the German sets and those made by the Mayer Company are large in comparison to the bowls. The figures are somewhat flattened rather than being modeled completely in the round. They are completely detailed on the reverse sides.

Jules Louis Charboneau was the designer of the Apostle spoons made by the Mayer Company. Apparently, they were first made with two types of bowls, the rounded, fig-shape and the more usual teaspoon bowl. The early teaspoon bowls were stamped inside with a cathedral and the back stamped with that cathedral's historical significance.

All of the above-mentioned sets have figures of the Apostles whose stance, emblems, and Gothic elements on the handles are virtually identical to the German set (Fig. 302–313) of extremely large size. These similarities point to a common source of design.

Apostle spoons seem to have had

their origin in Continental Europe and it was from there that thousands of them poured during the nineteenth century. The Low Countries, especially, were a prime source with France, Germany and Italy adding greatly to their numbers. Almost every country from Scandinavia south, including the Channel Islands, contributed.

Only a few American companies have been reported as makers of Apostle

301 Apostles, Gorham Company, c. 1888. Smaller set made by the Gorham Company. Left to right: SS. MATTHEW, THOMAS, JUDE, JAMES MAJOR, PETER, THE MASTER.
Left to right: SS. PAUL, JAMES MINOR, JOHN, PHILIP, BARTHOLOMEW, ANDREW.
312 St. Philip
313 St. Andrew

312

313

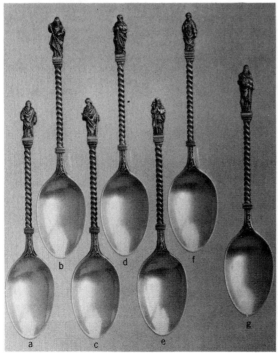

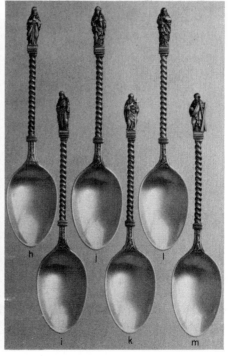

301

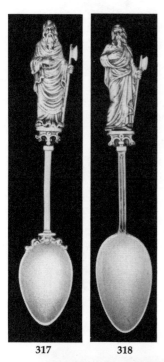

spoons. The Gorham Company seems to have been the first with their two sets, the first published record of these to come to our attention being printed in *The Watch Dial*, 1888. This trade publication carried a brief notice that "The celebrated silversmiths, Gorham & Co., of Broadway, New York, have recently issued a unique booklet of twenty pages entitled 'Apostle Spoons.' It is neatly bound in silver paper, and the text is printed on the fashionable

---

314 Apostles, Left to right: SS. ANDREW, SIMON, JAMES MINOR, PHILIP, BARTHOLOMEW, JUDE, PAUL, THOMAS, JOHN, PETER. James Major is missing. Marked: 19th century Nuremberg marks.

317 St. Matthew, marked: R. K. & Sons, Inc. STERLING.

318 St. Matthew, marked: "Crossed tools" "EJT" Compare 317 and 318 also with St. Matthew 314-g.

319 St. Jude, marked: JLC in an oval (for Jules Louis Charboneau, the designer), 8 STERLING.

317　　　318

319

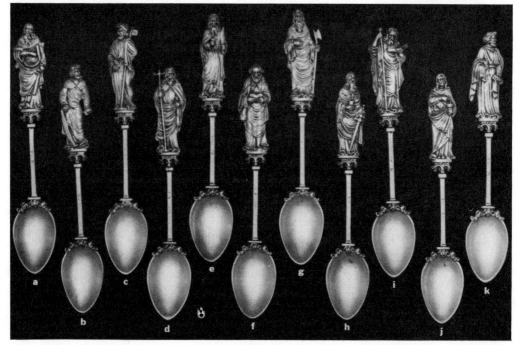

314

320

321

ragged-edge paper." Illustrations of their Apostle knives, forks and spoons appeared in their catalog issued in 1888. These Apostle spoons were made in two sizes, the larger ones being far more elaborate than the smaller. A full

---

315 **Left to right:** CATHEDRALS in the bowls—WESTMINSTER ABBEY, London; ST. PETERS, ROME; STRASBURG; BASILICA AND LEANING TOWER, PISA; ATHENS; TRONDHEIM; MILAN; THE KREMLIN, MOSCOW; NOTRE DAME, PARIS; ST. MARKS, VENICE; COLOGNE; and COPENHAGEN. The cathedrals are described on the backs of the bowls. The two illustrated are: left, Notre Dame and, right, Cologne. From a Joseph Mayer & Bros, Seattle, Washington, catalog c. 1915.

320 **The Master,** City Gates, St. Augustine, Florida in the bowl. Watson Co. trademarks used after 1910.

321 **The Master,** Eucharistic Congress, June 1926, Chicago in the bowl. Watson Co. trademarks used after 1910.

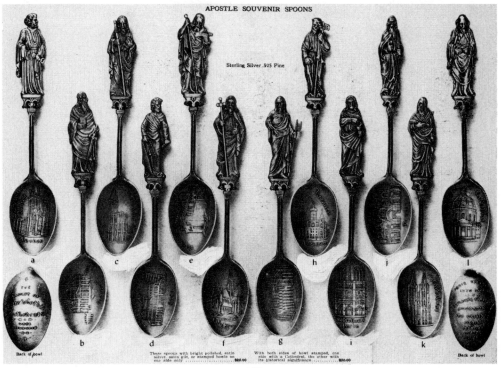

315

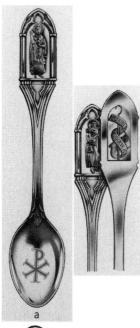

a

© FM 1973

322

set of each included the Master spoon. This larger set was reissued late in 1974.

The sets made by the Joseph Mayer Company of Seattle apparently did not include a Master spoon.

A set of Apostle Spoons very similar in appearance, but somewhat longer than those made by the

---

316 Apostles, left to right: SS. PETER, PAUL, JAMES MAJOR, THOMAS, SIMON, PHILIP, MATTHEW, JAMES MINOR, JOHN, BARTHOLOMEW, ANDREW, JUDE. Made by E. J. Towle Company from the old dies of the Joseph Mayer & Bros. Company. Average height 5 13/16" (147 mm.)

322 a-m Apostle spoons, a. THE MASTER, b.-m. The portion of the Apostles' Creed attributed to each Apostle is etched in the bowl. Maker: The Franklin Mint. Master: 6⅛" (156 mm.) Apostles: 5⅜" (134 mm.)

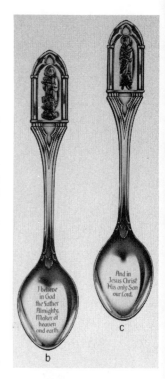

b   c

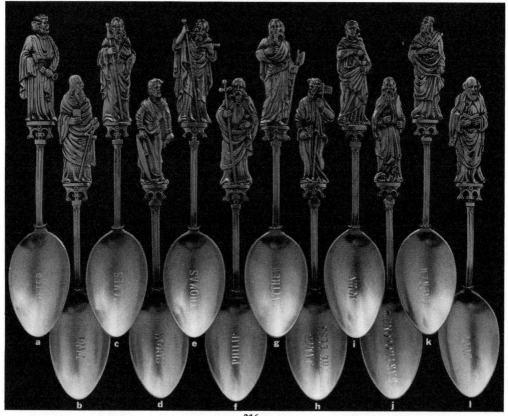

316

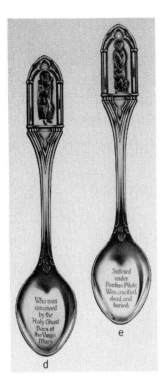

d

Who was
conceived
by the
Holy Ghost,
Born of
the Virgin
Mary,

e

Suffered
under
Pontius Pilate,
Was crucified,
dead, and
buried;

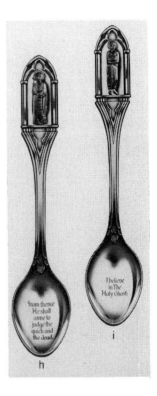

h

From thence
He shall
come to
judge the
quick and
the dead;

i

I believe
in The
Holy Ghost;

Gorham Company were made by Tiffany & Company in the 1880s.

Reports have been circulated that Apostle spoons were also made in this country by Andrew Warner of Baltimore and by Greenleaf & Crosby, jewelers and silversmiths of Florida. These reports have not been confirmed by actual examples, but in a record book which belonged to Andrew E. Warner, Jr., there is the following entry, "Nov. 6th (1882) Make 2 Apostle spoons for Miss Boyd No. 3 Cathedral St. to match one left to cost $6.50 each to be finished by Thursday sure" This entry is initialed either "WSP" or "NSP." Written across the entry in another hand is the notation "Finished by Nov 9/82."

Two spoons depicting the Master bear the Watson Company trademarks used after 1910. (Fig. 320-321) One of these can be dated by the bowl which commemorates the Eucharistic Congress held in Chicago June 1926.

In 1973 the Franklin Mint, of Pennsylvania, issued a set of Apostle spoons, including the Master. (Fig. 322a–m) They are distinguished by their unusual sculptural design. The front of each depicts the figure of one of the Apostles. On the back, the Apostle is identified along with his traditional symbol. Permanently etched into the bowl of each spoon is a portion of the Apostles' Creed attributed to the Apostle portrayed. Thus, the complete collection bears the full text of the Creed.

An English set was issued in 1973 as "Treasures of Goldsmiths' Hall." (Fig. 323–326) These spoons are limited edition replicas of an original set created by the London silversmith Benjamin Yates in 1626. They have the coat-of-arms of the Goldsmiths' Company engraved in the gilt bowls. Each Apostle is identified by name on the back of the handle.

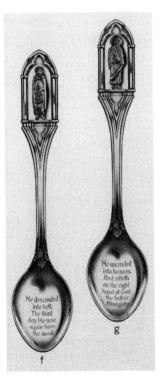

f

He descended
into hell.
The third
day He rose
again from
the dead;

g

He ascended
into heaven.
And sitteth
on the right
hand of God
the Father
Almighty;

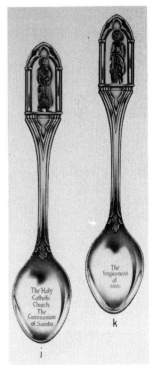

j

The Holy
Catholic
Church;
The
Communion
of Saints;

k

The
forgiveness
of
sins;

The resurrection of the body.

And the life everlasting.

m

l

FOUR EVANGELISTS

The Four Evangelists, SS. Matthew, Mark, Luke, and John, are also depicted on spoons. Strictly, speaking when these saints are depicted with evangelical emblems, the spoons should not be called "Apostle" spoons. Some spoons depict these saints as Apostles but with the addition of their evangelical symbols.

The earliest representations of the Evangelists shows them all with the emblem of a scroll or a book, or a book and pen, but about the fifth century, the "four Beasts" mentioned in Revelation (4:7) were assigned to them. They are: St. Matthew, a winged man (though more often represented by a book and pen); St. Mark, a lion (or a fig tree); St. Luke, the head of a calf or an ox; and St. John, an eagle.

The most familiar of these symbols perhaps is the winged lion of St. Mark. Several centuries after his death Venetian sailors took his body to Venice. St. Mark became the patron saint of that city, which adopted his emblem as its own. St. Mark and his winged lion are frequently represented in Venetian art.

According to legend, St. Luke was a painter and is supposed to have done several portraits of the Virgin Mary and Jesus. For this reason he is the patron saint of painters.

———— • •• ————

323-326 Treasures of Goldsmiths' Hall, part of set of Apostle spoons reproduced from a set in the collection of the Worshipful Company of Goldsmiths of the City of London. The original set was made by Benjamin Yates, London, 1626. This set marked: C·J·V in a shaped cartouche,   L
lion passant, r (1973). The leopard's head is stamped in the bowl. Each spoon had the coat-of-arms of the Goldsmiths' Company engraved in the bowl. ENGLAND is stamped on the back and the individual number of the set of the series of 1000 sets. 7 5/16" (187 mm.)

324

323

325

326

329

VIRGIN MARY
(Fig. 327–328)

In the latter part of the fourteenth century Maidenhead spoons first appeared (See also I, 18) and are thought to have been intended as representations of the Virgin Mary. They were made with only the head or bust of the figure while late nineteenth and early twentieth century representations are usually the full figure and sometimes include the Babe.

ST. NICHOLAS
(Fig. 329)

A St. Nicholas spoon would not have been included in a set of old Apostle spoons but one might have accompanied them as an extra spoon, and would, in the belief of that day, have protected them against loss or theft.

The spoon illustrated here is a reproduction of one which bears the London hallmark and date letter for 1528-29, with the Orb and Cross between the initials "I.C." (John Carswell) as the maker's mark. The spoon stem, while following the usual flattened hexagonal form of its period, is considerably heavier than most, presumably to accommodate the unusually heavy knop.

St. Nicholas was born of Christian parents in Papara in Lycia. While still a young man he was elected Bishop of Myra in Asia Minor. He devoted his life to the Christian cause and died in 342 A.D.

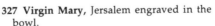

327 **Virgin Mary,** Jersalem engraved in the bowl.
328 **Virgin Mary,** no marks. 5¼" (133 mm.)
329 **St. Nicholas,** Chester, 1906-07. Marked:
 GN
 RH
 listed in Jackson, p. 395 but not identified by name. 6½2¼ (166 mm.) Other St. Nicholas spoons marked: G & S Co., Ltd., London. 6⅝" (169 mm.)
330 **St. Augustine, AD 354-430,** marked: Durgin trademark, STERLING, Greenleaf & Crosby (Florida retail jewelers). 4 15/16" (126 mm.)

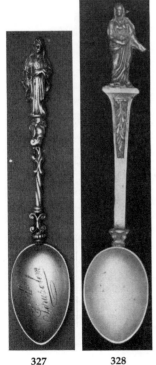

327   328

330

331

back

There are a number of legends associated with St. Nicholas. The one depicted on the spoon concerns the time he restored three of his boy pupils to life. For this miracle he was adopted as the protector and patron saint of children.

In another legend he was on a voyage to the Holy Land and the ship was threatened by heavy seas. St. Nicholas rebuked the waves and they subsided. For this miracle he became the patron saint of sailors and travelers and his image was raised in almost every seaport throughout the world.

On the death of his parents, St. Nicholas distributed his inherited wealth to the poor. A certain nobleman had lost all his money and his three daughters were to be sold into slavery. St. Nicholas provided a dowry for each by throwing bags of gold through the nobleman's window. Because his gift of the three purses was compared to gifts to the Christ Child by the three Magi, it became the custom in medieval times for people to give each other presents on the eve of St. Nicholas, December 6, and later in all the Germanic countries they were given on Christmas Day. To receive these "Gifts of St. Nicholas" stockings or wooden shoes were hung

332

333

---

331 **Mary and St. Olaf,** marked: Copenhagen town mark. Maker: H. Kyster. 7⅛" (181 mm.) Inscription in bowl. "Maria (Mother Mary) help me in my Distress and save me from eternal Death." (In Danish) Inscription on back: "Lord, pray for me." (In Latin) Inscription around handle: "Eat slowly, do not burn you." (In Danish) The figures in the bowl represent the Virgin with the Holy Child and St. Anne. The figure on the back represents St. Olaf. This spoon is a copy of an old spoon from Island (Iseland, one of the Scandinavian countries, not an island in the usual sense of the word) that is now in the National Museum in Copenhagen, Denmark.

332 **St. Olaf,** London, 1885-86. Maker: WC.

333 **Mary and St. Olaf** (See #331) This one marked: P. Hertz, Copenhagen .925. The figures and handle are accented in enameled colors.

334

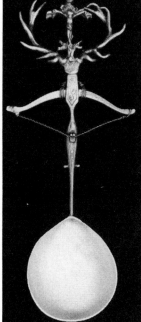

335

back

336

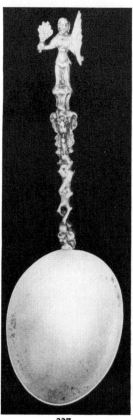

337

up. So, the legend of St. Nicholas gradually merged with the Christmas story and the familiar figure of Santa Claus.

St. Nicholas spoons were given to children with the hope that one day they too would bestow upon each other the love and kindness felt for them by their own patron saint.

ST. AUGUSTINE
(Fig. 330)

St. Augustine was born in Numidia (now Algeria), North Africa and educated in Carthage. Later, he studied law in Rome and became known for his learning. He was made Bishop of Hippo, in Africa, and died there of fever at the age of 76 during the siege of the city by the Vandals.

St. Augustine is usually represented wearing the habit of a bishop and bearing a book and pen, in reference to his writings. His *Confessions* and *City of God* have greatly influenced religious thinking. His special attribute is a flaming heart, sometimes pierced by an arrow.

ST. OLAV (OLAF)
(Fig. 331–333) (See IV, Fig. 565)

ST. BLAISE
(Fig. 334)

St. Blaise was Bishop of Sebaste in Armenia and was a physician by profession. He retired to a mountain cave for contemplation and was surrounded by wild animals. The animals did not attack him but fawned upon him. The emperor's huntsmen saw this and be-

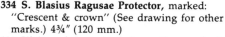

334 S. Blasius Ragusae Protector, marked: "Crescent & crown" (See drawing for other marks.) 4¾" (120 mm.)

335 Vision of Eustachius, inspection mark of Augsburg, Germany. Date letter worn, appears to be the Augsburg "pineapple" mark as used from 1686-1705. 9⅜" (237 mm.)

336-337 Angel Gabriel (?) Marks illegible. 6¾" (171 mm.)

338

340

lieved him to be a magician and took him prisoner. He was tortured by having his flesh torn with iron combs but his wounds were healed by divine help. In Renaissance paintings he is represented as an old man and carries an iron comb in allusion to his martyrdom. He is the patron saint of wild animals. He is invoked against sore throats because of the legend that he saved a child from choking on a fishbone.

THE VISION OF EUSTACHIUS
(Fig. 335)

Eustachius (Eustace) was originally called Placidus and was a captain of the guards under Trajan (Emperor 98-117) and later served under Hadrian (Emperor 117-138).

The legend about Placidus (Eustachius) relates that while he was still a heathen he was hunting and saw before him a white stag between whose horns appeared a bright light which formed a cross bearing the figure of Christ. Placidus fell on his knees and the apparition spoke to him, saying "Placidus, I am Christ whom thou has hitherto served without knowing me. Dost thou not believe"? The vision went on to say that Placidus would suffer many tribulations but that the Lord would not forsake him.

As a result of this vision, said to have taken place at Guadagnolo, near Rome, Placidus received baptism, together with his wife, Tatiana (Trajana). After baptism, their names were changed to Eustachius and Theopista.

As Christ foretold, Eustachius experienced much suffering. His wife was carried away by pirates and his sons by wild beasts. After fifteen years the family was miraculously reunited. But, when they refused to give thanks to the

---

338 **Noah,** marks illegible. 7½" (190 mm.)
339 **Noah,** London, 1864-65. 7¾" (196 mm.)
340 **Noah**
341 **Noah**

339

341

342

343

Roman gods, they were condemned to death in a heated brazen bull.

St. Eustachius has been honored for his martyrdom as one of the fourteen saints called Holy Helpers to whom persons in illness, peril, or want, often pray. He is a patron of the city of Madrid and of hunters.

A city in Canada bears his name as does a small island in the West Indies. It was in the harbor of Ft. Orange, on the island of St. Eustatius, on November 16, 1776 that the United States flag received its first foreign salute. The U.S. brig-of-war *Andrew Doria*, flying the flag of the new republic, roared out a national salute. After a short pause while Johannes deGraaf, the Governor, made a difficult decision as the Netherlands was then neutral, came the first salute to a flag of the United States.

NOAH
(Fig. 338–341)

Noah is represented by the anchor, symbol of Hope throughout the Christian world and by the raven which was sent out from the ark to find if the earth could be inhabited following the flood.

ADAM AND EVE
(Fig. 342–343)

Malum, the Latin word, means both evil and apple. This is the reason that the legend has grown up that the Tree of Knowledge in the Garden of Eden was an apple tree (Genesis 3:3).

---

342 **Adam and Eve,** Chester import marks for foreign plate for 1904-05. Other marks not traced. 5¾" (142 mm.)

343 **Adam and Eve,** marked: "Crowned N" "Rampant lion" Flli. COPPINI 800 "Caduceus".

344 **Crucifixion,** Chester import marks for foreign plate for 1903-04. Other marks not traced. 4½" (115 mm.) INRI on the Crucifix are the first four letters of the Latin words, "Jesus Nazarenus Rex Judaeorum" (Jesus of Nazareth, King of the Jews).

345 **Casting Out The Devil,** marked: N in a circle, "Crossed keys". 9⅜" (238 mm.)

344

345

CASTING OUT THE DEVIL
(Fig. 345)

The Archangels, members of the Third Hierarchy of angelic hosts, are the warriors of heaven and messengers of God to man. The winged figure in the center of the handle below Satan, is holding a sword. This is undoubtedly St. Michael who is frequently depicted doing battle with Satan. This refers to the dramatic description in Revelation (12:7-9), "And there was war in heaven: Michael and his angels fought against the dragon; and the dragon fought and his angels, and prevailed not; neither was their place found any more in heaven. And the great dragon was cast out, that old serpent, called the Devil, and Satan, which deceiveth the whole world: he was cast out into the earth, and his angels were cast out with him."

ST. MICHAEL
(Fig. 346)

St. Michael is one of the four Archangels mentioned by name in the Scriptures. According to Hebrew tradition, they sustain the throne of God. The name of the Archangel Michael means "like unto God." In Christian tradition he is described as the Captain-General of the hosts of heaven. It is he who will sound the last trumpet at the general resurrection (I Corinthians 15:52) and it is he who is to receive the immortal spirits when they are released from death and to weigh them in the balance (Daniel 5:27). St. Michael is frequently depicted holding the scales or balances in his role as Weigher of Souls.

346 St. Michael, marked: .934 quality mark for the Netherlands, British import marks for foreign plate for 1878. 7⅝" (195 mm.)

346

347

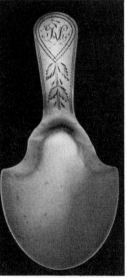

348

349

III
SPECIAL
TYPES OF
SPOONS

CADDY SPOONS
(Fig. 347–357)

The introduction of such expensive commodities as tea, coffee, and chocolate in the early part of the seventeenth century created a demand for new vessels for service, new containers for storage, and in the case of tea, before long, a new type of device for measuring.

Tea came from China and its introduction from that source had a profound influence on silver, porcelain, furniture, and other decorative arts.

Tea was shipped in containers called caddies, the name being derived from the Malayan word *kati*, indicating a measure of weight a little more than a pound (1 1/5 to 1 1/3 lbs.). Silversmiths created small silver boxes, holding about one-fifth that amount of tea, and to which the word *kati* was applied and soon Anglicized to *caddy*.

Because tea was expensive, these caddies were frequently made with locks or were kept in specially designed and locked boxes.

Tea caddies were first made with

---

347 **Caddy Spoon,** shell bowl, maker: WE London 1830-31.
348 **Caddy Spoon,** pastern or hoof-shape bowl, marked: Birmingham 1801-02.
349 **Caddy Spoon,** shell bowl, marked: London 1832-33.
350 **Caddy Spoon,** pastern or hoof-shape bowl, maker: Joseph Taylor, Birmingham 1813-14.
351 **Caddy Spoon,** sidewise oval bowl, maker: Joseph Taylor, Birmingham 1793,94.
352 **Caddy Spoon,** leaf shape bowl, maker: J. G. Birmingham 1898-99.

350

351

352

353

354

355

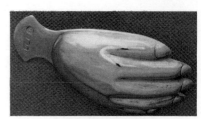

356

357

358

359

lift-off lids into which a small quantity of tea was measured and transferred to the teapot. Towards the middle of the eighteenth century tea caddies with hinged lids were introduced making it necessary to devise another means of measuring out the proper quantity of tea. It is thought that the short-handled medicine spoons which resemble a truncated teaspoon were first adapted to this purpose.

The first spoons made specifically for use as tea ladles were of shell design and originated in Sheffield, England. While London makers copied them and ultimately made more of them, it was in Sheffield in 1777 that the first fully hallmarked shell caddy spoon was made.

The shell motif may have been inspired by the sea shells packed with the tea chests by Chinese importers. These shells were scallop shape and served as inexpensive and readily available scoops. At least sixty variations of the shell motif have been found.

Some of the other early caddy spoons were made with scoop shape or deep oval bowls similar to sugar shells, though they had shorter handles. Decoration was often engraving, some of it bright-cut. These styles continued even after the advent of more elaborate ones. Other fancy shapes were not long in coming and silversmiths vied with each

353 **Caddy Spoon,** fig shape bowl, marked: London 1848-49.
354 **Caddy Spoon,** fig shape bowl, maker: HU Birmingham 1971-72.
355 **Caddy Spoon,** shell bowl; shell handle, maker: HU Birmingham 1971-72.
356 **Caddy Spoon,** maker: Francis Howard Ltd. Sheffield 1966-67. "Hand" caddy spoon is a reproduction of one made in 1805 by John Saunders of London.
357 **Caddy Spoon,** jockey cap, maker, Francis Howard Ltd. Sheffield 1966-67. Reproduction of an original "Jockey Cap" caddy spoon fashioned in the reign of George III.
358 **Shakespeare, Marked:** 10008. Brass
359 **Stratford,** no marks. Brass.

360

361

362

other to see who could produce the most unusual designs.

The inventive silversmiths of Birmingham put their talents to the creation of a wide variety of caddy spoons with a leaf motif, among which were the strawberry, grapevine, oak, ivy, tea, and acanthus. Other motifs attributed to a Birmingham origin are the "Eagle's Wing," the "Hand," and "Jockey Cap," all of which were made in many variations. The popularity of the "Hand" and the "Jockey Cap" remain so persistent that they are available today in reproduction. (Fig. 356-357).

Large numbers of caddy spoons were made of thin gauge silver, probably because heavy gauge metal would not be satisfactory for the die-stamping method of production. Some few appear to have been hand raised from flat sheets of silver.

A cast caddy spoon made by George Smith, London, about 1775 antedates others of this method of production by at least fifteen years as the first fully marked cast caddy spoon reported bears the London date of 1790. Other cast caddy spoons followed. Among them is the "Chinese Mandarin" in whose bowl is a portrait of that gentleman. It was made by Edward Farrell, London, 1816.

With the settlement of a colony of Italian craftsmen in the Clerkenwell district of London, there was introduced between 1790 and 1830 the technique of filigree work in the making of caddy spoons. Because of the delicate material used, these with only a few exceptions, bear no marks and are difficult to date except by style. These should not be

---

360 **Falstaff,** Brass.
361 **Charles Dickens,** no marks. Brass.
362 **Sam Weller,** marked: RGD. No. 698316:112817.
363 **Mrs. Bardall,** no marks. Brass.
364 **Fat Boy,** no marks. Brass.
365 **Drake,** no marks. Brass.

363

364

365

confused with the Indian and Chinese filigree articles which are generally darker in color and of finer wire. A later development was the creation of a simulated filigree in which the pattern was die-stamped, not made of the delicate wire.

A caddy spoon cast of brass and bearing the head of Britannia (or Minerva?) on the handle has been attributed to manufacture in China for the English trade c. 1830 (*Antiques* October 1965). During Victorian days caddy spoons were cast in silver in such forms as shells with handles of intertwined leaves and blossoms. Later Victorian spoons were cast in brass, their bowls being usually plain oval or round but with handles representing famous places and people, both real and storybook characters. Cast brass spoons of this type are still sold throughout the British Isles and Canada. An even more recent type is made of base metals and chromium plated.

Early tea caddy spoons were made primarily in England with the greatest numbers coming from Birmingham and London. They were also made by the provincial silversmiths of Sheffield, Exeter, York, and Newcastle. Those made in Edinburgh and Glasgow in Scotland, and Dublin, Ireland tend to be somewhat larger than those of English origin. American-made caddy spoons are a rarity. Other countries in which they were made are the Netherlands, France, Russia, China, Norway and Denmark.

Various materials were used. Early ones were made primarily of solid silver, some few being made of natural cowrie shells with silver mounts. "Old Sheffield Plate" was used but as the edges had to be covered to hide the "sandwich effect" too much time was consumed in their production thereby increasing their cost. With the advent of electroplating, numbers of caddy spoons were made but their design is usually of no great interest.

During the first twenty years of the nineteenth century caddy spoons with somewhat longer handles found favor. These handles were often of tortoiseshell, mother-of-pearl, boxwood, agate, bone, and ivory, the latter two being sometimes stained green, red, or yellow.

Niello work was used on some silver caddy spoons. Tortoise-shell piqué with gold or silver was an especially effective medium. Other materials used were china, glass, horn, and pewter.

SHAKESPEARE AND STRATFORD
(Fig. 358–359) (See also IV, Fig. 716 and VI, Fig. 1791–1795)

FALSTAFF
(Fig. 360)

The comic character, Sir John Falstaff, appears in two of Shakespeare's plays, *King Henry IV* and *Merry Wives of Windsor*.

Shakespeare's characterization was based on Sir John Oldcastle, whose story was obtained from *The Famous Victories of Henry V*, a crude and anonymous drama. He changed his character's name to Falstaff because the historical Oldcastle had contemporary descendants. The name itself may have been suggested by the historical Sir John Fastolf, who appears as a character in Part I of *King Henry VI*.

Falstaff appears in *King Henry IV* as a mountain of a man, jovial, and yet a cheat and a bully. He was a glutton and addicted to copious draughts of "sherris-sack" to which he renders immortal tribute which ends with, "If I had a thousand sons, the first human principle I would teach them should be to forswear thin potations, and to addict themselves to sack." One shudders to think of the blast he would loose at the thought of being portrayed on an instrument for the measuring of tea!

366

367

368

CHARLES DICKENS (1812–1870)
(Fig. 361–364)

The English novelist, Charles Dickens was christened Charles John Huffam (Huffham) Dickens. He was born in Landport, on the island of Portsea, Portsmouth, England, February 7, 1812. His father's improvidence and eventual imprisonment for debt forced young Dickens to support himself at an early age.

Dickens' first real literary success came with the publication of the *Pickwick Papers*, issued serially from about February 1836 to November 1837. This work was first intended to be a series of humorous illustrations with a running commentary on the activities of a group of amateur sportsmen. Dickens' idea of the main character brought about an entirely different development of the series. It is essentially a plotless narrative which reports the excursions and attendant experiences of Mr. Pickwick and is climaxed by a breach-of-promise suit brought against him by MRS. BARDELL (Fig. 363). The introduction of SAM WELLER (Fig. 362), Pickwick's shrewd servant with the amusing tricks of cockney speech, brought immediate popularity to the series and fame to its author. FAT BOY (Fig. 364) was another character in the *Pickwick Papers*.

DRAKE (1540–1595)
(Fig. 365)

Sir Francis Drake, the English naval hero, was the first English circumnavigator of the globe. His famous voy-

366 **Sir Walter Raleigh,** no marks. Brass.
367 **Robert Bruce,** no marks. Brass.
368 **Mary, Queen of Scots,** registry number illegible.
369 **Robert Burns,** marked: No. 564487. Brass.
370 **British Lion,** no marks. Brass.
371 **King George VI & Queen Elizabeth, Coronation 1937.** No marks. Silverplate.

369

370

371

71

age was undertaken in 1577 as part of a vast scheme of British expansion. He set out from Plymouth on December 13, 1577 with a fleet of three armed ships, the *Pelican* (later renamed the *Golden Hind*) in which he sailed, the *Elizabeth*, the *Marigold* and six auxiliary ships. The *Marigold* was lost in a violent storm and the *Elizabeth* returned home. After an eventful voyage he returned to England on September 26, 1580. Queen Elizabeth I visited him on board his ship at Deptford and knighted him on its deck.

SIR WALTER RALEIGH (1552–1618)
(Fig. 366)

Sir Walter Raleigh, English statesman, navigator, author, military and naval commander, was born at Hayes Barton, a farmstead in the parish of East Budleigh, Devonshire. He is best remembered for his voyages of discovery with Sir Humphrey Gilbert, his half-brother, and for winning the favor of Queen Elizabeth I.

During the years 1584 through 1589 he sent expeditions to Virginia which were unsuccessful in their efforts at colonization because the Queen forbade his personal participation.

It was through his efforts that the potato and tobacco plants were introduced into England.

Following the death of the Queen, Raleigh was sent to the Tower of London, accused of plots to prevent accession of King James to the throne. There he lived in relative comfort with his wife, son and personal servants for thirteen years. In 1616, on his promise to lead an expedition to a gold mine in America, Raleigh was released. The expedition failed to reach the mine and on his return to England Raleigh was executed by James I in the Old Palace Yard.

ROBERT BRUCE, (1274-1329)
(Fig. 367)

Robert VIII, son of Robert VII, earl of Carrick became king of Scotland.

Robert the Bruce is a name still honored in Scotland as he took up arms against Edward II of England and united Highlands and Lowlands in a single fierce fight for freedom. He is especially remembered for his decisive victory in the Battle of Bannockburn, June 24, 1314 though it was not until 1328 that the English king (Edward III) was forced to renounce his sovereignty over Scotland.

Robert Bruce is especially remembered for his perseverance in the face of defeat. The story is that six times he watched a spider attempt to swing from one beam to another to attach its web, only to end in failure, but the seventh try was successful. The king took this to be a good omen and resolved to resume his own struggle.

MARY, QUEEN OF SCOTS
(Fig. 368) (See VI, Fig. 1787)
ROBERT BURNS (1759-1796)
(Fig. 369)

Robert Burns, Scottish national poet and idol of the Scots was worn down in youth by hard toil on the farm. His songs and poems simply breathe the air of his native land where they hold foremost place. Burns was a man of conflicting emotions and experiences— often his own worst enemy. His immortal ballads give glimpses of his wasted genius.

BRITISH LION
(Fig. 370) (See IV Fig. 875–879, 848, 812)
KING GEORGE VI AND QUEEN ELIZABETH, CORONATION 1937
(Fig. 371–372) (See IV Fig. 838–841)
QUEEN ELIZABETH II
(Fig. 373) (See IV, Fig. 842–846)
ANCIENT CITY GATE, WELLS
(Fig. 375)

The ancient city gate in Wells, Somerset, England, is called Browne's Gate after Richard Browne, a shoemaker, who was living in the adjoining house in 1553. The gate was erected one hundred years earlier by Bishop Bekynton.

372

373

374

375

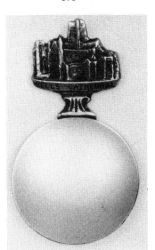

376

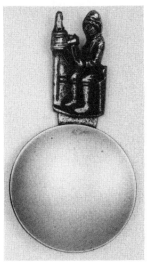

377

WELLS CATHEDRAL
(Fig. 374–379)

The Cathedral Church of Saint Andrew in Wells is thought to be one of the loveliest of all English cathedrals. Tradition has it that about the year 705, King Ina, by the advice of St. Aldhelm, Bishop of Sherborne, founded a church here in honor of Saint Andrew with a college of secular priests to serve it. When the bishopric of Wells was founded in 909, it is certain that this church became its Cathedral and these priests its canons.

The Cathedral now standing was begun by Bishop Reginald de Bohun between 1175 and 1185. The stone of which it was built was quarried at Dolting, and it is interesting to note that when replacement stones have to be made today, the stone still comes from the same quarry, some eight miles from Wells.

The central tower was raised to its present height in the fourteenth century. This considerable addition to its weight was so great that there was danger of its collapse. A major catastrophe was avoided when, inverted arches, which give additional strength to the columns supporting the massive weight, were built on three sides, the quire screen giving the necessary support on the fourth. The tower remains secure through this clever engineering device that is such a striking feature of the Cathedral interior.

A fourteenth century CLOCK (Fig. 378–379) stands in the north transept,

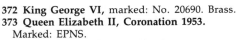

372 **King George VI,** marked: No. 20690. Brass.
373 **Queen Elizabeth II, Coronation 1953.** Marked: EPNS.
374 **Wells Cathedral,** no marks. Brass.
375 **The Ancient Gate House, Wells,** marked: Rd. Applied For 16034. Brass.
376 **Wells Cathedral,** marked: PEERAGE, ENGLAND, Brass.
377 **Jack Blandiver,** marked: Peerage, England, Brass.

378

379

380

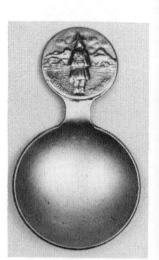

381

382

383

where on payment of a trifling fee today's visitors may watch as it strikes the hour. The importance of this famous timepiece is sometimes obscured by the jousting knights performing every hour, delighting all visitors. Not merely a mechanical toy, this beautifully decorated clock shows the hours on a twenty-four hour dial, the minutes, the days of the month and the phases of the moon, all on the interior clock face. It is the oldest complete mechanical clock in England, dating from 1392. It was invented by a man of Glastonbury called Peter Lightfoot. When the clock strikes the hour, so does the great bell on the tower strike and the puppet figures of knights on horseback joust. On the quarter hour, the figure of Jack Blandiver (Blandifer) (Fig. 377) sounds the note by kicking his heels against a bell. Two quarter-jacks dressed in fifteenth century armor, and standing four feet in height built of solid oak and finely carved, strike the bells above the outside dial. Visitors often join in reciting the Lord's Prayer after the clock strikes the hour.

THE LADIES OF PLAS NEWYDD, LLANGOLLEN
(Fig. 380)

During the eighteenth century the house called *Plas Newydd* was the home of Lady Eleanor Butler and the Hon. Sarah Ponsonby, two romantic and eccentric young women who fled there from their home in Ireland and came to be known as the "Ladies of Llangol-

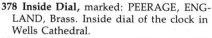

378 **Inside Dial,** marked: PEERAGE, ENG-LAND, Brass. Inside dial of the clock in Wells Cathedral.
379 **Outside Dial,** marked: PEERAGE, ENG-LAND. Brass. Outside dial of clock in Wells Cathedral.
380 **The Ladies of Plas Newydd, Llangollen.** Brass.
381 **Jenny Jones,** no marks. Brass.
382 **Jenny Jones,** no marks. Brass.
383 **Yarmouth,** no marks. Brass.

384

385

386

len." Determined to be intellectual and never marry, they kept busy knitting blue stockings (creating a new English expression). They were visited by notable people such as Wellington, Scott, Wordsworth and DeQuincey.

Llangollen is a lovely ancient town in northern Wales on the River Dee and is famous for the International Musical Eisteddfod, or singing festival held annually in July.

JENNY JONES
(Fig. 381–382)

Jenny Jones is a generic term that signifies any woman in typical Welsh costume. John Cambrian Rowlands (1819-1890), artist of the 1840s during the influx of tourists to Wales, encouraged the sale of prints of Welsh costumes and customs. These spoons may have been based on Rowland's drawing of "Jenny Jones" against a background view of Llangollen. A companion drawing shows a male character in the so-called Welsh national costume.

YARMOUTH, ENGLAND
(Fig. 383)

Yarmouth, Isle of Wight, England, is noted for its 145 narrow lanes at right angles to the main streets, known as the "rows" in which the houses were once the homes of wealthy burgesses. The lofty Nelson monument stands in the market-place, and the parish church founded in 1101, is the largest parish church in England.

The arms of Yarmouth consist of

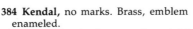

384 **Kendal,** no marks. Brass, emblem enameled.
385 **City of St. Andrews,** maker: A·J·B· Birmingham 1927-28·
386 **Houses of Parliament,** no marks. Silverplate and enamel.
387 **Oxford,** no marks. Silverplate and enamel.
388 **Weston-Super-Mare,** Marked: MADE IN ENGLAND. Silverplate and enamel.
389 **Cat & Fiddle,** marked: PEERAGE, ENGLAND. Brass.

387

388

389

half-lions and half-herrings which arose from the cutting in half of two shields—that of England and that of the Hanse.

KENDAL, ENGLAND
(Fig. 384)

Kendal, Westmorland, England is an old border town in the Lake District. Many of its houses were built around a central courtyard, accessible only through a single narrow gate—more easily defended during border clashes. Sitting among green hills in the Valley of the Kent River and because of its many gray limestone buildings, Kendal is known as "Auld Grey Town." It is a manufacturing center for shoes, cottons, soap, paper, carpets and farm machinery. Its woolen industry was introduced by Flemish immigrants and has long been famous. During the Middle Ages the cloth manufactured there was known as "Kendal Green."

CITY OF ST. ANDREWS
(Fig. 385)

The City of St. Andrews, Fifeshire, Scotland, received its name in the eighth century when the relics of Andrew the Apostle were taken there.

The first cathedral was built there in Celtic times; during the reign of David I (1124–1153) a second one was built. The third cathedral was built in 1318 but following a sermon by John Knox in 1559, the cathedral was partially destroyed. Although the cathedral is now largely in ruins, it was once the largest in the country.

St. Andrews present claim to fame is based on being the headquarters and birthplace of golf. There are four courses, including the Royal and Ancient Club founded in 1754.

HOUSES OF PARLIAMENT
(Fig. 386)(See also IV, Fig. 697)

OXFORD
(Fig. 387)

Oxford, Oxfordshire, England is best-known as the seat of Oxford University. It is an ancient city that was first mentioned as a "ford for oxen" over the Thames at Hinksey in the Anglo-Saxon Chronicles of 912 A.D.

WESTON-SUPER-MARE
(Fig. 388)

Weston-Super-Mare, Somerset, England was originally a fishing village and until 1800 had a population of no more than 100. It has little of historical interest but does have all the traditional features of a seaside resort.

CAT & FIDDLE
(Fig. 389)

The Cat & Fiddle on this spoon recalls the well-known nursery rhyme that says, "Hey, diddle diddle, the cat and the fiddle/ the cow jumped over the moon./ The little dog laughed to see such sport,/ and the dish ran away with the spoon."

EDINBURGH
(Fig. 391) (See IV, Fig. 749–753)
PORT GLASGOW
(Fig. 392)

Port Glasgow, Renfrewshire, Scotland, is a seaport on the estuary of the Clyde, twenty miles west and slightly north of Glasgow. It was there in 1662 that the magistrates of Glasgow purchased thirteen acres of land on which they built harbors and the first drydock in Scotland. Until the Clyde was deepened to allow large vessels to sail up to Glasgow, Port Glasgow was the seaport for the town.

According to legend, when the funeral procession of a girl who had died of consumption passed along the shore near Port Glasgow, a mermaid rose up from the water and recited this mournful verse:

"If they wad drink nettles in March,

390

391

392

And eat muggons (mugwort) in May,
Sae mony braw maidens
Wadna gang to the clay."

LONDON
(Fig. 393) (See also IV, Fig. 698–693)
WINCHESTER
(Fig. 394)

Winchester was a tribal center long before the Romans came to Britain. It was called *Caer-Gwent* by the Britons and *Venta Belgarum* by the Romans under whom it was an important place with a Christian church. The city was named *Wintanceaster* by the Saxons and became the capital of England under them when the country was united by Egbert in the first half of the ninth century.

Winchester Cathedral is the most important building in the town. The oldest parts date from the eleventh century but the greater part of it was erected from the thirteenth to the sixteenth centuries, much of it under William of Wykeham. There is said to have been a Christian church at Winchester in the latter part of the second century. Late in the third century it was converted into a temple to Woden.

Sometime in the latter half of the seventh century Winchester became an episcopal see and has had an unbroken line of bishops, including St. Swithin (Swithun). When Swithun died in 862, he was buried outside the church of that time, in accordance with his wishes to lie where the rain would fall on him. Nearly a century later, the

---

390 **Alsatian Wolf Dog,** marked: PEERAGE, ENGLAND. Brass.
391 **Edinburgh,** no marks. Silverplate and enamel.
392 **Port Glasgow,** marked: EXQUISITE PLATE, MADE IN ENGLAND. Silverplate and enamel.
393 **London,** marked: E.P.O.B. MADE IN ENGLAND. Silverplate and enamel.
394 **Winchester,** no marks. Brass and enamel.
395 **Leaf,** marked: L Sterling.

393

394

395

396

397

399

400

monks decided to move his tomb inside, and according to legend, St. Swithun's spirit was so angered by the move that it rained violently for forty days. Since that day, rain on St. Swithun's Day (July 15) has been an omen of continuing rainy weather.

GEORGE VI AND QUEEN ELIZABETH
(Fig. 397) (See also IV, Fig. 838–841 and III, Fig. 371–372)
WARWICK CASTLE
(Fig. 398) (See also IV, Fig. 714–715)
CITY HALL, TORONTO
(Fig. 399)

The City Hall at Queen and Bay Streets, Toronto, Canada, dominates the colonnaded Nathan Phillips Square. It was designed by the Finnish architect, Viljo Revell.

CHIEN D'OR, GOLDEN DOG, QUEBEC
(Fig. 400)(See also V, Fig. 1543)
NABOB
(Fig. 402)

Nabob is a tradename used by the Francis H. Leggett & Company, of New York City, since 1902. Included in the products carrying this label are tea, coffee, olives, dried fruits, jellies and other staple goods.

BLACKGANG SMUGGLER
(Fig. 406)

On the southwest coast of the Isle of Wight there is the Blackgang Chine (ridge or crest) which derives its name from the old smuggling gangs who must have found this 400 foot deep

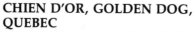

396 **Leaf,** marked: STERLING "Fleur-de-lis"
397 **George VI and Queen Elizabeth,** Crowned 1937, marked: Birmingham 1936-37.
398 **Warwick Castle,** marked: 16417. Brass.
399 **City Hall, Toronto,** marked: Rerd. Applied For. Brass.
400 **Chien D'Or, Golden Dog, Quebec,** no marks. Brass.
401 **Norway,** "Norge" on back.

401

78

402

403

404

ravine an ideal hideout as there is no way down to the beach from this stream-cut chine.

MARY, MARY, QUITE CONTRARY
(Fig. 407)

Many nursery rhymes are known to have been written originally, not for children, but as social commentaries. According to popular tradition the original Mary was Mary, Queen of Scots, whose gay ways displeased the dour Scottish Protestant reformer, John Knox. If she was the Mary of the nursery rhyme, "the pretty maids" might be the "Four Marys," her ladies-in-waiting. It is thought that the "cockleshells" were the decorations on a particular dress she was given by the Dauphin. All this is based on speculation. No proof has been found that the rhyme was known before the eighteenth century. However, there is a tune "Cuckolds all a row" in the 1651 edition of Playford's *Dancing Master*. The last line of the 1780 version of the rhyme reads "Sing cuckolds all on a row" could well be sung to the tune in the *Dancing Master*.

LINCOLN IMP
(Fig. 409–411) (See also IV, Fig. 719–720)
PIXIES
(Fig. 412–416)

Pixies are fairies or brownies—"the little people" of nocturnal habits whose chief amusements are music, dancing, laughter, and oftentimes, mischief. They make fairy rings in the meadow and turn the milk sour. They can also be helpful. There is the story told of Cornish pixies who fed a woman called

402 **Nabob,** no marks. Brass.
403 **Thistle,** mark illegible.
404 **Tobacco Leaf,** marked: HANDMADE IN RHODESIA. Copper.
405 **Owl,** marked: MADE IN ENGLAND. Brass.
406 **Blackgang Smuggler.** Brass.
407 **Mary, Mary, Quite Contrary.** Brass.

405

406

407

408

409

410

411

412

413

Anne Jefferies for six months and of the strange and wonderful cures she performed with the salves and medicines she received from them.

There have been many explanations to account for the belief in fairies. Stories and legends about "the little people" are common to cultures all around the world. According to some traditions, they are fallen angels, too good for Hell but not good enough for Heaven.

Some believe that the fairy faith is actually a cult of the dead, as in many stories it is difficult to distinguish between ghosts and fairies.

Others feel that when invaders arrived in an area and drove the original inhabitants into hiding, their skill at hiding in the woods seemed to give them the power of invisibility, and the memory of the early people lived on in tales about fairies.

Fairy stories have developed too out of early attempts to explain strange happenings.

Pixie Puck is the mischievous hobgoblin, half fairy and half human, who could change his shape at will. He was known in medieval mythology. His character and attributes are depicted in Shakespeare's *Midsummer Night's Dream*. Puck is known by a variety of names, Robin Goodfellow being one of them.

Country folk still put out little bowls of food and milk for the pixies. Skeptics say that the hedgehogs eat the food.

HORN OF ULPHUS, YORK
(Fig. 417)

Among the treasures preserved in

---

408 Dorothy, marked: RD. 777397 113 MADE IN ENGLAND.
409 Lincoln Imp, no marks. Brass.
410 Lincoln Imp, no marks. Brass.
411 Lincoln Imp, no marks. Silverplate.
412 Exmoor Pixie, marked: Rd. Applied For 14595. Brass.
413 Dartmoor Pixie, no marks. Brass.

414

415

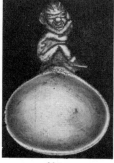

416

York Minster, the Cathedral Church of St. Peter, in York, is the Horn of Ulphus. This thousand-year-old horn is carved from an elephant tusk and is more than two feet long. The silver-gilt ornamentation on it is thought to be Italian work.

Ulphus (or Ulph) was a Danish chieftain who held lands in Western Yorkshire at the beginning of the eleventh century. When his eldest son, Adelbert, was killed in battle, Ulphus attempted to bypass the claims of his other three sons and to bequeath his lands to his granddaughter, Adelwynne. She persuaded him to give the lands to the Church. Ulphus filled his largest drinking horn with wine and knelt at the high altar in York Minster and, drinking the wine, laid the horn on the altar as a pledge for all time as title to his lands and wealth.

WITCH OF WOOKEY
(Fig. 418)

Near the village of Wookey, Somerset, England, the River Axe has carved out a series of caverns in whose chambers are many colorful stalagmites and stalactites. One of these stalagmite formations is said to be the Witch of Wookey, who was turned to stone for her wicked ways.

The witch is supposed to have lived in the caves with her familiars, a goat and its kid. Once crossed in love, she became vindictive and cast evil spells on the villagers. The frightened populace appealed to the Abbot of Glastonbury and he sent a monk to confront the witch. Evil cannot prevail against good. The monk sprinkled her with

414 **Cornish Pixie,** no marks. Brass.
415 **Pixie Puck,** no marks. Brass.
416 **Pixie,** no marks. Brass.
417 **York, Horn of Ulphus.** Brass.
418 **Witch of Wookey,** marked: 195. Brass.
419 **Cross Cercelée,** maker: SS Edinburgh
　　1960-61.

417

418

419

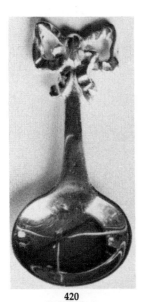

420

holy water and she turned to stone where she remains to this day.

Though this is a legend, in 1912 excavations in the caves revealed the bones of a woman of the Romano-British period. Nearby were the bones of a goat and a kid, together with a comb, a dagger and a round stalagmite which has been likened to a witch's crystal ball. The relics are in the Wells museum.

SOUTHERN RHODESIA
(Fig. 423)(See also IV, Fig. 1390)
UGANDA
(Fig. 424)

Uganda was a Protectorate in east central Africa under British administra-

420 Bow, no marks.
421 Horn, no marks. Scottish.
422 And One For Me, no marks. Brass. "And one for me" refers to the custom of using one measure of tea for every cup, and "one for the pot."
423 S. Rhodesia, no marks. Silverplate and enamel.
424 Uganda, marked: Chromium plate, Sheffield, England.
425-431 Dutch Spoons. Spoons of this type were made more for decoration than utility.

427

426

421

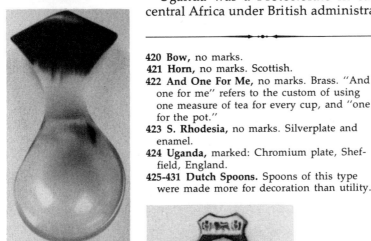

422

423

424

425

428

435

429

tion but gained its independence in 1962. It retained its badge displaying a crested crane and placed this at the center of a flag, striped horizontally in black, yellow and red.

BONBON SPOONS

After the middle of the nineteenth century simple ways of living were abandoned. The average American found that he no longer had to spend every waking moment in the pursuit of a living to maintain a family. There was a release from the pressure of time and economic factors which had prevented an expansion of ideas and ideals. With leisure time available there came the desire to spend it in pleasant surroundings and in agreeable company. Entertaining at home was in vogue and frequently took the form of elaborate dinners of many courses. Afternoon teas

---

432 **Dutch Bonbon Spoon**, marked: .833 standard mark, N$_2$.

433 **Dutch Bonbon Spoon**, marked: "Key" export stamp for silver.

434 **English Coat-Of-Arms Bonbon Spoon**, marked: STERLING.

435 **Bonbon Spoon**, maker: WC London 1890-91.

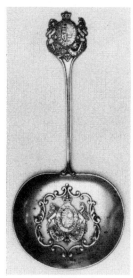

434

430

431

432

433

436

442

436 **Bonbon Spoon,** marked: Whiting Co., old trademark, STERLING. The handle is ivory.
437 **Bonbon Spoon,** marked: Arthur Stone trademark, STERLING B.
438 **Bonbon Spoon,** marked: "Pineapple" mark for Augsburg, Germany, 1674-1680; "R"; inspection mark; another illegible mark.
439 **Bonbon Spoon,** no marks. Copper and brass.
440 **Dragon Bonbon Spoon,** no marks. Probably Chinese.
441 **Chrysanthemum Bonbon Spoon.**
442 **Bonbon Spoon,** Gorham Company trademark, STERLING.
443 **Norwegian Dragon,** marked: 900S OXO.

437

443

back

438

439

440

441

444

451

were fashionable. Etiquette demanded a different type of silverware for the service and consumption of each dish. It simply would not do to serve tomatoes with the same server used for croquettes. The proliferation of "Fancy Pieces" as they were known in the trade, reached its height soon after the beginning of the twentieth century. World War I curtailed production of silverware for several years and in 1926 manufacturers adopted a simplified list of flatware, place pieces, and serving pieces. Most manufacturers still adhere, more or less, to these guidelines.

During the years of specialization in serving pieces some of the most ornate

---

444 Dutch Sugar Scoop, marked: (See drawing)
445 Norwegian Bonbon Spoon, marked: MH 830S M & I intertwined.
446 Danish Bonbon Spoon, marked: (See drawing)
447 Monkey Spoon
448 Monkey Spoon, marked: "Hatchet" O, other marks worn.
449 Monkey Spoon, marked: (See drawing)
450 Monkey Spoon
451 Monkey Spoon, marked: S .833 standard mark, export stamp.

450

445

446

447

448   449

452

453

articles made were the bonbon spoons without which no afternoon tea could have been conducted. Many were made in this country but great numbers were imported. The intended purpose of some of these imported spoons eludes us today and in many cases we can only speculate that they were used as scoops—for bonbons, nuts, mints, or sugar.

MONKEY SPOONS

Monkey spoons originated in the Netherlands, and later were found on the banks of the Hudson River during the seventeenth and eighteenth centuries. The affluent New York Dutch people bestowed monkey spoons upon

---

452 **Monkey Spoon**
453 **Monkey Spoon GEB?**
454 **Monkey Spoon N**
455 **Monkey Spoon,** marked: P "Crown" "L-ion"
456 **Monkey Spoon,** marked: HOLLAND .833 standard mark, export stamp. "Crown" B
457-458 **Monkey Spoons**
459 **Monkey Spoon.** This spoon measures 7⅞" (220 mm.). That is more than twice the length and four times the capacity of the average monkey spoon.

459

454

455

456

457

458

460

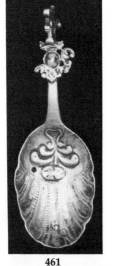

461

467

466

relatives and friends at funerals, weddings, and christenings.

The first person to delve into the history of these curious spoons was Mary P. Ferris who offered the following explanation of their purpose: "Among the Dutch drinking is called 'zuiging de monkey'. . .When a worthy burgher was ready for his morning meal, he went to the old sideboard and took his morning tonic of Santa Cruz rum, following it with a pinch of salt. This morning dram was to serve only as an

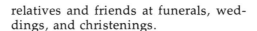

460 **Monkey Spoon,** marked: VC.
461 **Monkey Spoon**
462 **Monkey Spoon,** marked: N O "Fish" standard mark for less than .833.
463 **Monkey Spoon,** marks illegible.
464 **Monkey Spoon,** marks: State stamp; Amsterdam guild mark; The Hague guild mark; VDB; London import marks for foreign plate for 1898-99.
465 **Monkey Spoon,** marks: 930; C; "Lion" standard for .934 silver; "Key" export mark; Amsterdam guild mark; other marks not traced.
466-471 **Monkey Spoons.** #469 is marked: N_2 .934 standard for silver; "Key: export mark; Chester import marks for foreign plate for 1910-11; BML.

462

463

464

465

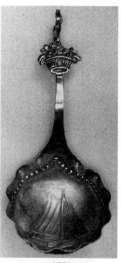

476

468

appetizer, and must be a small one, hence the use of the *monkey lepel* (monkey spoon) or liquor spoon with its shallow bowl. As the flowing bowl played a prominent part in the weddings and funerals of our worthy Dutch ancestors, it will be readily seen that a monkey spoon was a most significant token of esteem, and hence an appropriate gift.

Monkey spoons have curved handles, making it possible to suspend them from the rim of a punch bowl. Many have a monkey on the knop, but other decorations are also found, such as

472 **Monkey Spoon,** marked: Old English "n"; BM and Chester 1901 import marks for foreign plate.
473 **Monkey Spoon,** marked: "Key" export mark, "Fish" state stamp for silver less than .833 standard.
474 **Monkey Spoon,** marked: .833 standard mark; $\frac{16}{R}$ (Law of 1852 silver mark; (See drawing for other mark)
475 **Monkey Spoon Strainer,** marked: VB; .833 standard; export stamp; DS.
476 **Monkey Spoon.**

475

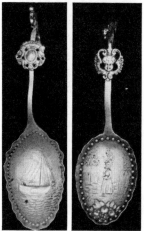

469   470

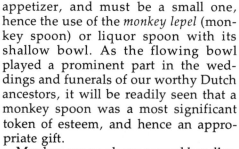

471

471   472   473   474

88

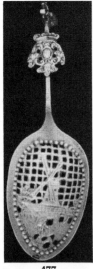

477

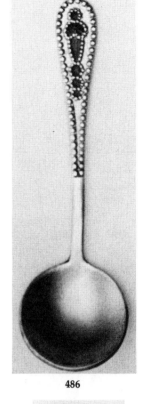

roosters, squirrels, birds and children. The majority of these spoons also have a boss directly beneath the knop, exhibiting a heart, rosette, cherub or other device. The bowls, round or oval, are nearly always decorated elaborately, sometimes with scenes symbolic of the occasion for which they were made. Some of the bowls are quite large, giv-

477 Monkey Spoon Strainer, marks: M G; D; .833 standard mark; "Key" export stamp; State stamp (Law of 1852); date letter for 1889.

478 Monkey Spoon

479 Salt Spoon, marked: IL/HL/CL, John, Henry & Charles Lias. London 1826-27

480 Salt Spoon, marked: French quality mark, first quality, maker's mark illegible.

481 Salt Spoon, marked: S. KIRK & SON STERLING

482 Salt Spoon, marked: Martin Hall & Co., Ltd. Sheffield 1870-80, RM/EH.

483 Salt Spoon, marked: W&H (Wood & Hughes, New York) trademark used after 1871.

484 Salt Spoon, no marks.

485 Seafood Salt Spoon, no marks.

485 Seafood Salt Spoon, no marks.

486 Russian Salt Spoon, marked: 2V HO, "Hammer & sickle" 875 within a star.

478

486

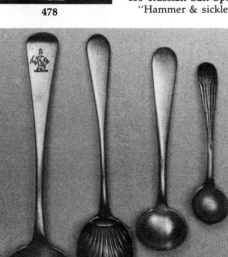

479   480   481   482   483   484   485

487 488

489 490

502 503

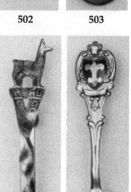

500 501

ing their users more than "just an appetizer" in the morning. In the Netherlands they are simply called 'Room lepel' (cream ladle).

487 English Victorian Salt Spoon, maker: George Angell, London 1854-55.
488 Michelangelo's David, no marks. Italian.
489 Thistle, marked: BM Co. STERLING
490 English Salt Spoon, coin bowl minted in 1914. The coin is three pence, no longer used.
491 Face Powder Scoop, marked: .925 ERR HECHO(?) EN MEXICO
492 Salt Spoon, no marks.
493 Salt Spoon, no marks. Mexican coin bowl.
494 Salt Spoon, marked: PRIMANS L. C. CO. SWEDEN
495 Salt Spoon, no marks.
496 Salt Spoon, marked: STERLING.
497 Salt Spoon, marked: T. K. CO.
498 Salt Spoon, marked: W. A. Birmingham 1902-03.
499 Salt Spoon, marked: Wm. BROWN 10. pz. 15.
500-504 Salt Spoons made into pins. #500 marked: 925. #501 no marks. #502 marked: Fine Arts Co. trademark, STERLING. #503 marked: STERLING. #504 no marks.

491   492   493   494   495   496   497   498   499

504

508

509

SALT SPOONS
(Fig. 479–504)

It was not until the advent of the more refined eating habits that came in during the eighteenth century that the tiny spoons used for adding salt or other condiments graced the dining table. They were made to accompany the sets of two, four, six, or even eight, salt cellars made during the first seventy-five years of that century.

Very few salt spoons earlier than 1800 of American make are still in existence. The styles of salt spoon handles followed those of larger spoons but the bowls were usually made rounder, or shell shaped.

It is possible to assemble a collection of salt spoons made after 1850 in variations of the "fiddle pattern" or in the numerous "fancy" patterns then coming into vogue. Salt spoons whose bowls were made of old coins make an especially intriguing collection.

505

SNUFF SPOONS
(Fig. 510–11)

The practice of snuff-taking was introduced into Europe from America during the sixteenth century and by the eighteenth had become quite common on the continent and in England. The capture of a large quantity of snuff by Sir George Rooke in Vigo Bay (Battle of Vigo Bay, Spain, 1702) made it readily available and the practice became widespread throughout England.

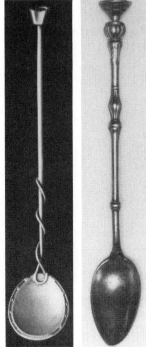

505 **Brandy Burning Spoon,** Renaissance pattern, patented in 1894. Marked: STERLING Dominick & Haff trademark. Brandy is poured into the spoon while it sits on a cup of coffee. A match is touched to the brandy and it is then gently lowered into the cup.
506 **Muddler,** marked: STERLING.
507 **Sugar Masher,** no marks. Pewter.
508 **Pipe Cleaning Spoon,** British made.
509 **Pipe Cleaning Spoon,** marked: STERLING. Hayden Mfg. Co. Newark, New Jersey trademark.
510-511 **Snuff Spoons,** no marks. Brass.

506   507

510

511

521

Snuffboxes were made in great quantities out of silver and gold and were often set with precious stones. Many were small ones to be carried in the pocket and were often accompanied by an *etui* that included a tiny spoon for taking up a pinch of snuff without soiling the fingers.

Table-top boxes were frequently accompanied by a small spoon with which one could refill the pocket box.

Snuff-taking was introduced into China in the seventeenth century and in the eighteenth became fashionable among the aristocracy. In that country it was the fashion to carry snuff in a beautifully decorated bottle. These bottles each had a spoon attached to the stopper and was used for dipping out

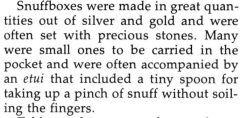

512-514 **Brass Spoons,** no marks.
515 **Ear Cleaning Spoon,** no marks.
516 **Ear Cleaning Spoon,** no marks. "KOREA" on front.
517 **Ear Cleaning Spoon** and tweezers, no marks. Silverplate worn.
518 **Ear Cleaning Spoon and toothpick.** Bone. Japan.
519-520 **Ear Cleaning Spoons,** no marks. One has bamboo handle and the other is tortoise shell. Japan.
521 **Mustache Spoon,** maker: William Hutton & Sons, Sheffield.

512   513

514

515   516   517   518

519   520

522

the snuff for inhaling. The bottles themselves are works of art. A wide variety of material was used: rock crystal, frequently painted on the inside; carved aquamarine; jade; bronze; lacquer; silver and gold; malachite; hornbill beak; glass; ivory; amethyst quartz and coral are some of the materials used. Spoons were made of wood, brass, ivory, silver and gold.

MUSTACHE SPOONS
(Fig. 521–523)

That Victorian badge of masculinity and household authority, the mustache,

---

522 Mustache Spoon, maker: Elkington & Co., Birmingham, c. 1889-90.

523 Mustache Spoon, maker: Reed & Barton. Made in silverplate and vermeil in both lefthanded and righthanded versions.

523a Advertisement from *Washington Post,* Washington, D. C.

523b Folder distributed with Reed & Barton's ''Master'' Mustache Spoons.

Reed & Barton's "Master" Mustache Spoon Banishes SASM* Forever

*SASM—Sloshed and Sopped Mustache

reed & barton silverplate mustache spoon
5.95

523a

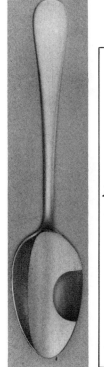

523

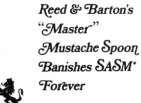

Reed & Barton's "Master" Mustache Spoon Banishes SASM Forever*

'SASM—
Sloshed and
Sopped Mustache

523b

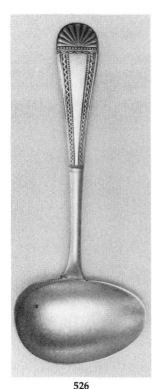

has once again assumed a place of importance and along with it mustache combs, spoons, trimmers, cups and brushes.

During their last heyday in this country equipment for the care of mustaches was the subject of many patents.* Twenty or more different mustache

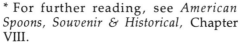

524 Pap or Caudle Spoon, marked: STERLING 90 Hartglanz 1½.

525 Pap or Caudle Spoon, marked: OW+6.

526 Pap or Caudle Spoon, marked: MH & CO S EP Pat. No 9446.

527 Pap or Caudle Spoon, marked: (See drawing for mark)

528-529 Infant Feeding Spoons, maker: Reed & Barton. Similar spoons illustrated in *The Strand Magazine*, January 1897.

* For further reading, see *American Spoons, Souvenir & Historical,* Chapter VIII.

527

526

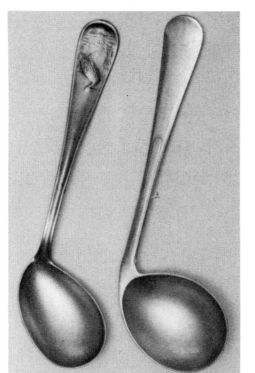

524   525   528   529

530

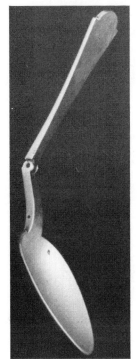

531

spoon styles were patented as well as all the waxes, oils and other paraphernalia necessary to the maintainance of such finery.

Mustache wearers of earlier days were not neglected in other countries as is attested by two examples of spoons shown from England. One style has a rather elegant handle whose design is based on the well-known *Onslow* pattern. The other English mustache spoon illustrated has a mustache guard with an asymmetrical and jaunty curve.

The recent popularity of mustaches has brought a revival in production of mustache spoons. This is most eloquently explained in the folder distributed by Reed & Barton with their spoons and reproduced here by permission.

PAP OR CAUDLE SPOONS
(Fig. 524–527)

Spoons for feeding pap or caudle to infants are so similar to some types of medicine spoons as to be virtually indistinguishable. Some may very well have been used for both purposes.

Caudle spoons similar to (Fig. 526) are currently sold throughout England with a matching bowl for porridge.

INFANT FEEDING SPOONS
(Fig. 528–529)

Spoons identical in appearance to these were illustrated in *The Strand Magazine*, January, 1897 above the caption, "Spoons for feeding through the nose." The body of the article dealt with the care and feeding of infants with no

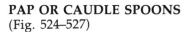

530 **Gibson Medicine Spoon,** no marks. Pewter.

531 **Folding Medicine Spoon**

532 **Folding Medicine Spoon,** marked: STERLING BALL & BALLOU

533 **Stettheimer's Patent Medicine Spoon,** marked: PAT. JAN 15.84 1 DRACHM. Similar spoons are marked: STANDARD SPOON CO., ROCHESTER, N. Y.

532

533

533a **Illustrated Price List,** C. ROGERS & BROS. catalog 1885.

534a **Medicine Spoon,** marked: Shiebler "Winged S" trademark; 8680 STERLING; A. A. GEORGE (retailer).

534 **Medicine Spoon** with corkscrew for attaching to cork of medicine bottle. Patent No. 350,499, William R. Noé, Newark, New Jersey, October 12, 1886.

535 **Medicine Spoon** with graduated bowl for powdered medicine. Patent No. 358,197, Elizabeth Guion, New York, February 22, 1887.

536 **Medicine Spoon** with two compartments for mixing medicine. Patent No. 1,095,469, Frederick W. Rice, Sayre, Pennsylvania, May 5, 1914.

538 **Spoon for Measuring and Dispensing Medicine.** Patent No. 3,054,184, Gerald E. Wyner & Richard T. Lee, Dallas, Texas, September 18, 1962. The spoon has a flat bottom to prevent rocking.

534

534a

C. Rogers & Bros. ✦ Meriden, Conn.

Unqualified Endorsements by the Medical Profession.

DIRECTIONS FOR USING

Stettheimer's Patent Medicine Spoon.

(ONE FLUID DRACHM.)

Figure 1 in cut shows spoon with cover drawn open ready to fill.

Figure 2 shows spoon with cover closed and inverted ready for use. When in this position, draw back the cover slightly, with the thumb on catch.

The spoon should be kept scrupuously clean, drying it after use with a piece of clean old linen.

We would respectfully invite your attention to the new patent Standard Medicine Spoon, an article indispensible in private families as well as in hospitals. With the use of the Standard Medicine Spoon, the administering of medicine becomes simple even in the hands of the unskilled. The advantages are numerous; the most prominent are as follows: The medicine can be given in just the prescribed quantity (as the spoon will hold one fluid drachm), without losing its contents in administering to the most rebellious patients, and also without producing to the most delicate person any disagreeable odor or taste of medicine, not injuring the teeth, as the medicine does not come in contact with them. Its advantages are great in all contagious diseases, such as measles, scarlet fever, diphtheria, etc., where it is highly necessary to use one particular spoon for the patients, to prevent the spreading of the disease to any other member of the family.

Furthermore, nauseating medicines are agreeably taken by putting the spoon on the back of the tongue, when the medicine can be readily swallowed without the disagreeable taste.

Each spoon is heavily silver plated and packed in a neat case. Retail price, $1.50. For sale by all leading druggists.

We will send a sample spoon free to any part of the United States on receipt of $1.50.

A special discount to the Trade. Address,

C. ROGERS & BROS., Meriden, Conn

533a

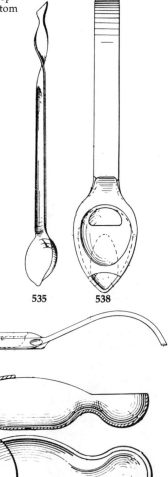

535   538

536

537 E-Z Feeding Baby Spoon for liquids or medicines. Prevents overflow and prevents blocking with the lips. Patent No. 2,640,263, Adolph Dieterich, Brooklyn, New York, June 2, 1953.

539 Porcelain, marked: WT in a diamond (Probably Whitall, Tatum & Co., N.Y.)

540 Pottery, marked: S.

541 Porcelain, no marks. Gold decoration.

542 Porcelain, no marks. Gold decoration.

543 Porcelain, mark indistinct.

544 Porcelain, no marks.

545 Porcelain, no marks. "Onion" pattern decoration in blue.

546 Pottery, marked: DENMARK. Overglaze decoration.

547 Pewter, marked: SHIRLEY.

548 Glass, marked: DUFFY'S PURE WHISKEY—A FOOD. Measurements of a teaspoon, dessertspoon and tablespoon are indicated by lines in the bowl.

549 Covered Medicine Spoon, porcelain, no marks. "Onion" pattern decoration in blue.

550 Medicine Spoon, no maker's mark. Measurements of dessertspoon and teaspoon indicated inside bowl. Outside stamped "R. THOMPSON, CHEMIST ELGIN COD LIVER OIL CREAM.

537

541

539

540

542

543

545

546

544

547

548

549

550

further mention of the spoons. Pediatricians advise that any such attempts would be followed by adverse, perhaps fatal, results.

MEDICINE SPOONS
(Fig. 530–562)

The problem of developing spoons for the accurate measurement of liquid medicine and for the administration of it to recalcitrant children has plagued designers ever since physicians and pharmacists devised the medicines. With the discovery of more potent drugs the problem became more acute until today a great many are administered in pre-measured capsule dosages or in dry form as pills.

Wrestling with these problems has produced some interesting types of spoons.

The earliest spoon designed especially for medicine appears to be one invented by a Charles Gibson, listed in London directories as a goldsmith. The Gibson medical spoon was described in Vol. 46 of the *Transactions* of the Society for the Encouragement of Arts, Manufactures, and Commerce, published in 1828. The earliest known example of a Gibson spoon is in the Wellcome Institute of the History of Medicine, London. It is of silver and bears the London date letter for the year 1827 on the inside of the bowl. Gibson's signature and address are inscribed on the stem.

Gibson medical spoons of this type may also be found in pewter, however, it should be noted that the pewter example illustrated here opens towards the handle rather than toward the spout as in the spoon illustrated in the *Transactions* and in the silver one in the Wellcome collection.

John Savory, also of London, in his *Companion to the Medicine Chest*, published in 1836, illustrated the Gibson medical spoon along with the following instructions for its use:

For administering medicine to children and adults, without their tasting, or being able to resist its passing into the stomach; and for giving medicine and food in a recumbant postion. This spoon is made to contain the quantity required, which is put in at the cover C, and then shut down tight; the tube G is then placed between the fingers, and the thumb pressed on the end of the tube N. When in the mouth, the thumb is removed.

It is hoped that this contemporary description of the method of use will dispel the notion, suggested by many, that the nauseous liquid was to be blown down the throat of the hapless patient. This very method, however, was specified in the patent of a spoon identical in appearance by patented by Hugh C. Middleton, Augusta, Georgia, on March 7, 1899.

Pewter spoons similar to the Gibson medical spoon were advertised and illustrated in the *Catalogue of Surgical Instruments* issued by J. & S. Maw in 1832. These same spoons were listed a few years later, marked "Maw Aldersgate" and in the 1869 and 1882 lists, the latter was issued under the name S. Maw, Son & Thompson, which reflected the change of firm name.

The Gibson medical spoons were widely known as "castor oil spoons." Their capacity varied from ½ oz. to one oz.

Other medical spoons, made of britannia metal, were marked "James Dixon & Sons," and were made by James Dixon & Sons of Sheffield, England, whose bugle trademark was so well-known on the tremendous quantities of britannia wares that came to this country from their establishment. According to their records, the Dixon company introduced their medicine spoon in 1839. It was illustrated in their catalog of that period as being available in three sizes—"small, middle and large."

American physicians and others interested in proper dosage and its ad-

551

553

552

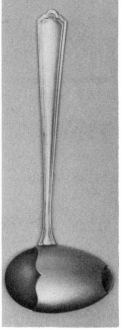

554

ministration were not far behind in their own efforts to solve the various problems. On February 17, 1852 Dr. I. C. Taylor of the West Liberty, Ohio, patented the first medicine spoon in this country (U.S. Patent No. 8,749). It had a sliding top under which a piston-action scraper pushed the medicine into the patient's mouth Dr. Taylor's patented medicine spoon was followed by many others.*

Countless medicine spoons were sold through pharmaceutical houses. Not all were made of silver, britannia or other metals. Maw, Son & Thompson, successors to Maw of Aldersgate, introduced and registered in England on March 22, 1873, a porcelain medicine spoon with graduations marked on the inside of the bowl indicating a teaspoon, dessert-spoon and tablespoon.

In New York City, Hagerty Brothers in 1879 offered for sale graduated medicine spoons of similar design made of glass. Whitall, Tatum Co., also of New York, featured these glass medicine spoons with the name of the druggist "pressed in the glass as an advertisement." Similar glass spoons were still being offered as late as 1900, some impressed with the names of druggists and others with slogans such as "DUFFY'S PURE MALT WHISKY—A MEDICINE," "ROMANTA WELLS, PHARMACIST, 21 WEST VAN BUREN ST. [CHICAGO?]" "COMPLIMENT'S

---

551 **Medicine or Measuring Spoon,** no marks. Silverplate. On handle: 2 TEASPOONS = 1 DESSERT SPOON 4 TEASPOONS = 1 TABLESPOON In bowl: TO OUTSIDE LINE CORRECT TEASPOON TO INSIDE LINE CORRECT HALF TEASPOON
552 **Medicine Spoon,** marked: STERLING
553 **Medicine Spoon,** no marks.
554 **Medicine Spoon,** marked: Webster Co. trademark, STERLING.

* For further reading, see *American Spoons, Souvenir & Historical,* Chapter XXI.

555

556

557

558

MONROE'S PHARMACY" and "PHILLIPS MILK OF MAGNESIA."

A late nineteenth century catalog of McKesson & Robbins, New York, offered eleven medicine spoons: one of earthenware in teaspoon size; six porcelain spoons, in tea and dessert size, two footed and one covered; Maw's Combination; a metal spoon similar to the Gibson spoon; Clayton's longhandled (a porcelain spoon with wire-strengthened handle); and Clayton's Combination which is a footed and covered, graduated porcelain spoon with a short handle.

Designers of medicine spoons were faced with multiple problems. First, the spoon should enable one to make accurate measurement of the medicine, second, there must be some means of keeping the spoon bowl level while filling it, the third requirement is to make the administration of the often nauseous liquid possible without undue strain on patient or nurse. Other factors were taken into consideration as well. The use of a medicine spoon designed specifically for that purpose did away with the danger of exposing other members of a family to contagious disease as would have been the case if an ordinary household spoon were used. The convenience of having a specific spoon always at hand was the inspiration for several types made to be attached to medicine bottles. The dilemma of the traveler was solved by folding medicine spoons, some of which have bowls of two sizes and were contained in leather cases for their pro-

---

555 **Folding Medicine Spoon,** marked: STERLING 20.

556 **Folding Medicine Spoon,** marked: TIFLING, Herbst & Wassal trademark, N.J., 1521.

557 **Folding Medicine Spoon,** marked: TIFFANY & CO. MAKERS STERLING 21938 M.

558 **Folding Medicine Spoon,** marked: Gorham trademark STERLING REF.

559

560

tection. There was a great vogue for these around the beginning of the twentieth century and lasting until World War I curtailed their production.

Regulations establishing the accurate determination of a teaspoon measure have been adopted. Even regulations to decide when a teaspoon is *full*—as the specific gravity of some liquids permits them to "heap up" above the level of the bowl. Efforts have been made to reach an agreement on whether a teaspoon contains 4 cc. or 5 cc. But, no universal standards have been adopted.

Medicine spoons in bewildering variety have come and gone. They have been designed by doctors, silver designers, housewives, anxious fathers, glass blowers, metalworkers and others but the problem of accurate measurement still remains.

As George Griffenhagen* points out, it "is ironical that the ancient Greek *cochliarion* was the equivalent of 4.5 cc, exactly halfway between the controversial 4 and 5 cc. measure."

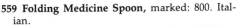

559 **Folding Medicine Spoon,** marked: 800. Italian.
560 **Folding Medicine Spoon,** marked: STERLING 30.
561 **Folding Medicine Spoon,** marked: MADE IN ENGLAND. Silverplate.
562 **Medicine Spoon,** marked: London 1867-68, TJ.

561

562

Journal of The American Pharmaceutical Association, April, 1959.

563

IV
THE
OLD WORLD

VIKINGS (Fig. 563, 600)

The Vikings or Norsemen who poured out of the north in their great longships inspired fear everywhere because of the ferocity of their raiding. They gave their name to the Viking Age, that period of history from the middle of the eighth through the eleventh centuries.

Arguments about the origin of the term Viking continue. Some say it comes from the Old Norse word *vik*, a bay or fjord, and the termination *ing*, meaning one who lurked in bays and sailed forth to plunder. Some say it was from *vig*, meaning battle, while others say it is from *Viken*, the Oslo region known as the Vik. Still others believe that the Latin word *vicus*, a district or settlement was the source. Still others hold that the verb *vikja*, meaning to deviate, gave rise to the noun, *viking*, or one who journeys from home.

The Vikings excelled in ship-building and were expert seamen. They were able to navigate across the open sea by the aid of the sun, moon and stars. Adventurous and daring, through their exploits and endurance they established kingdoms and settlements all over Europe from southern Russia to Britain (Fig. 564, 585, 600, 609, 610).

Preserved in Oslo are three Viking

565

---

563 **Viking.** Maker: Th. Marthinsen, marked: EPNS NORWAY.
564 **Viking Ship.** Maker: Th. Marthinsen, marked: EPNS NORWAY.
565 **Heilag Olav,** marked: TINN PEWTER NORWAY H-S.
566 **Runic Inscription.**

564

566

567

568

569

570

ships found in burial mounds between 1867 and 1904 where they had been interred in the protective blue clay and peat. Broad of beam and shallow of draft, they skimmed over the water like elongated saucers. The dreaded longships in which the Vikings ranged over most of the then known world were larger and more seaworthy. Old Viking sagas say that Canute, the Dane who became king of England in the eleventh century had a monstrous vessel 260 feet long—more than twice the length of the *Santa Maria* in which Columbus sailed to the New World five centuries later.

In addition to settlements, the Vikings left behind them the suffix "wich" a derivative of *vik*, in a great number of English place names. In France the Vikings were called Normans, as in the noun *nordmann* the "d" is silent.

HEILAG OLAV (Fig. 565)

Olav (Olaf) I, known as Olaf Tryggvesson, was king of Norway. About 990 he was in Ireland where he married Gyda, a Dublin princess and is supposed to have been converted to Christianity soon after. About 995 he returned to Norway and deposed the pagan ruler Earl Haakon and was accepted as king. He began the conversion of the Norwegians to Christianity and tried to unify all of Scandinavia into one kingdom under his own rule. According to tradition, on September 9, 1000 he met his death in a naval battle in the Baltic Sea when his defeat was evident and he leaped into the sea and was drowned.

───────── ❖ ─────────

567 **Norway, Coat-Of-Arms and Flag,** marked: 830S M. (The Norwegian flag as used 1898-1905 is on the handle.)
568 **Norway, Coat-Of-Arms and Flag,** marked: MH 900 M MADE IN DENMARK.
569 **Norway, Coat-Of-Arms and Flag,** marked: 900 STERLING.
570 **Norway, Coat-Of-Arms and Flag,** marked: 925 S (see drawing).

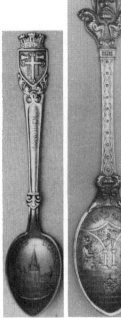

RUNIC INSCRIPTIONS (Fig. 566)

Runes are the characters, or alphabet of sixteen letters used by Teutonic tribes of northwestern Europe during the Viking era. They were written on tablets or slabs of stones, personal ornaments, jewelry and coins. Their origin is still not certain though they are known to be derived from the Helleno-Itallic family of alphabets. Three classes of runes are known, the Anglo-Saxon, German and Scandinavian. Only in Scandinavia were the runes more than an inscriptional alphabet, and even there the existing manuscripts are no older than the thirteenth century.

NORWAY, COAT-OF-ARMS AND FLAG (Fig. 565–570)

Norway was ruled by Denmark for 400 years until 1814 and used the Danish red flag bearing a white cross. At that time the golden lion of Norway, wearing the crown of St. Olav and holding in its forepaw a battle-axe, was placed in the canton. In 1821, because of confusion with the Danish flag, the lion was eliminated and a blue cross covering most of the white cross of the Danish flag was added.

TRONDHEIM, NORWAY
(Fig. 571–572)

The name of the city was originally Trondhjem but was changed to Nidaros January 1, 1930 and changed back again

574

571   **572**

573

- **571 Trondhjem,** marked: 830 NM NORWAY. (See #10)
- **572 Trondhjem,** marked: H. MØLLER 830. Since the earlier spelling of the city's name was used on both of these spoons, they must have been made prior to the name change.
- **573 Christiania,** marked: 925 (see drawing). "Det. Kgl. Slot" in the bowl represents the royal palace.
- **574 Christiania,** marked: 830 (see drawing; same mark on #575 and #14). "Christiania" inscribed on back of bowl.
- **575 King Haakon VII,** marked: S830 J. TOSTRUP 1906.

front   **575**   back

578

576

February 26, 1931 at the wish of the people. The old spelling of Trondhjem was changed to Trondheim.

CHRISTIANIA (OSLO) (Fig. 573–574)

Oslo, capital city of Norway was founded by Harald Haardraade in 1048–50. Burned several times, it was finally destroyed by fire in 1624. Christian IV commanded a new city to be built nearby which was named Christiania (Kristiania) in his honor. In 1878 the site of the old city was incorporated into the new and in 1925 the capital readopted its old name of Oslo.

KING HAAKON VII AND OLAV V (Fig. 575–576)

The "H7" stands for King Haakon VII. During World War II Norwegians often wrote H7 within the V for victory sign. King Haakon VII, originally Prince Carl, second son of Crown Prince Frederick (later Frederick VIII of Denmark) was elected king by the Norwegian parliament November 18, 1905 and crowned June 22, 1906, following Norway's separation from Sweden. King Haakon VII was a democratic king noted for his simple way of life. He died September 21, 1957 and was succeeded by his son as Olav V (Fig. 577), who in July, 1973 celebrated his seventy-fifth birthday by receiving Norway's highest decoration, the Gold Medal for Outstanding Civil Service.

BERGEN, NORWAY (Fig. 578)

Founded 1070–1075 by King Olav Kyrre (Olav III) as Bjorgvin on a site which, for natural beauty, no city has ever been able to surpass. It is situated in a natural harbor of a sheltered fjord

579

580

576 **H7 (King Haakon VII)**, marked: J. T. 830S.
577 **King Olaf V, Bergen**, marked: M. Asse 925 S.
578 **Bergen, Norway**, marked: 925S.
579 **Norge (Norway)**, marked: 925S.
580 **Norge (Norway)**, marked: (see drawing).

577

581

582

surrounded by seven majestic mountains. Bergen was the capital of the country from 1164 to 1299 and was an important trading post. Though it declined in importance during the last century it rose as a cultural giant. Four men of genius brought fame to the city—Ole Bull, violinist; Edvard Grieg, composer; Børnstjerne Bjørnson and Henrik Ibsen, both poets and dramatists.

NORGE (NORWAY)
(Fig. 579, 581, 589)

Norway, the land of fjords and the midnight sun, as depicted by travel posters is not a myth but a reality. Its spectacular fjords are one of the scenic wonders of the world. From its southernmost extremity to Nordkapp (North Cape) the country is 1,100 miles long but it is so deeply cut by fjords that the actual length of the coast is equal to about half the earth's circumference.

ÅLESUND (Fig. 582)

Ålesund has the largest fishing harbor in Norway and is situated on the islands of Nørvøy, Aspøy and Heissa, far out in the archipelago of islets on the western coast. It was almost destroyed by fire January 23, 1904 but has been rebuilt in stone.

NARVIK (Fig. 583)

Narvik became a town in 1902 and is of great importance as an ice-free harbor and the iron ore shipping port on the Norwegian coast. The town received world-wide prominence in World War II during the great naval engagement in the Ofot Fjord April 1940 when seized by the German forces. The ensuing campaign in which Norwegian troops, aided by British, French and Polish de-

583

581 Norge (Norway).
582 Ålesund, Norway.
583 Narvik, Norway.
584 Stalheim, Norway, marked: 60 GR HS.
585 Viking Ship, marked: NORWAY 830.

584   585

590   591

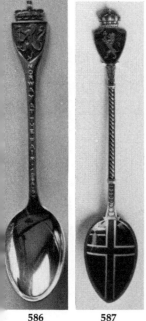

586   587

tachments, inflicted the first defeat of the war upon the Nazi military machine by recapturing the town.

NORWAY AT THE FAIR (Fig. 586)

One of the seventeen spoons designed for the New York World's Fair 1964–65 by Th. Marthinsen. They were made in sterling silver, sterling enamel and silverplate. The Marthinsen Company, silversmiths since 1883, also have designed spoons for all the fifty states of the United States, more than twenty cities and places of interest in those cities, as well as custom-made or special order spoons for colleges, churches, fraternal organizations, resorts, occasions and business promotions.

SPITZBERGEN, NORWAY (Fig. 588)

Spitzbergen is an archipelago in the Arctic Ocean and belongs to Norway. It was discovered by the Vikings in the twelfth century and named Svalbard by them. The islands were forgotten until their rediscovery by Willem Barents in 1596 and were subsequently visited by whalers and fur traders and in the nineteenth century by explorers and scientists. They served as a base for expeditions by Nordenskjöld, S. A. Andrèe, Roald Amundsen, Richard E. Byrd, Sir George H. Wilkins and others.

GUDVANGEN, NORWAY (Fig. 589)

Gudvangen is a small village two miles south-south-west of the entrance of Naerofjord, one of the steepest and narrowest fjords in Norway. A short drive takes one to Stalheim (see Fig. 584)

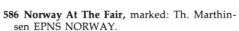

586 **Norway At The Fair,** marked: Th. Marthinsen EPNS NORWAY.
587 **Norway,** marked: 925 (see drawing).
588 **Spitzbergen, Norway,** marked: "Crescent & crown" 800 KFK.
589 **Gudvangen, Norway,** marked: "Crescent & crown" KFK.
590-591 **Gudbrandsdal, Norway,** marked: Bundadskjeer Fra Norsk Solvvareindustri A.S.
592 **Trondheim Fisherman, Norway.**

588   589   592

593

595

Turisthotell where a view of the dark valley far below with huge mountains towering on either side is one of the most impressive in all Norway.

GUDBRANDSDAL, NORWAY
(Fig. 590–591)

The Gudbrandsdal Valley, north of Oslo, is watered by the river Lågen. It is a favorite area for tourists, one of the attractions being the preservation of old customs. On special occasions villagers wear native costumes. At Lillehammer, the entrance to Gudbrandsdal, there is the famous Sandvig Collection at Maihaugen, an open-air museum. This collection of buildings and implements is unique and includes the Garmo Church (1030) and an entire farm of twenty-six buildings.

TRONDHEIM FISHERMAN, NORWAY (Fig. 592)

The Gulf Stream tempers the climate of the Scandinavian peninsula and brings in great shoals of cod, herring and other species of fish to the banks off Norway's west coast. Early Norwegians combined farming with fishing but new methods have created a class whose sole occupation is fishing.

FROGNERSAETEREN, OSLO, NORWAY (Fig. 593)

At Frogner Park, near Oslo, are the Gustav Vigeland sculptures—one hundred and fifty groups scattered over an area of several acres. Judgments vary from condemnation to unanimous praise. Best-known, perhaps, is the

---

593 **Frognersaeteren, Oslo, Norway,** marked: NORGE 40.
594 **1972 Norsk Christmas Spoon.** Maker: Th. Marthinsen.
595 **St. Olav(?),** marked: 830 S. "Bergen" engraved on back. The date 1578 has no significance in Norwegian history but may have been on the original spoon of which this is a copy.

monolith of more than a hundred figures of various sorts and shapes, struggling to reach the top of the fifty-six foot granite obelisk, supposed to represent all stages of humanity.

1972 NORSK CHRISTMAS SPOON (Fig. 594)

This was first in a limited edition series to be issued annually.

Borgund Stave Church is constructed of hewn timber. Its roof and siding are long round-tipped shingles. It was built in the middle of the twelfth century and presents a remarkable intermingling of pagan and Christian symbolism. In one wall is a small worn hole which we are told was the lepers' hole, through which those afflicted who were standing outside could hear the services.

SWEDEN'S FLAG (Fig. 596–597)

King Erik IX (r. 1150–1160), later known as St. Erik, and now the patron saint of Stockholm, undertook a religious expedition to Finland. When the ships were ready to cast off from Stockholm for the journey across the Bothnian Gulf, King Erik lifted his golden cross against the blue summer sky and cried, "In this sign we will win!" This was the origin of the Swedish flag which to this day displays a golden cross on a blue background. The flag dates from the sixteenth century and it was readopted in 1905 when the union of Sweden and Norway came to an end.

596

597

598

599

600

601

---

596 **Sweden, Kalmar Union,** marked: 925.

597 **Sweden, Kalmar Union and Flag,** marked: "Three crowns" S. "Stockholm" engraved on back of handle.

598 **Göteborg, Sweden,** marked: C.G.H. lima ALP A EPNS MADE IN SWEDEN.

599 **Sverige,** marked: Mena EPNS ALP SWEDEN.

600 **Viking,** marked: EPNS MADE IN SWEDEN.

601 **Sverige,** marked: SABEXTRAIMANSALP.

SWEDEN, KALMAR UNION
(Fig. 596)

The triple crown is a reminder of the Union of Kalmar, a stroke of political genius on the part of the great Danish queen, Margrethe, who united Denmark, Sweden and Norway under one crown in 1397. This Union lasted for 126 years and stretched from Finland, then part of Sweden, to Greenland. It created a powerful alliance of Atlantic and Baltic powers directed primarily against the growing influence of the Hanseatic League, a mercantile alliance of north German commercial towns. Sweden left the Union in 1523. Norway remained subject to the Danish crown until 1814 when it was ceded to Sweden; it gained its independence from Sweden in 1905. Iceland remained subject to Denmark until 1944. Greenland and the Faroe Islands are still Danish.

GÖTEBORG (GOTHENBURG), SWEDEN (Fig. 598)

Göteborg has been described as the "Gateway to the West" though actually it is the gateway to the world situated as it is on the western coast of Sweden. Compared to many European cities it is young, having been founded in 1619 by King Gustavus II but the area itself, ancient home of the Goths, has been settled some 4,000 years or more. East of Göteborg is Sweden's lake district, dotted with thousands of lakes of all sizes, including two of the largest in Europe, Vättern and Vänern. The 350-mile-long blue ribbon of the Göta Canal combines some of these lakes with rivers and man-made channels to make a water route from Göteborg to Stockholm creating one of the most scenic trips in all of Europe. Göteborg has long been noted as a center of shipping but recently has been identified with the production of Volvos.

SVERIGE (SWEDEN) (Fig. 599, 601)

This ancient name for Sweden was given to the country by early ruling tribes who took the name *Svea*, literally "we, ourselves";—*rige (rike)* means "kingdom." From this is Sverige, "our own kingdom."

STOCKHOLM (Fig. 602)

Stockholm is the capital and is located in southeastern Sweden on the Baltic Sea. The buildings on the handle of the spoon are KUNGL. SLOTTET, literally the King's Castle (Royal Palace); STADHUSET, the Town Hall, designed by Ragner Östberg and completed in 1923, a modern structure arising sheer above Lake Mälaren; KONSERTHUSET, the Concert Hall, built in 1923. During the early morning hours of July and August the Swedish flower market held in front of the Concert Hall presents one of the loveliest pictures to be found in Europe.

OSCAR II (Fig. 603)

Oscar II, king of Sweden and Norway, was born in Stockholm, January 21, 1829. He succeeded to the throne in 1872 on the death of his brother, Charles XV and became one of Sweden's most remarkable kings. He was an acknowledged expert in international affairs. The severance of the union between Sweden and Norway in 1905 was peaceful and is a tribute to his tact. Noted as a linguist, he spoke at least ten languages. He was well-versed in naval and military history and general literature. His reign was notable for the flowering of Sweden's literary and artistic life.

STOCKHOLM, NYA RIKSDAGHUSET (New Parliament Building, Sweden) (Fig. 604)

The edifice featured in the bowl is the former Parliament Building (Riksdag) of Sweden, built during the years 1894–1904 on the island of Helgeandsholmen in Stockholm. Built mainly of granite, the style is a German-inspired baroque, the drawings made by Aron Johansson.

602

603   604

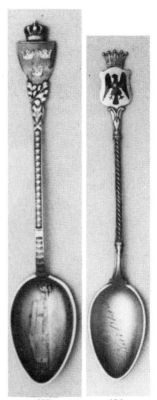

605   606

607

The Swedish Parliament was housed there 1905–1970.

The man on the handle is probably St Erik (Erik IX, ?–1160), the national saint of Sweden. He ascended the throne in 1150. According to tradition, the Swedish flag was born of his expedition to Finland to spread the teachings of Christianity and he held up a golden cross against the blue sky. He is buried in Uppsala, north of Stockholm and his picture is part of the seal and coat-of-arms of Stockholm.

KUNGL SLOTTET (King's Castle, Stockholm, Sweden) (Fig. 605)

The Royal Palace, replacing "Tre Kroner" the ancient royal castle, was begun in 1697 in Renaissance times, from the plans of the younger Nicodemus Tessin and completed in 1760 mostly under the direction of his son, Karl Gustav Tessin. A huge monument to grace and symmetry, it contains almost 700 rooms. The Royal Family lives in the east wing. The Palace Museum is housed in the cellars. Certain sections of the Palace are open to the public. Changing of the Guard on Wednesday and Saturday at 12, Sunday at 1 p.m.

KARLSTAD (Sweden) (Fig. 606)

Karlstad is the capital of the Swedish län (province) of Värmland. It was here that negotiations that resulted in the dissolution of the union between Sweden and Norway took place in 1905.

---

602 **Stockholm, Sweden,** marked: GABEXPNSALP.
603 **King Oscar II.** No mark.
604 **Stockholm, Nya Rikskaghuset** (New Parliament Buildings, Stockholm), marked: "Crescent & crown" 830 S. St. Erik on handle.
605 **Kungl Slottet** (King's Castle, Stockholm Sweden), marked: "Three crowns" 925.
606 **Karlstad** (Sweden), marked: 925.
607 **Danmark** (Denmark). No mark.

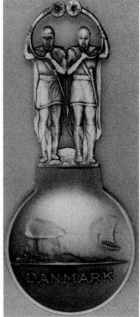

DANMARK (Denmark) (Fig. 607)

The national flag of Denmark, a white cross on a red field, is called the *Dannebrog* or "Strength of Denmark," and is reputed to be the oldest of the world's flags in continuous use. According to legend, it fell from heaven during the Battle of Lindanissa (now Tallinn) on June 15, 1219 when Valdemar II of Denmark defeated the Estonians. The Danish king and his troops were attacked and were about to be slain when the king saw the banner descend from the sky. He caught it and used it as a standard. He asserted that it became strength for him and saved Denmark.

608   609

CHRISTIAN X (1870–1947) (Fig. 608)

The two Kroner coin dated 1930 commemorates the 60th birthday of King Christian X. Carl Frederick Albert Alexander Vilhelm, king of Denmark and Iceland succeeded to the throne May 14, 1912. In 1915 he granted a new constitution which included the enfranchisement of women. During World War II he became a symbol of national resistance. He died April 20, 1947 and was succeeded by his son, Frederick IX.

PRIMA

611

DANMARK LURER (Fig. 611–612)

Lurer are Bronze Age wind instruments, all made by casting *à cire perdue*—the lost wax process. Each lur was cast in segments and dovetailed together with joints so fine they are scarcely visible. Their workmanship attests to a high degree of skill of Bronze Age metal workers.

A complete set of lurer consists of two instruments, corresponding in size, structure and decoration and tuned to

PRIMA
610

608 **Christian X.** No mark.
609 **Viking Ship,** marked: STERLING DENMARK.
610 **Danmark-Viking Ship,** (see drawing).
611 **Danmark-Lurer,** marked: (see drawing).
612 **Danish Lurer,** marked: STERLING SILVER.

612

613

614

615

approximately the same pitch but the tubes of each set are turned in opposite directions.

The first lurer were found in 1797, when in the Brudevaelt moor in North Zealand six were brought to light. Others were subsequently found in peat bogs or similar moist places, never in graves. When first found, lurer were generally regarded as war trumpets but under battle conditions, demanding speed and mobility, the lur seems unsuitable as a signaling instrument. Tests with lurer still in playable condition reveal that they must be blown while in a standing position or when walking very slowly. Correct position for holding the lurer was determined by signs of wear on the instruments. This was confirmed by rock carvings in which lur blowers were depicted, two or four together, some of them standing beside a ship and others inside. Some lurer may produce a series of seven to nine tones but whether they were used to produce "music" or solely to produce a trumpet-like "fanfare" is not known. The conclusion has been drawn that they are cult instruments but for what purpose Bronze Age people accompanied their cult ceremonies by lur-blowing is a question still unanswered.

DANMARK DYBBØL MØLLE
(Fig. 613–614)

Dybbol Mill, symbolic of the uncon-

616   617

613 Danmark Dybbøl Mølle, marked: (see drawing).
614 Dybbøl Mølle, marked: Copenhagen city mark 25 CFH.
615 Kronborg, Danmark, marked: Copenhagen city mark.
616 Red Cross, Denmark, marked: Copenhagen city mark "crown" M 925 CFH. On the back is the inscription, "OMNIA CUM DEO NIHIL SINE DEO" (All things with God, nothing without a day appointed.)
617 Danmark, 5 MAI 1945, marked: Copenhagen city mark 25 CFH.
618 Margrethe, Denmark, marked: A. MICHELSEN STERLING COPENHAGEN CF. "1940 XVI APRIL 1958" on back of handle.

618

querable spirit of the Danish people, is on the peninsula of Jutland near Sonderborg. Except where Jutland borders on Germany, Denmark is surrounded by the sea. For more than a hundred years battles have been fought near Dybbol Mill to determine whether the area would belong to Denmark or to Germany. The historic mill has been destroyed and rebuilt several times. Today it is a national museum considered by the Danes to rest on sacred ground.

The inscription: *Tvende gange skudt i grus atter rejst some møllehus* may be translated, "Twice leveled with the ground, erected again as a mill(house)."

KRONBORG, DANMARK (Fig. 615)

Kronberg Castle, at Helsingør, Denmark, was built about 1580 by Frederick II. Shakespeare used the castle as the setting for his great dramatic play, Hamlet. The Hamlet Festival, reviving the play, is held annually in June in the castle courtyard.

RED CROSS, DENMARK (Fig. 616)

The Denmark Red Cross spoon was made in 1908 in appreciation of the great work the late Queen Louise did in various humanitarian organizations. (See also Fig. 621)

DANMARK, 5 MAI 1945 (Fig. 617)

Made in commemoration of May 5, 1945 when Denmark was liberated from German rule.

MARGRETHE II, QUEEN OF DENMARK (1940–) (Fig. 618–620)

Margrethe II was born April 16, 1940, at Amalienborg Royal Palace, Copenhagen. She is the eldest daughter of the late King Frederick IX and Ingrid, Princess of Sweden. Upon Frederick's death, January 14, 1972 Margrethe became Denmark's first queen in more than six centuries. The first Queen Margrethe brought Denmark, Sweden and Norway under one rule which lasted from 1388 to 1412.

Margrethe II was given three other Christian names, Alexandrina, Ingrid and Thorhildur—the last out of regard to the then union with Iceland. Male succession had been the rule in Denmark until June 5, 1953 when Frederick IX signed a new constitution providing that women might succeed to the throne.

The new Queen had been educated at the universities of Copenhagen, Aarhus and Cambridge, and at the London School of Economics and the Sorbonne. She is an accomplished linguist and is interested in art and archaeology.

On June 10, 1967 she married a French diplomat, Count Henri de Laborde de Monpegat, who was given the title of Prince Henrik of Denmark. They have two sons, Prince Frederick (May 1968) who is first in succession to the throne, and Prince Joachim (June 1969).

SILVER WEDDING ANNIVERSARY OF KING FREDERICK VIII AND QUEEN LOUISE (Fig. 621)

King Frederick VIII of Denmark was born June 3, 1843. While still Crown Prince he and Louise, daughter of Charles XV of Sweden, were married. Frederick succeeded his father, Christian IX as king of Denmark in 1906 (See also Fig. 623 and 626). He fought in the war of 1864 in which Denmark lost Schleswig-Holstein and Lauenburg. Queen Louise was noted for humanitarian work (See Fig. 616). The dates "1869 28 Juli 1894" commemorate their 25th anniversary. The letters "G D C C L" and "T J H" intertwined with the scroll design in the bowl stand for the names of their children, Gustav, Dagmar, Christian (later King Christian X), Carl, Louise, Thyra, Ingeborg and Harald.

DANISH COMMEMORATIVE SPOONS (Fig. 622–628)

(Fig. 622) Commemorates the mar-

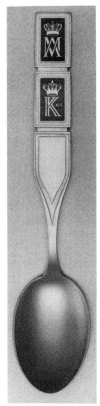

619

620

riage of Crown Prince Frederick (later King Frederick IX) and Crown Princess Ingrid of Sweden, May 24, 1935 (Fig. 622).

(Fig. 623) Commemorates the coronation of King Christian X and Queen Alexandrina May 15, 1915. To the left of the Danish shield is the initial of Christian IX, grandfather of Christian X and below is the initial of Frederick VIII, father of Christian X. At right top is the initial of Charles XV of Sweden, father of Louise (See Fig. 616, 621), who married Frederick VIII when he was crown prince (Fig. 623).

(Fig. 624) Commemorates the marriage of Princess Margaret of Denmark to Prince Renée of France, November 15, 1921.

(Fig. 625) Commemorates the Exposition which was to have been held at Malmo in 1914 but did not take place. The four coats-of-arms represent Sweden, Imperial Germany, Russia and Denmark.

(Fig. 626) Commemorates the coronation of Frederick VIII, January 29, 1906. He was sixty-three years old at the time. "HERREN.VAERE.MM.HIÆLPER.29 JAN. 1906" (The Lord be my Helper) appears on the back of the handle.

(Fig. 627) COPENHAGEN COAT-OF-ARMS "SAA.ER.BY.SOM. BORGER" (As the citizen is so is the city) is inscribed on the stem.

619 Margrethe, Denmark, marked: A. MICHELSEN STERLING COPENHAGEN CF. "18-IX" on back.
620 Margrethe II, Queen of Denmark, marked: A. MICHELSEN STERLING DANMARK M and I intertwined within a diamond-shaped shield. "15 JANUAR 1972" on the back.
621 Silver Wedding Anniversary of King Frederick VIII and Queen Louise, marked: P. HERTZ (Peter Hertz, Copenhagen silversmith 1810-1885, whose company by that name is still in business) 924.
622 Marriage of Crown Prince Frederik and Crown Princess Ingrid.
623 Coronation of Christian X and Alexandrina.

621

622   623

(Fig. 628) Frederick IX was born March 11, 1899 at Sorgenfri Castle near Copenhagen. He chose a career in the Navy while still crown prince and rose through the grades to captain in 1939 and to rear admiral in 1945. Also while still crown prince, he and Crown Princess Ingrid of Sweden were married May 24, 1935. On the death of his father, Christian X, he acceded to the throne on April 20, 1947. During World War II he remained in Denmark during the occupation and actively supported the resistance movement. May 24, 1960 King Frederick IX and Queen Ingrid celebrated their 25th wedding anniversary which is commemorated in this spoon. King Frederick died January 14, 1972 and was succeeded by his daughter, Queen Margrethe II.

628   **629**

DANMARK, QUEEN THYRA (950 A.D.) (Fig. 629)

Queen Thyra (Thyri) is honored by a runic inscription at Jellinge in Jutland dated about 935 which reads: "King Gorm erected this memorial in honor of his wife, Thyri, restorer of Denmark." The runic text leaves some doubt as to whether it is Gorm or Thyri to which it refers. Gorm did much for his country but Thyri seems to have an even greater claim to the title. According to tradition, it was she who recruited all able-bodied men in Denmark for work on the Danevirke, the barrier raised across the neck of Jutland against their southern enemies. She is said to have combined

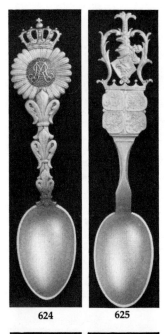

624   **625**

626   **627**

630

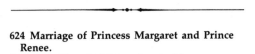

624 **Marriage of Princess Margaret and Prince Renee.**
625 **Exposition At Malmo** (not held).
626 **Coronation of Frederick VIII.**
627 **Copenhagen Coat-Of-Arms.**
628 **Silver Anniversary of King Frederick IX and Queen Ingrid.**
629 **Queen Thyra, Denmark,** marked: Copenhagen city mark CORTSEN CFH."1928 S.O.A." inscribed on back. 6 5/16" (161 mm.)
630 **København-Raadhuset (Denmark),** marked: (same as 570)

631

633

634

632

"the sagacity of Nestor, the astuteness of Ulysses and the wisdom of Solomon."

KØBENHAVN-RAADHUSET (DENMARK) (Fig. 630, 636)

The red-brick Raadhus or Town Hall was built 1892-1905 in the Danish version of the Renaissance style. Though completed in the twentieth century, it was made of handmade bricks to give it an older character. Over the main entrance is the figure of Bishop Absalon, the warrior-priest who founded Copenhagen as a Baltic fort in the twelfth century. The gilded copper figure was designed by V. Bissen. The most interesting feature inside is the astronomical clock, installed in 1955. The clock represents the life work of a Danish clockmaker, Jens Olsen. It is so accurate that it is not expected to lose more than one second in the next hundred years. In addition to the time, it shows the phases and eclipses of the moon and the positions of the stars for the next 3000 years. Copenhagen's municipal authorities are housed in the building.

KØBENHAVN-AMALIENBORG (DENMARK) (Fig. 631)

Amalienborg Royal Palace in Copenhagen is actually four separate palaces facing a huge square and is the winter home of the royal family. Entering the grounds from Sankt Annae Plads into Amaliegade through an imposing colonnade (which looks like stone but is actually wood), the palace facing you on the right is the royal residence. The other palaces contain guard rooms and

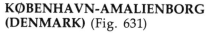

631 **Kφbenhavn-Amalienborg (Denmark),** marked: (same as 570)
632 **Kφbenhavn,** marked: STERLING BK DENMARK.
633 **Bishop Absalon,** marked: "Crown" M CFH Copenhagen city mark.
634 **Copenhagen,** marked: Copenhagen city mark VC 92.

639　　　　640

635　　　　636

royal reception chambers. During autumn and winter when the royal family is in residence the guards wearing their colorful uniforms topped by bearskin busbies and headed by their band, march through the city from the barracks adjoining Rosenborg Castle every day, to relieve the Amalienborg sentries at noon.

KØBENHAVN (DENMARK)
(Fig. 632–634)

Copenhagen, the capital city of Denmark, has been described as the "city of 1,000,000 people and 400,000 bicycles." It is also the city of impressive buildings, some of them topped by quaint spires, and interesting statues. Its atmosphere is gayer than many other cities and one of the centers of gaiety is the world-famous Tivoli Gardens. This unique combination of fun-fair, concert halls, band stand, restaurants and gardens was conceived in 1843 by Georg Carstansen.

Until the middle of the twelfth century Copenhagen was a small village strategically located on the Sound connecting the Baltic Ocean with the Kattegat and the North Sea and was constantly harassed by Venetian pirates. In 1167 Bishop Absalon decided to protect the little village by building a castle on the small central island of Slotsholmen. The name of the town was changed to Køpmannæhafn (Merchant's Haven) and grew rapidly within its protecting walls.

635 **Nikolaj Kirke (Nicolas Church)**, marked: 830S AC.
636 **Rosenborg Palace,** marked: 830S AC.
637 **Rådhuset or Raadhus (Town Hall)**, marked: 830S AC.
638 **Grundtvig's Church,** marked: 830S AC.
639 **Børsen (Stock Exchange),** marked: 830S AC.
640 **Vor Frue Kirke (Our Lady's Church),** marked: 830S AC.
641 **The Little Mermaid,** marked: "Viking warrior" B.

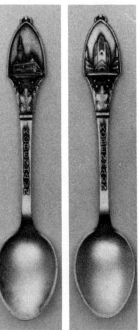

637　　　　638

641

642

644

KØBENHAVN-NIKOLAJ KIRKE (NICOLAI CHURCH, COPENHAGEN) (Fig. 635)

Lutheran services are held here, but it also houses the Naval Museum with its collection of three centuries of boat models, weapons and pictures.

ROSENBORG PALACE (Fig. 636)

Rosenborg Palace was built in 1632 in Renaissance style. It has been a museum since 1632 and contains the crown jewels, among the most magnificent in Europe, and regalia of Danish kings.

GRUNDTVIG'S CHURCH (Fig. 638)

Consecrated in 1940 and built in the style of the typical Danish village cathedral, this light buff-colored brick building stands in memory of N. F. S. Grundtvig, the poet, clergyman and founder of the Folk High School, whose name it bears.

BØRSEN (Stock Exchange) (Fig. 639)

This Dutch Renaissance style building with its many gables was built in the seventeenth century by Christian IV. The king himself is said to have had a hand in the construction of the incredible 180-foot spire made up of the twisted tails of four dragons standing on their heads. It is one of the most beautiful buildings in Copenhagen and claimed to be the oldest stock exchange in the world still trading in stocks and bonds.

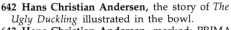

642 **Hans Christian Andersen,** the story of *The Ugly Duckling* illustrated in the bowl.
643 **Hans Christian Andersen,** marked: PRIMA SØLPLET.
644 **The Tinderbox,** marked: Copenhagen town mark M (Michelsen).
645-656 (inclusive) **HANS CHRISTIAN ANDERSEN FAIRY TALE SPOONS,** all marked: SH.
645 **The Little Match Girl.**
646 **The Little Mermaid.**

643

645   646

VOR FRUE KIRKE (Our Lady's Church) (Fig. 640)

Bishop Absalon is thought to have built a chapel here early in the thirteenth century. The church has a round tower topped with a plain, golden cross. It was ravaged by fire in 1728 and hit during the bombardment by Nelson in 1807, but restored soon afterwards. Inside is the famous Thorvaldsen statue, "Christ and the Twelve Apostles." Since 1924 it has been the Cathedral of Copenhagen.

HANS CHRISTIAN ANDERSEN (1805–1875) (Fig. 641–662)

Hans Christian Andersen was born in Odense, Denmark into a home of poverty and a family of eccentrics. He has been described as "surely the ugliest duckling who ever dreamt of sailing swan-like on the river of fame, and made the dream come true." Lanky, ill-clothed, ungainly and so full of fanciful notions that he was sometimes regarded as a lunatic, he left Odense for Copenhagen when only fourteen years of age. There he made successive futile efforts to become an actor, dancer, singer, playwright and novelist.

He was befriended by two musicians and a poet and after the publication of his first book in 1822, King Frederick VI underwrote the cost of his grammar school education.

In 1835 Andersen published the first of his immortal *Fairy Tales Told for Children*, a second series in 1838 and a third in 1845. Sales of these ended his financial woes but it was not until 1846 when Mary Howitt translated his best fairy

647 The Swineherd.
648 The Constant Tin Soldier.
649 The Emperor's New Clothes.
650 Great Claus & Little Claus.
651 The Shepardess and The Chimney Sweep.
652 The Real Princess.
653 The Tinder Box.
654 The Ugly Duckling.

647   648

649   650

651   652

653   654

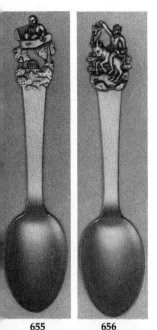

tales into English that his fame became widespread.

Andersen was a prolific writer, producing 168 stories in addition to novels, poems and plays. Of these, about 125 may be called fairy tales, though others contained more fantasy than fact. A few of his fairy tales were based on folklore but most were the creation of his lively imagination. His best fairy tales were published in 1845, later ones being full of moralistic teachings more suited to adult readers.

Literary immortality came to Andersen for his fairy tales but he always yearned to excel as a dramatist and novelist—for which he exhibited little talent. He continued writing until his 70th birthday, always seeing the world as through a child's eye.

CHRISTMAS COFFEE SPOONS, DENMARK (Fig. 664–670)

In 1969 the talented Danish silversmiths, Meka, started the production of their silverplated coffee spoons with gold finish and enamel inlay designs, each employing a well-loved Christmas design.

LONDON (Fig. 690–693)

London, the Roman city of *Londinium*, was founded after 43 A.D. at the furtherest point up the Thames River that sailing ships could reach on the tide and a place suitable for building a bridge. Londinium occupied roughly the same area as the modern city's "Square Mile." "The City," as it is usually called, was

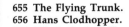

655 The Flying Trunk.
656 Hans Clodhopper.
657-662 (inclusive) Hans Christian Andersen.
Fairy Tale Spoons, all marked: SILVERPLATE DENMARK.
657 The Shepardess and The Chimney Sweep.
658 The Tinder Box.
659 The Swineherd.
660 Little Tiny.
661 Hans Clodhopper.
662 The Emperor's New Clothes.

655   656

659   660

657   658

661   662

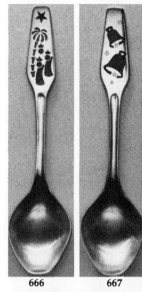

666   667

663

for almost a thousand years contained within the second-century Roman walls erected after Queen Boadicea sacked it in 60 A.D.

After the Norman Conquest the city stretched out a little beyond its walls to the west to Westminster. This westward population movement was accelerated by the Great Fire which devastated most of the city September 2, 1666, begun in an overheated baking oven in a timbered building. When the city was rebuilt all new buildings were required to be of brick or stone. A second Great Fire followed the blitz of December 29, 1940 and led to another massive rebuilding.

Today Greater London covers more than 620 square miles, annexing scores of towns, villages and hamlets. Its growth has always been haphazard and it has often been described as a "collection of villages," where each retains much of its distinctive character.

"The City" is the heart of London and is governed by a Lord Mayor and a Court of Alderman. The arms of "the City" date back at least to 1381. The white shield has the red cross of St. George bearing the red sword of St. Paul, the city's patron, in the canton.

668   669

ST. GEORGE AND THE DRAGON
(Fig. 694)

St. George is the patron of chivalry and tutelary saint of England. Very little is known about his life. According to the *Acta Sanctorum* (Deeds of the Saints), he was born of noble Christian parents in Cappadocia, became a distinguished

663 Child' Spoon (Denmark)
664-670 (inclusive) Christmas Coffee Spoons
  1966-1972, all marked: MEKA DENMARK.
664 Christmas Tree, 1966.
665 Christmas Angel and Star, 1967.
666 Three Kings, 1968.
667 Christmas Bells, 1969.
668 Peace Dove, 1970.
669 Madonna, 1971.
670 Church, 1972.
671 Suomi (Finland). No mark.

664   665

670   671

672

673

soldier, and after testifying to his faith before Diocletian, was tortured and put to death April 23, 303. His name was known in England as early as the eighth century but it was probably twelfth-century Crusaders who first invoked his aid in battle. About 1350 an order was instituted in his honor by Edward III and later was made the Order of the Garter with St. George as patron. The cult was steadily advanced by Henry V who was both warlike and devout, and thought by his followers to possess many of the saint's characteristics.

In the Church the slaying of the dragon symbolized the triumph of Christ over the powers of darkness. Outside the Church it represented strength. Probably the mingling of the two themes caused the frequent appearance of the beast in tales of chivalry.

BRITANNIA (Fig. 695)

Britannia was the ancient Roman name of Great Britain, especially the southern part. Later, a female figure was adopted to symbolize the country and is called Britannia. George Richardson, in his *Iconology; or A Collection of Emblematical Figures,** published in London in 1779, describes her as "a graceful woman, sitting upon a globe, and crowned with oak leaves. She holds a spear in one hand, and a branch of the olive tree in the other. . . . The cap of liberty by her side, is in allusion to the happy constitution of this country, to the equity of the laws and freedom of the

---

672 **Suomi (Finland).** No mark.
673 **Helsinki Lutheran Church,** marked: ALP.
674 **Iceland,** marked: Copenhagen city mark 38 C.K.H. S&J conjoined.
675 **Iceland,** marked: GB MADE IN ICELAND.
676 **Kvedja Fra Islandi (Greetings from Iceland),** marked: GB MADE IN ICELAND 925S.

* Based in part on a seventeenth century Italian publication by Cesare Ripa with the same title.

674   675

676

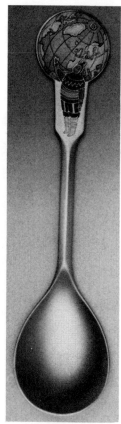

677

678

679

680

681

subject." The illustration of Britannia includes an oval shield displaying the British colors.

UNION FLAG (Fig. 696)

The flag of the British Empire, or Great Union Flag, has developed from the red cross on a white field, the emblem of St. George, which by 1277 formed the country's national flag. When James VI of Scotland became James I of England, he instructed his heralds to represent both countries on a combined national flag. His heralds placed the red St. George's Cross, bordered with white, on a field formed by the St. Andrew's emblem, to create the first Union Flag. In 1801 Ireland was admitted to the United Kingdom and had to be represented. St. Patrick's Cross, a red cross on a white field, was chosen. Because the Scottish cross was senior and had to be given precedence, the Irish emblem was placed below it in the hoist and above it in the fly (the outer half of the flag), the crosses being counterchanged or reversed to make the right-hand arms of the red cross higher than the left-hand arms, and vice versa with the white cross. This breaks the continuity of direction of the arms of St. Patrick's Cross but permits the Irish and Scottish crosses to be distinguished from one another.

HOUSES OF PARLIAMENT
(Fig. 697–698)

Officially called the New Palace of Westminster, Parliament stands on the site of the principal royal residence since the time of Edward the Confessor (b. 1002-d. 1066) to that of Henry VIII. The

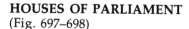

677 Greenland, marked: A. MICHELSEN STERLING DANMARK R.
678 Grönland, Danmark, marked: VIS SIL-VERPLATE.
679 Old Lapp Spoon, bone. No mark.
680 Old Lapp Spoon, bone. No mark.
681 Old Lapp Spoon, bone. No mark. 5⅛" (131 mm.)

old palace, long a meeting place for Parliament was almost entirely destroyed by fire in 1834, except for the Jewel Tower, the chapel crypt and the magnificent Westminster Hall. One of the first acts of the young Queen Victoria was to order a new building to be erected on the site. The present Gothic style buildings were completed in 1852. The House of Commons was destroyed by fire in an air-raid in 1941 but completely restored after the war. The Clock Tower by the House of Commons is world-famous for its bell, named Big Ben, named after the Commissioner of Works, Sir Benjamin Hall. The clock chimes every quarter-hour. These chimes are known throughout the world for many chiming clocks use its simple tune with the words:

"Lord, through this hour,
Be Thou our guide
So, by Thy power,
No foot shall slide."

TOWER OF LONDON (Fig. 699)

The official name of this medieval fortress is "Her Majesty's Royal Fortress and Palace of the Tower of London," and is not one but several buildings. There are thirteen towers defending the White Tower begun under William the Conqueror and slowly completed under his son, William Rufus. This is the "keep" or donjon of the fortress. The Outer Ward is defended by a second wall, flanked by six towers on the river face, and by two semi-circular bastions at the northwest and northeast.

The Tower has served many purposes. It was a royal palace until the time of James I, an observatory until the one at Greenwich was built in 1675, the Royal

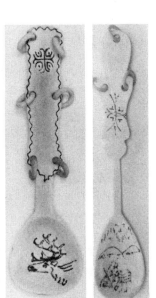

682   684

685

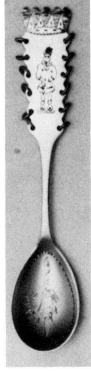

686

682 **Lapp Spoon,** made for the tourist trade.
683 **Lapp Drinking Spoon,** wooden bowl with bone handle. Dia. bowl 4 3/16" (111 mm.).
684 **Lapp Spoon,** made for the tourist trade.
685 **Lapp Spoon,** silver.
686 **Lapp Spoon,** silver, marked: FO "Three crowns" V8.

683

687

689

Mint from the thirteenth century until 1810, and for five centuries, until 1834, the site of the royal menagerie. It is its role as a prison that the Tower has imprinted itself on the popular imagination. Its prisoners have included kings of Scotland, France and England; queens, princes and pretenders; and a great many noblemen at odds with their sovereign. Two of the queens of Henry the VIII were beheaded here. The Crown Jewels are stored in Wakefield Tower and may be seen by visitors.

BRITISH COAT OF ARMS (Fig. 700)

The Queen's Royal Arms may be described in simple, non-heraldic terms as follows: Within the shield are the three golden lions representing England, the red lion rampant standing for Scotland, the golden harp speaking for Ireland. The supporters are the lion and the unicorn. Displayed in England, the lion is on the bearer's right (the observer's left) and the unicorn is on the left. But, when displayed in Scotland, the Queen's arms have the unicorn on the right and the lion on the left.

ST. PAUL'S CATHEDRAL (Fig. 701)

St. Paul's stands in the heart of "the City" and on almost its highest point, the summit of Ludgate Hill. It is the third cathedral on the site. The first was a Saxon building (c. 604); the second was originally Norman and afterwards had Early English additions (1087–1285). The present cathedral, Sir Christopher Wren's masterpiece, was begun in 1675, nine years after the medieval St. Paul's was destroyed in the Great Fire. Severely damaged in World War II, its in-

———— •·•· ————

687 **Lapp Spoon,** silver, marked: MH 830 S M.
688 **Lapp Spoon,** silver, marked, (see drawing) 830.
689 **Lapp Spoon,** silver, marked: MH M 830S NORDKAP in the bowl.
690 **London.** Maker: L & S, Birmingham 1907–08.

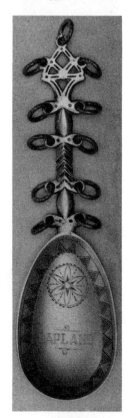

MM

688

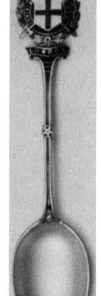

690

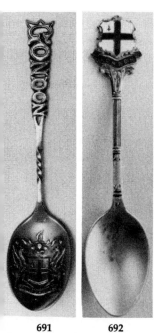

terior has been restored and enhanced by the replacement of bomb-damaged stained glass with clear glass as originally specified in Wren's design. A famous photograph of St. Paul's dome ringed with smoke and flames, during the blitz of December 29, 1940, became a symbol of London's faith in itself.

LONDON SILVER VAULTS
(Fig. 702)

At the northern end of Chancery Lane are the London Silver vaults which were established in 1882. There, deep underground, more than thirty individual silver merchants display in their strongrooms the largest collection of silver in the world. Percy's is one of them, receiving visitors with a warm welcome.

DR. SAMUEL JOHNSON—
YE OLD CHESHIRE CHEESE
(Fig. 703)

Ye Old Cheshire Cheese is a chophouse just off Fleet Street in the center of London's publishing district. It stands on the site of an old monastery. It was erected soon after the Great Fire. It is a favorite haunt of tourists and writers today because of associations with Dr. Johnson, Goldsmith, Dickens, Thackeray, Swift, Tennyson and others. No contemporary biographer of Johnson mentions it so it can hardly have been a favorite haunt though from its proximity

691 **London.** Maker: L & S , Birmingham 1902-03.
692 **London.** Maker: J.A.W., Birmingham 1949-50.
693 **Albert Memorial, London.** Maker: G & C, Birmingham 1903-04.
694 **St. George and The Dragon,** marked: London 1891-92.
695 **Britannia,** marked: CS FS, London 1889-90.
696 **Union Flag,** marked: London 1895-96.
697 **Houses of Parliament, London.** Maker: JMB, Chester 1912-13.
698 **Palace of Parliament, London.** Maker: CS FS. marked: R. G. No. 176644, London 1891-92.

691   692

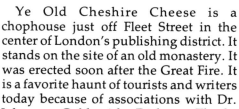

695   696

693   694

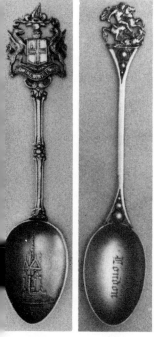

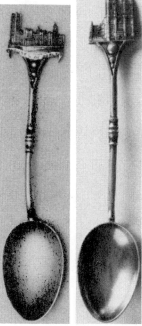

697   698

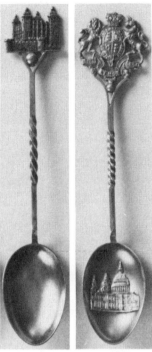

699

700

to his residences in the same neighborhood, it is difficult to believe he was never there. In what is called Dr. Johnson's Corner there is a copy of one of Reynolds' portraits with an inscription underneath: "The Favourite Seat of Dr. Samuel Johnson, Born September 18, 1709, Died December 13, 1784." The rather small armchair referred to in this inscription actually came from the Mitre Tavern.

BRIGHTON (Fig. 704)

Brighton began as a tiny fishing hamlet with a farming settlement on high ground behind. The fishing quarter has been almost entirely swallowed by the sea and the farming lands were swallowed by the maze of narrow streets called the Lanes which are lined with antique shops. The town became fashionable when the Prince of Wales, later George IV, visited there in 1783 and commissioned Henry Holland to build him a Royal Pavilion in Classical style with a Chinese interior. This was rebuilt in an Oriental style by John Nash and is one of the holiday attractions today.

Brighton's arms when fully displayed include martlets, heraldic birds closely associated with Sussex, which appear on the shield in the form of a border.

703　　　704

701　　　702

699 **Tower of London.** Maker: CS FS, London 1891-92.

700 **British Coat of Arms.** Maker: CS FS, Chester 1906-07. "St. Paul's Cathedral" (London) in bowl.

701 **St. Paul's Cathedral, London.** Maker: BB SLD Birmingham 1954-55.

702 **Percy's, London Silver Vaults.** Maker: CB & S, London 1957-58.

703 **Dr. Samuel Johnson—Ye Olde Cheshire Cheese,** marked: EPNS. "Ye Olde Cheshire Cheese Re-built 1669" on back.

704 **Brighton, England.** Maker: J F, Birmingham 1898-99.

705 **Chichester, England,** marked: S & Co. EPNS.

706 **Cheltenham, England.** Maker: A J B, Birmingham 1971-72.

705　　　706

detail

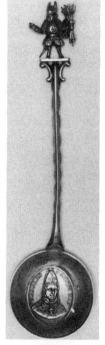

707

They enclose two swimming dolphins, reminders of Brighton's early fishing days. Two more dolphins, curving downwards between spurs of coral, form the crest.

CHICHESTER (Sussex) (Fig. 705)

The site of the modern city was occupied by the Regni tribe before the Romans built their new city of *Noviomagnus* (called Regnum in some accounts). It was captured by the Saxons in the fifth century. Aella, the first king of the South Saxons gave the *ceaster* (castle or town) to Cissa—according to tradition to his son. Cicca's Ceaster (both words pronounced with a "ch") eventually became Chichester. All traces of the castle have disappeared except the mound on which it stood. The city's Roman origin, however, is evident in its four main streets, meeting at right angles, the site of the octagonal Market Cross. This Cross of Caen stone was first erected in 1501 and is surmounted by a cupola fifty feet high put up in 1724. In spite of alterations and restorations, it largely retains its original form with massive central pillar from which spring flying buttresses.

Chichester Cathedral is chiefly early Norman and has one of the most graceful spires in the country. It has a detached bell tower, Perpendicular in style, and is the only one still standing in England.

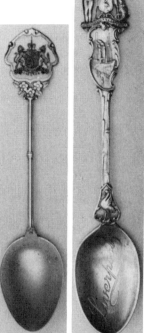

710   711

712   713

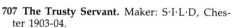

707 **The Trusty Servant.** Maker: S·I·L·D, Chester 1903-04.
708 **The Trusty Servant.** Maker: S·I·L·D, Chester 1902-03.
709 **Cheshire Cat, Chester, England.** Maker: L & S, Chester 1948-49.
710 **Chester (England) Coat of Arms.** Maker: A·J·B, Birmingham 1913-14.
711 **Liverpool, England.** Maker: L & S, Birmingham 1907-08. Rd. No. 353873.
712 **Saffron Walden, England,** marked: Birmingham 1907-08. Rd. No. 353873.
713 **Hatfield House,** marked: EPNS.

708   709

CHELTENHAM (Gloucestershire)
(Fig. 706)

Cheltenham is a fashionable inland spa and a lively center of music and art. It is noted for its splendid Regency houses and lovely parks. The Cheltenham arms are linked with the legendary beginnings of the town. Occupying the center and base of the shield is a chevron with two pigeons, one on each side, above it and an oak tree below. Another pigeon perched on a circle with wavy lines across it forms the crest. This circle represents the mineral waters which gave the town its importance as a spa and is said to have been discovered because pigeons were seen flocking around a spot from which a saline spring issued. The oak tree and the sprays on the crest represent the tree-shaded streets. Horizontally across the upper part of the shield are a cross and two open books. The cross is a reminder that at one time the Manor was held by Edward the Confessor and the books represent the town's excellent schools.

THE TRUSTY SERVANT
(Fig. 707–708)

In the entrance to the kitchen of Winchester College hangs a curious painting of a figure dressed in Windsor uniform and a wig. Beside the picture is an inscription which reads: "A Trusty Servant's portrait would you see,/This emblematic Figure well survey:/The Porker's Snout, not nice in diet shews:/The Padlock Shut, no secrets he'll disclose./Patient, the Ass his master's wrath will hear./Swiftness in errand, the Stagg's Feet declare;/Loaded his Left Hand, apt to labour saith;/The Vest, his neatness: Open Hand his faith./Girt with his Sword; his shield upon his arm;/Himself & master he'll protect from harm."

The picture was painted in 1809 by William Cave, replacing a much older wall-painting which had been repeatedly touched up for more than two centuries. The original, with Latin verses, had been produced by John Hoskyns, a scholar who entered the College in 1579. Hoskyns was not the inventor of the idea of the Trusty Servant, which is found expressed in proverbs in various languages and has been traced back in France as far as the thirteenth century.

The round bowl of the spoon contains a portrait of William of Wykeham and "Manners maketh man," the motto of his two foundations, Winchester College and New College, Oxford. Bishop Wykeham (1324–1404) built Windsor Castle and was chief keeper and surveyor of several royal castles. Both architect and statesman, he became lord chancellor of England 1367–71, 1389–91 and rebuilt the nave of Winchester Cathedral 1395–1405.

CHESTER (Cheshire) (Fig. 709–710)

The Romans established their major camp of *Deva* or *Castra Devana* (the camp on the Dee) here in 79 A.D. It was also known as *Castra Legionium*, from which its Welsh name *Caerleon* and its Anglo-Saxon name *Legaceaster*, shortened to *Ceaster*, were derived. Chester has well-preserved enclosing ramparts; much of the Roman wall survives but the towers and gates were added in the Middle Ages. Chester's galleried streets, called The Rows, form continuous passages along the first floor of the houses in the center of the old part of the city. Some of these half-timbered houses are genuinely medieval.

Chester is the county town of Cheshire—the perpetually grinning creature of that name being the cat that Alice encountered in Wonderland (*Through the Looking Glass*). He had the uncanny ability of slowly vanishing until only the grin remained.

Chester's coat of arms (Fig. 710) includes a sword, emblem of majesty and justice, and open-mouthed wolf heads that are from the arms of the eleventh century Earl of Chester.

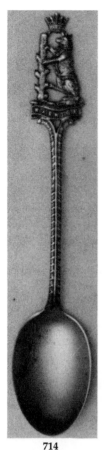

714

715

LIVERPOOL (Lancashire) (Fig. 711)

A settlement was established on the northern bank of the Mersey River, the first century A.D. and by 1207 the fishing village there was granted a charter by King John. The name of the city is of doubtful etymology. A mythical "Liver" bird, unknown to ornithologists, gave the city its name. The nearest equivalent, a cormorant, and a lyver (laver) seaweed in its mouth occupies the city's shield. Neptune holding a trident and a triton sounding a note on a seashell are the supporters and each also holds a banner. The crest is another cormorant. Dominating the busy waterfront scene in Liverpool is the Liver (pronounced Lie-ver) Building, offices of the Royal Liver Friendly Society. On its two main towers are "Liver" birds from which the city takes its name.

SAFFRON WALDEN (Essex) (Fig. 712)

An ancient town, the *Waledana* of the ancient Britons. There are remains of an Iron Age fort nearby, evidence of Roman occupation and the remains of a twelfth-century castle. The town derived its wealth from the wool trade and from its crop of saffron crocus, the growing of which was the most important industry from the reign of Edward III until c. 1790. Saffron was used as a dye and as a medicine and condiment; it is still the symbol of the town.

HATFIELD HOUSE (Hertfordshire) (Fig. 713)

Hatfield House, one of the most mag-

716

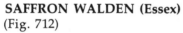

714 **Warwick, England,** Maker: Birmingham 1934-35. $\frac{BB}{sip}$

715 **Warwick, England.** Maker: BI, Birmingham 1962-63.

716 **Stratford-On-Avon, England.** Maker: WJH, Birmingham 1923-24.

717 **Lady Godiva,** marked: EPNS.

718 **Cross of Nails (Coventry Cathedral),** marked: OLD HALL, STAINLESS ENG.

717   718

nificent Tudor mansions, was built by Robert Cecil, first Earl of Salisbury about 1610. In the West Gardens is part of the Old Palace where Elizabeth I, then a princess, was imprisoned by Mary, her half-sister (1555–58). In the gardens at Hatfield House, seated under an oak tree, Elizabeth was first informed that she was to be Queen. Preserved here are some interesting personal relics of Elizabeth as well as other works of art.

WARWICK (Warwickshire)
(Fig. 714–715)

Warwick Castle is one of the most romantically storybook places in England and the "Bear and Ragged Staff" one of the most interesting. Originally, there was a borough fortification against the Danes. William the Conqueror gave the borough to Henry de Newburgh who became the first Earl of Warwick about 1088 and it was undoubtedly he who built the castle on the site of the old fortification. It stands on a high rock above the River Avon. Several of the original walls and towers date from the fourteenth century. Turned into a palatial mansion in 1604, it houses a magnificent collection of paintings and armor.

According to the earliest history of Warwick, much of which is legendary, the town of Warwick was destroyed by the Picts and Scots and then restored 1900 years ago by Caractacus, a British chieftain of the tribe of Catuvellauni. It was twice again ruined and then rebuilt by a king named Gwar, who named it Caer Gwar. There then lived one Arthal, Earl of Warwick, and as his name meant "Bear" he took the Bear as his sign. Then came another Earl, Morvidus, who slew a giant with a young ash tree, torn up by the roots, and who then took the sign of the Ragged Staff. From these two Earls, the crest of the Bear and Ragged Staff, long used by the Earls of Warwick, is derived.

STRATFORD-UPON-AVON (Warwickshire)
(Fig. 716; Fig. 1791–1795, VI; Fig. 359, III)

A Bronze-Age settlement was here and later a Romano-British village. Here, also, was a monastery founded in Anglo-Saxon days and by 1196 the town was granted the right to hold a weekly market. The town's growing prosperity led to independence and the establishment of a municipal government. In 1568 the office of bailiff was held by John Shakespeare, father of William Shakespeare, the poet and playwright born there about April 23, 1564, and the man most responsible for the town's present prosperity. Many buildings in Stratford are directly associated with him, among them his birthplace in Henley Street. It was built in the early sixteenth century in typical half-timbered style, with the spaces between its strong oak framing filled with wattle and daub. Another mecca for tourists is Anne's Cottage in the little village of Shottery, only a mile west of the center of Stratford. The "cottage" where Anne lived until she married Shakespeare c. 1582 is actually a thatched house of twelve rooms. One section was badly damaged in 1969 but has been completely restored.

LADY GODIVA, COVENTRY (Warwickshire), ENGLAND (Fig. 717)

The earliest accounts, written in Latin by two monks of St. Albans Abbey, Roger of Wendover in the twelfth century, and Matthew Paris in the early thirteenth century, say that she rode through the crowded market place of Coventry clothed only in her long hair. Later versions claim that everyone stayed indoors behind shuttered windows with the exception of the tailor, Tom, who was struck blind.

There was a real Lady Godiva. Her name was Godgifu and she was the wife of Earl Leofric of Mercia and Lord of

Coventry. She was wise, virtuous and charitable but her husband tyrannized the church and taxed the people mercilessly. According to the legend, when Godgifu begged him to lower taxes, the exasperated earl said that he would on the condition that she ride naked through Coventry on market day. While historical accounts do not entirely bear this out, it is possible that some historical Godiva performed some sort of penance in Coventry for the misdeeds of her husband.

It was not until the seventeenth century that the antiquary, William Camden first mentioned Peeping Tom. After a visit to Coventry in 1659, he said he had been shown a statue there which represented a man who had been struck blind for peeping at Lady Godiva. This statue was almost certainly the one now kept on the second floor of the Leofric Hotel. Another statue is above a shop front on Hertford Street and a third is on a clock overlooking Broadgate, the city's main square. As Lady Godiva crosses the clock, the head of Peeping Tom pops up into view. A bronze statue of Lady Godiva made in 1949 by Sir William Reid stands in the Broadgate. Her ride is still commemorated with an annual celebration in Coventry.

CROSS OF NAILS, COVENTRY CATHEDRAL (Warwickshire) (Fig. 718)

During the night of November 14, 1940 the fourteenth century cathedral church of St. Michael was reduced to

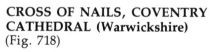

719 **Lincoln Imp.** Maker: T F H, Birmingham 1927-28.
720 **Lincoln Imp,** marked: Birmingham 1904-05.
721 **St. Mary's Abbey, York, England.** Maker: L & S , Birmingham 1908-09, Rd. No. 9610953. "St. Mary's Abbey" in bowl.
722 **Newcastle-Upon-Tyne Coat Of Arms,** marked: Birmingham 1906-07.
723 **Berwick-On-Tweed, England,** marked: R M M & S and London import marks for foreign plate 1934-35. STERLING P & B.

719   720   722

721   723

ruins by fire bombs. A few days after the bombing, two irregular pieces of the charred roof beams, twelve and eight feet in length, were fastened together by wire and set up in the ruins. This "Charred Cross" is now world-famous and stands behind the stone altar in the sanctuary of the ruins, having as its reredos the carving of the two words FATHER FORGIVE.

A second relic which became an inspiration is the "Cross of Nails." As the roof burned, large fourteenth-century hand-forged nails, which had fastened together the beams of the sanctuary, littered the floor. The inspiration came to form three of the nails into the shape of a Cross. This Cross has become the symbol of Coventry Cathedral's Ministry of International Reconciliation. Crosses of Nails have been formally presented to many cities throughout the world which have responded to the efforts of the cathedral to establish links of fellowship to study the meaning of Christian Reconciliation in a divided world, and to encourage exchanges of young people in that study.

As the ruins of the old cathedral still smoked, the resolve was made to rebuild. Rubble was cleared and two underground chapels were repaired and furnished. Reconstruction began June 8, 1954 and the new building consecrated May 25, 1962.

LINCOLN (CATHEDRAL) IMP (Lincolnshire) (Fig. 719–720; III, 409–411)

The city of Lincoln was the *Lindun Coritani* of the early Britons and became *Lindum Colonia* in Roman times. More than twenty centuries and five racial groups (Briton, Roman, Saxon, Danish and Norman) contributed to its being.

Lincoln Cathedral, built between the twelfth and fourteenth centuries, and rising to 365 feet, is a medieval masterpiece. It is especially noted for its Angel Choir which takes its name from the thirty sculptured angels seen high overhead in the traceries of the triforium. This supremely beautiful monument of English Geometrical Decorated work is said to be so lovely that the angels themselves must have built it. The Lincoln Imp, in the Angel Choir, is one of the many whimsical carvings to be found in cathedrals. This sculptured invader of sanctity is supposed to be climbing aloft to tease the angels. He is difficult to find. Locate the next to the last column on the left, raise your eyes above the dark lower portion of the column to a leafy decoration at the base of which sits the Imp, knees crossed and apparently resting between pranks.

YORK (Yorkshire) (Fig. 721)

The early British called it *Caer Ebrauc* and under the Romans, who called it *Eboracum*, it attained great importance after they built a fort there and garrisoned it in 71 A.D. Headquarters of the 6th Legion and capital of the province of Briton, it was often called *Altera Roma* (the Other Rome). The Danes captured and burnt the town in 867 and made it their capital in Britain for nearly a hundred years. They called it *Jorvik* and it is from this name that the present name, York, is derived.

The greatest attraction in York today is York Minster with its incredible wealth of early glass—three-quarters of all the fourteenth-century glass in the whole country. The Five Sisters, described by Dickens in *Nicholas Nickelby*, is a five-lighted lancet and one of England's most celebrated windows. The East Window, completed by John Thornton of Coventry in 1408 (for the princely sum of fifty-five pounds) measures 78 feet by 31 feet, larger than a regulation tennis court.

The York Arms consists of a red cross of St. George on a shield with five golden lions on the cross, thus combining royal, national and religious symbols. Crossed behind the shield are a sword and a mace, showing civic power and

724

725

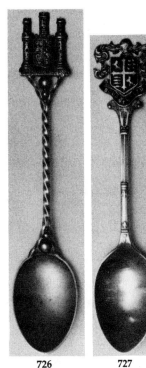

726 727

728

dignity. The effect is enhanced by a chapeau, or ceremonial hat placed above the shield.

St. Mary's Abbey (shown in the bowl), founded by Stephen of Lastingham in 1089, is now in ruins but still impressive. Much dating from the thirteenth century is still visible.

NEWCASTLE-UPON-TYNE (Northumberland) (Fig. 722)

Newcastle began as a minor fort built upon a Roman wall and known as *Pons Aelii*. After the Romans came an obscure religious colony known as Monkchester and then the Normans. The name Newcastle comes from the Norman castle built in 1080 by Robert Curthose, eldest son of William the Conqueror; this was replaced by the existing castle built by Henry II between 1172–1177.

The expression "to carry coals to Newcastle" is a tribute to the size of the city's once principal industry, the export of coal.

On the city's Arms are three towers each surmounted by three turrets displayed on the shield; another forms the crest. These same arms were adopted by Newcastle's goldsmith's hall. Above the tower on the crest is a royal lion. The lion holds a staff and pennon of St. George. The motto, "Triumphing by brave defense," was adopted during the Civil

724 **City Of Bath, England.** Maker: L & S, Birmingham 1903-04, Rd. No. 371236. Motto: INSIGNIA CIVITATIS BATHONIA (Insigne of the City of Bath).

725 **Bath Abbey & Bath, England.** Maker: L & S, Birmingham 1908-09. Left (handle): shield of the West front of Bath Abbey. Right (handle): shield of the City of Bath.

726 **Dorchester, England.** Maker: JMB, Birmingham 1896-97, Rd. No. 269478.

727 **Bournemouth, England.**

728 **Plymouth, England.** Maker: PP & I, London 1911-12, No. 433575. "PLYMOUTH-1620" on back. Motto: TURRIS FORTISSIMA EST NOMEN JEHOVA (The name of the Lord is our strength.)

War, probably following the stubborn resistance maintained in 1644.

BERWICK-UPON-TWEED (Northumberland) (Fig. 723)

The northernmost town in England, it was once a part of Scotland, and during the succession of Border Wars between the Scots and the English, Berwick, founded c. 870 A.D. changed hands thirteen times. It was finally surrendered to the English in 1482. Berwick has had two sets of protecting walls. The first walls were completed in the reign of Edward II (1307–1327) but little is left of them. New fortifications were raised by Elizabeth, starting in 1558, and built according to the New Italian design. They were completed in 1565, some ten feet thick, and were designed especially for gunpowder warfare. A two-mile walk along this wall provides a superb view of the town, the river and the sea.

BATH (Somerset) (Fig. 724)

According to legend, the city of Bath owes its history and its name to the mineral waters which produce some 500,000 gallons a day at 120° F. Prince Bladud, favorite son of Hudibras and father of King Lear, was founder of the city to which he gave his name, Bladud. (Bad-Lud—Bath-waters.) Banished when he contracted leprosy, he was forced to become a swineherd to earn a living. His pigs wandered into a warm, swamp marsh and on driving them out, Bladud discovered he was cured. After being restored to favor, he converted the swamp into a spa.

More probably the first discoverers were the Romans who turned a primitive township into a fashionable resort in 44 A.D. which they called *Aquae Calidae, Aquae Solis,* or *Aquae Sulis,* from *Sul,* a Celtic goddess, who was also identified with Minerva. By the Saxons who captured Bath in 577, it was known at first as *Akemanceaster* and later as *Aet Bathun.*

In early medieval times Bath was a textile center but the baths themselves were almost lost to view. They had fallen into ruins or were destroyed sometime between the departure of the Roman legions and the capture of the city by the West Saxons in 577. Rediscovered in 1879, archaeological work disclosed the sophistication and luxury enjoyed by the citizens of Bath during the 400 years of its existence as a Roman city.

By the beginning of the eighteenth century Bath had developed into a fashionable resort with Beau (Richard) Nash the celebrated arbiter of civic entertainment. Prominent visitors flocked to the city.

The rebuilding of the city had begun by the end of the seventeenth century but it was John Wood who laid the foundation of the elegant Georgian city we know today. His architectural dreams were translated into squares and terraces and crescents and were continued by his son in the stately Royal Crescent, an open design of thirty houses in a sweeping semi-ellipse facing a sloping lawn.

The beginning of the nineteenth century brought Bath to its gradual subsidence into a pleasant, provincial town. Post-war years have brought housing developments to the grassy slopes of former estates.

BATH ABBEY (Fig. 725)

For more than 1200 years a Christian church has stood near the site of the largest of the hot mineral springs, *raison d'être* for the city of Bath. A nunnery founded at *Hat Bathu* in 676 received its first royal endowment from Osric, sub-king of Wiccia. This was converted into a Benedictine monastery by King Edgar, crowned there in 973. Soon after the Norman Conquest (1066) William Rufus appointed his own physician and chaplain, John de Villula, to be Bishop of Wells. He was given the responsibility of replacing the little abbey with a vast

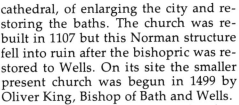

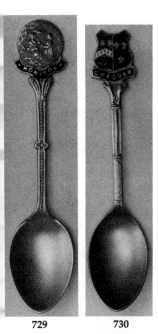

cathedral, of enlarging the city and restoring the baths. The church was rebuilt in 1107 but this Norman structure fell into ruin after the bishopric was restored to Wells. On its site the smaller present church was begun in 1499 by Oliver King, Bishop of Bath and Wells.

Bath Abbey is the last great church to be built in the Perpendicular period. It was designed in this most English of all architectural styles by the brothers Robert and William Vertue.

The west front, with the face of its turrets decorated with angels ascending and descending from heaven, represents the dream which inspired Bishop Oliver King to build it. At the side of the doorway are the sixteenth-century figures of SS. Peter and Paul.

DORCHESTER (Dorset) (Fig. 726)

The history of Dorchester, now the county town of Dorset, goes back to the Stone Age, Bronze Age and Iron Age, and was later *Durnovaria*, a Roman stronghold in 70-400 A.D. Poundbury Camp and the Maumbury Rings, a Stone Age stone circle, was adapted by the Romans as an amphitheater capable of seating 10,000 people. It was used in the Middle Ages for bull- bear- and badger-baiting and as late as 1767 for Hanging Fairs, or public executions. By 660 A.D. Dorchester was a Saxon center and under Athelstan (925-39) a mint town. It was taken by the Normans who built a castle there which is thought to have been one of the hunt-loving King John's numerous temporary residences. The plague and a great fire in 1613 caused death and destruction. The city became Puritan in the seventeenth cen-

732

729 Honiton, England.
730 Cheddar, England, marked: EPNS.
731 Glastonbury Abbey, marked: EPNS.
732 Canterbury, England: Maker: A·J·H, Birmingham 1971-72.
733 Thomas A Becket. Maker D & F, Birmingham 1894-95.

729   730

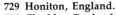

731

733

tury and a shipload of its residents, led by John White, left there to establish a church at Dorchester (originally called Mattapan), Massachusetts c. 1628.

Thomas Hardy was born nearby at Higher Bockhampton and used the area as the setting for many of his novels. Dorchester is the "Casterbridge" of his novel *The Mayor of Casterbridge*.

BOURNEMOUTH (Hampshire) (Fig. 727)

Bournemouth is situated at the mouth of the valley formed by the river Bourne, and is almost Mediterranean-like in its atmosphere. Two centuries ago the area was worthless but is now a favorite summer resort and is characterized by its pine woods and beautiful "chines" (ridges) that interrupt the line of cliffs. Bournemouth was the setting of Thomas Hardy's novel, *Tess of the D'Urbervilles* under the name of "Sandbourne." Robert Louis Stevenson lived there (1884–87) and it was there that he completed *Kidnapped* and *Dr. Jekyll and Mr. Hyde*.

PLYMOUTH (Devonshire) (Fig. 728)

Plymouth was known as Sutton in the Domesday Book and received its charter in 1439. It was fortified soon after and has ever since played an important role in the maritime history of England. Plymouth was the point of departure for many of the expeditions of Sir Francis Drake, Sir Humphrey Gilbert, Captain James Cook and Sir John Hawkins. Of more interest to Americans is the fact that it was from the barbican that the Pilgrims set out on September 6, 1620 on their momentous voyage to "settle in New Plymouth and to lay the Foundation of the New England States."

Plymouth's civic arms are embossed on the back of the spoon with its motto: *Turris Fortissima Est Nomen Jehova* (The name of the Lord is our strength). This motto was frequently recalled by Plymouth residents during the blitz of World War II.

HONITON (Devonshire) (Fig. 729)

Honiton was once famous as a wool town but from the sixteenth through the nineteenth centuries it was lace that brought it fame. Handmade lace is still made there with as many as 400 bobbins used to weave one intricate pattern. This specialty of Honiton, pillow-lace, was introduced by Flemish refugees during the reign of Queen Elizabeth I, but is now not made in great quantity. Honiton lace resembles Brussels lace and examples may be seen in the Honiton and Allhallows Public Museum. Old and new Honiton is exhibited along with a collection of different types of Continental lace.

CHEDDAR (Cheshire) (Fig. 730)

Cheddar is a small village at the foot of the famous Cheddar Gorge. Several caves in which Stone Age tools and weapons have been found by archaeologists are open to the public.

The cheese to which the town gave its name has long been imitated elsewhere. It was made in local farmhouses as early as the twelfth century but barely survives there now as a cottage industry.

GLASTONBURY ABBEY (Somerset) (Fig. 731)

Set among towering trees and well-kept lawns are the ruins of Glastonbury Abbey. These fragments are all that remain of one of the greatest monasteries of medieval England. After the dissolution of the monasteries by King Henry VIII in 1539 the buildings were stripped and left in neglect for three hundred years. The walls were used as a quarry from which much of the town of Glastonbury is built.

According to legend, St. Joseph of Arimathea brought the Holy Chalice of the Last Supper to the area and buried it under the waters of a spring on the

slopes of Glastonbury Tor (hill) and that when he thrust his thorn staff into the ground and leant upon it in prayer, the staff took root and grew into the distinctive Glastonbury winter-flowering thorn-tree—a sign that he should settle and found a religious house. The holy thorn on Wirrall Hill, believed to have grown from his staff was destroyed in the Civil War but a thorn-tree in the Abbey grounds is said to have been grown from a cutting. Cuttings from this tree have been sent around the world to religious institutions.

While there is no historical evidence for the legend about Joseph, there was probably a religious foundation at Glastonbury by the fifth century. The Abbey was the last of several built on the site, the first having been founded in 688 by King Ine of Wessex.

Another legend says that King Arthur and Queen Guinevere were probably buried at Glastonbury. In 1191 the monks identified a tomb in the ancient cemetery, south of the Lady Chapel, as that of the king and his consort. In April 1278 they were magnificently entombed in a shrine in the center of the quire. During archaeological excavations, the base of this shrine was discovered in 1934; it has now been covered and a marker identifies the site.

One of the outstanding features of Glastonbury Abbey is the Abbot's Kitchen, still standing. It is a massive building 70 feet high, its eight stone ribs crowned with a lantern 12 feet across. The kitchen is actually a square building

734 **Japan-British Exhibition 1910 (London),** marked: Rd. 55489.
735 **British Empire Exhibition, Wembley 1924.** Maker's mark worn. Marked: Birmingham 1923-24.
736 **Franco-British Exhibition 1908 (London).** Maker: S & Co., Birmingham 1907-08.
737 **Festival Of Empire Exhibition & Bicentennial of London 1911 (Crystal Palace).** Maker: E & C, Birmingham 1911-12.
738 **Malta.** No mark.

734   735

737

736

738

but appears octagonal as the corners are cut off to accommodate a fireplace in each; it has an octagonal roof. The fireplace flues are carried up outside the vaulted center to the lantern on the roof. The kitchen was an addition to the Abbot's House in the middle of the fourteenth century.

CANTERBURY (Kent) (Fig. 732)

THOMAS À BECKET (Fig. 733)

The modern city of Canterbury stands on a site which had been occupied since the Iron Age (300 B.C.) because of its natural advantages. When the Romans arrived in Britain in 55 B.C. they found a settlement of the Germanic Belgae tribe who had settled there c. 75 B.C. at the ford across the River Stour. The Romans met resistance and it was not until the Roman Conquest in 43 A.D. that they were able to establish their encampment fortress of *Durovernum*.

The era immediately following the Roman occupation which ended in the fifth century is obscure but by the middle of the sixth century Canterbury had become the capital of the kingdom of Kent under King Ethelbert who began his rule in 561. The first cathedral was built there in 597 A.D. when St. Augustine arrived from Rome in the Saxon town, then called *Cant-wara-byrig*—"the borough or fortress of the people of Kent"—to baptize the king and to pave the way for Christianity in England.

In 851 Norsemen invaded the city and for the following two centuries it was constantly in danger of attack. In 1011 the city was sacked by the Danes. Its turbulent history did not end there. It was the Norman invasion, following the Conquest (1066), that founded the modern city of Canterbury.

Nothing remains of the cathedral that Augustine built. Soon after the Conquest the cathedral burnt down and was entirely rebuilt, with many additions through the centuries. It was in the Trinity Chapel that Thomas à Becket, archbishop 1162–1170, was murdered by four knights of Henry II after his long and bitter feud with the king. The Shrine of St. Thomas was visited by thousands of pilgrims for more than 300 years until it was despoiled and plundered for its jewels by King Henry VIII.

The Canterbury Arms display the coughs (birds) taken from the Arms of Thomas à Becket and the lion of England. On the Arms together they recall the bitter and eventually tragic dispute.

BRITISH EXHIBITIONS
(Fig. 734–737)

England can claim the distinction, by more than thirty years, in holding the first industrial exhibiton. The Society of Arts exhibited in April 1761, in a warehouse leased for two weeks, all machines or models of machines that had been awarded prizes in competitions the previous year. At the expiration of their lease the exhibits were moved to the Society's cramped quarters where there was established a permanent repository whose models, with later additions, had a profound effect in the development of new machinery.

In Paris shortly before the beginning of the nineteenth century there was held the first exhibition in which the products of industry were exhibited rather than merely its tools.

It was in London in 1851 at the Crystal Palace that the Great Exhibition of the Industry of All Nations was held. At first planned as another *national* exhibition, Prince Albert, Consort of Queen Victoria, urged that it be made *international* in scope. So successful was this exhibition that America's response was to open her own in New York in 1853. Since that time international exhibitions have been held all over the world, interrupted only during war times.

The Franco-British Exhibition, held at the White City, London, in 1908 was restricted to the products of the two na-

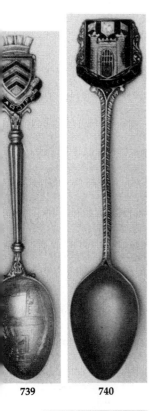

739   740

741

tions. The popular appeal of the dazzling white buildings, especially the Indian architecture of the Court of Honour with its fountain and pools attracted a tremendous number of visitors. Two years later equally large crowds went again to the White City to see the Japan-British Exhibition held in 1910 to celebrate the Anglo-Japanese alliance.

After World War I it was the British who organized the first major exhibition. The British Empire Exhibition, held at Wembley in 1924 and 1925 had originally been planned for 1915. It was concerned mainly with the products and development of the British Empire. Featured there was the Never-Stop Railway which worked on the principle of the underground escalator and ran without drivers.

MALTA (Fig. 738)

The ancient name of this British Crown Colony in the Mediterranean was Melita. It was held in turn by Phoenicians, Greeks, Carthaginians and Romans. Arabs seized the island in 870 and from 1090 to 1530 it was attached to Sicily. Emperor Charles V bestowed it on the Knights Hospitalers of St. John of Jerusalem who defended the island against the Moslems, changing the name of the order to the Knights of St. John of Malta. Malta was seized by Napoleon in 1798. Finally at the request of the people Malta was made a British protectorate and annexed by the Treaty of Paris (1814).

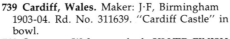

739 **Cardiff, Wales.** Maker: J·F, Birmingham 1903-04. Rd. No. 311639. "Cardiff Castle" in bowl.
740 **Swansea, Wales,** marked: SILVER FINISH SFNS.
741 **Scottish Highlander,** marked: FOREING EPNS.
742 **Braemar, Scotland,** marked: EXQUISITE EPNS.
743 **Aberdeen, Scotland.** Maker: L & S, Birmingham 1911-12. "Municipal Bldg." in bowl.

742

743

141

Because of its strategic importance, the island is strongly fortified, especially Valletta, the capital (shown in the bowl of the spoon) headquarters of the British Mediterranean Fleet.

The Maltese Cross, Emblem of the Knights of Malta, has an ecclesiastical meaning and symbolizes regeneration, being an attribute of St. John the Baptist, the patron saint of the order.

According to some accounts, the eight-pointed white cross which is the emblem of Malta, is supposed to represent the eight Beatitudes.

CARDIFF (Glamorganshire), WALES (Fig. 739)

A great seaport city on the Bristol Channel, Cardiff and coal have been practially synonymous. The nearby Rhondda Valley is particularly rich in coal.

Cardiff Castle (in the spoon bowl), in the center of the town is a Norman fortress dating from 1093 and built on the site of a first century Roman camp whose name has been lost. The castle was ordered built by William the Conquerer and is one of more than a hundred remaining as a safeguard against the turbulent Welsh chieftains.

Cardiff became a county borough in 1888, became a city in 1905 and had been the capital of Wales since 1955.

SWANSEA (Glamorganshire) (Fig. 740)

Swansea, the second largest city in Wales, is in a beautiful setting at the mouth of the River Tawe. The city would have become a picturesque and fashionable spa had not the development of copper and other metals turned it into an industrial center. The Industrial Museum of South Wales is there.

SCOTTISH HIGHLANDER (Fig. 741)

The Scottish Highlander in full dress wears a costume consisting of a kilt or *féile-beag* and plaid of the tartan of his clan, with hose of the same tartan pattern or knitted in a check of the tartan's colors in proper portions; a doublet (jacket) of cloth, velvet or tartan with lozenge or diamond-shaped silver buttons; low-cut shoes, silver-mounted sporran; broad bonnet with badge or crest; a brooch to fasten the plaid; a waist-belt and a baldric or sword-belt.

Everyday wear consists of the kilt, jacket, and vest of tweed, known as "hill checks," with horn buttons, strong shoes or *brogs* (brogues), plain knit hose, garters and a "Balmoral" style bonnet. The kilt should reach the center of the knee cap. The best way to test the length is for the wearer to kneel on the floor. In this position the kilt should just touch the floor.

BRAEMAR, SCOTLAND (Fig. 742)

Braemar is a small resort village, perhaps best-known as the site of the Royal Highland Gathering held each September and usually attended by the members of the royal family.

Near Braemar is Balmoral Castle, known in the fifteenth century as Bouchmorale, Gaelic for "majestic dwelling." Queen Victoria and Prince Albert bought it in 1853 and had it rebuilt and enlarged as a castle in Scottish baronial style. It is still often occupied by the royal family. The public is admitted to the grounds when the royal family is not in residence.

ABERDEEN, SCOTLAND (Fig. 743)

The present name of the city may have been derived from its location on the mouth of the Dee River, or from Denburn, a small tributary beside which the town was founded as Devana about 700 A.D. Little is known about the town prior to the settlement there of a group of Flemings about 1130. The bishopric, previously located at Mortlach, was transferred to Aberdeen about 1137, and the town received its first royal charter in 1179 from William the Lion. Between

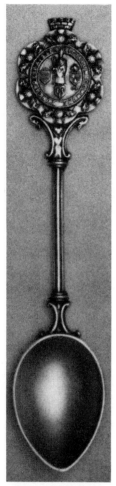

744

747

the twelfth and fourteenth centuries a Scottish royal residence was located there. Robert the Bruce, in the early fourteenth century, was the city's greatest benefactor.

Aberdeen is sometimes called "The Silver City by the Sea" because of its gleaming gray granite buildings. It was here that the building of St. Machar Cathedral, Great Britain's only granite cathedral, was begun in the fourteenth century. Industrially, Aberdeen is still important as a granite center.

PAISLEY, SCOTLAND (Fig. 744)

Paisley was the medieval town of *Passeleth* and was once a Roman station named *Vanduara*. It was once noted for the fine Paisley shawls produced there but are no longer made. Paisley is now the largest thread manufacturing center in the world.

The town grew up around a Cluniac abbey founded in 1163 by Walter, son of Alan, ancestor of the Stewarts. The nave is still in use as the abbey church. Parts of the old abbey building are included in the seventeenth-century Palace of Paisley, which has been restored as a war memorial.

OBAN, SCOTLAND (Fig. 745)

Oban is situated on the Bay of Oban, an arm of the Firth of Lorn, from which it gets its name Obe-an, meaning "little bay." It is protected from Atlantic gales by the Island of Kerrera which forms an almost land-locked harbor. Protected by

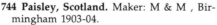

744 **Paisley, Scotland.** Maker: M & M , Birmingham 1903-04.
745 **Oban, Scotland.** Maker JC & S, Birmingham 1906-07.
746 **Glasgow, Scotland,** marked: STAINLESS CHROMIUM PLATE, BIRMINGHAM, ENGLAND.
747 **Glasgow University, Glasgow, Scotland.** Maker: L & S, Birmingham 1905-06, Rd No. 364971.
748 **Glasgow Cathedral, Glasgow, Scotland,** marked: Birmingham 1903-04.

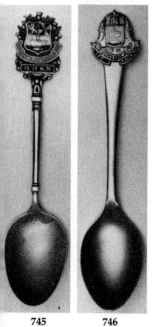

745   746

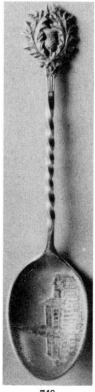

748

high mountains which rise picturesquely north and east of town, it has an exceptionally mild climate which makes it a favorite tourist resort of the west highlands.

On a high bluff overlooking the sea stands the ruins of Dunollie Castle, once the seat of the Lords of Lorn who once owned a third of Scotland. Gylen Castle, home of the MacDougalls, dating back to 1587, is on the island of Kerrera. One of the most ambitious, though unfinished, follies of the late nineteenth century is McCaig's Folly, a replica of the Coliseum in Rome, built by John Stuart McCaig in 1890 as a memorial to his family.

GLASGOW, SCOTLAND
(Fig. 746–748)

According to tradition, Glasgow, the "green-hollow" was founded by St. Kentigern ("chief lord"), also called St. Mungo ("dear friend"), who built his church there in 543 A.D. St. Kentigern, who is better known by his affectionate name of Mungo, is the patron saint of Glasgow.

The progress of the settlement is shrouded in obscurity for several centuries after Kentigern's death in 603. In 1136 a cathedral was erected over his remains and was added to piecemeal from the twelfth to the sixteenth centuries. It is basically in Early English style and is the finest and best preserved Gothic church in Scotland.

The University of Glasgow celebrated its 500th anniversary in 1951 having been founded on January 7, 1450-51 when at the request of James II, King of

749   750

752

751

753

749 **Edinburgh, Scotland,** marked: CHROMPLATE. MADE IN ENGLAND.
750 **Edinburgh, Scotland.** Maker: L & S, Birmingham 1908-09. RD No. 371236.
751 **Edinburgh, Scotland.** Maker: JC & S, Birmingham 1933-34.
752 **St. Giles', Edinburgh, Scotland.** Maker: W & S, Edinburgh 1907-08.
753 **Edinburgh Castle, Edinburgh, Scotland.** Maker: HT, Edinburgh 1913-14.

758

Scots, Pope Nicholas V gave papal authority for its establishment. The new college or *Universitas*, was poorly endowed and met in the chapter house of the cathedral or in the Black Friars' monastery. It was not until 1460 that a permanent building was secured with four acres of ground. Subsequent gifts of land and funds furthered its growth and development.

Glasgow's arms depict a robin perched in a tree. The bird was supposed to have been a pet of St. Serf and was accidentally killed by another student but was miraculously brought to life by St. Kentigern. The two salmon which support the shield recall another miracle he performed. The Queen of Stratclyde gave a ring, which had been a present from her husband, to her lover. The king found the lover wearing the ring as he slept by the side of the River Clyde and threw it in the river. When ordered by her husband to show him the ring she prayed to St. Kentigern who caused it to turn up in a salmon caught by her servants.

EDINBURGH, SCOTLAND
(Fig. 749–757)

Unlike many of Britain's ancient cities which rose along river valley, Edinburgh was built on crags. The origin of the city is lost in the mists of antiquity but there is evidence of human occupation on the slopes of Castle Rock, Calton Hill and Arthur's Seat, dating back to the

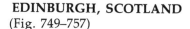

754 **Scottish Thistle,** marked: Edinburgh FH 1934-35.

755 **Scottish Thistle.** Maker: WJ & S, Birmingham 1969-70.

756 **Edinburgh, Scotland,** marked: Edinburgh 1889-90. Cairngorm stone set in handle.

757 **Edinburgh, Scotland.** Maker: H & I, Edinburgh 1927-28.

758 **Scottish Thistle.** Maker: WJ & S, Birmingham 1970-71. Cairngorm stone set in handle.

759 **Scottish Thistle,** marked: Birmingham 1904-05. "Auld Brig O'Doon" Allainay, Ayr. in bowl.

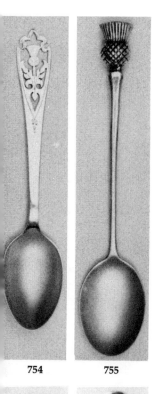

754   755

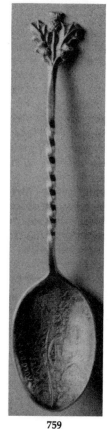

756   757

759

760   761

762

Iron Age. According to an old chronicle Edinburgh Castle was built by a "ruler of Britayne" called Ebranke, who lived nearly a thousand years before Christ and who had "twenty-one wyves, of whom he received twenty sonnes and thirty daughters." It is believed that the Iron Age fort was the scene of struggle between the Picts and the Saxons of Northumbria and that in the seventh century it was rebuilt by Edwin, king of Northumbria, from whom the city is thought to have received its name.

Castle Rock, like nearby Arthur's Seat, is an extinct volcano, a basalt plug which withstood glacial movement from west to east and formed the head of a crag-and-tail formation. Though we may never know exactly how long the Rock was in use as a place of refuge, the re-building of the castle by Edwin is re-corded. The most reliable records, how-ever, date from the eleventh century when King Malcolm III and his Queen Margaret, great-niece of Edward the Confessor, built the beautiful little Norman Chapel still in use in the Castle Citadel. Malcolm Canmore, son of the Duncan who was murdered by Mac-beth, reigned in Scotland as Malcolm III from 1057 to 1093. The Queen who was known for her piety and charity became St. Margaret.

Edinburgh Castle has always been as-sociated with the fortunes of the Scottish kings. One outstanding event in the

763   764

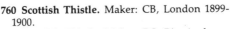

760 **Scottish Thistle.** Maker: CB, London 1899-1900.
761 **Scottish Thistle.** Maker: RC, Birmingham 1908-09.
762 **Stirling Castle, Stirling, Scotland.** No mark.
763 **Scottish Thistle, Edinburgh, Scotland.** Maker: JA, London 1930-31.
764 **Scottish Thistle,** marked: STERLING SCOTLAND IONA C.A.1. Cairngorm stone set in handle.
765 **Scottish Thistle,** marked: EPNS.
766 **Scottish Thistle,** marked: REGᴅ Birmingham 1891-92 S & I.

765   766

Castle's history was the birth there on June 19, 1566 of James, son of Mary Queen of Scots, under whose reign the crowns of Scotland and England were to be united. James was crowned as James VI (and later also James I of England) at Stirling when he was one year old. The Scottish Regalia, or Honours of Scotland, are displayed in an iron cage in the Crown Room of the old Palace. Here is the Crown which probably dates back to Robert the Bruce but was certainly re-fashioned before 1540. Also seen here is the Sceptre given by Pope Alexander VI to James IV in 1494 and the Sword of State presented by Pope Julius II in 1507. These regalia were last used when carried before Queen Elizabeth II on her Coronation Visit to Edinburgh in 1953.

The High Kirk of St. Giles', is the principal church of Edinburgh. The oldest parts of the existing building are the four octagonal pillars supporting the tower on which rests the spire or Crown of St. Giles'. These are thought to be part of the Norman church erected in 1120 and destroyed in 1385. The present building erected between 1387 and the middle of the fifteenth century stands on a site occupied by earlier churches as far back as the ninth century.

SCOTTISH THISTLE (Fig. 758–766)

The stemless *Cirsium acaule*, or thistle is an emblem of Scotland. The thistle in Scotland is significant because of The Order of the Thistle, an honorary order of knighthood ranking second among nineteen such orders in Great Britain. The Order was formally established by

767

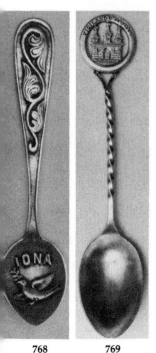

768   769

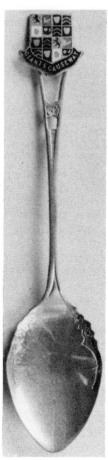

770

771

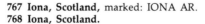

767 **Iona, Scotland,** marked: IONA AR.
768 **Iona, Scotland.**
769 **Kirkcaldy, Fife, Scotland.** Maker: C & S, Birmingham 1902-03.
770 **Belfast, Northern Ireland.** Plated spoon, marks not clear. Inscription on coat-of-arms reads: PRO TANTO QUID RETRIBUAMUS.
771 **Giant's Causeway, Northern Ireland,** marked: EPNS.

147

Queen Anne in 1703 and is limited to the sovereign and sixteen knights companion. The Order's badge depicts St. Andrew bearing the Cross and is supported by a collar of gold, formed of alternate thistles and sprigs of rue.

Cairngorms, often called the Scottish topaz, are used on some of the Scottish thistle spoons. They range in color from almost colorless to brown and may be found in the western United States, Switzerland, Ireland and Brazil. The finest ones are mined in the Cairngorm Mountains of east-central Scotland.

STIRLING CASTLE, SCOTLAND
(Fig. 762)

Stirling Castle, perched on a rocky crag overlooking the Forth Valley, was a Scottish royal palace until 1603, when James VI became King of England.

IONA, SCOTLAND (Fig. 767–768)

It was on the tiny island of Iona off the western coast of Scotland that St. Columba established his abbey when he went there from Ireland in 563 A.D. to convert Scotland to Christianity. This monastery became a center of the Celtic Church. Missionaries were sent out from the island and pilgrims flocked there from many lands. The island was raided by Norsemen in the eighth and ninth centuries and the monastery burned. It was restored by St. Margaret, consort of Malcolm III of Scotland, who is said to have built in 1080 St. Oran's Chapel, the oldest remaining building on the island. A Benedictine monastery was founded there in 1203 and dismantled in 1561. The Cathedral of St. Mary built in the late fifteenth and early sixteenth centuries, and later restored, survives. Points of interest on the island today are the Iona Cross which possibly dates to the ninth or tenth century and St. Oran's Cemetery, the oldest Christian cemetery in Scotland and the burial place of forty-eight Scottish kings, including Duncan, murdered by Macbeth

in 1040, four kings of Ireland and eight kings of Norway and Denmark.

Among the surviving pieces of medieval silver in Scotland, the earliest are the Iona spoons, now preserved in the National Museum of Antiquities. Four of them were found with a gold fillet under a stone in the Nunnery on Iona and were probably for ceremonial use. Three of the spoons were in poor condition but the fourth is complete and in good condition. It has a shallow, fig-shaped bowl with gilt border and engraved floral design and a narrow stem ending in a knop resembling a mulberry in a calyx. There is a step-junction between stem and bowl similar to the Coronation spoon.

KIRKALDY, FIFE, SCOTLAND
(Fig. 769)

Kirkaldy is an industrial town often known as "Lang Toun" because of its main street more than a mile in length. Ravenscraig Castle, built there about 1440 by James II is one of the treasures of Britain.

The city emblem depicts an abbey of three pyramids, each assigned with a cross pattie or (each surmounted by a golden cross).

BELFAST, (County Antrim), NORTHERN IRELAND (Fig. 770)

Belfast has been since 1921 the capital of that division of Great Britain, Northern Ireland. Until the middle of the eighteenth century it was a place of little importance being overshadowed by Carrickfergus. The city's modern development is the result of the introduction of linen manufacture and the establishment of large-scale shipbuilding.

GIANT'S CAUSEWAY, (County Antrim), NORTHERN IRELAND
(Fig. 771)

The Giant's Causeway is a remarkable geological phenomenon two and a half miles north of Bushmills, County An-

772

774

773

775

trim, Northern Ireland. The causeway is part of an overlying mass of basalt, 300 to 500 feet thick, which covers much of the county. It is of volcanic origin and is believed to have been formed when enormous quantities of basalt cooled into thousands of three- to nine-sided columns. These prismatic columns present many curious and spectacular formations to which have been given fanciful names. Seen from a distance the effect is of an uneven platform. The name of the causeway is derived from a legend that it was the beginning of a road to be built by giants across the channel to Scotland.

KILLARNEY, (County Kerry), IRELAND (Fig. 772)

Killarney is a small market town forty-five miles northwest of Cork. It's name is derived from the Gaelic *Cill Airne*, "Church of the Sloe." Killarney is a tourist center whose popularity is based on the beautiful setting amid the three Lakes of Killarney.

Killarney is most admired for the beauty of its mountain and lake scenery, but there are man-made attractions too. Among these is Muckross Abbey founded for Franciscan friars by Donal MacGarthy Mor, about 1340 on a site said to have been settled by St. Finian in the sixth century. The buildings have been in ruins since they were destroyed by Cromwell's troops in 1652.

GALWAY, (County Galway), IRELAND (Fig. 773)

Galway, located on Galway Bay at the mouth of Lough Corrib is said to be "the

---

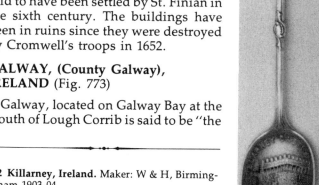

772 **Killarney, Ireland.** Maker: W & H, Birmingham 1903-04.

773 **Galway, Ireland.** Maker: W & H, Birmingham 1903-04.

774 **Blarney Castle.** Maker: L & S, Birmingham 1904-05.

775 **Blarney Castle.** Maker: L & S, Birmingham 1904-05.

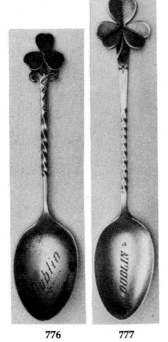

most Irish of all Irish cities." It was founded by the Normans who settled there and built a high-walled town to keep the Irish out. There are remains of the thirteenth-century town walls and the Spanish architecture of many of the buildings is a reminder of Galway's extensive trade with Spain during the later Middle Ages.

One of the principal buildings is the cruciform church (Episcopal) of St. Nicholas founded in 1320. It is the largest medieval church in Ireland and has a profusion of fine carvings, much of it dating from the fifteenth and early sixteenth centuries when Galway was most prosperous.

BLARNEY CASTLE, (County Cork), IRELAND (Fig. 774–775)

"There is a stone there, whoever kisses,/Oh, he never misses to grow eloquent!" So, tradition says. The Blarney Stone in Blarney Castle is known the world over for the eloquence it is said to impart to those who kiss it. Eloquence comes especially in the telling of hanging backwards and being held by the feet to kiss the stone. It is set into the wall just below the battlements. Those brave enough to hang by their heels and poke their heads through the machicolations of the castle keep, almost eighty-five feet above the ground, are justified in their subsequent boasting.

Blarney Castle was built in 1446 by the

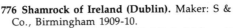

776 **Shamrock of Ireland (Dublin).** Maker: S & Co., Birmingham 1909-10.
777 **Shamrock of Ireland (Dublin).** Maker: JC & S., Birmingham 1894-95.
778 **Shamrock-Harp of Ireland,** marked: Birmingham 1910-11.
779 **Harp of Ireland,** marked: Birmingham 1910-11.
780 **Harp of Ireland,** marked: Edmond Johnson, Dublin 1893-94. "IRISH VILLAGE CHICAGO ILL." on back of bowl.
781 **Celtic Cross,** marked: Birmingham 1910-11.
782 **Dublin Ireland,** marked: CHANCELLOR DUBLIN.

783

784

785

786

McCarthys of Muskerry. The McCarthys retained their hold on Blarney until the Cromwellian confiscation and recovered it after the Restoration, only to lose it again at the Williamite revolution. It has been for many years only a hollow shell, only the walls remain. Visitors reach the top by means of the winding staircase set into an angle-tower. The view from the top is one long remembered.

SHAMROCK OF IRELAND
(Fig. 776–778)

The shamrock is worn on St. Patrick's Day, March 17, both in Ireland and in the United States and other countries where large numbers are shipped to those of Irish extractions—or those who wish they were Irish. The name is anglicized from Gaelic *seamrog* which means trefoil or three-leaved. It is sometimes applied to a number of plants and which is the true one might be left to the Irish if they agreed, but they do not. The black medic *(Medicago lupulina)*, *Oxalis acetosella* and various clovers such as the common red clover *(Trifolium pratense)* and the common low, white clover *(T. repens)* are all claimed by some to be the one picked by St. Patrick as a symbol to illustrate the Holy Trinity.

HARP OF IRELAND (Fig. 778–780)

The harp is the oldest of the stringed musical instruments. It was the favorite instrument of the old Irish poets and has come to be one of the emblems of Ireland. When displayed with the royal crown it is one of the Royal Irish Badges.

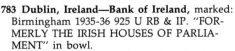

783 **Dublin, Ireland—Bank of Ireland,** marked: Birmingham 1935-36 925 U RB & IP. "FORMERLY THE IRISH HOUSES OF PARLIAMENT" in bowl.

784 **Anointing Spoon.** Maker: BG & Co. London 1901-02. 9-9/16" (243 mm.)

785 **Anointing Spoon,** marked: Birmingham 1901-02. 4-5/16" (111 mm.)

786 **Anointing Spoon,** marked: London 1902-03. 9-7/8" (226 mm.)

CELTIC CROSS (Fig. 781–782)

The Celtic (Irish) Cross, is also called the Cross of Iona because of an ancient one found there. Basically, it is a Latin cross with a circle, expressive of eternity, at the intersection of the arms. They were erected by the early Irish Christians between the tenth to the thirteenth centuries. Some forty-five of them are still standing in Ireland.

DUBLIN (County Dublin), IRELAND (Fig. 776–777, 782–783)

The site of the city was inhabited in remote times as shown by a prehistoric burial site 4000 years old in Phoenix Park. Situated as it is at a ford on the River Liffey with a natural harbor provided by the river mouth it must have been important in Celtic times as well. There were churches and monasteries there in the early historic period but Dublin's real beginning as a city started with the building of a defended shipstead by Norse Vikings in 841 A.D. It was built by the Black Pool (Gaelic *Duibhiln* Norse *Dyfflin* from whence the English *Divelin* and eventually Dublin was derived). The black pool was, of course, the peat-stained waters of the River Liffey. The official modern Gaelic name of the city is Baile Atha Cliath whose English meaning is "the town of the ford of the hurdles." This name came from the fact that one of the seven roads that led to Tara, the prehistoric capital of Ireland, crossed the river by a ford at this point and was protected by hurdles because of its strategic importance.

BANK OF IRELAND, DUBLIN (Fig. 783)

The Bank of Ireland in Dublin occupies an imposing building that was formerly the Old Parliament House. This building was begun in 1729 from the design of Sir Edward Lovat Pearce and in 1785 the eastern portico in Corinthian style was designed by James Gandon. It is regarded as one of the finest examples of eighteenth century architecture.

CORONATION or ANOINTING SPOONS (Fig. 784–788)

The English coronation can be traced from the *ordo* drawn up by Archbishop Dunstan. This service was for King Edgar at Bath in 973. In the Edgar coronation all of the essential features of a modern coronation ceremony appear, in primitive form. The service has been revised frequently, with English taking the place of Latin after the Reformation.

The present coronation service in Westminster Abbey consists of four parts. The first part includes the entry, recognition and oath. The second is the consecration of the sovereign by anointing. The third part is the investiture of the anointed sovereign with the royal robes and insignia culminating with the crown and the last, the enthronement and homage followed by a communion service.

The Coronation spoon is among the oldest objects of the Royal Regalia. In all probability it owes preservation to the time when the more obvious attributes of royalty were destroyed at Charles I's execution in 1649. His death was followed by the systematic destruction of the royal ornaments (some probably dating from the early Middle Ages and possibly from the time of Edward the Confessor), and a new set was made in 1661 for the coronation of Charles II. However, they are intimately connected with the most solemn moment of the entire ceremony when the holy oil, poured from the beak of the golden eagle on the Ampulla into the coronation spoon, is applied by the officiating bishop or archbishop to the head, breast and palms of the new sovereign. The spoon's decoration suggests an early date, the handle showing a pattern of strapwork and filigree scrolls characteristic of the late twelfth century. Reproductions of the anointing spoon have been favorite

787

788

souvenirs of these important ceremonies. The earliest ones seen were made after Victoria's death at the coronation of Edward VII.

CORONATION CHAIR (Fig. 789–791)

The Coronation chair was made around 1297, by the order of Edward I, to enclose the Stone of Scone. According to legend, this stone was originally the pillow of Jacob at Bethel. After wanderings, only equalled by the most peripatetic of the patriarchs, it reached Scone about A.D. 850. Here it was enclosed in a wooden chair. From the coronation of Malcolm IV to that of John Baliol, all Scottish kings were crowned here. Tradition has it that Edward I was crowned King of Scotland on the Stone of Scone after his defeat of Baliol at Dunbar in 1296. Edward I took the stone and Scottish regalia and placed them near the Confessor's shrine in 1297. Attempts were made to regain the famous stone and Edward III did consent to restore it. Although the regalia were allowed to return, Londoners wouldn't part with the stone.

The Coronation chair, made of oak, is now worn and colorless. Originally, it was covered with gilt gesso work, wrought into patterns. During Coronation services the chair is covered with a cloth of gold. On its back was the figure of a king enthroned (probably intended to represent Edward the Confessor), with his feet on a lion. Edward II and all succeeding sovereigns have been crowned in this chair, except Edward V and Edward VIII.

---

787 **Anointing Spoon.** Maker: CS & FS. London 1903-04. 4-⅞" (121 mm.)

788 **Anointing Spoon.** Maker: Birmingham 1952-53. STERLING ENGLAND. $^{BB}_{SL^B}$

789 **Coronation Chair,** marked: London 1902-03.

790 **George V & Queen Mary.** Maker: BHJ., Birmingham 1910-11.

789

790

RICHARD I (1157–1199 A.D.)
(Fig. 792)

Richard I was called Coeur de Lion (the Lionhearted) and was born at Oxford September 8, 1157, the third son of Henry II of England and Eleanor of Aquitaine. On the death of his father he was crowned king in 1189 but went with Philip Augustus of France on the Third Crusade in 1190. The Crusade was a failure and on his return home Richard was taken prisoner by Leopold, duke of Austria, and handed by him to the emperor, Henry VI, who imprisoned him. He was ransomed at great cost to the country and returned to England in 1194. He was killed while storming a town in France in 1199. Sismondi (Jean Charles Leonard Simonde, Swiss historian and economist, 1773–1842) said of him, "A bad son, a bad brother, a bad husband, and a bad king." He had a certain naive magnanimity and courage which gained him the title of Coeur de Lion.

It is said that Richard took the first swans to Britain from Cyprus after the Third Crusade, and for centuries afterwards the swans have been royal property.

HENRY I (1068–1135 A.D.) (Fig. 793)

Henry I, called Henry Beauclerc, was the fourth son of William the Conqueror and Matilda of Flanders. He is said to have received a good education. He fought with his elder brothers, King William II and Robert II, duke of Normandy but made peace with the former. On the evening of August 2, 1100, William II, nicknamed "Rufus" because of his red hair led a hunting party in the New Forest. The king and seven companions were all armed with the long-bow and arrows. Two stags dashed into a clearing and arrows were loosed. The king fell mortally wounded. Though nearly 900 years have passed the mystery of the king's death has not been solved. No one knows for sure whether it was a political murder, a hunting accident or a ritual killing. Henry's immediate actions aroused suspicions. William was killed at 7:00 p.m. on a Thursday, his body was taken to Henry on Friday morning at Winchester where he was buried by noon. By afternoon Henry had seized the Treasury, had himself elected king, instead of Robert who was on his way home from the First Crusade, and was on his way to London to be crowned. The official version of the king's death was that an arrow shot by Walter Tyrrel, a friend of the king, was deflected by the thick hair on the stag's back and ricocheted into William's heart.

To reconcile the people to his usurpation of the crown, Henry issued a charter which was the basis of the Magna Carta.

The figures on Fig. 792 and 793 may be based on the statues in the late fifteenth-century choir-screen at York Minster where there are fifteen statues depicting the kings of England from William the Conqueror to Henry VI.

HENRY VIII (1491–1547 A.D.)
(Fig. 794)

Henry VIII was the second son of Henry VII (called Henry Tudor) and Elizabeth of York. He received a good education and became an accomplished poet and muscian. He was created Prince of Wales in 1503 and was betrothed to his brother Arthur's widow, Catherine of Aragon, whom he married soon after his succession to the throne in 1509. Henry's desire for a male heir and his marital difficulties involving six wives are better remembered than other events of his reign. During this time the union of England and Wales was completed in 1536 and Ireland was made a kingdom in 1541. The passage of the Six Articles by Parliament in 1539 (known as the Six-stringed Whip or Bloody Statute from the merciless persecutions which followed) and his creation of a national

791

792

793

794

795

church marked the real beginning of the English Reformation.

TUDOR ROSE (Fig. 795)

The rose in English history began with the golden rose of Provence, a badge of Eleanor of Provence who married Henry III in 1236. King Edward I took his mother's badge and it remained a royal badge until the death of Richard II in 1399, when the Lancastrians succeeded, and brought the red rose to the English throne. The red rose of Lancaster came from Edmund "Crouchback," the first Earl of Lancaster and second son of Henry III and Queen Eleanor. As the second son he had to vary the color of his badge and adopted the red rose.

A white rose was the badge of the next dynasty, the House of York. It came from the badge of Roger Mortimer, Earl of March, brought by Anne Mortimer to Richard Plantagenet, Duke of York. Anne Mortimer was the granddaughter of Lionel, Duke of Clarence, the third son of Edward III. By virtue of his descent, the House of York alleged its superior right to the throne over that of the House of Lancaster, which was descended from the fourth son of Edward III. This led to the War of Roses (1452–85). Finally, in 1486 Henry VII, head of the House of Lancaster, was married to Princess Elizabeth Woodville, eldest daughter of Edward IV, and heiress of the House of York, and the red and white roses were united, giving the Tudor rose as we know it today, five white petals inside and five red outside.

791 **George VI & Queen Elizabeth.** Maker: illegible, marked: Birmingham 1936-37.
792 **Richard I,** marked: BHM Chester (England) import marks 1912-13 (other marks, see drawing). 8-1/16″ (205 mm.)
793 **Henry I,** marked: BHM Chester (England) import marks 1912-13 (other marks, see drawing. 8-1/16″ (205 mm.)
794 **King Henry VIII,** marked: E.J. Ltd. Birmingham 1972-73.
795 **Tudor Rose,** marked: E. J. Ltd. Birmingham 1972-73.

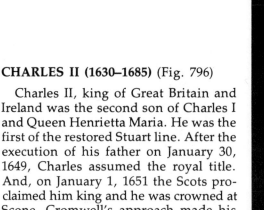

CHARLES II (1630–1685) (Fig. 796)

Charles II, king of Great Britain and Ireland was the second son of Charles I and Queen Henrietta Maria. He was the first of the restored Stuart line. After the execution of his father on January 30, 1649, Charles assumed the royal title. And, on January 1, 1651 the Scots proclaimed him king and he was crowned at Scone. Cromwell's approach made his stay in Scotland unsafe and he left for England, with Cromwell in swift pursuit. After a succession of narrow escapes, including the episode of taking shelter in the celebrated Royal Oak at Boscobel, he reached Shoreham and there fled to France where he remained for nine years in exile. Following Cromwell's death in 1658 the English became dissatisfied with the Protectorate and invited Charles to return. He was proclaimed king in London on May 8, 1660 and was joyfully received. This joy was short-lived as the court of Charles II is considered the most immoral in English history.

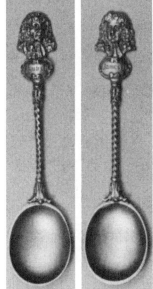

JAMES II (1633–1701) (Fig. 797)

James II was king of England and, as James VIII, of Scotland (1658–88). He was the second son of Charles I and Queen Henrietta Maria, sister of Louis XIII of France. Shortly before his father's execution in January 1649 he was forced to flee and escaped to Holland and then to France where he served with distinction in the French and Spanish armies. He returned to England with his elder brother, Charles II, at the Restoration (1660) and was appointed Lord High Admiral and made Warden of the Cin-

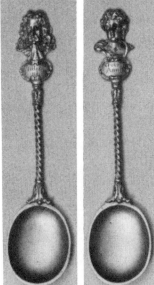

796   797

798   799

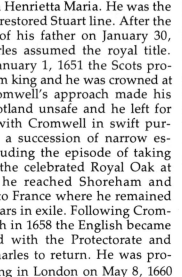

800

801

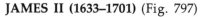

796 **Charles II,** marked: German "Crescent".
797 **James II,** marked: German "Crescent".
798 **William III,** marked: German "Crescent".
799 **Queen Anne,** marked: German "Crescent".
800 **William and Mary.** No mark. Dutch, 17th century.
801 **William and Mary.** Pewter reproduction.

156

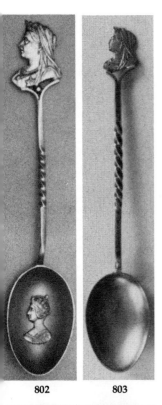

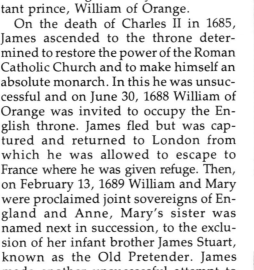

que Ports. His second marriage was to a Catholic princess, (1673) Mary Beatrice of Este but in 1677, at the insistence of Charles II, he assented to the marriage of his eldest daughter Mary to the Protestant prince, William of Orange.

On the death of Charles II in 1685, James ascended to the throne determined to restore the power of the Roman Catholic Church and to make himself an absolute monarch. In this he was unsuccessful and on June 30, 1688 William of Orange was invited to occupy the English throne. James fled but was captured and returned to London from which he was allowed to escape to France where he was given refuge. Then, on February 13, 1689 William and Mary were proclaimed joint sovereigns of England and Anne, Mary's sister was named next in succession, to the exclusion of her infant brother James Stuart, known as the Old Pretender. James made another unsuccessful attempt to regain the throne, was defeated, and spent the rest of his life in France.

806   **807**

WILLIAM III (1605–1702) (Fig. 798)

See William and Mary spoons Fig. 800 and 801.

QUEEN ANNE (1665–1714) (Fig. 799)

Anne, Queen of Great Britain and Ireland was the second daughter of James II and Anne Hyde, daughter of the first Earl of Clarendon. The last Stuart ruler of

802 **Queen Victoria.** Maker: CS & FS., London 1896-97.
803 **Queen Victoria,** marked: London 1900-01.
804 **Queen Victoria.** Maker: CS & FS., London 1894-95.
805 **Queen Victoria,** marked: P. W. Ellis & Co. " maple leaf" trademark, STERLING. "Yarmouth, N.S." in bowl.
806 **Queen Victoria,** marked: P.W. Ellis & Co. "maple leaf" trademark, STERLING. "Toronto" in bowl.
807 **Queen Victoria's Diamond Jubilee,** marked: London 1896-97.
808 **Queen Victoria's Diamond Jubilee.** Maker: MH, marked: 924.

808

809

England, she was a rather dull and obstinate woman. However, she was called "Good Queen Anne" because of her deep religious convictions. She was married to George, Prince of Denmark, in 1683 and had seventeen children, none of whom survived her. On the death of William III in 1702, Anne became queen. At her death in London, August 1, 1714, the crown passed to the nearest Protestant heir, the Elector of Hanover, who became King George I.

The name of Queen Anne is applied to the decorative arts of that period that are characterized by simplicity and little or no ornamentation. The plainer surfaces and sturdy proportions of Queen Anne's reign were soon replaced by the ornate rococo style which had become fashionable in France.

WILLIAM AND MARY (Fig. 800–801)

William III, king of Great Britain and Ireland and hereditary stadholder of Holland, was born at The Hague November 4, 1650, the posthumous son of William II of Nassau, Prince of Orange, and his mother was Henrietta Mary Stuart, daughter of Charles I of England. Mary, his wife, whom he married in 1677, was the elder daughter by Anne Hyde of the Duke of York, afterwards James II of England. Mary was born April 30, 1662 and was presumptive heir to the throne. In January 1689, Parliament offered the crown to William and Mary jointly with William holding the executive power. Mary died childless in 1694 and William died as the result of a fall from his horse February 21,

809 **Queen Victoria's Diamond Jubilee.** Maker: Roden Bros. Ltd., Toronto. STERLING.

810 **Queen Victoria's Diamond Jubilee.** Maker: Messrs. Ahronsberg Bros., Birmingham 1894-95.

811 **Queen Victoria's Diamond Jubilee.** Maker: CS·FS., Birmingham 1896-97. "1837-97" inscribed on back of handle.

812 **Edward VII and Queen Alexandra.** Maker: M Bros., Birmingham 1902-03.

811

810

812

813

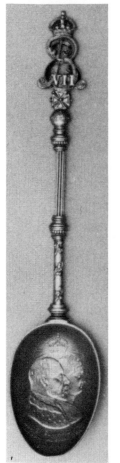

814

1702. They were succeeded by Queen Anne, sister to Mary.

QUEEN VICTORIA (1819–1901)
(Fig. 802–811)

Alexandrina Victoria, Queen of the United Kingdom of Great Britain and Ireland and Empress of India, reigned sixty-three years, seven months and two days, the longest reign known in English history. She was the daughter of Edward Augustus, Duke of Kent and Victoria Mary Louisa, fourth daughter of Francis Frederick Antony, reigning duke of Saxe-Coburg and Saalfeld, Germany. There was a possibility that the first offspring of this union would become heir to the English throne; therefore, Victoria's parents were given residence in Kensington Palace, London, where she was born May 24, 1819.

On the death of William IV, June 20, 1837, Victoria became Queen at the age of eighteen. Coronation ceremonies were held at Westminster Abbey June 28, 1838.

Leopold, king of the Belgians, and uncle to Victoria, suggested that the young Prince Albert of Saxe-Coburg-Gotha was a suitable match for the young queen. He and his elder brother arrived in England and during the social events that followed he and the queen met. Court etiquette required that the queen propose marriage and Victoria exercised her royal prerogative. They were married February 10, 1840 in the chapel of St. James' Palace, London. Their marriage was one of unusual felicity. After the death of the Prince Consort

---

813 **Edward VII and Queen Alexandra,**
   marked: STERLING.
814 **Edward VII and Queen Alexandra,**
   marked: Birmingham 1902-03.
815 **Edward VII and Queen Alexandra.** Maker:
   SB & SL., Birmingham 1901-02.
816 **Edward VII and Queen Alexandra,**
   marked: P. W. Ellis & Co. "maple leaf"
   trademark, STERLING.

815

816

817

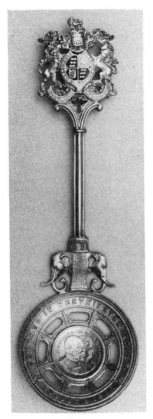

818

in 1861 Victoria went into semi-seclusion and never fully recovered from her bereavement.

Great numbers of spoons were made to commemorate Victoria's Diamond Jubilee in 1897. The Victorian Sexagenary spoon (Fig. 810) illustrates the accomplishments of the nation during her reign. The front of the handle is surmounted with the Imperial Crown and the bust of the Queen. Peace is represented by a reproduction of one of the most powerful men-of-war in the British navy, H.M.S. *Thunderer*, the vessel representing the navy, which guarantees peace. Commerce is typified by a vessel of the merchant service. Electricity is represented by two winged messengers, and under the scroll is a scene depicting Britannia committing the charge of the home defense to the rifle volunteers. Steam is represented by a railway train, and penny postage by a modern postman.

On the back of the handle, immediately under the crown, is the rose, shamrock and thistle and the Union Jack and Royal Standard. The British possessions are represented by the Star of India surrounded by palm branches, and Australia, Canada and Cape Colony on ribbons interspersed with laurel leaves. In the bowl is the coronation scene of Queen Victoria, in repousse, after the picture of Sir George Hayter, bearing distinct portraits of Queen Victoria, the Duchess of Kent, the Duchess of Cambridge, the Archbishop of Canterbury, the Duke of Wellington and Viscount Melbourne.

819

817 **Edward VII and Queen Alexandra,**
marked: STERLING.
818 **Edward VII and Queen Alexandra,**
marked: RD. 1902. STERLING.
819 **Edward VII and Queen Alexandra,**
marked: TIMO. A STERLING reg'd.
820 **Edward VII and Queen Alexandra,**
marked: STERLING RD 1902.

820

821

EDWARD VII AND QUEEN ALEXANDRA (Fig. 812–827)

Edward VII, born November 9, 1841 at Buckingham Palace, London, was the eldest son of Queen Victoria and Prince Albert. He was created Prince of Wales and Earl of Chester shortly after his birth. He studied at Edinburgh, Oxford and Cambridge Universities and was greatly interested in international affairs. Queen Victoria excluded him from affairs of state and kept him occupied with ceremonial appearances. In 1863 he married Princess Alexandra (1844–1925) of Denmark, daughter of King Christian IX. Deprived of the opportunity to render real service to his country, he became a patron of the arts and sciences. He managed, however, to found the Royal College of Music and improved relations between his country and India.

On the death of Queen Victoria, January 22, 1901, "Bertie" became king, choosing to reign under the name Edward VII. His coronation ceremonies were set for June 26, 1902 but illness caused a postponement until August 9th of that same year. (Some spoons bear the earlier date.)

During his reign, Edward VII restored the ceremonial splendors of the monarchy which action created a wave of gaiety and elegance in dress that relieved the austerity of the Victorian era.

Edward VII died May 6, 1910 and was succeeded by George V.

GEORGE V AND QUEEN MARY (Fig. 828–834)

George Frederick Ernest Albert, King of Great Britain, Ireland, and the British

822a

821 **Edward VII and Queen Alexandra,** marked: STERLING.
822 **Edward VII.** Maker: BHJ, Birmingham 1900-01.
822a **Edward VII.** Maker: John Lawrence & Co. Birmingham 1901-02.
823 **Edward VII and Queen Alexandra.** Maker: WD. Birmingham 1901-02.

822

823

824   825

826   827

Dominions Beyond the Seas, Emperor of India, was born at Marlborough House, London on June 3, 1865, the second son of King Edward VII and Queen Alexandra. He became heir presumptive to the throne on the death of his elder brother, Albert Victor, the Duke of Clarence. His father was Prince of Wales at that time and therefore heir apparent. Prince George and his brother, Prince Albert Victor entered the Royal Navy as cadets on the training ship *Britannia*. Prince George remained in the Naval service becoming a vice-admiral in 1903.

George V succeeded to the throne on the death of his father on May 6, 1910; coronation ceremonies were held in Westminster Abbey June 22, 1911. His coronation as Emperor of India was held in Delhi on December 12 of that same year. He did not revel in the pomp and circumstance as had his father but was noted for the great devotion to his family and eventually won the great affection of his people. A Silver Jubilee lasting three months celebrated twenty-five years of reign in 1935. He died January 20, 1936 and was succeeded by his eldest son, the Prince of Wales, as Edward VIII.

Victoria Mary of Teck, consort of George V was born in London on May 16, 1867, daughter of Francis, Duke of Teck and Princess Mary Adelaide of Great Britain (granddaughter of George III). She was betrothed first to Albert Victor but after his death married his brother George in 1893. Mary shared the duties of the throne with her husband

828   829

------

824 **Edward VII and Queen Alexandra.** Maker: SB & SL. Birmingham 1900-01.
825 **Edward VII and Queen Alexandra.** Maker: JP FP London 1894-95.
826 **Edward VII.**
827 **Queen Alexandra.**
828 **George V.**
829 **Queen Mary.**
826-829 **(inclusive)** all marked: CB & S, Sheffield 1936-37.
830 **George V and Queen Mary,** marked: (see drawing).

M?CF ◎ 925 Ⓟ

830

831

832

833

834

and took an active interest in the social and educational problems of the country. During both world wars she worked to organize relief and visited the wounded.

EDWARD VIII (Fig. 835–838)

Edward VIII, Edward Albert Christian George Andrew Patrick David, King of Great Britain and Ireland was the eldest son of King George V and Queen Mary. He was born at Richmond, Surrey, on June 28, 1894. He was created Prince of Wales and Earl of Chester and became Duke of Cornwall in 1910 when his father ascended to the throne. On the death of his father in 1936 he became the first bachelor king of England in 176 years. He wished to marry someone twice a divorcee and make her his queen. Opposition from church, the public and the government developed into a constitutional crisis and he abdicated December 11, 1936 in favor of his brother, the Duke of Clarence, who became King George VI. Edward's reign from January 20th to December 11th was the shortest in English history since that of Edward V. During that historic year of 1936 England had three kings. George V, Edward VIII and George VI. After his abdication he was given the title of Duke of Windsor. He died June 1, 1972.

GEORGE VI AND QUEEN ELIZABETH (Fig. 838–841)

Albert Frederick Arthur George, King of Great Britain and Northern Ireland was born at Sandringham, England December 14, 1895, the second son of King George V and Queen Mary. Known in his early years as Prince Albert, he re-

---

831 **Queen Mary,** marked: London 1910-11.
832 **George V,** marked: London 1910-11.
833 **George V and Queen Mary,** marked: London 1910-11.
834 **George V and Queen Mary,** marked: Birmingham 1911-12. "Tria Juncta in Uno" in the bowl.

835   836

837

ceived his education at Osborne and Dartmouth naval colleges and later transferred to the Royal Naval Service in which he won his wings as a qualified pilot. He was created Duke of York in 1920.

On April 26, 1923 he was married in Westminster Abbey to Lady Elizabeth Bowes-Lyon, daughter of the fourteenth Earl of Strathmore. To them were born two daughters, Princess Elizabeth, later Elizabeth II, and Princess Margaret Rose.

On the abdication of his elder brother, Edward VIII, on December 11, 1936, the Duke of York ascended the throne and with his queen was crowned in Westminster Abbey on May 12, 1937.

The reign of George VI was one of the most troubled in English history, but he and his queen won the admiration and affection of his subjects, especially during the war years when they remained at Buckingham Palace in London and shared with their people the bombings and other wartime perils and austerity.

In 1939 the king and queen visited Canada and the United States, becoming the first English monarchs to visit North America.

After a long illness George VI died in his sleep on February 6, 1952.

———— ◄•►◄ ————

835 **Edward VIII.** Maker: Mappin. STERLING. "Windsor Hotel, Montreal" in the bowl.
836 **Edward VIII.** Maker: IF & Son, Ltd. London 1936-37.
837 **Edward VIII, and George VI.** Marked: Reg. 8130 MENTO EPNS.
838 **George V, Queen Elizabeth and George VI, Edward VIII.** No mark. "Souvenir of the Coronation of King George VI and the historic year of 1936 during which England had three Kings" inscribed on the back of the handle.
839 **George VI and Queen Elizabeth.** Maker: W & Co. London 1936-37.
840 **George VI and Queen Elizabeth.** Maker: International Silver Co. "Commemorating the visit of the King and Queen of the British Empire to the United States in 1939" inscribed on the back of the handle.

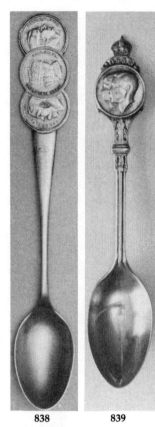

838   839

840

QUEEN ELIZABETH II (Fig. 842–846)

Elizabeth Alexandra Mary, Queen of the United Kingdom of Great Brtain and Northern Ireland was born in London, April 21, 1926, the elder daughter of King George VI and Queen Consort Elizabeth.

At the age of ten she became heiress presumptive to the throne upon the abdication of her uncle, Edward VIII and the accession of her father, George VI.

Elizabeth and her sister, Princess Margaret Rose, were educated at home by a Scots governess. After her father succeeded to the throne, Elizabeth's education stressed constitutional history and law to prepare her for her future position as queen, and she made early public appearances as part of that training. During World War II she was eager to join the Auxiliary Territorial Service, the women's branch of the British army, for which she finally won her father's permission in March 1945.

On November 20, 1947 she married Philip Mountbatten, formerly Prince Philip of Greece, who was created Duke of Edinburgh on the eve of their marriage. They both made visits of state to other countries and assumed many ceremonial duties. Their projected five-month tour that was to have taken them to Ceylon, New Zealand and Australia was cut short on February 6, 1952

845 846

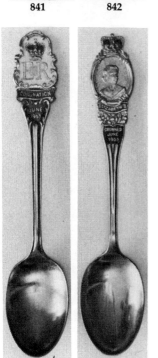

841 **George VI and Queen Elizabeth,** marked: EPNS.

842 **Queen Elizabeth II,** marked: ECCO STERLING

843 **Queen Elizabeth II.** Maker: $^{BB}_{SL^B}$ STERLING ENGLAND.

844 **Queen Elizabeth II.** Maker: $^{BB}_{SL^B}$ STERLING ENGLAND

845 **Queen Elizabeth II.** Maker: E & Co. Birmingham 1952-53.

846 **Queen Elizabeth II.** Maker: HCP. Birmingham 1952-53.

847 **Prince of Wales' Investiture,** marked: ENGLAND E.P.A.1.

848 **Order of the Garter.** Maker: SB & S L. London 1911-12.

841　　　842

843　　　844

847　　　848

849

850

851

by the sudden death of her father. Coronation ceremonies were held in Westminster Abbey on June 2, 1953.

On the accession of Elizabeth as Queen, her son, Prince Charles, Duke of Cornwall became heir apparent.

PRINCE OF WALES (Fig. 847)

Prince Charles, Duke of Cornwall and heir apparent to the British throne was born November 14, 1948 the eldest son of Queen Elizabeth II and Prince Philip, Duke of Edinburgh. In July 1969, in a ceremony rich with medieval splendor, the Queen crowned Prince Charles as the 21st English Prince of Wales. This Investiture took place in the courtyard of Caernarvon Castle, Wales.

THE ROYAL ARMS AND ORDER OF THE GARTER
(Fig. 812, 815–819, 848)

The Royal Arms of Great Britain have undergone many changes but on the accession of Queen Victoria the present form came into use. The famous Plantagenet golden lions occupy quarters one and four. The second quarter contains the arms of Scotland and shows the Royal Tressure, "flory counter flory," which refers to the *fleur-de-lis* pointing alternately in and out of the border enclosing a rampant lion. The third quarter contains the Irish Harp. It no longer represents all the Emerald Isle. The golden harp with silver strings represents Northern Ireland and not Eire, the Republic of Ireland. It was first introduced into the royal arms at the Union of the Crowns in 1603 and had previously appeared on Irish coins of the Tudor era.

The circle surrounding the shield represents the Order of the Garter, established by Edward III in 1348. A cele-

---

849 **18th Century Woman,** marks not traced.
850 **18th Century Woman**
851 **18th Century Dutchman.**
852 **Lute Player.**

852

853

bration following the capture of Calais, the king picked up a garter dropped by Joan, Countess of Salisbury. As he wrapped it about his own knee he rebuked jesting onlookers with the words *Honi soit qui mal y pense*, which is usually translated as "Shamed be he who thinks evil of it." There are twenty-four members of the Order, plus the sovereign, who is its head. Certain princes of the blood are admitted as supernumerary members, among them Prince Charles, heir to the throne, knighted in 1968. There are also four Ladies of the Garter, Queen Elizabeth II, Queen Elizabeth the Queen Mother, Queen Juliana of the Netherlands and Princess Margaret.

The crest of the royal arms is the Crown thereon a gold lion statant guardant (facing). The supporters of the royal arms are the crowned lion rampant on the dexter and on the sinister, a silver unicorn. The motto below is *Dieu et mon droit*, (God and my Right).

When displayed in Scotland there are certain differences in the royal arms. Crest and supporter of the Scottish kings have always borne precedence over those of the English, the arms of the Kingdom of Scotland being displayed on the first and fourth quarters, the English lions occupying the second quarter.

THE NETHERLANDS (Fig. 849–863)

Dutch silver has always been in great demand for its fine craftsmanship. Much of it was made directly for the English market as silver was not widely used in Dutch households until about 1850 when a wave of prosperity created a new market at home.

In the nineteenth century when travel became possible for more and more

855

856

854

853 **18th Century Dutchman.**
854 **Court Attendant,** marked: Antwerp?
855 **Dairy Maid.**
856 **Dutch Musician.**

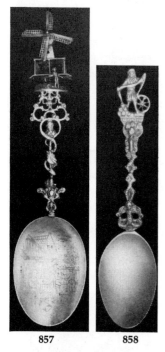

people, silversmiths of the Netherlands met travelers' demands for easily carried mementoes of their travels. Spoons filled part of that need. Because of the reputation for fine quality, it is not surprising that there was a big demand for Dutch spoons.

Lacking the powerful ecclesiastic influence of countries where Apostle spoons were made by the thousands to be sold in or near the cathedrals, the Dutch silversmiths turned instead to the production of spoons that depict everyday scenes on the farms, in the taverns and city streets, and of the people one might meet in these places. People of fashion and court attendants are found on others. The Dutch love of flowers also finds expression on these silver souvenirs.

Unlike other countries, the Netherlands had no laws forbidding the punching of old hallmarks. Several makers specialized in the reproduction of antique pieces and made new designs as well, all of which were allowed by law to be punched with period hallmarks provided that (a) the articles were sold for export and (b) in addition to the marks used for one town they struck additional marks which would not normally be found in combination. Therefore, we find many spoons of nineteenth century and early twentieth century manufacture bearing some odd and confusing combinations of marks. The Dutch marks are often accompanied by English import marks for foreign plate.

's GRAVENHAGE, THE NETHERLANDS (Fig. 864–870)

The formal Dutch name of the city is 's *Gravenhage* but *Den Haag*, the German

860

857 Dutch Windmill.
858 Dutch Spinner.
859 Dairy Maid.
860 Tavern Scene
861 Netherlands' Coat-Of-Arms. Maker: W. Y. Z., marked: .833 quality mark.

857   858

859

861

862

863

form, is more commonly used. In French the name is *La Haye* and in English *The Hague*, all of which mean *The Hedge*, in reference to the hunting lodge which the Counts of Holland built there in the thirteenth century. The town began when Count William of Holland began construction of a castle there in 1248 and a settlement grew up around it.

The city is the actual seat of the Netherlands Government as it is the residence of the sovereign and the meeting place of her States-General (Parliament). The city appears less crowded and less commercial than most Dutch cities. Near the center of town is the Binnenhof, a complex of buildings begun by William II, which includes the administrative offices of the state, two chambers of the legislature, and the Ridderzaal (Knight's Hall) where the Queen arrives on the third Tuesday of September every year to open the States-General.

The Hague is especially noted for its beautiful buildings, fine parks and outstanding museums. Among the latter are the Academy of Fine Arts (reproductions of monuments and statues), the Meermanno Westreenlanum Museum (manuscripts), the Bredius Museum (porcelain, silver, glassware), the Mesdag Museum (late nineteenth century art) and the Municipal Museum. The Mauritshuis or Royal Museum of Painting since 1821, was at one time the residence of Prince Maurits of Orange, the seventeenth-century stadholder and is regarded by many as one of the finest museums of Europe. There are also museums of specialized interests such as the Torture Museum, the Netherlands

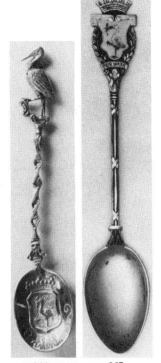

864   865

866

862 **Dutch Ship,** marked: quality marks and date letter for 1860.
863 **Dutch Ship.**
864 **Den Haag, Netherlands.**
865 **Den Haag, Netherlands.** Maker: WS, marked: "Crescent & crown" 800.
866 **Den Haag, Netherlands.**

867

868

869   870

Costume Museum, the Royal Numismatic Museum and the Orange-Nassau Museum, the last containing many of the gifts presented to the royal family of the Netherlands.

Near The Hague, and now virtually part of it, is Scheveningen (Fig. 867), a popular spa. In addition to its streets of amusements and a magnificent park, the Scheveningse Bosjes, there is boating and swimming and all the usual offerings of a health resort.

Perhaps the most unusual exhibit in The Hague is Madurodam, a miniature city spread over several thousand square feet along one of the canals leading to Scheveningen. Madurodam was established in 1952 as a monument to all Dutchmen who gave their lives in World War II. Its name honors George J. L. Maduro, former resident of Willemstad (Curacao) and student at Leiden University and Dutch patriot executed by the Nazis at Dachau. He displayed such conspicuous courage as a reserve officer of the Hussars that he was posthumously awarded the country's highest military order, the Militarie Willemsorde. This miniature city is designed on a scale of 1/25th of life size and is unbelievably real. It is mechanized to simulate the industry and traffic of an actual community. Windmills turn, ships sail the harbor and trains move along on more than two miles of railroad. Automobiles compete with swarms of bicycles in the streets, music fills the air and at night more than 45,000 lights illuminate this modern Lilliput.

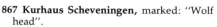

867 **Kurhaus Scheveningen,** marked: "Wolf head".
868 **Coat of Arms. 's Gravenhage, Netherlands.**
869 **The Hague, Netherlands.** No mark. In the bowl is a reproduction of the young man in a painting by Jan Steen.
870 **The Hague, Netherlands.**
871 **Dutch Windmill,** marked: "Crescent & crown" 800 (also see drawing).

871

170

872

The stork with an eel in its beak is emblematic of the Hague.

DUTCH WINDMILLS (Fig. 857, 871, 877, 881, 884, 887, 889, 893)

It would be impossible to tell the history of the Netherlands without reference to the work of the thousands of windmills in their valiant battle against the charging forces of wind and wave. For centuries the windmills made it possible for people to live below sea level by removing the water with pumps. Many windmills were of enormous size and were used to turn the wheels of industry as well as to pump the superfluous water from the lowlands up to the sea. A century ago as many as 9,000 windmills were at work; today there are only 300 in use.

Though correctly applied only to one province, the name Holland, meaning according to some "hollow country," has been applied to all of the Netherlands—and with reason. Most of the Netherlands is a marshy region of sand and mud and being hollow, much of it actually below sea-level, it was forever invaded by the sea. The swampy area in early times reached from the mouths of the Scheldt to the estuary of the Dollart. Only North Holland and Friesland were inhabited—by a wild population the Romans could not subdue. When Pliny the Elder visited Friesland in 50 B.C. he remarked that "no one could tell whether it [the country] belonged to land or sea." As a protection against tidal water the Fresians lived on

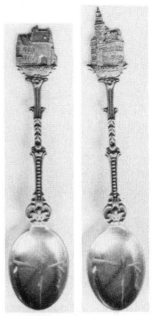

875   876

877

872 Dutch Hanging Spoon.
873 Museum Boymans, Rotterdam, Netherlands, marked: HH 90.
874 Grootekerk, Rotterdam, Netherlands, marked: HH 90.
875 Gevangenpoort, Den Haag, Netherlands, marked: HH 90.
876 Stadhuis 's Gravenhage, Netherlands, marked: HH 90.
877 Amsterdam, Netherlands, marked: $\frac{N}{N}$

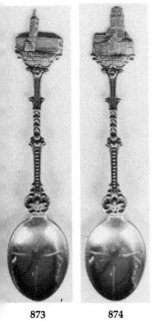

873   874

878

artificial mounds called *terpen*. As these mounds were gradually linked to one another by causeways, the modern system of dykes evolved. As early as 800 A.D. 800 "polders" (land reclaimed from the sea) were under construction by surrounding flood-prone land with dykes of reed, clay and pebbles. These fragile dykes gave way with every storm and had to be rebuilt. To add to their troubles there was a continual sinking of the ground level at a rate of 9-12 inches every hundred years. Water accumulated in low areas, the formation of some of them hastened by the cutting of peat for fuel. The Rhine and Maas rivers, by their constant silting raised their beds and caused great damage during seasonal floods. Then, in 1300, the North Sea inundated thousands of acres, swallowing up hundreds of villages and created the Zuider Zee (now an enclosed lake, the Ijselmeer).

The time had come for organized dyke-building and land reclamation. An association for fighting the waters had been founded in Walcheren, Zeeland in 1293 and later groups banded together for the fight. Soon after 1400 the first windmills appeared and from that time, though battles were lost, the war was won. For four centuries wind-power alone kept away the invading waters. The procedure was this: they built a dyke and canal around the area to be drained. Windmills were built along the canal to pump away the water and as the water level sank, more windmills were built below. These lower windmills pumped the water until it reached a main drainage canal. The dykes became foundations for roads and a network of

880

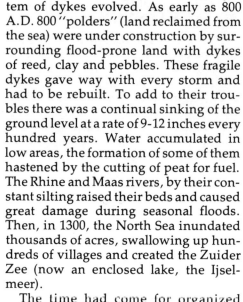

---

878 **Amsterdam, Netherlands.** No mark.
879 **Amsterdam, Netherlands.** Mark illegible.
880 **Stork-Windmill.** No mark. Pewter.
881 **Dutch Windmill,** marked: DD .833 standard mark, state stamp for 1965.
882 **Dutch Country Life,** marked: MADE IN HOLLAND.

879

881

882

883

884

canals provided continual drainage of the reclaimed land. Between 1500 and 1600, 105,000 acres of land were reclaimed; 130,000 between 1600 and 1650. By 1836 the steam-pump was used to reinforce the windmill. Today almost all the pumping is done by electricity.

Unknown to most visitors is that windmills have a language of their own, spoken through their sails. The language varies from district to district but there are some standard positions used throughout the country. When the sails are set directly, horizontally and vertically, that is at 90 degrees to one another, it means that the mill has been working and is about to start again. Set purely diagonally, that is at 45 degrees to the vertical, it means that the mill will be resting for a while. A joyous occasion, such as a birth or wedding, is announced if the sails are set sloping, with the top wing just below the vertical and horizontal. A death in the family is indicated when the sails are turned just past the working position. During World War II the language of the windmills was used for transmitting important messages to the Resistance Movement and to pilots of Allied aircraft.

MUSEUM BOYMANS, ROTTERDAM, THE NETHERLANDS
(Fig. 873)

The Boymans-van Beuningen Museum is thought by some to be a stunning building, ideally designed to house the collections of paintings and sculpture, ceramics and furnishings inside; other deplore it. The collections, strongest in Dutch and Flemish works—Bosch, Hals, Steen, Rubens, and Rembrandt and including the best

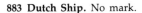

883 **Dutch Ship.** No mark.
884 **Dutch Windmill,** marked: MADE IN HOLLAND.
885 **Dutch Parrot,** marked: Quality mark VH C.
886 **Dutch Shoes,** marked: .833 standard AL3 (state stamp).

885

886

173

group of French Impressionist paintings in the Netherlands, is first rate. There is also a distinguished collection of sculpture by Rodin, Degas and Aristide Maillol.

GROOTEKERK, ROTTERDAM
(Fig. 874)

Only the walls and tower of the more than 550-year-old St. Lawrence's Church (Grootekerk) survived the war. The interior was completely burned out and all the windows were gone from the city's largest and most historic religious edifice. Restoration and reconstruction plans began immediately and it has been completely rebuilt.

GEVANGENPOORT, DEN HAAG, THE NETHERLANDS (Fig. 875)

The Gevangenpoort, a prison-gatehouse on the north side of the square, contains a collection of instruments of torture and is open to the public as a museum. Built in the fourteenth century, the Gavengenpoort was formerly a gatehouse of the palace of the Counts of Holland.

STADHUIS, 's GRAVENHAGE, THE NETHERLANDS (Fig. 876)

The Stadhuis (Town Hall), built in the thirteenth century was formerly the residence of the Counts of Holland. It was renovated between 1620-30.

AMSTERDAM, THE NETHERLANDS
(Fig. 877–879)

Amsterdam can trace its beginning to 1204 when Giesebrecht van Amstel built a fortress there. In 1240, his son Giesebrecht III built a sea wall and a dam there so remarkable that the people became known as the people of the *Amstel Dam* or *Amstelredamme*. Atop the Dam they laid out their main square. It was called simply The Dam, and still is. The little fishing village or Amstelredamme grew up in the marshes and peat bogs between the Zuider Zee and the junction of the two rivers, the Amstel and the Ij ("Eye"). It passed into possession of the Counts of Holland in 1296, and by 1482 was important enough to be a walled city.

The city is built in semicircle with four concentric main canals: Prinsen, Keizer's, Heeren, and Singel, with the Dam in the center. The city itself fans out from the great broad plaza of the Dam along two main thoroughfares, the Damrak and the Rokin. Most of the people of modern Amsterdam live beyond the outer canal, the Singelgracht, but it is within its sweep that the historical city lies.

From the beautiful restaurant on the top floor of the 14-story Havengebouw or Harbor Building, a magnificent view is afforded of the entire city. From here it is easy to trace the lines of the tree-garlanded canals, the docks in the harbor and the industrial area which has developed on the far shore of the Ij. A more intimate acquaintance may be made, however, by way of the slender power boats that tour the canals of the old part of the city.

Amsterdam's many buildings rest upon piles that are driven from 14 to 60 feet through sand and mud to solid clay. Some idea of the immensity of the building problem may be gained when one learns that the Royal Palace stands on more than 13,000 wooden piles. It was built from 1648 to 1655 and was formerly the town hall.

Amsterdam is a city of squares connected by broad avenues and winding canals. One of these is the Muntplein, a busy square whose chief feature is the Munttoren (Mint Tower) with its clock and bells more than three centuries old. Another square of special interest to visitors is the Museumplein, the site of both the Rijksmuseum and the Stedelijk Museum. The Rijksmuseum is worth a visit if only to see the famous Rembrandt painting, "The Company of Captain Frans Banning Cocq and Lieutenant Wil-

lem Van Ruytenburg," painted in 1642 and traditionally, but incorrectly referred to as "The Night Watch." The Stedelijk Museum houses collections of van Gogh drawings and paintings, There are also specialized museums such as the Scheepvaart Museum (maritime), the Amsterdam Historical Museum, the Jewish Historical Museum, the Allard Pierson Museum (archaeology), the Willet Holthuysen Museum (eighteenth century decorative arts), and the Bijbelmuseum (biblical history).

Amsterdam is known as the diamond capital of the world, with Antwerp in second place. Since 1948 Israel has been a serious contender for the title. Since the Middle Ages Amsterdam and Antwerp have been the centers of the diamond industry. A diamond in the rough receives only a passing glance but a perfectly cut diamond is the ultimate in gems. The diamond cutters of Amsterdam have brought that art to precise perfection and a number of the diamond-cutting firms in the city welcome visitors. No pressure is brought to bear, but many a girl has taken advantage of her visit to acquire a "girl's best friend."

890

DELFT, THE NETHERLANDS
(Fig. 884, 886, 888)

Delft, only a few miles from the Hague on the way to Rotterdam is steeped in the past. The name of the city is pronounced "deluhft" by many of its citizens. It is known principally for the charming blue and white pottery that bears its name. During the seventeenth and eighteenth centuries Delftware was at the height of its popularity. Delftware is still made there, and in other towns also, principally Gouda, and while it

887

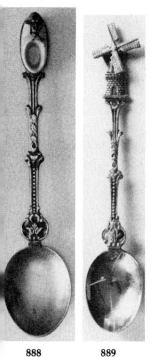

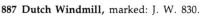

887 **Dutch Windmill,** marked: J. W. 830.
888 **Dutch Shoe,** marked: HOLLAND.
889 **Dutch Windmill,** marked: HH 90.
890 **Rotterdam Coat-Of-Arms.**
891 **Scene of Dutch Life.**

888   889

891

892

893

894

may be technically superior, many feel that it lacks the charm of old examples which may be found in antique shops.

ROTTERDAM, THE NETHERLANDS (Fig. 890)

During the bombardment on May 14, 1940 all of the city center of Rotterdam was destroyed by fire, so what one sees today is a new city. The old town, with its houses and shops that dated back to the fifteenth and sixteenth centuries was obliterated. Rotterdam suffered a second destruction, perhaps more disastrous than the first, when in 1945 the defeated enemy before retreating systematically destroyed five miles of wharves, the very life of the largest port in Europe. Rotterdam refused to die. Destruction of her port might have meant the end for a lesser people, but the Dutch who had fought successfully against the sea for centuries chose to restore the vital shipping facilities even before they erected new homes. Their foresight and determination has rebuilt Rotterdam again into the second busiest port in the world.

LIÈGE, BELGIUM (Fig. 902)

Liège is Belgium's third largest city. The Liègois are proud of their turbulent history and of their reputation for stubbornness, their rebellion and resistance to oppression. "La Fontaine de Perron" represented on the spoon is a reminder of the freedom of the city from the oppression of the king, count or landlord during the Middle Ages.

---

892 **Dutch Parrot.**
893 **Dutch Windmill.**
894 **Dutch Seaside Scene.**
895 **Brussels, Belgium,** marked: 935.
896 **La Dentelliere Brussels, Belgium,** marked: HUMA H.S.
897 **Palace of Justice, Brussels, Belgium.** No mark.
898 **Brussels, Belgium,** marked: MADE IN HOLLAND.

895   896

897   898

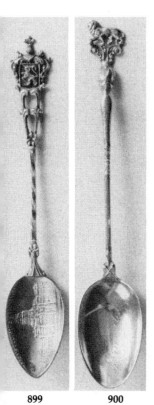

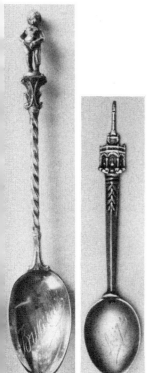

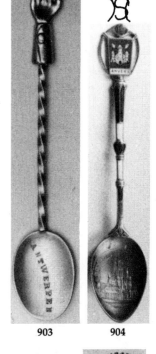

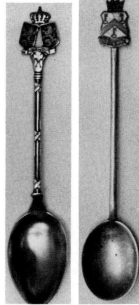

ANTWERP, BELGIUM (Fig. 903–904)

(French, ANVERS; English, ANTWERP: German and Flemish, ANTWERPEN)

The name of the city literally means "at the wharf" (*aan het werf*) but according to local legend it is the place where hands (*hand*) were thrown (*werpen*) into the Scheldt by a giant Druon Antigonus, who was the legendary founder of Brabant. The legend goes on to say that a Roman named Salvius Brabo, related to Caesar, defeated the giant and cut off *his* hand. Two severed hands appear on Antwerp's coat-of-arms but scholars explain that this had assumed its present form two centuries before the Brabo legend.

Antwerp's outstanding monument, the Cathedral of Our Lady (Fig. 904) is one of the most remarkable Gothic buildings in western Europe. It is also one of the largest. The cathedral was begun in 1352 and was more than two centuries in the building. At one time plans were drawn to make it the largest by enlarging it to twice its present size. Its richly ornamented spire was to have been matched by a second. The interior of the cathedral was stripped of its windows and much of its splendor in 1584 and again during the French Revolution and today seems stark in relation to its elaborate exterior.

GAND, BELGIUM (Fig. 905)

(Dutch, GENT; French, GAND; English, GHENT)

Ghent began with a monastery

---

899 **Palace of Justice, Brussels, Belgium,** marked: 800 "Crown".
900 **Brussels, Belgium.** No mark.
901 **Manikin Pis, Brussels, Belgium.** No mark.
902 **Liège, Belgium,** marked: 830.
903 **Antwerp, Belgium.** No mark.
904 **Antwerp, Belgium,** marked: DEPOSE "Crescent & crown" 800 (also see drawing).
905 **Ghent, Belgium,** marked: 800 SM.
906 **Ostende, Belgium.** Maker: WJH. Birmingham 1925-26.

899   900

901   902

903   904

905   906

907

909

founded early in the seventh century at the confluence of the Scheldt and Leie Rivers. The monastery was built by Christian missionaries who were making desperate efforts to convert the inhabitants of Ghent which is reputed to have been the last stronghold of paganism in Gaul. The city has a long history of violence and internal strife which is reflected in its architecture.

Two thirds of Belgium's linen is produced in Ghent which also has a monopoly on the cotton fabrics.

Thousands of visitors flock to Ghent each year to visit the Cathedral of St. Bavon, not to see the building itself, but to see the famous polyptych, *The Adoration of the Lamb*. Variously attributed in the past, it is now generally believed to have been painted by both Hubert and Jan van Eyck.

OSTENDE, BELGIUM (Fig. 906)
(Flemish, OOSTENDE; French, OSTENDE; English, OSTEND)

Ostend is a seaport town and resort on the North Sea almost exactly midway along the coastal strip of the country. It is the oldest town on the coast; Crusaders sailed from there. In the fifteenth century Ostend was a fortress and at the end of the sixteenth it was the last stronghold of the Dutch in the Southern Netherlands. Since mid-nineteenth century it has become an important seaside resort.

BRUXELLES (BRUSSELS), BELGIUM (Fig. 895–901)

The name of Belgium's capital city, *broeck* (brook), *sele* (dwelling) may be from its location on the River Senne,

908

910

907 **Belgium 50th Anniversary of Independence.** No mark. Coin is 2 Francs.
908 **Waterloo, Belgium.** No mark.
909 **Dinant, Belgium.** Maker: AD. French quality mark.
910 **Luxembourg,** marked: "Crescent & crown" 800 (also see drawing). Adolphe Bridge in the bowl.

911

913

which now courses through the city underground and unseen.

The Church of Saint Gudule (Fig. 895) (formerly the Collegiate Church of St. Michael and St. Gudule) is the finest of many fine churches in Brussels. It was constructed over a period of six centuries beginning in 1010. Reconstruction was begun in 1220 and carried on until the seventeenth century. It is richly adorned with sculptures and paintings.

The Palais de Justice (Fig. 897, 899) is a magnificent modern building of colossal proportions built in the classical style. It is called the biggest building in Europe. It covers an area of six and one-half acres, twelve percent greater than St. Peter's in Rome. Its crowned dome towers to a height of 400 feet.

Brussels has long been famous for hand-made lace, both needlepoint and bobbin lace. Until a few years ago lacemakers could often be seen at work in doorways and on sidewalks in fair weather. They are few in number now because machine-made lace has largely replaced the handmade.

The most photographed curiosity of Brussels is the *Manneken Pis* (Fig. 901), the statue of a small boy supplying water for a fountain as small boys will. He stands in a niche in the little side street Rue de l'Étuve, the undisputed symbol of the city. He was created in the seventeenth century by the well-known sculptor, Dequesnoy. According to one legend, the boy represents the king's son who was lost and the searchers found him in that particular pose. The statue has been stolen four times (to 1968) but new ones are created from the

---

911 **L'Opera (Opera House), Paris, France,** marked: IMPORTE.

912 **Paris, France,** marked: Paris 1890 quality mark, M "Wine glass" J.

913 **Paris, France,** marked: "Wolf head" quality mark, J "Ladder" G.

914 **Eiffel Tower, Paris, France,** marked: AUGIS AA LYON

912

914

original molds. It has been the custom for visiting dignitaries to present him with a costume. More than eighty of these are on display at the Maison du Roi.

BELGIUM'S 50TH ANNIVERSARY OF INDEPENDENCE (Fig. 907)

The Belgians revolted against Dutch rule on August 25, 1830 and one month later, September 25, 1830, a provisional government was constituted which proclaimed Belgium's independence.

WATERLOO, BELGIUM (Fig. 908)

In the bowl of this spoon is a picture of the farm "La Belle Alliance" where the French troops stayed during the battle of Waterloo. The emblem on the handle is "Aigle de France," the eagle chosen by Napoleon as his symbol—perhaps because the word in French also means "genius" or "mastermind."

DINANT, BELGIUM (Fig. 909)

The town dates from the sixth century. It has had a turbulent history. The citadel on the summit of the cliff behind the town occupies the site of a fortress built in 1040. The town was sacked in 1466 by the Burgundians under Charles the Bold and by the French in 1554. It was seized by Louis XIV in 1675 and held by the French for nearly thirty years.

Dinant is the most popular resort on the Meuse River. Among the several natural wonders near there are the grotto, the *Hall of Diana* and *La Merveilleuse* which is all brilliantly white within and a pleasure even to those who do not ordinarily enjoy spelunking.

Centuries ago Dinant was renowned for its copper and brass ware, called *dinanderie*. Unhappily, the hammered copper which festoons the shops today is not made with the old craftsman's skill.

LUXEMBOURG (Fig. 910)

The Grande Duchy of Luxembourg is an independent state in western Europe and is slightly smaller than the state of Rhode Island. Its capital is the City of Luxembourg sited on a rocky plateau, bounded on the east and south by two deep valleys which divide Old Luxembourg from the modern town and the railway station. Great viaducts such as the Adolphe Bridge shown in the spoon bowl, connect the two. Luxembourg's size is not impressive but its location is for it occupies one of the most dramatically beautiful heights in Europe. On the ruins of an ancient Roman fortification overlooking the valleys of the Pétrusse and the Alzette, a citadel was built in the tenth century. The old city grew up around this citadel and in later years bridges were built across the gorges and all but the most precipitous cliffs planted as parks. The city eventually outgrew the old ramparts and by the twentieth century the buildings were an architectural miscellany. The Ducal Palace is an excellent example being primarily of Italian Renaissance influence with an admixture of Spanish—on which there was emblazoned the arms of Burgundy. Only part of it is used by the reigning family today; the rest is used by the legislature.

PARIS, FRANCE (Fig. 911–921)

Paris was founded more than two thousand years ago but reached its present development because of its political role. Now capital of France, it began as a tiny Celtic village of "Lutetia" and was mentioned in a communiqué in 51 B.C. Nothing is known of the little village and nothing remains with the exception of a few objects found in the rubble of the Île de la Cité one of the islands in the River Seine where the first settlers established a refuge. It is thought that two footbridges connected the La Cité and the marshy mainland where the inhab-

itants lived by fishing and some farming. The present name of the city seems to have been derived from a Gallic tribe of Parisii. At the beginning of the fourth century it took the name, the city of the Parisians from a military milestone engraved in 307 A.D.

The mural crown, on the city seal, established the symbol as one of civic significance, not of an individual or family.

L'OPÉRA (Fig. 911)

The Paris Opera House or National Academy of Music was designed by Charles Garnier. Construction began in 1861 and was completed in 1874; it has since been modernized. A museum and library under the Opera House contains a collection of the great recorded voices in music.

919

EIFFEL TOWER (Fig. 914–917)

Symbol of Paris, the Eiffel Tower is the most prominent landmark of that city. It stands at the western end of an ancient military parade ground known as the *Champs de Mars*. The tower was built in 1889 by Alexandre Gustave Eiffel for the Paris International Exposition. Constructed of 12,000 girders held together by 2,500,000 rivets, this slender skeleton of steel weighs only 7,000 tons. It is 984 feet high, the tallest structure in Europe. Stairways and elevators lead to observation platforms at the top, from which visitors can see all of the city. At the very tip is a television transmitter.

915 **Eiffel Tower, Paris, France.** Mark illegible.
916 **Eiffel Tower, Paris, France.** Maker: J-M.
917 **Eiffel Tower, Paris, France,** marked: French quality mark L "Scythe" P.
918 **Arch of Triumph, Paris, France.** No mark.
919 **Arch of Triumph, Paris, France.** Maker: L & P, French quality mark.
920 **Paris Exposition, 1900,** marked: "Animal" L, French quality mark. "PALAIS DE L'ELECTRICITE, PARIS 1900" in bowl.

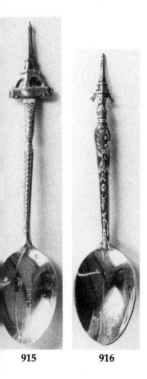

915   916

917   918

920

921

ARC DE TRIOMPHE DE L'ÉTOILE
(Fig. 918–919)

The Arc de Triomphe de l'Étoile is more than a monument to the glory of Napoleon. It is the symbol of France. It is located in the center of the Place de l'Étoile whose twelve avenues radiate like rays of light from the center circle. The main facades are ornamented with colossal groups in high relief: *Le Départ, La Resistance, Le Triomphe* and *La Paix*, representing four great episodes in the life of a people who went to war in spite of their dislike of it. The eternal flame of the Tomb of the Unknown Soldier burns within its arch. The Arc de Triomphe is for Parisians a symbol of some of France's most glorious days. It has known the joy of victory processions and the sadness of enemy parades, and is where Parisians gather when storm clouds arise.

PARIS EXHIBITION, 1900
(Fig. 920–921)

Thirty-nine million people visited the exhibition held in Paris in 1900. Three of its buildings were designed as permanent structures. The Grand Palais which housed the display of contemporary art later became the site for many important salons. The Petit Palais became the Paris Museum of Fine Arts and the ornate Pont Alexandre III linking the Champs Elysées with the Esplanade de Invalides. This bridge was built by two engineers, Resal and Alby. The first stone was laid in 1896 by Tsar Nicholas II. Three hundred and fifty-one feet (107 meters) long and 131 feet (40 meters) wide, it is

923

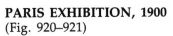

922

921 Paris Exposition, 1900. Maker: Armand Gross, French quality mark. "PONT ALEXANDRE III, PARIS 1900" in bowl.

922 Colmar, France. Maker: K.F.K. "Crescent & crown" 800.

923 Strasbourg, France. No mark.

924 Strasbourg, France. Maker: AD, French quality mark 2nd standard.

925 Strasbourg, France, marked: "Crown" (similar to Sheffield city mark) 950 M.

924   925

926

decorated with statues, golden lions and numerous lamps.

COLMAR, FRANCE (Fig. 922)

With its old painted and sculptured houses and "Venetian Quarter," Colmar is one of the loveliest towns in Alsace. The city is famous for its Unterlinden Museum with its awe-inspiring Isenheim altarpiece by Matthias Grünewald.

STRASBOURG, FRANCE
(Fig. 923–926

Strasbourg is sometimes called "The City of Storks." It is one of the largest inland ports of Europe and was originally a Celtic settlement. During the Roman occupation it was called by them *Argentoratum* and was an important military station. It was destroyed by the Huns in 455 A.D. and rebuilt as Strateburgum and annexed to the Frankish empire. It became a free city of the Holy Roman Empire in the thirteenth century. A center of medieval German literature, it was here that Johann Gutenberg perfected his printing press in the fifteenth century. A monument to him stands in a square. (See also Frankfort-am-Main.)

Strasbourg contains some fine old buildings. One of its architectural treasures is the Gothic cathedral begun early in the eleventh century and noted for its fourteenth century astronomical clock. The hour is struck by a figure representing Death, while the Apostles receive the blessing of Christ and the cock crows in memory of Peter's denial. The clock actually operates at 12:30 p.m. although it is listed for noon in most guidebooks.

In the last hundred years Strasbourg has changed hands four times between France and Germany. It was French be-

928

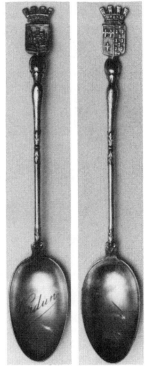

929   930

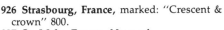

926 **Strasbourg, France,** marked: "Crescent & crown" 800.
927 **St. Malo, France.** No mark.
928 **Chaumont, France.** No mark.
929 **Verdun, France.** No mark.
930 **Brest, France.** No mark.

927

fore 1870 when Bismarck's army marched across the Rhine and took possession of Alsace and Lorraine and it became German. In 1918 the French returned to Strasbourg. In 1940 Hitler made the city German again, and in 1944 it was once again part of the French Republic.

ST. MALO, FRANCE (Fig. 927)

St. Malo was named for the Welsh monk, St. Maclou, or Malo, who became the city's first bishop in the sixth century. This city is surrounded by medieval ramparts on four sides and by the sea on three. Only these massive ramparts and a medieval tower, *Tour-Quic-en-Groigne* survived World War II. Since, St. Malo has been rebuilt. The symbol on this spoon is the Ermine—crest of Anne of Brittany and Claude of France.

CHAUMONT, FRANCE (Fig. 928)

Chaumont is a small city in the richly forested area of northeastern France, at the confluence of the Marne and Suize Rivers southeast of Paris. Its quaint, turreted houses are reminiscent of a bygone era.

The emblem at the top of the spoon is the Salamander, crest of Francois I.

VERDUN FRANCE (Fig. 929)

Verdun is a fortified town in northeastern France in the Meuse Valley. It is best remembered for its gallant resistance during the cruel siege of World War I when some of the heaviest fighting and most severe artillery fire the world has ever seen occurred there.

BREST, FRANCE (Fig. 930)

The magnificent landlocked harbor of Brest has made the city an important northwestern Atlantic commercial and naval port. It was the port of debarkation for United States troops during World War I and was subject to constant bombardment in World War II. Ninety percent of the city was destroyed but has been rebuilt and modernized.

NORMANDIE, FRANCE (Fig. 931)

Normandy was an ancient province of northwestern France and was originally inhabited by Celtic tribes. Its name is derived from the Northmen who began raiding its coasts in the middle of the ninth century.

In 1066, William, Duke of Normandy, conquered England and united Normandy with it. Normandy was regained by Philip Augustus in 1204. It was retaken by the English in the Hundred Years' War in the fifteenth century and once again regained by Charles VII at the Battle of Formigny in 1450. In 1791 the province was divided into five departments—Seine-Inférieure, Orne, Calvados, Manche and Eure. Normandy suffered heavily in World War II.

Honfleur, inscribed on the back of this spoon, is important as the birthplace of the Impressionist school of art.

DUNKERQUE, FRANCE
(Fig. 932–933)

Dunkerque (English, Dunkirk) was founded in the seventh century by Saint Eloi and was for many years a fishing village. An important link in the German defensive-offensive system during the German occupation of France in World War II, it is best remembered as the scene of the heroic retreat of the British in 1940 when yachts, little motorboats and everything that could float was used to evacuate 350,000 men.

NANTES, FRANCE (Fig. 934)

Before the Roman conquest of Gaul, Nantes was the principal town of the Namnetes, a leading Gallic tribe of Brittany. Three times in the ninth century it was overrun by Norse raiders and almost entirely destroyed. Its turbulent history has included near total destruction by fire in 1118 and repeated suffering during the Hundred Years' War.

The outstanding event in the history of Nantes was the famous edict issued by Henry IV (Edict of Nantes) on April

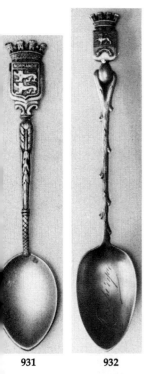

30, 1598, securing the free exercise of religion by Protestants and making them eligible for all civic and military employment. This edict was revoked by Louis XIV in 1685.

CHAMONIX, FRANCE (Fig. 935–936)

Chamonix is a valley of southeastern France in the Savoy Alps. It was inhabited by Benedictine monks in the eleventh century. The first ascent of Mont-Blanc (1787) brought the valley to the attention of tourists and made the valley internationally famous as a resort center.

CHAMBÉRY, FRANCE (Fig. 937)

Chambéry is located in a fertile valley at the juncture of the Albane and Leysse rivers. It was founded about the tenth century. Its principal landmark is the old château of the princes of Savoy.

ROUEN, FRANCE (Fig. 938)

Rouen, called by the Romans *Rotomagus,* has been the capital of Normandy since the beginning of the Christian era. It was here that Joan of Arc was burned at the stake on May 30, 1431.

LA PORT DES PÊCHEURS (Fisherman's port or harbor), BIARRITZ, FRANCE (Fig. 939)

Biarritz is a fashionable summer and winter resort on the southern Atlantic coast of France. It was first made famous by Empress Eugenie and later by Queen Victoria and Edward VIII.

BORDEAUX, FRANCE (Fig. 940)

Bordeaux was the *Burdigala* of the ancient Romans and lies on the Garonne River, about sixty miles from the Bay of Biscay. One of the world's wine capitals,

931   932

934

931 Normandie, France.
932 Dunkerque, France. No mark.
933 Dunkerque, France, marked: French standard mark.
934 Nantes, France. No mark.
935 Chamonix, France. No mark.

933

935

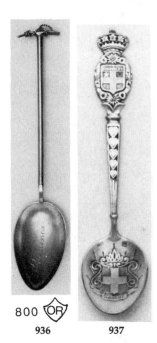

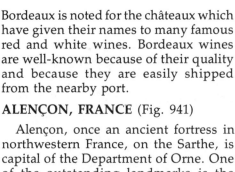

Bordeaux is noted for the châteaux which have given their names to many famous red and white wines. Bordeaux wines are well-known because of their quality and because they are easily shipped from the nearby port.

ALENÇON, FRANCE (Fig. 941)

Alençon, once an ancient fortress in northwestern France, on the Sarthe, is capital of the Department of Orne. One of the outstanding landmarks is the fourteenth-eighteenth century Church of Notre Dame. The city has long been famous for the manufacture of *point de' Alençon,* a kind of lace. It is still a lace-making center, examples of which may be seen in an unusual museum there.

LOURDES BASILIQUE ET LA GROTTE (Fig. 942)

Lourdes, France is best known for its Roman Catholic shrine. The history of this world-famous shrine dates from February 11, 1858, when Marie Bernarde, a fourteen-year-old peasant girl, better known as Bernadette, said she had seen the Virgin Mary in a grotto and that at her direction she had uncovered a spring. Soon afterward the first of the miraculous cures attributed to the waters of this spring was reported. Each year about 2,000,000 people visit Lourdes. Marie Bernarde reported that the Virgin said, "Go drink at the spring and bathe in its waters." In the Domaine de la Grotte, a 60-acre enclosure where most of the religious ceremonies take place, are twenty taps where pilgrims may drink. There is also a gray marble bath house with nine tubs where, clad in dark blue wraps, they may bathe.

800 (OR)

936

937

938

940

---

936 **Chamonix, France,** marked: (see drawing).
937 **Chambery, France,** marked: AUGIS AA LYON
938 **Rouen, France.** No mark.
939 **Biarritz, France.** Maker: Solingen, 900 "Crescent & crown".
940 **Bordeaux, France.** No mark.
941 **Alencon, France,** marked: 800 "Crescent & crown".

939

941

942

943

ST. JEAN CATHEDRAL, LYON, FRANCE (Fig. 943)

Lyon, the oldest city in France, celebrated its 2000th anniversary in 1957. It was founded in 43 B.C. by Munatius Plancus as *Lugdunum*. The Romanesque-Gothic Cathedral of St. Jean is noted for its stained glass and astronomical clock.

NANCY, FRANCE (Fig. 944)

Nancy, the historic capital of Lorraine lies 175 miles east of Paris. It is a commercial center because of its situation on the Eastern and Marne-Rhine canals and on the Meuthe River near its junction with the Moselle. The factories of Nancy make furniture, glassware and electrical equipment. The city has a university founded in 1572 and a school of forestry and mining.

Around the Place Stanislas (shown in the bowl) are the Hôtel de Ville, Grande Hôtel, Arc de Triomphe, theater and art gallery, fine examples of 18th century French architecture.

AIX-LES-BAINS, FRANCE (Fig. 945)

Aix-les-Bains was the ancient *Aquae Gratianae* of Roman times and is in eastern France. It is a fashionable spa visited each year by many thousands for the warm alum and sulphur springs. The baths were first established there in 125 B.C. by the Romans. A renewed interest in the town dates from the building of a bathhouse in 1779 by the king of Sardinia. There are extensive Roman ruins which include the Arc of Campanus, a structure of the third or fourth century A.D. Another Roman building of the

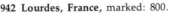

942 **Lourdes, France,** marked: 800.
943 **Lyon, France,** marked: 800 SM. "Cathedrale St. Jean" in bowl.
944 **Nancy, France.** No mark "Place Stanislaus" in the bowl.
945 **Aix-Les-Bains, France.** Maker: LP, French quality mark.
946 **Nice, France.** Maker: LM, French quality mark.

944

945   946

second or third century is still standing and was made part of a château early in the sixteenth century and is now the town hall.

Interesting excursions may be made to nearby Lake Bourger, Mount Revard and the Abbey of Hautecomb, used by the Princes of the House of Savoie since 1189.

NICE, FRANCE (Fig. 946–951)

Nice was founded in 350 B.C. by the Greeks of Marseilles and given its Latin name of *Nicea* in honor of their victory, or *nike*, over the neighboring Ligurians. Under the Greeks it was only a modest trading post and even under later Roman rule was largely by-passed in favor of Cimiez which was later reduced to nothing by barbarian and Saracen invasions. A turbulent era followed and it finally came under the protection of the princes of Savoy who retained control for the next four centuries. And, except for a few short interruptions, Nice belonged to the House of Savoy until 1860 when it became part of France.

The historical center of the city rests on a limestone hill above the newer section and lies within the curve of the Baie des Anges (Bay of Angels) in a natural amphitheater of flower-covered hills that bask in the Mediterranean sun.

Nice is frequently called the "Queen of the Riviera"—a title well-deserved for the wonderful temperate climate and beautiful setting. Between Nice and Menton the Alps plunge right down to the blue Mediterranean. Each of the Riviera Corniches affords spectacular views, the most breathtaking being the Grande Corniche built by Napoleon a-

947

948

949

947 **Nice, France.** No mark.
948 **Nice, France.** No mark.
949 **Promenade Des Anglais, Nice, France,**
marked: "Pine tree" 800, three indistinct marks.
950 **Promenade Des Anglais, Nice, France.** No mark.

950

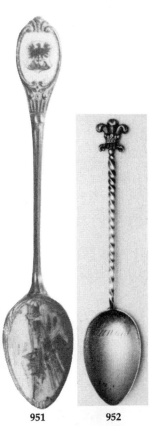

951   952

954

long the route of the ancient Aurelian Way. It is the highest of the three roads and passes through La Turbie from where one may look down on the Principality of Monaco.

The old and new sections of Nice itself are divided by the mountain torrent the Paillon. The old town lies at the foot of a rocky promontory which was once the site of a citadel. It is best seen on foot as only by walking can one fully appreciate the old houses, ruined palaces and picturesque atmosphere.

The new town is noted for its fine hotels, handsome villas, beautiful shops and wide boulevards.

The Promenade des Anglais, shown in the bowls of Figures 949, 950 and 951 is one of the world's famous streets. A century and a half ago a path led along the shore from the Rocher du Château. It was rough, broken and uneven. When English visitors began to visit Nice in 1822 they decided to underwrite the construction of a coastal path which was the origin of the present promenade and gave it its name. They changed this mule path to a splendid seaside boulevard, more than four miles long. The land side is lined with white, Mediterranean-style luxurious hotels, mansions and public buildings including the Palais de la Méditerranée, Nice's newest casino, and the Masséna Museum. A-cross the street is the boardwalk along the sea and a narrow pebbly beach where one may bask in the sun or be served a luxurious lunch.

CANNES, FRANCE (Fig. 952–953)

Cannes, eighteen miles west of Nice, is also on the French Riviera. Somewhat

951 **Promenade Des Anglais, Nice, France,**
   marked: IMPORTE DE CHECOSLOVAQUIE.
952 **Cannes, France.** "March 4, 1892" engraved
   on back of bowl.
953 **Cannes, France,** marked: 800; other marks
   rubbed.
954 **Menton, France,** marked: 800 SM.
955 **Monaco,** marked: 800.

953

955

956

957

958

958a

smaller in size than Nice, it is neverthe-less an elegant resort famous for its festivals. Among them are the battles of the flowers, the international regattas, the mimosa festival and the Internation-al Film Festival.

Probably colonized by the Romans, it is known that as far back as the eighth and tenth centuries a little cluster of houses stood at the foot of the rock known today as Mount Chevalier. The little settlement was of sufficient impor-tance to attract the attention of Moorish raiders who sacked and destroyed it on two separate occasions. Until the eight-eenth century it was little more than a fishing village. Its growth as a summer resort is credited to Henry Peter Brough-am, Lord Chancellor of England, who was on his way to Nice in 1834 and was prevented from reaching there by an outbreak of cholera and so returned to Cannes. The small fishing village pleased him so much that he built a house there for the remaining thirty-four years of his life, left the winter fogs of London for the Mediterranean sun-shine of Cannes. Others of English aris-tocracy followed his example.

MENTON, FRANCE (Fig. 954)

Menton, situated at the extreme east-ern tip of the French Riviera, consists of two distinct towns. In the old town covered alleys interlace as they rise from the harbor to the old castle and are lined with typical Mediterranean buildings and Italian baroque churches. The new town has modern buildings and broad avenues.

956 **Monaco.**
957 **Monaco,** marked: 800, IMPORTE. 8-15/16" (226 mm.)
958 **Prince Rainier III & Princess Grace.** Maker: AR LYON
958a **Switzerland,** marked: 800 JR within a shield. "Zurich 22 July 1904" in bowl.

959   back

960   back

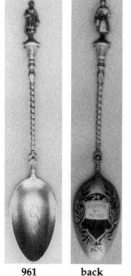

961   back

MONACO (Fig. 955–958)

The Principality of Monaco is a sovereign state of only eight square miles—smaller than New York City's Central Park. It is divided into four distinct sections: Monaco, the old town; Monte Carlo, the new town; La Condamine, where most of the people live and Fontvieille, the new, expanding industrial section. Old Monaco, high on a rock, contains the palace of the Princes of Monaco, built on the foundation of a thirteenth-century Saracen stronghold. Monte Carlo is famous throughout the world for its casino, rich villas, luxurious shops and beautiful flower covered terraces.

The Prince's Palace was once a fortress guarding Monaco and is now the home of the Grimaldi family which is responsible for the rise of the tiny country into its present importance. In 1308 a member of the Grimaldi family bought the Domain of Monaco from the Genoese. Prince Rainier III, a descendant of the House of Grimaldi, is the present ruler. In 1956 he married American actress Grace Kelly of Philadelphia.

The Casino of Monte Carlo began in 1856 when the Prince of Monaco authorized the opening of a gambling house to raise revenue. This was a small affair and poorly patronized. After a few years the concession was taken over by M. Blanc, the director of the casino at Bad-Homburg, the Hesse spa in Germany. He lent his talents and capital and succeeded where others had failed. The present casino stands in beautifully landscaped gardens. The building itself was built in sections, the first by Charles

959-965 (inclusive). **Swiss Cantons,** all marked: JR 800.
959 **Neuchâtel.**
960 **Thurgau.**
961 **Vaud.**
962 **Basle.**
963 **Schaffhausen.**
964 **Lucerne.**

962   back

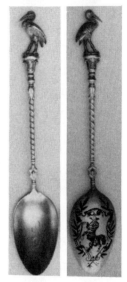

963   back

964   back

191

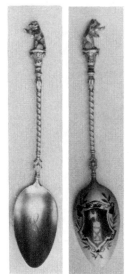

965 back

966 967

Garnier in 1878, the most recent dates from 1910. From the central hall and throughout the entire complex the interior is fitted with marble, huge mirrors, crystal chandeliers, fine paintings and other sumptuous decorations. The citizens of Monaco are prohibited by law from gambling in the casino.

HELVETIA (Fig. 958a)

(English; SWITZERLAND; French, LA SUISSE; Italian, LA SVISSERA; German, DIE SCHWEIZ; Latin, HELVETIA)

This spoon may be an idealized representation of "Helvetia" symbolizing the Confederation of Switzerland and a reminder of the Helvetii, an ancient Celtic group which had originally inhabited south Germany but about 200 B.C. migrated to what is now western Switzerland. The country in which they settled came to be known as Helvetia, which is still the Latin name for Switzerland.

SWISS CANTONS (Fig. 959–965)

The canton is a political division and comes from the Italian word *cantone*, meaning a corner or angle. Each of the twenty-two states that make up the Swiss republic is known as a canton. Seven of them are represented here. They are (Fig. 959) Neuchâtel whose present coat of arms dates from the proclamation of the Republic of Neuchâtel in 1848. The white cross on a red background commemorates its adhesion to the Confederation. (Fig. 960) Thurgau,

968 969

970 971

965 St. Gallen.
966 Bern Bear, Bern, Switzerland, marked: SCH & W "Crescent & crown".
967 Bern Bear, Bern Switzerland, marked: 800 "Crescent & crown" "Crossed hammers".
968 Bern Bear, Bern, Switzerland.
969 Bern Bear, Bern, Switzerland, marked: 800 E.
970 Geneva, Switzerland, marked: 800 "Crescent & crown". "Geneva" engraved on back of bowl.
971 Geneva, Switzerland. No mark.

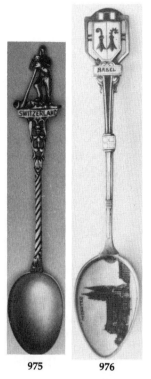

whose two lions in the coat-of-arms were borrowed from the arms of the Counts of Kyburg. (Fig. 961) Vaud, whose green flag was adopted with the Lemanic Republic was founded in 1798; the white flag with "Liberté et Patrie" when Vaud joined the Confederation in 1803. (Fig. 962) Basle, whose arms include a bishop's crosier (red for the District, black for the Town) since this town was the seat of the prince-bishop for several centuries. (Fig. 963) Schaffhausen, means "the houses of sheep." Near Schaffhausen is the Rhine Falls—the greatest waterfall in Europe. (Fig. 964) Lucerne, whose blue and white shield represents both the town and the canton founded in 750. Once under the Austrian yoke, it has been part of the Swiss Confederation since 1332. Under the Helvetic Republic it was the seat of government. (Fig. 965) St. Gallen, whose fasces on the shield is a reminder of the union of the various district which were joined in 1803 when the canton was formed.

972   972a   975   976

BERNE, SWITZERLAND
(Fig. 966–969)

(German, BERN)

According to a fifteenth century chronicle the Duke Berchtold V of Zähringen founded the city of Berne in 1191 where it is on the advice of his huntsmen and chief master of the hounds and agreed to give it the name of the first animal caught at the hunt. It so happened that this was a bear (Bär). The Duke then named the town Bärn (Berne) and gave it a bear as its coat of arms.

---·•·---

972 **Geneva, Switzerland.**
972a **Swiss Flag.**
973 **Schweiz,** marked: SWISS MADE 90.9 SR.
974 **Swiss Chalet.**
975 **Alpenhorn,** marked: 800 SILTA.
976 **Basel, Switzerland,** marked: DEPOSE "Crescent & crown" 800.
977 **Valais, Switzerland.** No mark.
978 **Lausanne Cathedral, Lausanne, Switzerland.** No mark.

973   974

977   978

Modern philologists agree that the Zähringen family was responsible for the development of the town but doubt the story of the bear and attribute the name to a local variation of the name of an Italian city, Verona, from which some of the early settlers were supposed to have come. B and V are sounded much alike and they say that Berne is Verona with a Swiss accent. Whatever the source of the name, the bear is on the city's arms and there is a fifteenth century Bärengraben (bear pit) at the end of the Nydeggbrücke (Nydegg Bridge) that is a great tourist attraction. Bears of wood, stone, metal, chocolate and gingerbread are found all over the city.

GENEVA, SWITZERLAND
(Fig. 970–972)

(French, GENEVE; German, GENF)

The arms of the canton of Geneva reflect the origins of the cosmopolitan and independent people living at the junction of the Rhône and the Arve. The city of Geneva was an imperial town and is represented by the half-eagle; as a bishopric it is represented by the golden key encircled by a pale. It was often defended by its rulers from attacks of neighboring territorial powers before the Reformation. The liberal rights granted it by its Prince-Bishop Adhémar Fabri in the fourteenth century are an indication of the city's political and economic evolution. Its independent and cosmopolitan character were further enhanced by the religious outlook of Calvin.

The International Red Cross founded in 1863 by Jean Henri Dunant, has permanent offices in Geneva.

The Jet d'Eau (Fig. 970) whose great plume plays up to 50 feet above Lake Léman is the highest fountain in the world and is a symbol of Geneva.

SWISS FLAG (Fig. 972a–974)

The Swiss flag consists of a white cross on a red field and is said to date from the time of the Crusades. Swiss forces in 1339 were said to have been distinguished by the sign of the Holy Cross, a white cross on a red shield, as they believed that the freeing of their nation was for them a cause as sacred as the deliverance of the Holy Places.

When the Red Cross was recognized at the International Conference held in Geneva in 1863, their search for a distinguishing emblem brought about the adoption of the colors of Switzerland counterchanged, the red cross on a white ground.

SCHWEIZ (Schwyz), SWITZERLAND
(Fig. 973)

It is said that this small town, capital of the canton of the same name, has the honor of having given to the Swiss Confederation both its name and its red flag with a white cross. The shield of Schweiz (Schwyz) was once plain red but was later charged with a white cross.

ALPHENHORN (Fig. 975)

At one time these mighty trumpets, usually fashioned of a curved root of the forest pine or Alpine pine tree, were blown on mountain tops to warn distant friends of the approach of enemies. They later became musical instruments with a scale similar to the B-flat French horn.

BASEL, SWITZERLAND (Fig. 976)

(French, BÂLE; English, BASLE; German, BASEL)

Basle occupies a site originally settled by Celts and there in 374 A.D. the Roman Emperor Valentinian I built a royal residence, or *Basilea*. In the Middle Ages it became a free imperial city but joined the Swiss Confederacy in 1501. The city is divided into Gross-Basel and Klein-Basel by the Rhine but connected by five bridges. The old thirteenth-century wooden bridge, so long a feature of the city, was replaced by a granite one in 1905. The cathedral, or minster,

979

980

was consecrated in 1019 and contains the tomb of Erasmus.

Basle was the seat of a prince-bishop for several centuries and that is why the city's arms include a bishop's crosier— red for the District, black for the Town. (See also Fig. 962)

VALAIS, SWITZERLAND (Fig. 977)

While there has been some impressive industrial development of the Valais, there is also a survival in the high valleys of the most ancient ways of life. The Valais is rugged; there is the country of the Matterhorn and Monte Rosa. There are high mountain landscapes dotted with chalets and *raccards* or *mazots*—small barns perched on piles and used as granaries or storehouses. Though in some areas Valasian peasants have to carry soil washed down by the rain, back up to their narrow terraces, they produce magnificent vineyards and are noted for the many varieties of red and white wines.

CATHEDRAL OF NOTRE DAME, LAUSANNE, SWITZERLAND (Fig. 978)

Lausanne was originally built by the Romans on the shore of Lake Léman, southwest of its present site, and was destroyed by the Alemanni in the fourth century. When the people rebuilt their town they relocated it on five hillocks which location lends it much of its picturesque beauty. Neolithic skeletons have been found on the site and part of the former "Lousanna" has been excavated disclosing a section of Roman road.

The Cathedral of Notre Dame is the finest Gothic building in Switzerland. Its construction began about 1175 and it was consecrated in 1275 by Pope Greg-

979 Interlaken, Switzerland, marked: 800.
980 Montreux, Switzerland, marked: 800.
981 Zurich, Switzerland. No mark.
982 Zurich, Switzerland, marked: 0,800.

981

982

983

ory X. It occupies the highest elevation in the city a spot shared by the castle built by the bishops in the early fifteenth century.

INTERLAKEN, SWITZERLAND
(Fig. 979, 984–85)

Interlaken is the gateway to the Bernese Oberland and is situated as the name implies "between the lakes" of Thunersee and Brienzersee on a narrow strip of land through which flows the River Aare. The city was built for the sole purpose of accommodating summer visitors and is the point of departure for those climbing the Jungfrau, for the Jungfrau circuit by rail and for several other excursions. It grew up around an Augustinian monastery of which traces can still be found in the block of buildings formed by the castle and the Reformed church.

Each summer there is a traditional performance of Schiller's *William Tell.* (See Fig. 991–994)

MONTREUX, SWITZERLAND
(Fig. 980)

The mild climate and Mediterranean atmosphere of Montreux make it the most frequented resort on Lake Léman (Lake Geneva). The coat of arms on the spoon represents the canton of Vaud (See also Fig. 961).

ZÜRICH, SWITZERLAND
(Fig. 981–983)

Zurich is the capital of a Swiss canton by the same name. It is the largest city in

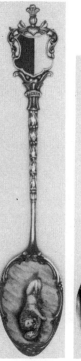

986   987

983 **Zurich, Switzerland,** marked: DEPOSE 800.
984 **Interlaken, Switzerland.** No mark.
985 **Interlaken, Switzerland,** marked: 800 "Crescent & crown."
986 **Lucerne, Switzerland,** marked: 800 "Crescent & crown."
987 **Lucerne, Switzerland,** marked: 800 KFK "Lion".
988 **Lucerne, Switzerland,** marked: 800 "Crescent & crown".

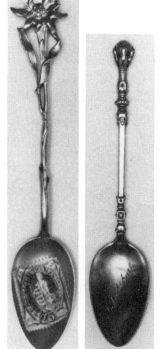

984   985

988

Switzerland and one of the most beautifully situated in its setting between the blue of Lake Zurich and the green of the wooded hills. It is the economic capital of the confederation and is modern in appearance.

There are four very fine museums: Schweizerisches Landesmuseum (Swiss National Museum); Kunsthaus (Fine Arts Museum); Rietbergmuseum (Rietbert Museum—formerly Wesendonck Villa) and Kunstgewerbemuseum (Museum of Decorative Arts).

The twin towers on the left hand side of the picture on the handle of Fig. 983 are Zurich's Cathedral, or Gross Munster, built in the eleventh-thirteenth centuries.

989

LUCERNE, SWITZERLAND
(Fig. 986–994)

(German, LUZERN)

Lucerne is the capital of the canton of Lucerne. This old town, a monastic settlement about 840 and later a fisherman's village, after the opening of the St. Gotthard route in the thirteenth century became an important staging point between Flanders and Italy. It is in a beautiful setting in the northwest end of Lake Lucerne and the point of departure for excursions to Mt. Rigi and Mt. Pilatus, the ascent of the latter being by rack-railway (cogwheel mountain railway) or cablecars. Mt. Pilatus, a 7,000 foot triangular crag, according to legend, is where Pontius Pilate was wafted by the devil after the Crucifixion.

Lucerne's symbol and mascot-protector, the lion (Fig. 986–987, 989–990) is commemorated by a colossal statue sculptured in living rock in a natural grotto in the city. The monu-

992a

992b

---

989 **Lucerne, Switzerland,** No mark.
990 **Wilhelm Tell,** marked: 950 M & W.
991 **Wilhelm Tell,** marked: 800 "Crescent & crown." "Lucerne" on back.
992a-992b **Wilhelm Tell,** (b) marked: "Crescent & crown" 800 "Pine tree"

990   991

993

ment was erected in memory of the Swiss soldiers who gave their lives in defense of the Tuileries when the storm of the French Revolution broke in Paris in 1792. The artist was Bertal Thorvaldsen, a Danish sculptor born in Copenhagen in 1770. The actual carving was done by Eggenschwyler and Lucas Ahorn in 1821.

The spires of the Hofkirche (Cathedral of St. Léger) (Fig. 989, 992) dominate the skyline. The collegiate church was dedicated to St. Léodegarius, the patron saint of Lucerne, which is said to have derived its name from him. It was founded in 735 and in 1633 all except the Gothic towers were destroyed by fire and it was rebuilt in the Renaissance style.

WILLIAM TELL (Fig. 991–994)

According to legend, William Tell, a Swiss folk hero was a peasant of Bürglen and lived during the first half of the fourteenth century. Tell protested against a decree that all Swiss must uncover their heads before the hat belonging to Gessler, the tyrannical Austrian bailiff of Uri. For his refusal he was forced to shoot an apple from the head of his own son. He succeeded but then confessed that he had a second arrow concealed on his person that was intended for punishment of the tyrant if he had failed and injured his son. Therefore, he was kept a prisoner and while in a small boat with Gessler a violent storm broke. Tell was a skillful helmsman and managed to leap ashore as did Gessler but William Tell shot him with his bow and arrow. The death of Gessler signaled the beginning of a war between

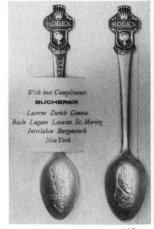

With best Compliments
BUCHERER
Lucerne Zurich Geneva
Basle Lugano Locarno St. Moritz
Interlaken Burgenstock
New York

995a   995b

994

---

993 **Wilhelm Tell Chapel.** No mark. "MON NOV. REIP LUCERNENS" and shield and crown on back.

994 **Wilhelm Tell Chapel.**

995a-995b **Rolex Spoons,** marked: $^{CB}_{M}$ 69 BUCHERER OF SWITZERLAND.

996 **Liechtenstein,** marked: 800 GESCH.

996

997

998

the Swiss and Austrians that lasted until 1499. No proof of William Tell's actual existence has even been uncovered and similar stories occur in other cultures. But, for generations William Tell has been a folk hero and chapels such as the one on the shores of Lake Lucerne were erected to his memory.

ROLEX SPOONS (Fig. 995a–995b)

Visitors staying in the hotels of Lucerne, Zurich, Geneva and some other Swiss cities are given Rolex spoons with the compliments of the Bucherer Watch Company of Switzerland. These two are examples from among at least eight different styles.

LIECHTENSTEIN (Fig. 996)

Liechtenstein is a tiny principality whose territory of only sixty square miles is nestled in the verdant countryside between Switzerland and Austria. Liechtenstein was founded in 1719 for the benefit of Prince Hans Adam of Liechtenstein. The present regent is Franz Josef II who has ruled since 1938. Vaduz is the capital and contains the 700-year-old castle, home of Prince Franz Josef II. Citizens live an almost fairy-tale existence in a country that has no army, no navy, no air force, cities, nightclubs, department stores, strikes or beggars—and virtually no crime. The main industry is the production of finely engraved postage stamps which depict scenes of the countryside and reproductions of the royal art collection.

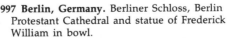

997 **Berlin, Germany.** Berliner Schloss, Berlin Protestant Cathedral and statue of Frederick William in bowl.
998 **Berlin, Germany,** marked: 800 "Crescent & crown". Reichstagsgebäude in bowl.
999 **Berlin, Germany,** marked: 800 "Crown & crescent" and "Pine tree". Brandenburger *Thor* in bowl.
1000 **Berlin, Germany,** marked: 800 C&C. Reichstagsgebäude on handle.

999

1000

1001

1002

BERLIN, GERMANY (Fig. 997–1015)

Berlin began with a small village called Kölln (Cölln), built by Slavs around 400 A.D. The city's early history is shrouded in mystery as its first five centuries are not recorded, but it is known that a neighboring village, called "Das Berlin," grew up across the River Spree. The Germans arrived there in 1134 under Albert I, called Albrecht the Bear (1100-1170), margrave of Brandenburg. Berlin received its charter as a free town in 1230 and eventually merged with the town across the river, Kölln. The rampant bear, Berlin's coat of arms, was once that of Albrecht the Bear.

Shown in the bowl of Fig. 997 are the former Royal Palace (Berliner Schloss), later the Palace (Schloss) Museum, erected by the Elector Frederick II as a castle in 1443-1451 and after 1538 converted into a palace by Joachin II; the Berlin Protestant Cathedral, and the statue of Frederick William (Fig. 1012), the Great Elector, designed by the noted sculptor Andreas Schlüter and standing in the palace court of honor.

The Reichstagsgebaüde (Fig. 998, 1000, 1002, 1006) (Reichstag Building) or lower house of the German parliament was built 1884-94. On February 27, 1933, just a month after Hitler became chancellor, the central part of the building was set afire. The cause was not definitely established. The building was rebuilt but suffered heavy damages a-

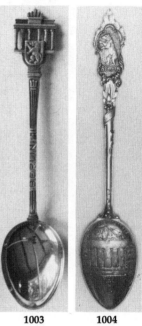

1003   1004

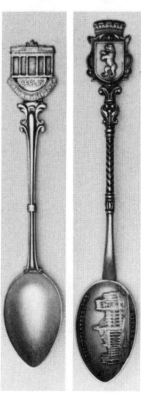

1005   1006

1001 **Berlin, Germany,** marked: 800 "Crescent & crown". Brandenburger Tor in bowl.
1002 **Berlin, Germany,** marked: 800 "Pine tree". Reichstagsgebaüde in bowl.
1003 **Berlin, Germany.** No mark. Brandenburger Tor on handle.
1004 **Berlin, Germany,** marked: 800 RS "Crescent & crown". Brandenburger Tor in bowl.
1005 **Berlin, Germany,** marked: 90. Brandenburger Tor on handle.
1006 **Berlin, Germany.** No mark. Reichstagsgebaüde in bowl.

gain in World War II and once again was completely restored.

The Brandenburger Tor (Brandenburg Gate) (Fig. 999, 1001, 1003–1005, 1007), a triumphal arch forming a gateway to the city at the beginning of "Linden" (Unter den Linden) was once the city's emblem; it has in recent years become the symbol of the division existing in the country as well as the city. The Brandenburg Gate was built in 1789 by K. G. Langhans. Its design was inspired by the Propylea of the Parthenon. Six Doric columns form part of the stone arch walls supporting an antique-style coping. The Gate is surmounted by a reconstruction of the famous Victory quadriga by Schadow. The quadriga, all ten tons of it, was taken on Napoleon's instructions, to Paris and kept there from 1806 to 1814. It was bombed during a pathfinder raid during World War II.

SIEGESSÄULE (VICTORY COLUMN) (Fig. 1001–1014)

The figure of the winged victory atop the 222 foot high column commemorates the campaigns of 1864, 1866 and 1870. This monument is a landmark which can be seen when traveling along any of the roads leading into Berlin. After a climb of 285 steps one is rewarded with a view of the Tiergarten and the Spree and in the distance can be seen the domes of the churches of East Berlin and the red tower of the old Town Hall built between 1860-69.

1011

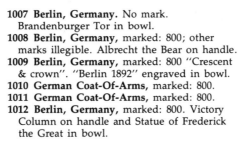

1007 **Berlin, Germany.** No mark. Brandenburger Tor in bowl.
1008 **Berlin, Germany,** marked: 800; other marks illegible. Albrecht the Bear on handle.
1009 **Berlin, Germany,** marked: 800 "Crescent & crown". "Berlin 1892" engraved in bowl.
1010 **German Coat-Of-Arms,** marked: 800.
1011 **German Coat-Of-Arms,** marked: 800.
1012 **Berlin, Germany,** marked: 800. Victory Column on handle and Statue of Frederick the Great in bowl.

1007   1008

1009   1010

1012

1013

1014

1936 OLYMPIC GAMES, BERLIN
(Fig. 1015)

The modern Olympic Games, an international series of amateur sports competitions, were inaugurated in 1896 as a revival of the ancient Greek festivals and follow the four-year cycle of the old Greek competitions. There is one significant difference, however. The ancient Greek states suspended their wars in order to celebrate the games but world wars have forced the cancellation of the games in 1916, 1940 and 1944. The 1963 Olympic Games were held in Berlin.

NATIONALDENKMAL AUF DEM NIEDERWALD (National Statue of the Niederwald) (Fig. 1016–1018)

Near Rudesheim am Rhein in the Niederwald stands the National Niederwald Monument erected September 28, 1883 to commemorate the re-establishment of the German Empire in 1871 following the War of 1870-71. The height of the monument is 115' (35 m.) while the figure of Germania stands 44' (13.3 m.). The site selected for this monument is in wooded country above the Rhine River near the confluence of the Nahe and the Rhine at the opening of the Bingen Gap. This memorial, erected as a hopeful symbol of the "Unified Germany" of 1871 is also known as the Wacht am Rhein.

BREMEN, GERMANY (French, BRÊME) (Fig. 1019–1026)

Bremen is Germany's second largest port. The town, extending some twelve miles along the Weser River is divided into four distinct sections: the Alstadt

---

1013 **Berlin, Germany.** No mark. Souvenir of the International Mechanical (or Mining) Engineers Convention, June 27, 1913.

1014 **Berlin, Germany,** marked: "Crescent & crown" 800.

1015 **Berlin, Germany-1936 Olympic Games.**

1016 **National Statue of the Niederwald.** No mark.

1015

1016

1017

1019

(old town), with its crooked, narrow streets and ancient fortifications on the north side of the river; the Vorstadt, a residential section surrounding the old town; the Neustadt, on the south side of the river, with many modern business houses; and the suburbs of Südervorstadt and the Woltmershausen around it. Many fine old buildings still stand in the town, including the Rathaus (town hall) and the twelfth century St. Peter's Cathedral.

The Rathaus, built in the fifteenth century, stands in the market square and a giant 30 foot statue of Roland (Fig. 1022) stands before it, signifying civic power. The knight bears the sword of justice and a shield with the imperial eagle.

The badge of the free city of Bremen is red and bears an antique key of silver (Fig. 1019, 1021, 1023–1026).

BREMERSTADMUSIKANTEN (Street Musicians of Bremen) (Fig. 1027)

At the corner of the west wing of the Rathaus stands the statue of the Street Musicians of Bremen, characters from the story by the brothers Grimm. Four animals, a donkey, a dog, a cat and a rooster who had served their masters faithfully but who had been turned out on growing old, met on the road to Bremen. During a series of adventures they joined forces to make strange and joyful music.

COLOGNE, GERMANY (German, KÖLN) (Fig. 1028–1033)

The history of the city of Cologne can be traced back to its beginnings as the

1018

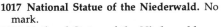

1020   1021

1017 **National Statue of the Niederwald.** No mark.
1018 **National Statue of the Niederwald.**
1019 **Bremen, Germany.** No mark. "Bremen" in bowl.
1020 **Bremen, Germany,** marked: 800. "Bremervorde" (Bremen) on handle.
1021 **Bremen, Germany,** marked: "Crescent & crown" 800. "Bremen" on back.

203

1022

chief seat of the German Ubii and was called *Oppidum* (or *Ara*) *Ubiorum* by the Romans. Cologne's name dates from 50 A.D. when the Roman Emperor Claudius established a colony for war veterans and called it *Colonia Agrippina* in honor of his wife. Agrippina (Nero's mother) had been born there when it was still only a military outpost. Her name was eventually dropped from the city's title which was shortened to *Colonia*, then later changed to its present form, the German "Köln" and the French "Cologne."

The great Gothic cathedral of Cologne, whose twin spires rise to 515' (157 m.) was modeled after the cathedral at Amiens, France and was begun in 1248. According to legend, the architect who designed it tricked the Devil into giving him the plans. Satan told him that the cathedral would never be completed. This prophecy held for almost six and a half centuries because work was suspended in 1437. Building was not resumed until after 1842 when Neo-Gothic fever gripped Romantic Germany and in 1880 the cathedral was at last completed according to the original plans.

The twin spires of the cathedral have been compared to bristling giant pine trees. The facade is particularly characteristic of the full Gothic style with its stepped windows and gables slimly in line with tier after tier of sharp slender arches rising to the tips of the pinnacles.

Cologne Cathedral's most prized possession is the reliquary said to contain the skulls of the Three Wise Men (called The Three Kings in Cologne) who fol-

1025

1022 **Bremen, Germany.** No mark. "Bremen" in bowl.
1023 **Bremen, Germany,** marked: 800 KFK.
1024 **Bremen, Germany.** No mark.
1025 **Bremen, Germany,** marked: "German eagle" 800 "Crown & crescent". "Bremen 1892" engraved in bowl.
1026 **Bremen, Germany,** marked: 800; other marks illegible. Rathaus-Dom u. Börse in bowl.

1023   1024

1026

1027   1028

back

1029   1030

lowed the star of Bethlehem with gifts for the infant Jesus. The reliquary of pure gold by the goldsmith Nicholas Verdun, was made in the form of a miniature temple, and encrusted with jewels. Figures of the Three Magi, whose names were Melchior, Gaspar, and Balthasar, are studded on the front. According to legend, the skulls of the Magi were presented to the Archbishop of Cologne by Frederick Barbarossa in 1164 and attracted so many pilgrims that the city became known as the "German Rome." The crowns of the Three Kings are part of Cologne's coat of arms.

EISERNE JUNGFRAU, NÜRNBERG
(Iron Maiden of Nuremberg)
(Fig. 1034–1038)

These torture instruments used in Germany during the Middle Ages are thought by some to have originated in Spain and from there were transplanted into Germany during the reign of Charles V (Holy Roman Emperor and, as Charles I, king of Spain died 1558), who reigned over both countries. Another name for the instrument is the Spanish Mantle.

The very existence of Iron Maidens was stoutly denied by the citizens of Nuremberg. The Jungfern Kuss or Kiss of the Virgin, was a well-known phrase in Germany though its import was little understood. A general impression reigned that in certain towers and pris-

1031

1027 **Bremerstadmusikanten** (Musicians of Bremen), marked: 800.

1028 **Cologne Cathedral, Cologne, Germany,** marked: 800.

1029 **Cologne Cathedral, Cologne, Germany,** marked: (see drawing).

1030 **Cologne Cathedral, Cologne (Köln), Germany.** No mark. Made in solid silver and silverplate.

1031 **Cologne Cathedral, Cologne, Germany,** marked: "Crescent & crown" 800 (also see drawing).

1032 **Cologne Cathedral, Cologne, Germany,** marked: 800 S.

1032

1033

1034

handle—open view

ons there was a terrible engine, which not only destroyed life but also annihilated the body of the person sacrificed; and this, from being constructed in the form of a young girl, was called the "Virgin."

The first man to demonstrate that such instruments actually existed was R. L. Pearsall, an English antiquary. About 1838 Pearsall heard rumors and while he searched through some of the halls and dungeons he found no evidence. About to dismiss the matter as a fable, he came across a passage in a book entitled, "Materlalen zu Nürnbergerischen Geschichte harausgegeben von D. J. Siebenkees, Nürnberg, 1792." The passage was represented to have been extracted from an old chronicle, and was to this effect:

> In the year of our Lord, 1533, the Iron Virgin was constructed for the punishment of evil-doers, within the walls of the Frosch Thurm [Frog's Tower] . . . . Therein was an iron statue, seven feet high, which stretched abroad both its arms in the face of the criminal. Death by this instrument was said to send the poor sinner to the fishes in hidden waters.

Mr. Pearsall went to Nuremberg and found other torture instruments but no Iron Virgin. Inquiry revealed that two or three days before the entry of the French into Nuremberg, the Virgin and other instruments of torture were taken away by night in a cart. The actual spot on which the Iron Virgin had been was discovered. In the center of the floor of a

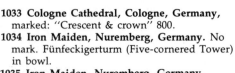

1033 **Cologne Cathedral, Cologne, Germany,** marked: "Crescent & crown" 800.
1034 **Iron Maiden, Nuremberg, Germany.** No mark. Fünfeckigerturm (Five-cornered Tower) in bowl.
1035 **Iron Maiden, Nuremberg, Germany,** marked: 800. "Nürnberg" engraved in bowl.
1036 **Nürnberg, Germany,** marked: DEPOSE "Crescent & crown" 800 H&S intertwined. Fünfeckiger Turm in bowl.

1035

handle—open view

1036

206

1037

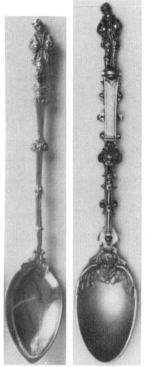

1039   1040

dark chamber was a square hole, on the side of which were the remains of hinges, which showed that it had once been covered with a trap-door. In a line with this hole, on the opposite wall, were four holes, the position of which made it evident that some important piece of machinery had once been fixed there.

At length Pearsall learned that an Iron Virgin might be seen in the collection of antiquities belonging to a Baron Diedrich who said that he had "bought it of a person who obtained it with the left hand [illegally] during the French Revolution . . . in a cart with several things which had formerly belonged to the arsenal of Nürnberg. . . ."

The figure is attired like the costume of Nuremberg in the sixteenth century, which is precisely the time when the Virgin is said to have been constructed there. It is just seven feet high, Nuremberg measure, and is entirely made of iron. It stands on a sort of low pedestal, hollow and square. A skeleton, formed of bars and hoops, is coated over with sheet iron, which is laid on and painted to represent a Nuremberg citizen's wife of the sixteenth century in the mantle then generally worn by persons of that class. The front of the figure opens like folding doors, the two halves of the front part of it being connected by hinges with the back part. On the inside of the right breast are thirteen quadrangular poniards. There are eight of these on the inside of the left breast, and two on the

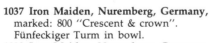

1037 Iron Maiden, Nuremberg, Germany, marked: 800 "Crescent & crown". Fünfeckiger Turm in bowl.
1038 Iron Maiden, Nuremberg, Germany. Pewter.
1039 Gooseman Fountain, Nuremberg, Germany. No mark.
1040 Gooseman Fountain, Nuremberg, Germany. No mark. "Nürnberg 1891" engraved on back.
1041 Gooseman Fountain, Nuremberg, Germany, marked: "Crescent & crown" 800.

1038

1041

1042

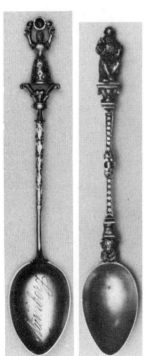

1043   1044

inside of the face. These last are clearly intended for the eyes of the victim. The mechanism which caused it to operate was no longer attached but holes and sockets indicated the points of insertion.

A 1902 Baedeker guidebook describes the pentagonal tower of Nuremberg's castle and states that the tower contains a torture chamber with "the Iron Virgin, a hollow figure with iron spikes in the interior into which a victim was thrust. . . ." Yet, Pearsall, in 1838 found no Iron Maiden there. It is certain that an Iron Maiden was exhibited there between 1890 and 1945 when it was "liberated" from the bombed tower by American soldiers or others.

An article in *Country Life*, July 22, 1965, tells of an Iron Maiden which sold at Sotheby's, London, for £2,200. One is in the Hinckeldey Museum in Rothenburg ob der Tauber where it is claimed that she is the real Iron Maiden of Nuremberg. Others have also been recorded.

GÄNSEMÄNNCHEN (Gooseman Fountain) NÜRNBERG
(Fig. 1039–1041)

Considered by many to be Nuremberg's most popular fountain is the Gänsemännchen (Gooseman Fountain) with its bronze figure of a peasant carrying a goose under each arm. The wooden model for it (circa 1540) can be seen in the museum. The little Gooseman Fountain was given a cement overcoat during World War II and survived.

1042 Bratwurstglöcklein, Nuremberg, Germany.
1043 German Wager Cup Miniature, Nürnberg, Germany, marked: 800.
1044 Hans Sachs, marked: "Crescent & crown" 800.
1045 Hans Sachs Haus.
1046 Nuremberg, Germany, marked: "Crescent & crown" 800. Kgl Burg (Kaiserburg or Nürnberg Castle) in bowl.

1045

1046

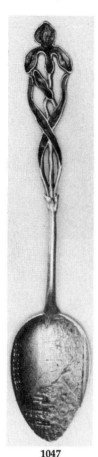

BRATWURSTGLÖCKLEIN, NÜRNBERG (Fig. 1042)

Near the thirteenth century church of St. Sebaldus was the celebrated Bratwurst Glöcklein, where the people of lusty appetites consumed prodigious portions of sausages and sauerkraut and seas of foaming beer for more than four centuries. It was blitzed to the ground in World War II and never rebuilt.

JUNGFRAUENBECHER (Maiden cup) (Fig. 1043)

German wager cups of the sixteenth century were so named because of the custom of filling the larger and smaller bowls at the same time and offering them to guests who competed in draining both without spilling the wine. They are sometimes called "marriage cups," in which case the smaller cup was reserved for the bride and the larger for the groom. They originated in Germany during the last quarter of the sixteenth century in the Nuremberg Jamnitzer family goldsmiths.

HANS SACHS (Fig. 1044–1045)

Nuremberg was the home of Hans Sachs, real life prototype of the Meistersinger and inspiration for both Goethe and Wagner. Wagner's opera, "Die Meistersinger von Nürnberg," was based on stories of the medieval equivalent for barber-shop quartets.

An inscription on the back of the spoon (Fig. 1045) reads, "Wir einmal

1047

1050

1048   1049

1051

1047 **Heidelberg, Germany,** marked: 800. "Heidelberg" in bowl.
1048 **Heidelberg, Germany,** marked: 800 KFK.
1049 **Perkeo,** marked: 800.
1050 **Perkeo,** marked: 800 "Crescent & crown".
1051 **Perkeo,** marked: "Crescent & crown" 800.
  Inside bowl: 1716   HALT 204 FUDER
        1664 in Heidelberg 30 HM. 4VIRT
on back of bowl: VON CARL LUDWIG BIN ICHERBAVT DEM CARL PHILLIP WURD ANUERTRAVT DA DIESERZUR RE GIRUNG KAHM UND VON DEM LAND DIE HAND-TREVNAHM

1052

1053

nür in Schurnberg war, Der Kämgern wie die jides Jahr." (He who once visits Schurnberg would happily go back every year.)

NÜRNBERG KGL BURG (Nuremberg Castle) (Fig. 1046)

Nuremberg Castle (Kaiserburg) looks down on the city from the north. It was lived in by the burgraves and emperors of the eleventh to the fifteenth centuries. Severely damaged during World War II, it has been completely restored.

HEIDELBERG, GERMANY (Fig. 1047–1053)

Heidelberg (Heather hill) is picturesquely located on the south bank of the Neckar River. It is noted especially for its university and its castle. Heidelberg is the oldest university town in Germany and has been enlivened by students since 1386.

Heidelberg Castle is an immense ivy-covered complex, partly in ruins. It is located above the city on a high hill from where one may view the town, the Neckar River and the Old Bridge. The castle was begun in the thirteenth century and added to from time to time until the eighteenth. Portions have been extensively reconstructed and are in excellent condition.

A famous castle curiosity is a huge wine vat, the Heidelberg Tun (Fig. 1050–1051), 28 feet long with a capacity of 49,000 gallons. The vat is guarded by the grotesque wooden figure in the cellar, the court jester, Perkeo. Perkeo, a favorite figure in Joseph Viktor von Scheffel's popular romance, "Der Trompeter von

1054   1055

 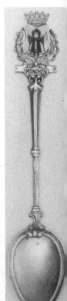

1056   1057

1052 **Perkeo**, marked: N. "Heidelberg" stamped on back.
1053 **Perkeo**, marked: 800.
1054 **Munich, Germany**, marked: 800.
1055 **München (Munich), Germany**. No mark.
1056 **Munich, Germany**. No mark. "München" on back.
1057 **München (Munich), Germany**. marked: "Crescent & crown" 800 "Pine tree".

1058

1060   1061

Säkkingen," was known for his hair-raising alcoholic capacity and his ingenious clock, now part of Heidelberg folklore.

MÜNCHEN, GERMANY (English, Munich) (Fig. 1054–1059)

Munich was established in the ninth century near a Benedictine abbey and took the name of its monks—in German *Mönche*, High German *Munichen*. From this comes the town's emblem a little monk *(Münchner Kindl)* that is used on the coat of arms. Atop the tower of the "new" rathaus, built 1867-1908, is a statue of the little monk, two fingers of his right hand raised in benediction, his left hand holding a book. On spoons, the child monk is often shown with a Krug (mug) in one hand and a radish in the other. The mug is in honor of the brewing industry and the radish is what is eaten with beer.

The bowls of the spoons (Fig. 1058–1059) feature the Marienplatz with the column to the Virgin (Mariensaule), city patron, in the center. On this same square near the old town hall (Altes Rathaus, fifteenth century) is the new town hall (Neues Rathaus) in the Gothic style with stepped gables crowned by bell turrets. Its carillon (Glockenspiel), the largest in Germany, is set in motion every morning at 11:00 o'clock. Some of the mechanical figures do a cooper's dance while others are dressed as knights in armor on horseback and fight a mock battle.

OBERAMMERGAU, GERMANY (Fig. 1060–1067)

Oberammergau is best known for its Passion Play performed every ten years.

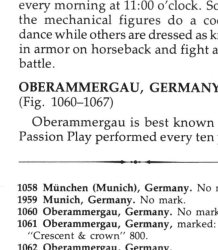

1059

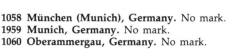

1058 **München (Munich), Germany.** No mark.
1959 **Munich, Germany.** No mark.
1060 **Oberammergau, Germany.** No mark.
1061 **Oberammergau, Germany,** marked: "Crescent & crown" 800.
1062 **Oberammergau, Germany.**

1062

211

1063

1065

1066

After a terrible plague epidemic in 1632, which miraculously stopped just short of Oberammergau, the village people vowed to give a presentation of this play every ten years, the first one taking place in 1634. The seventeenth century text has been rewritten twice, in 1750 and 1850, to meet contemporary taste.

Some 500,000 spectators witnessed the ninety performances given from May to September in 1970. Each presentation lasts all day, with only a short intermission for the midday meal. The amateur actors prepare for their arduous roles a long time in advance. They are local citizens who have resided in Oberammergau for twenty years, and female members of the cast must be unmarried. The participants are chosen by election. All amusements are prohibited during the entire years of preparation for the Passion Play.

SPOON OF ROTHENBURG, GERMANY (Fig. 1068)

One of the early silversmiths in Rothenburg ob der Tauber designed this spoon about 1650. They are now made in the shop of Claus Hinrichs, the silversmith in the shop that has been in operation since 1527. The design is made in all sizes of spoons and serving pieces.

ROTHENBURG CITY SEAL (Fig. 1069)

The spoon with the city seal of Rothenburg is also made in Claus Hinrichs' shop. The design of the seal is a remind-

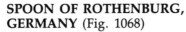

1063 **Oberammergau, Germany.**
1064 **Oberammergau, Germany,** marked: "Crescent & crown" 800.
1065 **Oberammergau, Germany,** marked: MF .800 "Crescent & crown".
1066 **Oberammergau, Germany,** marked: 800.
1067 **Oberammergau, Germany,** marked: DEPOSE 800 "Crescent & crown" S & H conjoined.

1064

1067

1068

1069

1072

er of the walls and towers surrounding the old city.

DER MEISTERTRUNK (The Master-draught of Burgermeister Nusch) (Fig. 1070–1071)

During the Thirty Years' War, Rothenburg ob der Tauber was captured by the imperial forces of General Tilly (Johan Tserclaes, Count of Tilly, the septuagenarian general of the Duke of Bavaria) who ordered the executioner to behead the entire town council. The Cellar Master persuaded Tilly to spare the people if there was one among them who could down six and one-half pints of wine held in a huge goblet, without stopping to take a breath. Burgermeister (Mayor) Nusch accomplished the feat and saved the town.

Every day at 11:00, 12:00, 1:00 and 2:00 o'clock the shutters of a double window at the "Drinking Hall" in Rothenburg fly open and reveal two figures. At the left, Tilly raises his baton. At the right, Nusch raises the goblet and tilts back his head. Tilly then turns a face of wooden amazement toward the spectators. These spoons, with movable arms so that Nusch can lift the goblet to his lips, commemorate the event.

OSNABRÜCK, GERMANY (Fig. 1072–1074)

Osnabrück grew in the ninth century around the episcopal quarter and the market town. From the eleventh century

---

1068 **Rothenburg, Germany.** Maker: Claus Hinrichs, Rothenburg, 835 OT.
1069 **Rothenburg, Germany.** Maker: Claus Hinrichs, Rothenburg, 835 OT.
1070 **The Master-Draught of Burgermeister Nusch, Rothenburg, Germany.** Maker: Claus Hinrichs of Rothenburg; marked: 835.
1071 **The Master-Draught of Burgermeister Nusch, Rothenburg, Germany.** Maker: Claus Hinrichs of Rothenburg. No mark.
1072 **Osnabrück, Germany,** marked: D800 M "Pine tree" F.
1073 **Osnabrück, Germany,** marked: KFK 800.

1070   **1071**

1073

1074

1075

1076

onwards a new town spread around the church of St. John. The two were united within a single city wall about 1300 and Osnabrück became an important commercial center. The city lent its name to the coarse linen known among English-speaking people as osnaburgs. However, the linen trade has been replaced by metal products and paper.

The Dom, or St. Peter's cathedral (in the bowls of both spoons) is a thirteenth century Transitional Gothic style building. Its squat outline is distinguished by large towers which differ in size and design.

FRIEDRICHSHAFEN, GERMANY
(Fig. 1074)

Friedrichshafen is an industrial town and port on the northern shore of Lake Constance. Between 1900 and 1945 it was the home of the German dirigible industry, founded by Count Ferdinand von Zeppelin. Zeppelin blimps and the Dornier seaplanes were made there. The Zeppelin works were damaged in World War II and subsequently dismantled. Today Friedrichshafen is the home of the Zeppelin Museum.

HANNOVER, GERMANY (French, HANOVRE; English, HANOVER)
(Fig. 1075–1076)

Hannover, former capital of the kingdom of Hannover and subsequently of the Prussian province of that name, is situated at the confluence of the Ihme with the Leine River. The prancing stallion was the coat of arms of the ancient province of Hannover. It was also used by the Land of Lower Saxony, which came into existence after World War II. The prancing stallion became the heral-

1077

1074 **Friedrichshafen, Germany.** Maker: C. F. Schuzt KFK 800 "Crescent & crown".
1075 **Hannover, Germany,** marked: 835.
1076 **Hannover, Germany,** marked: KFK 800.
1077 **Freiburg, Germany,** marked: "Crescent & crown". "Freiburg 1892" on back.

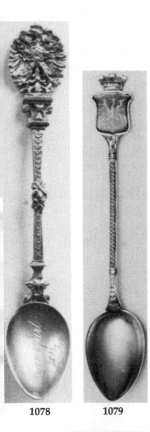

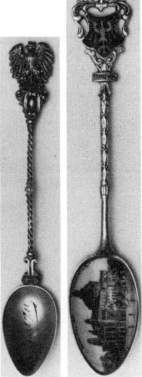

dic figure of the province of Hannover because this province is famous for horse-breeding.

The Rathaus (in the bowl of Fig. 1076), Old Town Hall, was built between 1439 and 1455. It now contains civic archives and houses a museum of antiquities. The view from its dome is magnificent.

FREIBURG IM BREISGAU, GERMANY (French, FRIBOURG-EN-BRISGAU) (Fig. 1077)

The old university town of Freiburg-im-Breisgau, one of the most attractive cities in southern Germany, was founded in 1120 by Conrad, Duke of Zähringen. The city has had a turbulent history; it passed to the Hapsburgs in 1368, to the Swedes in the Thirty Years' War, to France in 1679, to Austria in 1697, to Baden in 1805 and to French troops in 1945 after much of the older section was destroyed by Allied air raids.

The heart of the city is its Gothic cathedral. Its open-work spire is one of the most striking sights in Germany.

Martin Waldseemüller, the geographer who first used the name "America" on a map, lived in Freiburg.

FRANKFURT AM MAIN, GERMANY (French, FRANKFORT-SUR-LE-MAIN; English, FRANKFURT-ON-MAIN) (Fig. 1075–1082)

Frankfurt was founded in 793 and by 843 was the capital of the Eastern Franks. When Frederick I was elected in 1152 the city became the place of election of the German kings, a custom made law by the Golden Bull of Emperor Charles IV

1078 1079

1080

1083

1078 **Frankfurt, Germany.** Marks illegible.
1079 **Frankfurt City Coat-Of-Arms,** marked: STER 900.
1080 **Römer, Frankfurt, Germany.** No mark.
1081 **Frankfurt, Germany.** No mark.
1082 **Schauspielhaus, Frankfurt, Germany,** marked: ABK 800.
1083 **Hamburg, Germany.**

1081 1082

1084

1085

in 1356. From 1562 to 1792 it was the coronation city of the emperors. Its present importance is as a transportation center and commercial city. Frankfurt has the largest airport in Europe, ranks third among Germany's inland ports and has seven railroad lines.

Frankfurt was the home of the international banking family, the Rothschilds, the poet Johann Wolfgang Goethe and the philosopher Arthur Schopenhauer.

There is a centuries-old rivalry among several German cities over their respective claims to Johann Gutenberg, reputed father of printing. Most authorities agree that he was born in Mainz but that Strasbourg, Frankfurt and Venice share with his birthplace the honor of his first printing. Monuments to him stand in Frankfurt, Strasbourg and Mainz.

The Römer (in bowl of Fig. 1080) is a diverse block of reconstructed fifteenth-century burgher's houses and was once the town hall and coronation palace. The Zum Römer house in the center gave the name to the entire group. It is the most ornate and since 1405 has been used by the municipality.

HAMBURG, GERMANY (French, HAMBOURG) (Fig. 1083–1087)

Hamburg was founded by Charlemagne between 808 and 811. He built a citadel and church as a protection against neighboring pagan Slavs. In spite of frequent devastation by Danes and Slavs, Hamburg became an important commercial city and in 1241 and 1249 it joined with Lübeck and Bremen in forming the Hanseatic League. Hamburg has endured occupation by Napoleon (1806), the Russians (1813) and has

1086

1087

1084 Hamburg, Germany.
1085 Hamburg, Germany. No mark.
1086 Jungfernstieg, Hamburg, Germany, marked: "Crown" 800 SM.
1087 Jungfernstieg, Hamburg, Germany. No mark.

1088

1090

from time to time been a free state. During World War II it suffered devastating air attacks and was captured by British forces. Rebuilt after the war, Hamburg's new architecture shows traces of the medieval buildings that once were present.

The Jungfernstieg (Fig. 1085–1087) is a well-known road in Hamburg. It runs along the Binnenalster Basin and is the town's cosmopolitan artery. There is a half-moon landing stage where the Alster boats come alongside, a coffee pavilion and large shop windows. At one time there was situated there the dam belonging to Reese, the owner of a windmill, the Reesendamm, and lovely Hamburg ladies enjoyed the path on which to saunter. From this custom, the promenade received the nickname of "Jungferstieg" (Virgin's Walk).

The people of Hamburg love to point out that the hamburger, so popular in America, originated in their city.

WILDBAD, GERMANY
(Fig. 1088–1089)

Wildbad is in the Scharzwald (Black Forest) and has all the quaint charm associated with it. It also has all the amenities of a modern thermal spa and holiday resort. Summer activities include fishing, miniature golf, swimming and tennis. Tobogganing and skiing on slopes with an elevation of more than 3,000 feet are available in winter.

LUDWIG II and NEUSCHWANSTEIN CASTLE
(Fig. 1090–1091)

The fortress, Neuschwanstein Castle, is a formidable mass of cold gray granite bristling with towers and pinnacles,

1089

1091

1088 Wildbad, Germany.
1089 Wildbad, Germany, marked: 800 "Pine tree" "Crescent & crown".
1090 Ludwig II, München, Germany, marked: "Crescent & crown" 800.
1091 Neuschwanstein Castle.

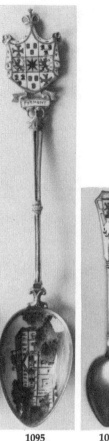

rising from a spur cut at its eastern end by the Pöllat Gorge and was the dream of the mad King Ludwig II of Bavaria. The first sketches were drawn by a theatrical decorator, not an architect, which explains the castle's dream-like, fairy-tale atmosphere.

The unfortunate Ludwig stayed at Neuschwanstein only 102 days. It was here on June 10, 1886 he learned from the Governmental Commission hastily sent from Munich that he had been deposed, and he died three days later.

STUTTGART, GERMANY
(Fig. 1092–1093)

Stuttgart was first mentioned in 1229 and after 1265 was the favorite residence of the counts of Württenberg. The city developed rapidly as an industrial center in the nineteenth century. It is the center of southern German publishing trade. Among other industries are manufacture of electrical equipment, machinery, textiles, automobiles and furniture. The Daimler-Benz Automobile Museum, on Mercedestrasse, tells the history of the firm which in 1899 became the world's leading car manufacturer.

The Stiftskirche (Collegiate Church) in the bowl of Fig. 1094 was rebuilt after the war.

BIBERACH, GERMANY (Fig. 1094)

Biberach is an industrial city in Württemberg on the Riss, a small affluent of the Danube. Old walls still partially remaining give the town a medieval aspect. Among its old buildings is a

1092   1093

1095   1096

1094

1097

1092 **Stuttgart, Germany,** marked: 800 W.
1093 **Stuttgart, Germany.** No mark. Stiftskirche (Collegiate Church) in bowl.
1094 **Biberach, Germany.** No mark.
1095 **Bad Pyrmont, Germany,** marked: 800 KFK "Crescent & crown".
1096 **Barmen, Germany,** marked: "Crescent & crown" DEPOSE 800 KFK.
1097 **Dom Zu Aachen, Aix-La-Chapelle, Germany,** marked: "Crescent & crown".

1098

1099

front

1100   back

1101

church dating from 1100. The town is noted for its bell foundries.

BAD PYRMONT, GERMANY
(Fig. 1095)

Bad Pyrmont's saline springs, brine and mud baths have been known and used for more than 400 years. The town is situated in a valley near the River Emmer. One of the loveliest parks of Europe is found here.

BARMEN, GERMANY
(Fig. 1096)

Barmen, a former city in Germany on the Wupper River, was chartered in 1808. It was a textile manufacturing and metalworking center. In 1929, Barmen was incorporated with Elberfeld and other neighboring towns to form Wuppertal.

AACHEN, GERMANY (French, AIX-LA-CHAPELLE) (Fig. 1097)

Aachen was once the *Acqui Granum* or *Acquae Grani* of the Romans, who were attracted to the area by its hot springs. It was the residence of Charlemagne who died there in 814. Charlemagne's love for his "Ais, le Capele" is celebrated in the *Chanson de Roland*. The tomb of the emperor lies in the cathedral along with his treasure and the holy relics he collected.

Aachen is still renowned as a health resort for rheumatism because of its sulphuric sodium chloride baths in the hot springs.

WIESBADEN, GERMANY
(Fig. 1098–1099)

Wiesbaden is a large spa or health resort. The Kurhaus was built in a Greek style in 1905–07 to the plans of Fr. von

1098 **Wiesbaden, Germany.** No mark.
1099 **Wiesbaden, Germany,** marked: 800.
1100 **Bavarian Taler.** Maker: Shreve & Co., San Francisco.
1101 **Bad Tölz.** One Kreutzer coin bowl.

Thiersch. The shell room, its walls covered with innumerable shells rather like the decorated external walls of one of those cottages that one sees sometimes in Donegal, was the idea of Kaiser Wilhelm. The Kurhaus is now primarily an international meeting place. On either side of the esplanade, two colonnaded buildings extend the vista: to the north, the Brunnen Kolonnade, which contains the thermal fountain fed by the famous Kochbrunnen spring, concert and exhibition halls; to the south, the theater.

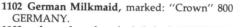

1102 **German Milkmaid,** marked: "Crown" 800 GERMANY.

1103 **a, b, c, d, e, f, g, h, i, j, k, l.** GERMAN MUSICIAN SPOONS.

1104 **Helgoland, Germany,** marked: 800 "Crescent & crown" KFK.

1102

1104

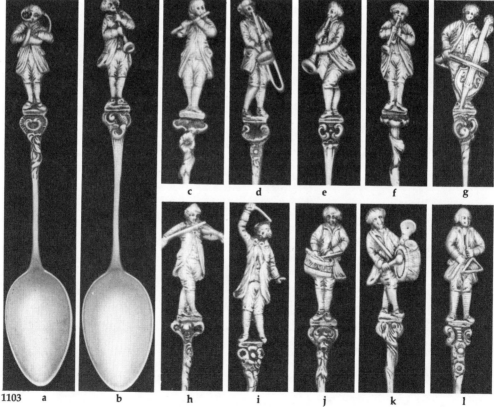

1103 a   b   c   d   e   f   g   h   i   j   k   l

1105

1106

BAVARIAN TALER (Fig. 1100)

The Bavarian Convention taler of the Madonna type was struck in the name of Maximiliam III Joseph, the eldest son of Karl Albert. He was born in 1727, became elector and vicar of the Holy Roman Empire in 1745 and died in 1777 leaving no heir to the throne.

BAD TÖLZ, GERMANY (Fig. 1101)

Bad Tölz is an old city. The Romans had a settlement there in the fifth century named *Tollusium*. This spa is actually twin towns lying on either side of the Isar River south of Munich. The old town faces a modern spa with wide streets, the latter having been exploited since 1845 to take advantage of the richly iodized waters.

GERMAN MILKMAID (Fig. 1102)

Windmills and bucolic scenes on spoons are frequently associated with the Netherlands but are also found on German and Danish spoons as well.

MUSICIAN SPOONS (Fig. 1103)

Sets of German spoons depicting individuals engaged in their various occupational endeavors were made in great numbers with musicians being among them.

HELGOLAND (HELIGOLAND), GERMANY (Fig. 1104–1106)

Helgoland (Danish for "holy land") is a small island in the North Sea. Formerly under Danish rule, it was taken from them in 1807, ceded to Great Britain in 1814 and transferred to Germany in 1890. They made it into a great fortress to which no visitors were allowed. Under the Treaty of Versailles, Germany

1107

1108

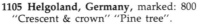

1105 **Helgoland, Germany,** marked: 800 "Crescent & crown" "Pine tree".
1106 **Helgoland.** No mark.
1107 **Imperator,** marked: "Pine tree" 800.
1108 **Imperator,** marked: Birmingham 1912-13.

1109

1110

1111

was forced to dismantle the fortifications. Helgoland is now a popular sea-bathing resort. Fishing is the main occupation of the inhabitants.

IMPERATOR (Fig. 1107–1108)

German oceanic shipping had its beginnings between the second half of the nineteenth century and the out-break of World War I. The Hamburg-Amerika Line was founded in 1847 and the Norddeutscher Lloyd in 1857. These steamship lines assumed great importance because of the favorable geographic position of Hamburg which made it a vital link as a port of transshipment and an outlet to several central European countries.

The Hamburg-Amerika Line at one time built the largest steamers in the world. The first of the series was the *Imperator,* later the Cunard *Berengaria.* She was launched in 1912 and her name, *Imperator* meaning "general," or one who exercises supreme power, was fitting for the vessel, her dimensions being 886.38 feet by 98.3 feet by 57.1 feet; gross tonnage 51,969.

LUCANIA (Fig. 1109) and KAISER WILHELM II (Fig. 1110)

The *Lucania* launched in 1893 was one of the luxury ships of the Cunard Line. She was the first ship to require a crew of more than 500 men. Marconi conducted his wireless experiments aboard her. The *Lucania* and her sister ship, the *Campania,* were the most popular ships on the ocean. They cut down the Atlantic record to about five days and eight hours, the *Lucania* making a famous run

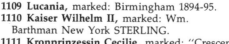

1109 **Lucania,** marked: Birmingham 1894-95.
1110 **Kaiser Wilhelm II,** marked: Wm.
Barthman New York STERLING.
1111 **Kronprinzessin Cecilie,** marked: "Crescent & crown" KFK C. F. Schutz.
1112 **Dresden, Germany.** No mark.
1113 **Dresden, Germany,** marked: "Crescent & crown" 800.

1112   1113

of 560 nautical miles in one day. In 1902 the *Lucania* lost her laurels for speed to *Kaiser Wilhelm II* of the Norddeutscher Lloyd line.

KRONPRINZESSIN CECILIE
(Fig. 111)

The *Kronprinzessin Cecilie* was launched by the Norddeutscher Lloyd line in 1906.

DRESDEN, EAST GERMANY
(Fig. 1112–1122)

The name Dresden immediately brings to the collectors' minds the beautiful hard-paste porcelain of that name. This so-called Dresden china was the first hard-paste porcelain made in Europe. The original factory was not located in Dresden, but in Meissen, fourteen miles northwest of Dresden. The ware came to be called Dresden from the fact that it was sold there rather than at the factory.

Dresden porcelain was first made by Johann Friedrich Böttger in 1709 after much experimentation in an attempt to imitate the glazed, white porcelain being imported from the Far East.

A city of Slavic origin, Dresden was formerly called the "Florence of the Elbe" because of is extraordinary art galleries, museums, palaces, churches and theaters. The treasures of the Green Vaults, the name generally given to the series of rooms on the ground floor of the Zwinger Palace, are world-famous. They consist of ivories, enamels, bronzes, gold and silver objects and jewels.

Among the many beautiful buildings

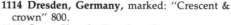

1114 **Dresden, Germany,** marked: "Crescent & crown" 800.
1115 **Court Church, Dresden, Germany,** marked: 900.
1116 **Court Church, Dresden, Germany,** marked: 800 "Crescent & crown" M.F. "Pine tree".
1117 **Dresden, Germany,** marked: 800 "Crescent & crown".

1114

1116

1115

1117

1118   1119

1120

is this Roman Catholic Hofkirche (Fig. 1115–1117) or Court Church, built 200 years ago for Saxon kings in the eighteenth-century baroque style.

LEIPZIG, EAST GERMANY
(Fig. 1123–1124)

Leipzig was first mentioned in 1015 and received its town charter between 1156 and 1170. It is still noted for its fairs which had become important as early as the fourteenth and fifteenth centuries. Since the eighteenth century Leipzig had become Germany's leading publishing and printing center and because of the importance of German science and music, its products were known and distributed all over the world. The air attack of December 4, 1943 destroyed their large storehouses of books and musical literature and Communist censorship has rendered recovery impossible.

POTTSDAM, EAST GERMANY
(Fig. 1125)

The palace of Sans Souci in Pottsdam is a low building on fine terraces, its historical associations quite out of proportion to its poor appearance. It is surrounded by fine French gardens.

ERFURT, EAST GERMANY
(Fig. 1126)

Erfurt, in the former Prussian Province of Saxony and now included in the German Democratic Republic (East Germany) is dominated by the Domberg,

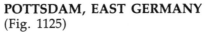

1118 **Dresden, Germany,** marked: "Crescent & crown" 800 KW.
1119 **Dresden, Germany.**
1120 **Dresden, Germany,** marked: KFK 800. Hoftheater on handle.
1121 **Dresden, Germany,** marked: 800 "Pine tree" and "Crescent & crown."
1122 **Dresden, Germany,** marked: "Crescent & crown" 800 S & H conjoined. Köngle Hoftheater, in bowl.
1123 **Leipzig, Germany,** marked: "Crescent & crown" 800 SM.

1121   1122

1123

1124

1125

on which stands the two largest churches —the cathedral (shown in the bowl of this spoon) begun in the twelfth century, and the neighboring church of St. Severus. During World War II the cathedral was severely damaged.

BERNBURG, EAST GERMANY
(Fig. 1127)

Bernburg, first mentioned in 961 was important in the Middle Ages as it lay on an ancient trade route. It consisted of two almost completely separate communities, both of which acquired civic rights in 1278. The castle was probably built in the tenth century and later converted into a Renaissance style chateau.

DESSAU, EAST GERMANY
(Fig. 1128)

Dessau was founded by Albrecht the Bear in the twelfth century and became a city in 1213. Because it was the site of the Junker airplane factory, the city suffered much damage from bombings during World War II.

The Bauhaus of Dessau became between two world wars the cornerstone of modern art and architecture.

STEPHANS DOM (Cathedral of St. Stephen), WIEN (Vienna) AUSTRIA
(Fig. 1129)

St. Stephen's Cathedral in Vienna is the city's landmark. It is one of the most important Gothic buildings in Europe. The belfrey rises to a height of 450' (137 m.) in the heart of the city.

During recent restoration work the existence was discovered of a Romanesque sanctuary built about the middle of the twelfth century. Another later

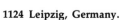

1124 Leipzig, Germany.
1125 Pottsdam, East Germany, marked: "Crescent & crown" 800 SM.
1126 Erfurt, East Germany, marked: 800 SM GERMANY.
1127 Bernberg, East Germany, marked: 800 KFK.

1126

1127

STERLING 925 HELDWEIN

1131   1132

1128

basilica, built in late Romanesque style, was badly damaged in the fire that ravaged Vienna in 1258 and all that remains of those early buildings are the Giants' Doorway (Riesentor) and the Towers of the Pagans in the west facade.

The Romanesque building was gradually replaced by a Gothic edifice at the beginning of the fourteenth century. This too was damaged by the Turks during their seige of the city in 1683 and the cathedral fared even worse in 1945. Russian and then German bombardments resulted in almost total destruction. Funds were given from all over Austria for its complete restoration.

ÖSTERREICH (AUSTRIA) COAT-OF-ARMS (Fig. 1130, 1132)

The arms of the Austrian monarchy consisted of a black double-headed eagle crowned, the double head signifying the former Holy Roman Empire. Above the eagle appeared the crown of Austria. In one claw the eagle held a sword and scepter and in the other an orb. On its breast was a shield divided equally into three vertical sections (Fig. 1132). The eagle now has only one head and carries a hammer and sickle (Fig. 1130).

PESTSÄULE AM GRABEN (Plague Column on the Graben) WIEN (Vienna) (Fig. 1131)

In a city noted for the splendors of its architecture and music, it seems impossible that the burghers could have at one time so totally neglected public health. At the end of the seventeenth century,

900 H&S

1133   1134

1128 **Dessau, East Germany.** No mark.
1129 **Stephans Dom (Cathedral of St. Stephen), Vienna, Austria,** marked: HD 800.
1130 **Osterreich, Austria Coat-Of-Arms,** marked: HD 800.
1131 **Pestäule Am Graben (Plague column in the Graben),** marked: (see drawing).
1132 **Austrian Coat-Of-Arms,** marked: "Crescent & crown" 800.
1133 **Wien, Austria,** marked: (see drawing).
1134 **Wien, Austria,** marked: (see drawing).

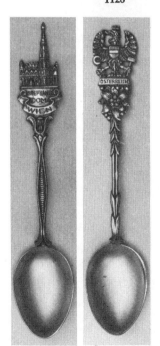

1129   1130

1135

1136

the creeks flowing across Vienna to the Danube were filled with filth. Scavengering rats and garbage thrown from windows into the narrow streets contributed to Vienna's reputation as the city of bubonic plague. In 1678, when the celebrations for the birth of a son to the Emperor Leopold I were scarcely over, this terrifying sickness decimated the city and threatened complete annihilation. Paul de Sorbait, the great Belgian doctor, arrived at the height of the epidemic and established his Plague Order de Sorbait. Drastic measures of hygiene brought complaints from businessmen who said that the economic life of the city was imperiled. However, the plague abated and then vanished. The city was saved. After Sorbait's death his tomb was placed in St. Stephen's Cathedral.

In Vienna, as in many other Austrian towns, columns dedicated to the Virgin or to the Holy Trinity were set up at the end of the seventeenth century to commemorate their delivery from two scourges, the plague and the Turks. The Plague Column on the Graben, dedicated to the Holy Trinity and Nine Angelic Choirs, was erected to fulfill a vow by the Emperor Leopold I. The first column was of wood. This was replaced 1682–93 by the present more elaborate one in stone. The design by Mathias Rauchmiller is of nine angels being swept heavenwards in the company of many cherubs on a column of clouds topped by the Trinity.

WIEN, ÖSTERREICH (French, VIENNE, AUTRICHE; English, VIENNA, AUSTRIA) (Fig. 1133–1135)

The land on which Vienna stands has

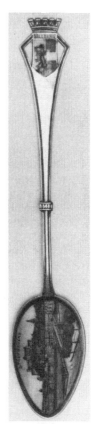

1137

1138

1135 **Wien, Austria,** marked: 800.
1136 **Festung Hohen-Salzburg.** No mark.
1137 **Salzburg, Austria,** marked: 800 KFK. Stadtbrücke in bowl.
1138 **Innsbruck, Austria,** marked: 800. Annesäule (St. Anne's Column) in bowl.

been occupied for many centuries. Archaeological remains have been found dating back to the Stone Age. Illyrians, settled there during the early Iron Age, achieved a certain degree of culture when the Celts introduced the La Tène culture around 400 B.C. Roman legions in the reign of Augustus set up a camp near the Danube near the frontier fort at Carnuntum. Around 100 A.D. this camp was moved to the present location of the Hoher Markt and was *Vindobona*. The city was overcome and pillaged by Attila about 450 and conquered by Charlemagne about 791. The capital of the Margraviate of Austria in the twelfth century, municipal privileges were given it in 1221. In 1278 Vienna became the seat of the Hapsburg dynasty whose influence is still deeply marked.

Vienna's location on the Danube River and being only 44 miles (70 km.) from the Iron Curtain made her of strategic importance in ages past as well as the present. The narrow, twisting streets that grew up around St. Stephen's Cathedral during the Middle Ages with sharp corners to turn would have made trouble for an attacker as would the seventeenth century city walls. The city grew and spilled beyond the walls and by 1857 the Emperor Franz-Josef ordered the removal of the bastions and the formation of a belt of boulevards around the old town, creating the world-famous "Ring" which turned the capital city into a great building site. Foreign as well as Austrian architects created the magnificent buildings for which Vienna is so well-known. Among them are the Votive Church, the New University, the Burgtheater, the Town Hall, Parliament, the Academy of Fine Arts, the Fine Arts and Natural History Museums, and the Opera, all of which are enhanced by their settings of beautiful public gardens and fine vistas.

In Vienna, music has held a place of honor ever since the thirteenth century under Archduke Albert I, but it was in the eighteenth and nineteenth centuries that Gluck, Haydn, Mozart, Beethoven, Schubert, Czerny, Joseph Launer, Johann Strauss (both father and son), Edward Strauss, Otto Nicolai, Brahms and Schumann made the city of the Hapsburgs the world's capital of glorious music.

FESTUNG HOHEN-SALZBURG (Fortress Hohen-Salzburg) (Fig. 1136)

This fortress, former stronghold of the prince-bishops, was begun in 1077 by Archbishop Gebhard, as a result of a controversy between the emperor and pope. Gebhard, faithful servant of the pope, found himself in considerable danger and wished to secure a safe retreat from the threats of princes of South Germany who were supporting the emperor. It is the largest and best-preserved medieval fortress standing. It attained its present aspect through 600 years of enlarging and strengthening. Visitors may reach the fortress by means of a funicular railway. Guided tours take visitors through the State rooms formerly occupied by the arch-bishops. From a watch-tower there is a circular panorama of the Tennengebirge and the Berchtesgaden Alps.

SALZBURG, AUSTRIA (French, SALZBOURG) (Fig. 1137)

About 20,000 B.C. the valley where the city of Salzburg now lies was a prehistoric lake. About 3000 B.C. the level of the water gradually lowered and the first authenticated settlers arrived. There was salt-mining a little south of Dürrnberg. In 1800 B.C. there were Bronze Age settlements; by 1000 B.C. the Indo-Germanic tribe, the Illyrians, came; 500 years later there was an important Celtic settlement in the immediate vicinity of the present town, on the Rainberg. Salt-mining continued on the Dürrnberg.

Roman rule began in the area in 15 A.D. when the Emperor Claudius raised

the town of *Juvavum*, built where the Old Town now stands, to the rank of a Municipium. Soon Juvavum developed into an important road junction.

In 477 St. Severin began to preach in Juvavum and that same year the town was destroyed by the East Germanic tribe of the Heruli from northern Hungary, under their General, Duke Ottokar. Eleven years later the remaining Romans left the district.

In 696 Bishop Suffragan Rupert (Hruodprecht or Hruodbert in old German meaning "of glorious renown") was sent from Worms on the Rhine by Duke Theodo II as a missionary. On the ruins of Juvavum he founded the Monastery of St. Peter and also founded the Benedictine Abbey on the Nonnberg. It was probably here that the "Salz Burg" (salt citadel) stood, which guarded the salt-traffic down the river and gave the town its name. The name of the town is first recorded in 755 in the "Life of St. Boniface."

Today, Salzburg is noted as a resort town and tourist center. Its world-famous Salzburg Festivals were founded in 1920 by Max Reinhardt and Hugo von Hofmannsthal and attract thousands of visitors.

Hundreds of Protestant peasants left Salzburg and went to Pennsylvania where they were described as Dutch immigrants. Others left there to establish the city of Savannah, Georgia.

INNSBRUCK, AUSTRIA
(Fig. 1138–1139)

Innsbruck, or Innspruck (Bridge over the Inn River) derived its name from the ancient Roman one of *Œnipontium* and is

1139

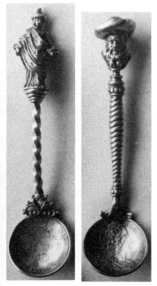

1142

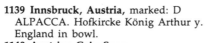

1139 Innsbruck, Austria, marked: D ALPACCA. Hofkircke König Arthur y. England in bowl.
1140 Austrian Coin Spoon.
1141 Austrian Coin Spoon.
1142 Portugese Coat-Of-Arms, no marks.
1143 Portugese Coat-Of-Arms, mark illegible.

1140   1141

1143

locally called Schpruck. Innsbruck is the capital of the Tyrol and one of the most beautifully situated towns in the world. The view along the Maria-Therese-inenstrasse towards the steep slopes of the Nordkette is one that is traditional for photographers who visit the city.

St. Anne's Column (Annesäule) shown in the bowl of Fig. 1138 placed in the center of the thoroughfare in 1706 commemorates the birthday, July 26, 1703, of St. Anne, when the Bavarian invaders retreated during the war of the Spanish Succession.

Among the outstanding buildings in Innsbruck is the Hofkirche, containing the cenotaph of the Emperor Maximilian I. It is one of the most splended monuments of its kind in Europe. It was intended to glorify the splendors of his reign and to record the flawless legitimacy of the Holy Roman Empire as the heir of the Caesars. Included in the original plan were forty large statues, 100 small bronzes of saints and thirty-four busts of Roman emperors. The plans were not fully completed but in 1584 the casting of the kneeling statue of Maximilian which crowns the structure marked the end of the work. Twenty-eight of the statues were completed, all in bronze but two which are in copper and all more than life size. They stand guard over the empty tomb. The choice of figures is sometimes surprising but took into consideration ties of blood and marriage. The royal families of Hapsburg, Burgundy and Austria are represented as are also the heroes of chivalry and precursors of medieval Christianity —King Arthur (Fig. 1139) in armor, Theodoric and Clovis.

AUSTRIAN COIN SPOONS
(Fig. 1140–1141)

The bowls of both spoons were made of Austrian coins, Fig. 1140 a 20-Kreuzer (Tirol) coin dated 1809 (The Tyrol became part of Austria in 1805, a settlement imposed by the Congress of Vien-

na). The other coin is dated 1740 and the reverse features the double-eagle with crown. The inscription reads CAROL · V · I · D · G · R · I · S · A · G · E · HI · HU · BO · REX.

PORTUGUESE COAT-OF-ARMS
(Fig. 1142–1144)

The coat-of-arms consists of a large silver shield upon which five small blue ones are arranged in the form of a cross, each one bearing five silver plates. Around the shield is a red border upon which are seven golden castles. Alfonso I defeated five Moorish princes in the battle of Ourique, and he adopted the five blue shields commemorating this triumph. The five white spots on the small shield represent the five wounds of Christ. The red border was added by Alphonse III in 1252, after his marriage. The circle of gold upon which the shield and border are imposed, and the green of the flag, which is that of St. Benedict of Aviz, commemorate the fame of Prince Henry, the Navigator.

Spoon Fig. 1192 has the coat-of-arms on the handle as well as in the bowl. The device in the bowl has the date 1818 and JOANNES · D · PORT · REGENS · ET · BRAS · D. The back of the spoon bowl shows an armillary sphere and an inscription around the sphere reads: STAB · SUBQ · SIGN · NATA. The bowl appears to be a coin design but is rough for a real coin.

Spoon Fig. 1143 also appears to be a coin, or a facsimile of one. The back side has a cross with the motto "In hoc signo vinces" (By this sign thou shalt conquer).

LISBOA (Fig. 1145–48)

Lisboa (Lisbon), Portugal, was largely destroyed by fire in 1755 but today has been rebuilt and is one of the most beautiful capitals on the Continent.

The ancient name for the city was Olisipo. The city is remembered as being the port from which Vasco da Gama's fleet set out on July 9, 1497 and completed the voyage to India by way of the Cape of Good Hope, thereby establishing a new trade route between Europe and the Orient.

CASINO ESTORIL (Fig. 1149)

Estoril, Portugal's "Riviera" offers gambling, swimming, yachting, golf, horseback riding, trap shooting, tennis, fishing and many other attractions to its visitors. The most famous after-dark spot in the nation is the Casino at Estoril.

VASCO DA GAMA'S VOYAGE TO INDIA (Fig. 1150)

The spoon bowl is made out of a 500 reis Portuguese coin struck in commemoration of the 400th anniversary of Vasco da Gama's voyage to India.

The Portuguese were discouraged when Columbus returned from his voyage and it was realized that he had not found a westward route to India. Vasco da Gama was sent out with orders to go around Africa to India or die in the attempt. His round-trip distance was 24,000 miles and a much more dangerous voyage than that of Columbus. He arrived on the Malabar (west) coast of India in 1498. After an equally difficult return trip he arrived back in Lisbon on August 29 (September 9th, according to some), 1499. His heroic voyage opened up new trade routes and brought wealth and fame to Portugal.

The reverse side of the coin has a cross with the motto *In hoc signo vinces* (By this sign thou shalt conquer).

Carlos I (1863–1908) and his queen, Marie Amélie, are on the obverse.

front   1144   back

1145   1146

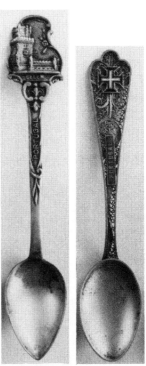

1147   1148

1149

1144 **Portugese Coat-Of-Arms,** no marks.
1145 **Lisboa,** marked: TOPAZIO
1146 **Lisboa,** no marks.
1147 **Belem Tower, Lisbon,** mark illegible.
1148 **Portugal,** no mark.
1149 **Casino Estoril,** mark rubbed.

1150

1151   1152

THE LEGEND OF THE COCK
(Fig. 1151–1153)

In beautiful Barcelos, Portugal, there still exists an ancient stone cross engraved with the images of the Virgin de Pilar, St. Paul, as well as the Moon and the Sun, above which there is a Christ on a cross. On the opposite side of the cross is St. Tiago of Compostela holding a man hanging from the gallows. Below another Christ on the cross is a cock.

Once upon a time the inhabitants of Barcelos were alarmed when a crime was committed and the criminal was never caught. One day a Spaniard from Galacia, a stranger in Barcelos, was arrested and condemned as guilty of the crime. Although the man repeatedly pleaded his innocence, he was forcibly dragged to the gallows. Here he had a vision inspired by St. Tiago, and he begged to speak to the judge who condemned him. When taken to the judge's home, he again denied being guilty, but the judge would not believe him. The man looked at the roasted cock which was being served and cried out: "It is as true that I am innocent as this roasted cock will crow when they hang me." Although everyone present laughed, the fact was that the roasted cock did crow when the man was being hanged, saving his life. Some years later the ex-convict returned to Barcelos where he had a stone cross built in remembrance of his odyssey. On the cross is St. Tiago holding the convict in order to prevent the rope from being tightened. The cock above these figures symbolizes kindness, hospitality and good luck. The Moon and Sun represent the Light and the Dragon is symbolic of Darkness and Evil, which the devotion of St. Tiago, St.

1150 **Vasco Da Gama's Voyage To India,**
    marked: "Boar's head" with II underneath; another illegible mark.
1151 **Legend of the Cock,** marked: TOPAZIO.
1152-1153 **Legend of the Cock,** no marks.
1154 **Mallorca (Majorca),** no marks.

1153

1154

Paul and the Virgin de Pilar defeated with Faith and Truth.

MALLORCA (MAJORCA) (Fig. 1154)

Mallorca, largest of the Balearic Islands, lies a little more than one hundred miles off the eastern coast of Spain. It has an area of about 1,400 square miles. Like the rest of the Balearic Islands, it was seized successively by the Phoenicians, Carthaginians, Romans, Vandals, Byzantines and in 797, by the Moors from whom it was recaptured in 129 by James I the Conqueror, king of Aragon. It is presently a Spanish possession.

The island has a very ancient tradition of folk dances such as the *copeo* and the *mateixz,* considered by some to be of Moorish origin.

Its only large city and its capital, Palma, is one of the loveliest cities in Mediterranean Spain.

SPANISH COAT-OF-ARMS
(Fig. 1155–1156)

When the monarchy was overthrown in 1931 new arms were adopted. They contain a yellow triple-towered castle on a red field for Castile; a red lion rampant on a white field for Léon; four vertical stripes on a yellow ground for Aragón; yellow chains on a red ground for Navarre; and a pomegranate on a white ground for Granada.

MADRID'S COAT-OF-ARMS
(Fig. 1157)

The coat-of-arms of Madrid includes a standing bear eating the fruit of the Madroño tree.

1159

1155 **Spanish Coat-Of-Arms,** marked: Q35.
1156 **Spanish Coat-Of-Arms,** marked: II.
1157 **Madrid, Spain,** no mark.
1158 **Bullfight,** marked: MADE IN SPAIN PAT 18933.
1159 **El Prado, Madrid, Spain.**
1160 **Cartagena, Spain,** marked: 0900
1161 **Cadiz, Spain,** marked: 800.

1155 **1156**

1157 **1158**

1160 **1161**

BULLFIGHTS (Fig. 1158)

Bullfighting, once popular in Greece and Rome, was probably introduced into Spain by the Moors. It soon became a favorite of the Spanish gentry and its popularity has continued, attended by much pomp and ceremony. In Portugal, bullfights are exhibitions of skill, grace and courage. The horns of the bull are padded, and the fighter makes his encounter unarmed, on horseback, and therefore the bulls are never killed.

EL PRADO (Fig. 1159)

El Prado in Madrid, Spain, is one of the first stops for any art lover. Housed in a magnificent eighteenth century building are treasures painted by El Greco, Velázquez, Goya, Rubens, Van Dyck, da Vinci, Murillo and many others. The museum also contains works of classical sculpture, collections of coins, enamels, silver and gold work.

CARTAGENA, SPAIN (Fig. 1160)

Cartagena is well-known for its harbor, one of the largest and safest in the Mediterranean. Ruins of four old castles stand on the summits of four hills which adjoin the town.

Ancient *Carthgo Nova* (Cartagena) was founded by the Carthaginians circa 225 B.C., who were the first to work the copper mines there. In 210 B.C. the city became a Roman colony when it was taken by Scipio Africanus.

CADIZ, SPAIN (Fig. 1161)

The seaport of Cadiz is one of Spain's handsomest cities, and is capital of the province of Cadiz. It was founded by the Phoenicians about 1100 B.C. The city reached its greatest prosperity after the discovery of America at which time it became the European emporium for the New World.

BARCELONA, SPAIN (Fig. 1162)

Archaeological remains show that the area that is now Barcelona was first settled by an Iberian tribe at Layte on Montjuich, then an island. Romans founded a town there called Taber. It was later called Barcino and became the capital when occupied by the Visigoths in 415.

Deposit banking is said to have originated in Barcelona with the establishment of the Bank of Barcelona in 1401.

SEVILLE, SPAIN (Fig. 1163)

Seville, capital of the province, is on the left bank of the Guadalquivir River. The city is an architectural treasure house. Among its many imposing buildings is the Alcazar, built in 1181 as the palace of the Moorish kings and later used by the Spanish sovereigns. Another magnificent building is the Gothic cathedral, built 1402–1519, which houses a wealth of works of art and historical treasures.

TOLEDO, SPAIN (Fig. 1164)

Toledo's founding is ascribed variously to Tubal, grandson of Noah, to Hercules, and to Jews who, exiled by Nebuchadnezzar, founded a settlement there and named it *Toledoth*, "Place of Generations." Under Roman rule in 193 B.C. it was raised to the status of a colonia. Today the city has little commercial or political importance. It has a wealth of art, architecture and history. El Greco lived there, and his house is now a museum.

Toledo is famous for the production of "Toledo blades," swords of remarkable quality, celebrated since Roman times.

GRANADA, SPAIN (Fig. 1165)

Granada, in southern Spain, is another historic city that was once capital of a powerful Moorish kingdom. Developed early in the Middle Ages, it became the seat of the kingdom of Granada in 1238. A noted center of Moslem culture and learning, it was the last Moorish stronghold in Spain to be conquered by the Christians. The city fell in

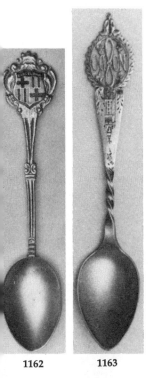

1492 to forces led by Ferdinand V and Isabella. A Gothic chapel adjacent to the city's sixteenth-century cathedral contains the tombs of these two powerful rulers.

SAN SEBASTÍAN, SPAIN (Fig. 1166)

San Sebastían, a fashionable seaside resort is capital of the province of Guipúzcoa. It is situated on the Bay of Biscay in northern Spain. Late in the nineteenth century the royal family began spending its summers there, thus setting a fashion. Today San Sebastían's chief occupation is catering to the visitors who throng there annually. Among its principal points of interest is the Casino.

LAS PALMAS (Fig. 1167)

Las Palmas, capital of Grand Canary Island and also of Las Palmas Province, is built on seven hills and extends along the shore for nearly six miles. On either side of the city are two golden beaches, *Las Alcaravaneras* and *Las Canteras*.

The famous Canary sack, a sweet white wine, is produced there. Canaries bred on the island are sold in small wicker cages in front of many of the city's shops.

The house where Christopher Columbus stopped on his first voyage to America in 1492 is still standing.

ANDORRA (Fig. 1168)

The semi-autonomous republic of Andorra on the south slope of the eastern Pyrenees is under the joint sovereignty of the Spanish bishop of Urgel and of France.

1162 **Barcelona, Spain,** mark illegible.
1163 **Seville, Spain,** marked: No 800 V. FRANCO.
1164 **Toledo, Spain,** mark rubbed.
1165 **Granada, Spain,** no mark.
1166 **San Sebastian, Spain,** marked: ARGENT FBE 800
1167 **Las Palmas,** no mark.
1168 **Andorra,** no mark.

1162   1163

1164   1165

1166

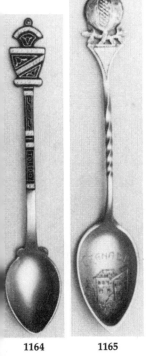

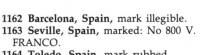

1167   1168

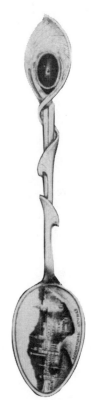

The name Andorra is said to have come from the Iberian words "and" and "ore," meaning "greatest iron deposits." The valleys of Andorra were known for their rich deposits of iron ore almost as early as 2,000 B.C.

A unique feature of Andorra is its lack of postage for internal service. All mail delivered inside the country is free. Spanish and French authorities supervise postal service. For mail sent outside the country, stamps are issued.

Andorra has always had the reputation of being a nation of smugglers; their location along the mountain passes of the Pyrenees Mountains being an ideal location for such activities.

GIBRALTAR (Fig. 1169–1171)

The name, Gibraltar-*(gebel al Tariq, rock of Tariq)*, is derived from Jebel Tarig, named after Tarig Ibn Said who captured the rock in 711 A.D. Before that, the Rock had been fought over by Romans, Greeks, Carthaginians, Goths, Visigoths, and Arabs. The latter held it until the Spaniards drove them out six centuries later. Then it was taken over by the Sultan of Fer. And so it went on, one garrison after another capturing it until it was taken by the British aided by the Dutch fleet in 1704 and has since been British.

This famous Rock towers 1,398 feet above the Mediterranean Sea. The summit can be reached by cable car or road.

Known to ancient geographers as one of the Pillars of Hercules, it was an important submarine station during World War I and a key base in the Allied Mediterranean defenses during World War II.

1169 **Gibraltar,** no mark.
1170 **Gibraltar,** no mark.
1171 **Gibraltar,** marked: 800 KFK "Crescent & crown." "Rock from Commercial MDI.E" in bowl.
1172 **Marienbad, Czechoslovakia.**
1173 **Karlsbad, Czechoslovakia,** marked: 800 "Crescent & crown".

1169   1170

1171

1172

1173

The badge of Gibraltar, shown on the spoon handles, is a castle and a key—symbolizing its strategic value as a fortress and as the "key to the Mediterranean." The Latin motto on the scroll below is *"Montis Insignia Calpe"* (The badge of Mount Calpe), a reminder that the classical name of the great Rock was Mons Calpe.

MARIENBAD (Mariánske Lázné), CZECHOSLOVAKIA (Fig. 1172)

Once-active volcanoes left the hot springs of Marienbad and Karlsbad, Czechoslovakia. Marienbad was once a famous spa and enjoyed its greatest popularity around the turn of the nineteenth century when its therapeutic resources were used by Chopin, Wagner and Goethe. It is delightfully situated at the mouth of a valley protected by mountains.

1174

KARLSBAD (Karlovy Vary), CZECHOSLOVAKIA (Fig. 1173)

Karlsbad's widely celebrated hot mineral springs were once among the most aristocratic watering places in Europe. Set in magnificent scenery, it was frequented by royalty and other celebrities.

To visitors it appears that the whole town stands on a vast cauldron of steaming water and only the safety valves of the springs prevent it from bursting.

The town's founding is ascribed to the Emperor Charles IV (1347) and it was made a free town by Joseph I.

PRAHA (Prague), CZECHOSLOVAKIA (Fig. 1174)

The KARLŮV TÝN KARLSTEIN or

1176

1174 Karlův Týn Karlstein, Prague,
   Czechoslovakia. No mark. "PRAHA" on back.
1175 Fiume, Yugoslavia.
1176 Budapest, Hungary, marked: "Crescent & crown" ND 800. City shield on handle and "Budapest Parlament" in bowl.
1177 Budapest, Hungary, marked: "Crescent & crown" 800.
1178 Warsaw, Poland, marked: (see drawing).

1175

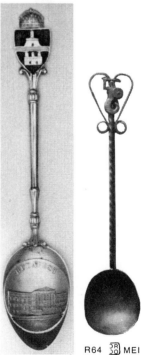

R64 ⅃Ꝺ MEI

1177   1178

237

1179

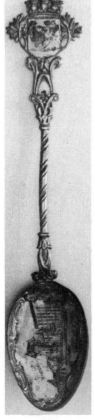

1180

castle of Charles IV on the handle of the spoon is located between Prague and Pilsen. The Emperor Charles IV built this castle to house the imperial regalia. The picturesque little town of Carlstein is situated at its feet.

FIUME, YUGOSLAVIA (Fig. 1175)

In Roman times this seaport on the Adriatic was known as *Tersatica* or *Tharsaticum*. The Romans found there an ancient community populated by Illyrian-Celtic Liburnians and Japudians (Iapydians). Tersatica was completely destroyed in 802 A.D. Nothing is known of it until 1281 when it was referred to as Flumen. The city was united with Croatia in 1776; in 1779 passed to Hungary; betwen 1809–13 it was part of Napoleon's Illyrian Province; from 1849–70 it was part of Croatia; was under Hungary until the end of World War I; seized in 1918 by Croat troops and in 1924 given to Italy; in World War II the city was occupied by German troops which were ousted in November 1944 by Yugoslavs; assigned to Yugoslavia under the terms of the peace treaty following World War II. Under Yugoslav sovereignty the city is kown as Rijeka.

BUDAPEST, HUNGARY
(Fig. 1176–1177)

Budapest consists of the united towns of Buda and Obuda on the east bank of the Danube River, and Pest, on the west. The two towns were united in 1872 yet maintain their individuality. Buda is the site of the famous Roman camp, *Aquincum*, and contains buildings of historic interest. Pest is the commercial, cultural, industrial and po-

1181

1182

1179 **Bad Flinsberg, Poland.** No mark.
1180 **Danzig, Poland.** No mark.
1181 **Breslau, Poland,** marked: "Crescent & crown" 800 S & H conjoined, DEPOSE. "Rathaus Breslau" in bowl.
1182 **Roma (Rome), Italy.** She-wolf on handle.

1183   1184

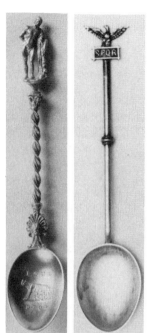

1186   1188

litical center. Parliament (in the bowl of Fig. 1176) opened in 1896.

The Budapest coat-of-arms, shown on the handles of both spoons, includes the Lion and the Griffin, guardians against harm. These supporters that flank the shield are omitted from both spoons. The upper castle represents Pest, the lower Buda. On top rests the traditional symbol of Hungary, the crown of St. Stephan, the first monarch of the Hungarian state.

WARSAW, POLAND (French, VARSOVIE, POLOGNE; German, WARSCHAU, POLEN) (Fig. 1178)

Warsaw is believed to have originated in the hamlet adjoining a thirteenth-century castle built by a duke of Masovia. After the burning of Cracow in 1595 Warsaw became the capital of Poland.

Warsaw was almost completely destroyed in World War II but has been skillfully rebuilt, even the famous Old Town.

The mermaid on the handle of the spoon is Warsaw's emblem. According to legend, she met a prince and then a fisherman named Wars and his wife, Szawa at the site of the present city and directed the prince to build a city there.

BAD FLINSBERG, POLAND (Fig. 1179)

Bad Flinsberg is in Lower Silesia, named Wroclaw province after 1945, near the Czechoslovakia border. It is a health and winter resort. The city was chartered after 1945 and was for a brief time called Wieniec Zdroj.

1183 **Roma (Rome), Italy.** She-wolf on handle.
1184 **Roma (Rome), Italy.** She-wolf on handle.
1185 **Roma (Rome), Italy.** She-wolf on handle and Pantheon in bowl. No mark.
1186 **Roma (Rome), Italy.**
1187 **SPQR** (*Senatus Populusque Romanus*, the Senate and People of Rome), ROME, ITALY. Marked: "Crescent & crown." View of Roman Forum in bowl.
1188 **SPQR, Rome, Italy.**

1185

1187

DANZIG, POLAND (Fig. 1180)

Danzig, now called Gdánsk, is Poland's largest port on the Baltic Sea. Its favorable location made the city one of the leading ports of Central Europe. Danzig was the capital of West Prussia, a province of the German Empire until the establishment of the Polish republic at the end of World War I. Under the Treaty of Versailles it was created a free city under the protection of the League of Nations. Nazi demands that the city be returned to Germany provoked hostilities with Poland and precipitated World War II. With the recovery of the city by Allied forces in 1945 it was returned to Poland which restored to it the ancient name of Gdánsk.

The famous Hoist Gate (Krantor) shown in the bowl of the spoon, was built in 1444.

BRESLAU, POLAND (Polish, WROCLAW) (Fig. 1188)

Breslau is a city in the southwestern section of Poland and is capital of the Wroclaw department. Before World War II because of its location in a mining district, it was the chief industrial chief of Lower Silesia. The city was destroyed by the Mongols in 1241 and rebuilt chiefly by German settlers. In 1526 it was acquired by the Hapsburgs and conquered by Frederick II in 1741. Again its turbulent history continued when it was besieged by Russians from February to May 1945 and fighting ended only with Germany's surrender. The city was provisionally assigned to Poland by the Potsdam Conference of 1945. That same year the Gothic city hall shown in the bowl, built between the fourteenth and sixteenth centuries, was destroyed.

ROME, ITALY (Fig. 1182–1191)

(English and French, ROME; German, ROM)

According to legend, Rome was founded by Romulus, one of twin sons of Mars, God of War, and Thea Silvia, a Vestal Virgin. The boys were cast into the Tiber River and saved and suckled by a she-wolf until a sheperd, Faustulus, found them and they were reared by his wife. In 753 B.C. Romulus, who was a born leader, laid out the walls of a city with a plow and decreed that whoever crossed the furrow outside the gates would be put to death. Remus defied his brother and was killed by Romulus who declared himself king of Rome. In order to populate his new city, Romulus invited all adventurers who cared to settle there. He acquired them wives by carrying off the Sabines, women of a neighboring tribe.

Historical research indicates that Rome, like other cities of Latium, developed from an agglomeration of several villages, the earliest nucleus of which was on the Palatine Hill, a natural stronghold on which Romuus was reputed to have built his *Roma Quadrata*.

The Pantheon (in the bowl of Fig. 1185) was built by the Emperor Agrippa in 27 B.C. to honor the divine ancestors of Caesar. It was remodeled a century and a half later by Hadrian. It became a Christian church in the seventh century. In spite of looting of its interior marble and bronze during the Renaissance, it still is the most perfectly preserved building of ancient Rome. Its great, unsupported dome is one of the architectural wonders of the world.

The remains of the Roman Forum are shown in the bowl of Fig. 1187. Here was the center of public life in Rome until the days of Empire. There were monuments, basilicas and temples, including the Tomb of Romulus, the Arch of Septimius Severus, the Temples of Saturn, Castor and Pollux, Julius Caesar, Vestus, Antonius and Faustine, the Arch of Titus and the Curia where the Senate met.

The Column of Marcus Aurelius (bowl of Fig. 1191) was erected between 176 and 193 A.D. and celebrates the victories of Marcus Aurelius over the Germans

and Sarmatians. On top is a statue of St. Paul, placed there by Sixtus V in 1589. This column was made in imitation of the Column of Trajan and stands in the Piazza Colonna while the Trajan Column stands in the remains of the Trajan Forum.

VATICAN CITY, ITALY
(Fig. 1182–1291)

The Vatican is a city within a city, an independent state within a state. It is the world headquarters of the Roman Catholic Church and is governed by the Pope and his Cardinals.

The Vatican mints its own money (Fig. 1197–1200), issues its own postage stamps, maintains a radio station that broadcasts all over the world, publishes its own newspapers and magazines, has its own postoffice, railroad station and industries.

The world's smallest state, it contains the world's largest church, St. Peter's Basilica. It can accommodate 70,000 at one time. It is built on the site of Nero's circus, over St. Peter's tomb and the spot where he was martyred. The first basilica was built at the beginning of the fourth century on command of the Emperor Constantine. It was rebuilt and enlarged several times, the present facade being completed in 1614. This facade is adorned with figures of the Redeemer, St. John the Baptist and the Apostles.

St. Peter's Square is regarded by many as the most beautiful in the world. It was designed by the Neapolitan, Gian Lorenzo Bernini, son of the Florentine sculptor, Pietro Bernini. The colonnade

1191

1189 **Rome, Italy.** Italia and Roma shields on handle.
1190 **Roma (Rome), Italy.** Italia map in bowl.
1191 **Roma (Rome), Italy.** No mark. Column of Marcus Aurelius in bowl.
1192 **Vatican City Coat of Arms.**
1193 **Vatican City Coat of Arms.** "Anno Santo Roma 1900" in bowl.

1189

1190

1192   **1193**

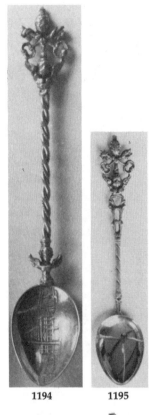

1194   1195

1196   1197

has encircling arms which seem to extend an invitation to all.

The Vatican has gathered great art treasures from all over the world and has assembled the world's most valuable collection of manuscripts and ancient books. Among the treasures of sculpture is the Apollo Belvedere (Fig. 1201), a copy of a bronze statue executed soon after the death of Alexander. The original is attributed to Leochares.

The symbol on the handles of Fig. 1192–1195 is derived from the Vatican flag and includes the Pope's triple-tiered crown above two crossed keys. One of the keys is gold, representing the heavenly kingdom. The other key is silver, for the worldly realm. The papal crown and keys are used by each Pope who adds his own coat-of-arms.

DUOMO DE MILANO, ITALY
(Fig. 1202–1205)

Milan is the bustling commercial and industrial city of northern Italy. It is also famous for its beautiful cathedral. This marvel of white marble, bristling with belfries, gables, 135 pinnacles and 3,000 white marble statues, stands at one end of a great paved esplanade. An important example of Italian-German Gothic

1198

1194 **Vatican City Coat of Arms.** "St. Peter's Cathedral" in bowl.
1195 **Vatican City Coat of Arms,** marked: 800.
1196 **Roma (Rome), Italy,** marked: "Crescent & crown" DEPOSE. "St. Peter's Cathedral" in bowl.
1197 **Vatican Coin Spoon.** "Petrus II D. G. Const. Imp. Et Perp. ? DEF. 1856" on coin. "IN HOC SI GNO VINCES" on head.
1198 **Vatican Coin Spoon.** "Pius VII Pon. M. An. III" on coin. "1802 AVXILIVM" on reverse. Perhaps a papal medal as Pius VII was Pope from 1800-23.
1199 **Vatican Coin Spoon.** "AVXIL???UE SANCTO 1775 SACROSAN BASILIC: LATERAN POSSESS PIUS VI PONT·M·A·I" on coin.
1200 **Vatican Coin Spoon.** "PIUS IX PONT MAX·AN·XII" on coin front. "20 BAIOCCHI 1858" on back.

1199   1200

ornament, it was begun in 1386 under the patronage of the first Duke of Milan. By 1402 more than fifty German architects appear to have been employed and it was these men who gave the structure its principal features, although the matchless tracery spire, which arises at crossing is attributed to the Italian architect Filippo Brunelleschi. Building continued through the fifteenth and sixteenth centuries. The facade was not completed until 1805–09, by order of Napoleon.

The Milan Cathedral is the world's largest medieval cathedral, with the exception of Seville Cathedral in Spain. It is constructed largely of white Italian marble and exhibits in its pinnacles, parapets and windows some of the most delicate, lacelike ornamentation found anywhere. Many of the more than 3,000 white marble statues may be admired in detail by going up on the roof and from there to the top of the Tiburio or central tower which is surmounted by a small but much venerated statue, the Madonnina.

1204

1201

BOZEN (BOLZANO), ITALY
(Fig. 1206)

The city of Bozen, to use the name it bore prior to World War I, when it was still part of the Austrian Tyrol, has since that time been within the Italian borders and is now known as Bolzano.

The Hotel Bristol (in the bowl) has been for many years one of the outstanding hotels of Bozen. A number of years ago the name was changed to Grifone-

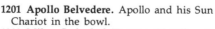

1201 **Apollo Belvedere.** Apollo and his Sun Chariot in the bowl.
1202 **Milan Cathedral (Duomo Di Milano), Italy.** No mark.
1203 **Milan Cathedral (Duomo Di Milano), Italy.** No mark.
1204 **Milan Cathedral (Duomo Di Milano), Italy,** marked: 800 "Pine tree" MF "Crescent & crown."
1205 **Milan Cathedral (Duomo Di Milano), Italy.** No mark.

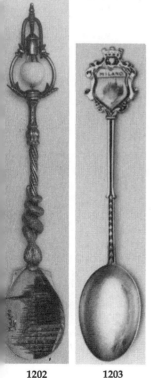

1202   1203

1205

1206

1209   1210

Bristol and more recently to Grifone-Greif. The hotel is situated in extensive gardens and enlarged in the last ten years by the addition of thirty-five new rooms.

SAN REMO, ITALY (Fig. 1207)

A large and popular resort, San Remo has for years been the luxurious center for the socially prominent and wealthy. It has earned the name "Queen of the Italian Riviera" with its scores of fine and fashionable hotels, miles of beaches, yacht basin, airport to accommodate private planes, elegant gardens and two famous promenades—the English Walk and the Empress' Walk.

GENOA, ITALY (Fig. 1208)

According to legendary traditions, Genoa was founded earlier than Rome. It was mentioned by Livy (Titus Livius, the Roman historian 59 B.C.–17 A.D.) under the name *Genua*. Genoa's situation on the Gulf of Genoa and the Bisagno River at the foot of the Appenines, has made it Italy's greatest seaport. Its medieval churches, sixteenth-century palaces and importance as a seaport justify the city's title of "La Superba" (The Proud).

Among the famous Genoese are Christopher Columbus shown in the bowl of the spoon.

RIVA, ITALY (Fig. 1209)

Riva is an attractive little health resort at the northern extremity of Lake Garda north of Verona. The old section of town, near the harbor, is especially

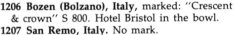

1206 **Bozen (Bolzano), Italy,** marked: "Crescent & crown" S 800. Hotel Bristol in the bowl.
1207 **San Remo, Italy.** No mark.
1208 **Genoa, Italy,** Christopher Columbus in bowl.
1209 **Riva, Italy,** marked: DEPOSE 800 A "Crescent & crown."
1210 **Bologna, Italy,** marked: 800. Asinelli and Garisenda Towers in bowl.
1211 **Leaning Tower of Pisa, Italy.** No mark.

1207   1208

1211

1212

1213

charming. Among the interesting buildings is the thirteenth century Aponale Tower. The Rocca, a castle of the twelfth century was made into a barracks by the Austrians and now contains a museum.

BOLOGNA, ITALY (Fig. 1210)

Bologna was the Etruscan city of *Felsina* and the Latin *Bononia*. The city owes its fame principally to its university, the oldest in western Europe.

Bologna's best-known landmarks are the two twelfth-century towers called Torre degli Asinelli, 320 feet high (100 m.) and four feet out of line and Torre Garisenda, left unfinished at 146 feet, seven feet ten inches out of line. They were named for two local noble families. They are called the "Towers of Nobility." Such towers were built in towns in the Middle Ages by noble families who designed them for use as keeps (places of security) during the power struggles between the Guelphs and the Ghibellines. Later, for reasons of prestige, local lords built their own towers as high as they could. The towers often lean; some think this is because of their height and weight which has caused the earth to settle; others think they were made to lean to display the architect's skill.

LEANING TOWER OF PISA, ITALY (Fig. 1211–1215)

Pisa, capital city of Pisa Province, in Tuscany, is located on a flat plain on both banks of the Arno River and about six miles from the Ligurian Sea. It was possibly founded as a Greek Colony, was a Ligurian and an Etruscan town and became a military colony under

---

1212 Leaning Tower of Pisa, Italy. No mark.
1213 Leaning Tower of Pisa, Italy. No mark.
1214 Leaning Tower of Pisa, Italy. No mark.
1215 Galileo—Leaning Tower of Pisa, Italy. No mark.
1216 Lion of St. Mark, Venice (Venezia), Italy, marked: "Crescent & crown" 800. "St. Mark's Cathedral" in bowl.

1214   1215

1216

245

1217

1218

Roman rule. It was a busy commercial port and a rival of Genoa and Venice in the eleventh century. Until the Middle Ages the sea reached the city but an accumulation of silt has made Pisa an inland town, connected now with the port of Leghorn by a ship canal. The quiet appearance of the town now gives little evidence of its past glory.

Pisa is noted now mainly for its art treasures, especially for its unique Leaning Tower which is part of the architectural ensemble in Piazza del Duomo, consisting of the cathedral, the baptistry, the cemetery and, of course, the campanile. The Leaning Tower was begun in 1174 by Bonnano Pisano and completed in the fourteenth century. It is made up of eight superimposed marble arcades, is 180 feet (54 m.) high, 52 feet (10.5 m.) in diameter, and 14 feet (3.9 m.) out of perpendicular because the foundations gave way on one side. The famous bell tower began to develop a tilt before completion as the earth sank under one side. Work on it ceased but four centuries later a new architect, adding the top four galleries, attempted to rectify the inclination. The angle of tilt increased with each passing year.

A climb of 294 steps inside the campanile is rewarded by a panoramic view of the city. As one climbs, there is the curious sensation of being drawn to the lower side and some visitors experience a feeling of vertigo even on entering the first floor.

During World War II a group of G.I. pranksters took powerful trucks and complicated blocks and tackles to Pisa

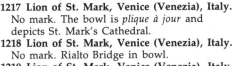

1217 **Lion of St. Mark, Venice (Venezia), Italy.**
No mark. The bowl is *plique à jour* and depicts St. Mark's Cathedral.
1218 **Lion of St. Mark, Venice (Venezia), Italy.**
No mark. Rialto Bridge in bowl.
1219 **Lion of St. Mark, Venice (Venezia), Italy,**
marked: "Crescent & crown" 800 H & S intertwined. Palazzo Ducale in bowl.
1220 **St. Mark's Cathedral, Venice, Italy,**
marked: ITALY. Handle is mosaic.

1219

1220

1221

1224

and told the people they would straighten the tower for them. They called off their joke when the unhappy Pisans thought their chief tourist attraction would be ruined.

It was from the Leaning Tower that Pisans believe that late in the sixteenth century Galileo dropped a ball and a feather to demonstrate that weight has no influence on the speed of falling bodies.

Inside the cathedral, opposite the pulpit, hangs the sixteenth-century bronze lamp which inspired Galileo's (Fig. 1215) theory of the movement of the pendulum when the sacristan set it swinging.

VENEZIA (VENICE), ITALY
(Fig. 1216–1226)

The great amphibious city of Venice basks under a golden sun in a blue lagoon as it sprawls over 117–120 (no agreement on this) islands separated by 150 canals but connected by almost 400 bridges. There is a fascination about Venice that charms people from all over the world and an atmosphere that invites *farniente* (idleness). Traffic moves about by *vaporetti* (small steamers) or *motoscafi* (motorboats) or by gondolas, the latter constituting one of the most distinctive features of the city.

The beginnings of Venice are shrouded in mystery but historians generally agree that before 452 A.D. when Attila invaded northern Italy, the islands of the Venetian lagoon had a small population of fishermen who had sunk oak piles as foundations for their rude a-

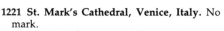

1221 **St. Mark's Cathedral, Venice, Italy.** No mark.
1222 **St. Mark's Cathedral, Venice, Italy,** marked: 800.
1223 **Lion of St. Mark, Venice, Italy,** marked: VENEZIA. St. Mark's Cathedral in bowl.
1224 **Venetian Gondola, Venice, Italy,** marked: 800.
1225 **Venetian Gondola, Venice, Italy.** No mark. St. Mark's Cathedral in bowl.

1222   1223

1225

1226   1227

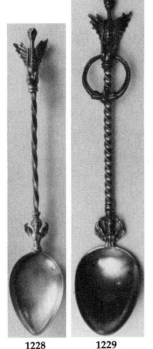

1228   1229

bodes. In 811 inhabitants of Malamocco near the Lido, fled from the Franks and guided by pigeons carrying little crosses, according to legend, they settled on the Rivo Alto, known today as the Rialto, and so founded the present city of Venice. Thirteen years later the bones of St. Mark the Evangelist were taken there from Alexandria, and he became the patron saint and protector of Venice.

The LION OF ST. MARK (Fig. 1216–1219, 1223, 1226) is a symbol of Venice and other cities once under Venetian rule. The lion holding the open book signifies that a town joined the Serenissima voluntarily. On the open pages is written, "Peace unto you, Mark, my Evangelist." The lion holding the closed book indicates that Venice conquered a city by force. In 1797 Bonaparte occupied parts of Italy and obliterated Venetian symbols everywhere. Some of the lions seen today are modern replacements of the originals.

The first patron saint of Venice was Theodore, a minor Byzantine saint inexplicably coupled with a crocodile. In 823 or 828 two Venetian merchants stole the body of St. Mark from a church in Alexandria. His familiar, or symbol was the winged lion of Ecclesiastes which became the symbol of Venice. Two tall antique columns, one carrying the earliest winged lion and the other St. Theodore standing on his crocodile, stand in present-day Venice.

1230   1231

———— •◦• ————

1226 Lion of St. Mark, Venice, Italy. No mark.
1227 Harpy-Horse Tether Ring, Florence, Italy. No mark.
1228 Harpy, Florence, Italy, marked: "Crown."
1229 Harpy-Horse Tether Ring, Florence, Italy, marked: 800.
1230 Harpy, Florence, Italy. No mark. "QUATRINI CENTO 1856 FIORINO" and the Fleur-de-lis, symbol of the City of Florence, in bowl.
1231 Lion of St. Mark, marked: 800. Fleur-de-lis and "FIRENZE" in bowl.
1232 Street Light, Florence, Italy, marked: U. PRILLI FIRENZE.

1232   1233

1234

1235

The CATHEDRAL OF ST. MARK (Fig. 1216–1217, 1221–1222, 1225) is a fine example of Byzantine and European architecture. It was begun in 829 to house the tomb of St. Mark. The basilica has a rich exterior with five great domes and superb facades with magnificent mosaic and reliefs. Interior lower walls are covered with rare, exquisite marbles and sculpture and in a golden background overhead are some of the world's most beautiful mosaics. Above the central doorway of the facade are the four bronze horses brought from Constantinople by Doge Dandolo in 1204. In 1797 Napoleon I had them taken to Paris but after the fall of the French Empire, they were returned.

The PALAZZO DUCALE (Doges' Palace) (Fig. 1219) was a symbol of Venetian power and glory as well as the residence of the doges and the seat of government. Built in the twelfth century, it replaced an early building built in 814 and destroyed in 976 during a plot against Candiano IV. Again destroyed by fire in 1105 it was rebuilt again. It has undergone reconstructions and modifications to assume its present Venetian-Gothic style. It houses treasures of art and ancient relics.

Both Palladio and Michelangelo were competitors in the competition for the construction of THE RIALTO BRIDGE but the contest was won by Antonio da Ponte for this graceful single-arch. It was built in the years between 1580 and

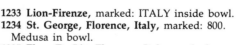

1233 **Lion-Firenze,** marked: ITALY inside bowl.
1234 **St. George, Florence, Italy,** marked: 800. Medusa in bowl.
1235 **Fleur-De-Lis, Florence, Italy,** marked: "Caduceus" MADE IN ITALY FILLI COPPINI 800. Medusa in bowl.
1236 **David, Florence, Italy,** marked: ITALY.
1237 **Christ Child, Florence, Italy,** marked: ITALY.
1238 **Christ Child, Florence, Italy.** No mark. "Florence" engraved on back.
1239 **Winged Infant with Dolphin.** "Florence" engraved in bowl.

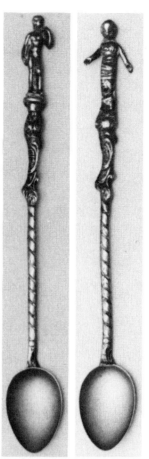

1236   1237

1238   1239

1240

1241

1591. The bridge was designed to permit an armed galley to pass under it and has therefore, a pronounced "hump." The bridge is in the center of the business district and is lined with shops.

FIRENZE (FLORENCE), ITALY
(Fig. 1227–1240)

Florence began as a small Etruscan village. In the second century B.C. it was a little marketplace at the foot of the hill on which was found the Etruscan town of *Faesulae* (now Fiesole). During the reign of Augustus (27 B.C.–14 A.D.) the Romans established a military colony there which grew in importance when the Cassian Way cut through the village. By the year 1000, Florence was a city of importance and took a stand as a Guelph community, siding with Rome's popes against the emperors attempting to u-surp their power. The city continued to rise in importance and by the fifteenth century found its ruler in the powerful Medici, Lorenzo the Magnificent. Under his leadership Florence rose to prominence in Italy's Renaissance in art. During the sixteenth century Florence became the capital of the Grand Duchy of Tuscany. In 1860 Florence and all Tuscany joined a united Italy, for which this city of art and culture served as the capital from 1865 until 1871 when, following the Franco-Prussian War, a plebiscite overwhelmingly favored the annexation of Rome and made that city the capital.

The emblem of Florence is the FLEUR-DE-LIS (Fig. 1230–1231, 1233, 1235, 1240), a medieval symbol whose origin is obscure (see also VI, Fig. 1803–1807). It is thought by some to be connected with a possible derivation of the name *Fiorenza*, or *Floria*, city built in a flowery

1242

1243

1240 **She-Wolf—SPQR (Rome) Italy.** No mark. Fleur-de-lis in bowl.
1241 **Vesuvius, Napoli (Naples), Italy.**
1242 **Napoli (Naples), Italy,** marked: 800.
1243 **Napoli (Naples), Italy,** marked: 800.

1244

meadow, from the abundance of the flowers and lilies growing in the plain of the Arno River. Others feel that it was named from Fiorinus, one of Caesar's generals. Most of the scholars hold the first to be true. Whatever the origin, the fleur-de-lis appears on almost every public building in Florence. Its most dramatic representation perhaps is on the shield held by Donatello's marzocco, the heraldic lion which stood for Florentine's power. (Marzocco is thought to be a corruption of *Martocus*, "little Mars," Roman god and first patron of the city).

It is said that the king of France in 1465 gave Piero de Medici the privilege of adding the fleur-de-lis to the *palle* or balls on his coat-of-arms as a token of Piero's friendship for France.

The huge rings which are a prominent feature on the sides of buildings in Florence were used originally in the fourteenth century to tie up horses and are called HORSE TETHER RINGS (Fig. 1227, 1229). Once useful articles, they later became just a typical decoration of the city. They are found throughout the city but are especially numerous on Tournabourni Street.

Strange, winged creatures called HARPIES (Fig. 1227–1230) are found on several spoons from Florence. The Harpies (Greek *Harpuiai*, swift robbers) were the goddesses of storms. Poets and artists vied with each other in depicting them in hideous forms—feathered wings, human arms with claws, a white breast and human legs terminating in the feet of a fowl, or the face of a young woman with the ears of a bear. According to mythology, they were the daugh-

1247

1244 Vesuvius, Naples, Italy.
1245 Vesuvius, Napoli (Naples), Italy.
1246 Napoli (Naples), Italy.
1247 Artemis (Diana)—Naples, Italy. Apollo and his Sun Chariot in the bowl.
1248 Artemis (Diana)—Naples, Italy, marked: STERLING. "A. L. K. 1904" inscribed on back of bowl.

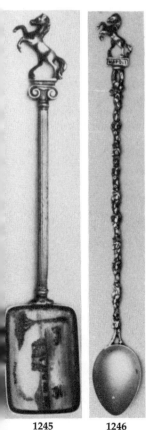

1245   1246

1248

251

ters of Thaumas and Electra and were tempest-goddesses. It was their habit to snatch and devour food from tables, or to soil the food, causing famine. When the soothsayer, Phineus, was condemned by Zeus to eternal old age and everlasting hunger, the Harpies stole the food put before him, soiling what they could not carry away. There is said to be a "Madonna of the Harpy" in Florence.

Many of the LAMPS (Fig. 1232) that light the streets of Florence have huge spikes or prongs at the top. These lamps were put on the corners of buildings, mostly by wealthy families (lesser folks used rush lights) in the fifteenth and sixteenth centuries. Most of them were made by a celebrated locksmith Niccolò Grosso, who is known by the nickname of "il Caparra," after the design of Benedetto da Majáno. The richest and most elegant models adorn the corners of Strozzi Palace.

The figure on the handle of Fig. 1234 is a statue of ST. GEORGE by Donatello, a fifteenth century Florentine artist. It is in the Bargello, or National Museum in Florence.

The bowls of two spoons (Fig. 1234–1235) are thought to be representations of MEDUSA. According to Homer, the three frightful phantoms of Hades were Stheno, Euryale and Medusa. Their hair was entwined with serpents and they turned to stone all those who looked upon them.

The figure on the handle of Fig. 1236 (also spoon III, Fig. 488) is a poor representation of the famous statue of DAVID by Michelangelo, now in the Galleria Accademia in Florence. A copy of the statue stands in Piazzale Michelangelo, the beautiful square overlooking the city.

The CHRIST CHILD (Fig. 1237–1238) is another poor representation of a famous work of art. This is the Christ Child in swaddling clothes from a terra cotta by Luca Della Robbia.

The Palazzo Vecchio Courtyard in Florence is enlivened by Verrocchio's delightful WINGED INFANT WITH A DOLPHIN (Fig. 1239).

NAPOLI (NAPLES), ITALY
(Fig. 1241–1248)

The rampant horse is the symbol of the city of Naples and has an ancient origin. It was the symbol of one of the "Seggi" (administrative divisions of the city). This particular Seggio was called "the bird's nest" and existed from the Middle Ages until the last century. The rampant horse was from its coat-of-arms and has been used more recently to symbolize the entire city.

According to legend, the siren Parthenope lent her name to a village that grew up near her tomb and for this reason Naples is called the Parthenopaean City. Historians say that Naples was founded by Greeks from Cumae, in the seventh century. The settlement was known as Parthenope, Palaepolis and Neapolis. This settlement was conquered by the Romans in the fourth century B.C. In the sixth century it was taken by the Byzantines but gradually became independent. The Norman conquest of southern Italy brought an end to this independence and became part of the Kingdom of Sicily. It was annexed to Sardinia (Italy after 1861).

VESUVIUS (Fig. 1244 bowl) is one of the few still active volcanoes of Europe. It was long thought to be extinct but proved to be extremely lively in the earthquake of 63 A.D. and the eruption of 79 A.D. which buried Herculaneum and Pompeii.

The figure of ARTEMIS (DIANA) (Fig. 1247–1248) as a Huntress, is modeled after the well-known statue in the National Museum in Naples. Diana is accompanied by a hind, the adult female of the red deer. She wears a short tunic which does not cover her knees. This is actually the Dorian chiton which has

1249

1250

been turned up and the folds retained by a girdle. Her feet are shod with the *cothurnus* or laced buskin.

POMPEII, ITALY (Fig. 1249–1253)

The city of Pompeii was founded, according to Strabo, by the Oscans about the fifth century B.C. It came under Greek influence by the sixth century but later felt Roman domination. It became a fashionable resort for the wealthy people of Rome as it was near the sea and had the glamour of Greek elegance. It was shaken in 63 A.D. by an earthquake and then buried under a shower of pumice and ashes from Vesuvius in 79 A.D. The city was preserved almost intact. Few of its inhabitants escaped. The fall of ashes reached a depth of twenty feet. A second fall of molten lava and cinders formed a crust of volcanic rock and so the city was lost to the rest of the world. Pompeii was rediscovered in the seventeenth century by the architect, Fontana, when he was building a road but no attention was given to the buried city until 1748 when valuable finds were made by a peasant digging a well. Systematic excavations began and the archaeological finds had a tremendous effect on the arts of Europe bringing about a revival of the antique and development of the so-called Pompeiian style. It was the disinterment of these Greco-Roman relics that brought about the Adam Period of architecture and decorative art (1760–94).

PALERMO, ITALY (Fig. 1254–1255)

Palermo is the capital of Sicily and lies on the head of a wide bay of the Tyrrhenian Sea at the foot of Mt. Pellegrino. One of the oldest seaports on the

---

1249 Pompeii, Italy, marked: 800.
1250 Pompeii, Italy, marked: 800 "Pine tree".
1251 Pompeii, Italy, marked: "Crescent & crown" 800 S & H intertwined.
1252 Pompeii, Italy. No mark.
1253 Pompeii, Italy. No mark.

1251

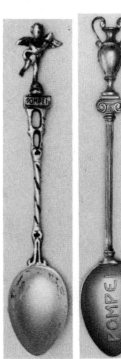

1252   1253

1254

1255

Mediterranean, it was founded by the Phoenicians between the 600s and 500s B.C. It became part of Italy in 1860.

SIENA, ITALY (Fig. 1256)

Siena, famed for its medieval appearance and numerous works of art is a living representation of the Middle Ages and the Renaissance in Italy. In the center of the city is the fan-shaped *Piazza del Campo;* eleven streets lead into it. Here stands the massive thirteenth-century *Palazzo Pubblico,* or town hall, with its graceful soaring *Torre del Mangia,* or bell tower.

SORRENTO, ITALY (Fig. 1257)

Sorrento, celebrated in music and song for the beauty of its gardens, for the magnificence of its sunsets, and the irresistible charm of its people, is on the southern shore of the Bay of Naples. It was here that Ulysses resisted the lure of the sirens only by plugging the ears of his crewmen with wax and making them lash him to the mast of his ship. Visitors by the thousands each year are unable to resist the luxuriant beauty that surrounds them in Sorrento and vow to return.

Torquato Tasso (1544–1595) on the handle of this spoon was an Italian poet of the late Renaissance period. He was born in Sorrento. His birthplace is near St. Francis' Church (San Francesco). Tasso's masterpiece, *Jerusalem Delivered,* was written in 1575. This epic was concerned with the First Crusade and delivery of the sacred tomb from the infidels.

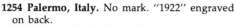

1254 **Palermo, Italy.** No mark. "1922" engraved on back.
1255 **Palermo, Italy.** No mark.
1256 **Siena, Italy.** Palazzo Pubblico (town hall) and Torre del Mangia (bell tower) in bowl.
1257 **Torquato Tasso—Sorrento, Italy,** marked: 900.

1256

1257

1258

AMALFI, ITALY (Fig. 1258)

The charming town of Amalfi is nestled in the ravine of the Valle dei Molini twenty-four miles southeast of Naples on the Gulf of Salerno. Originally a Byzantine settlement, it equalled Venice and Genoa in importance for its considerable trade with the East during the ninth century. The city enjoyed its greatest prosperity in the eleventh century when shipping in the Mediterranean was regulated by the *Ravole Amalfitane* (Amalfi Navigation Tables), the oldest maritime code in the world and now preserved in the town hall.

Amalfi has for many years been a favorite resort for writers and composers. Its breath-taking Amalfi Drive along the Gulf of Salerno, is probably the most scenic in Europe.

CAPRI, ITALY (Fig. 1259–1260)

Capri (pronounced CAPri) in the Bay of Naples is often called "the isle of dreams." The island is formed of two rocky massifs, its almost inaccessible coast is honeycombed by wave-cut grottoes, the beautiful Blue Grotto being the most famous.

In Greek mythology, Capri was the home of the Sirens whose music enchanted Ulysses and his crew.

Less romantic writers have suggested that the island, named from the genus *Capra*, to which goats belong, received the name because only goats dared the island's precipitous cliffs.

The story is told that during the reign

1260   1261

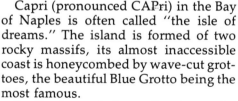

1258 **Amalfi, Italy,** marked: .900.
1259 **Capri, Italy,** marked: ALPACCA. "Isle of Capri" in bowl.
1260 **Capri, Italy,** marked: 800 and another illegible mark.
1261 **Centaur.** No mark. "Athens, Greece" engraved on back.
1262 **Centaur.** No mark. Triskelion design in bowl.
1263 **Triskelion,** marked: "Crescent & crown" 800.

1259   1262   1263

1264

1265

of Tiberius, the passengers of a ship heard a loud noise proclaiming that the god Pan was dead. In a Christian legend this incident was associated with the birth of Christ.

CENTAURS, ATHENS (ATHINAI), GREECE (Fig. 1261–1262)

Centaurs were monstrous creatures in Greek mythology depicted as men with the hindquarters of a horse. The name actually means "those who round up bulls" and possibly once referred to a primitive people who herded cows. Though most were unlettered and crude, a few were known for their wisdom. Among them was Chiron, teacher of heroes. After Chiron was wounded by an arrow, Zeus placed him among the stars as part of the constellation Sagittarius.

TRISKELION (Fig. 1262–1263)

The triskelion or triskele (Greek *triskele*, three-legged) is a three-legged device of booted and spurred human legs bent at the knee as though running, and jointed at the hip to form a radiating design. This design goes back to Athenian coins of 600 B.C. From Athens the triskelion spread to the Greek colonies in Sicily. When King Alfred III of Scotland became King of Man in 1266, his wife, sister of the Queen of Sicily, introduced it to the Isle of Man where it was used on the coinage from 1709.

AΘHNAI (ATHENS), GREECE (Fig. 1264–1265)

Athens was named for Athena, goddess of wisdom and patroness of the ancient city. The founding of the city is

1266   1267

1264 **Ancient Warrior.** AΘhnai (Athens), Greece.
1265 **Athens Owl,** marked: 800 "Crescent & crown".
1266 **Knossos—Lictor, Greece,** marked: 800.
1267 **Knossos, Greece,** marked: 800.
1268 **Acropolis, Athens, Greece,** marked: 800.
1269 **Delphi, Greece,** marked: 800.

1268   1269

1270   1271

1272

lost in tradition but it is known that Athens is the oldest surviving capital of the modern world. The earliest record is the memory of Eleusis regarding its independence (683 B.C.). Athens' great creative period was the sixty years following the Perisan Wars (499–479 B.C.).

In 1834 Athens succeeded Nauplia as capital of Greece. Severe damage was incurred by industrial establishments, harbor, docks and warehouses during World War II but the ancient monuments were spared.

The OWL OF ATHENA (Fig. 1265) was sacred to Athena, goddess of the city. It was the symbol of wisdom and appeared on Athenian coins from the sixth century onwards. Both the owl and the ancient warrior stood stand on columns of the Grecian Ionic order. The PARTHENON (Greek *parthenos*, a virgin) (Fig. 1265 in bowl, Fig. 1270) is a shrine built between 447 and 438 B.C. and dedicated to Athena. It is a temple of the Doric order and has been much copied for churches, banks and other public buildings. More than 2,000 years ago, in the Age of Pericles, the Greeks created the most beautiful temples and statues in the ancient world and placed the best of these on the ACROPOLIS (Fig. 1268) which rises abruptly about 500 feet (15.2 m.) in the heart of the city Athens.

KNOSSOS (Fig. 1266–1267)

Knossos, an ancient city on the Greek Island of Crete was the center of Cretan civilization in the Bronze Age and occupied before 3000 B.C. In 1900 Sir Arthur Evans began excavations there that revealed the immense palace of King Mi-

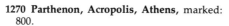

1270 **Parthenon, Acropolis, Athens,** marked: 800.
1271 **Island of Rhodes,** marked: RHODES 850.
1272 **Moscow,** marked: DEPOSE 900.
1273 **Leningrad,** no marks.
1274 **Moscow,** marks: Moscow assay office mark, AA 1891, 84.

1273

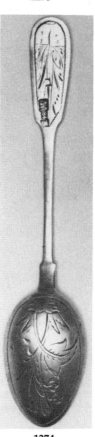

1274

nos, built about 2000 B.C. and rebuilt perhaps following an earthquake about 1700 B.C.

DELPHI (Fig. 1269)

Delphi is famous as the seat of the Oracle of Pythian Apollo, usually referred to as the Delphic Oracle. Delphi was the religious meeting place of the Greek city-states. Its influence endured for more than a thousand years from the seventh century B.C. to the fourth century A.D. Representatives were sent once a year to confer with the Oracle on important social, religious and political matters. The responses were expressed in verse in an ambiguous form which could be interpreted in more than one way, making accuracy difficult to refute afterwards.

ISLAND OF RHODES (Fig. 1271)

The Island of Rhodes, or "Island of Roses" lies between Crete and Asia Minor in the Agean Sea. It was at one time the sronghold of the Knights of the Order of St. John.

The symbol of the island is an antlered deer. The name of Rhodes is said to have been derived from the Greek word, *rhodon*, meaning "rose," a flower said to have been "so abundant in Hellenic days that its scent could be perceived by mariners at sea."

MOSCOW (Fig. 1272)

The first mention of Moscow in ancient documents was in 1147 when it was a small village on the site of the present Kremlin. The city was founded as a trading post in the twelfth century and remained small until Alexander Nevsky's son in the late thirteenth century unified the duchy of Moscovy, the nucleus from which the present U.S.S.R. has grown. The city's central location in European Russia was ideal for her growth as a trading center.

Ivan the Terrible, Moscow's ruler in 1547 took the title of Czar (Caesar) and called the city the Third Rome. Moscow became the capital until 1711 when Peter the Great moved it to St. Petersburg (now Leningrad). Following the Bolshevik Revolution in 1918, the capital was moved back to Moscow by Lenin.

LENINGRAD (Fig. 1273)

Leningrad is the second largest city of the Soviet Union and, under the name of St. Petersburg, was for two centuries the capital of czarist Russia.

The city was founded in 1703 by Peter the Great. Its name, St. Petersburg, was changed in 1914 to the Russian form, Petrograd, because of Germany's opposition to Russia in World War I. When Vladimir Ilich Lenin died in 1924, the city was renamed for him.

The equestrian statue on the spoon handle is that of Peter the Great in Peter the Great Square. The buildings in the bowl seem to be the Senate Building and St. Isaac's Cathedral.

RUSSIAN IMPERIAL CROWN
(Fig. 1275)

The Russian Imperial Crown, shown here on the back of the spoon bowl, was made in 1724 for the coronation of Catherine I. It has more than forty large diamonds. The five largest form a cross at its top, supported by an uncut ruby.

The flags shown on the spoon are the Russian merchant flag designed by Peter the Great when he was learning shipbuilding in the Netherlands. He first took the colors of the Dutch flag, a tricolor of red, white and blue and turned them upside down but when it was pointed out that this would be taken for *their* flag flown as a signal of distress and disaster, he revised his flag, putting the white at the top and the red at the bottom, with the blue in between.

RUSSIAN LACQUER (Fig. 1276)

Colored, and occasionally opaque, varnishes are applied to objects of wood or metal to produce lacquer ware such as

1275

1276

this. The name is derived from the resin *lac,* the basic ingredient of lacquer.

The scene here is of two people being driven in a *troika* at full gallop in a snowy landscape.

NICHOLAS II (Fig. 1277)

Nikolai Aleksandrovich, Nicholas II, was the last czar of Russia. He was born on May 18, 1868 in St. Petersburg. At his father's death, November 1, 1894, Nicholas ascended to the throne reluctantly. Later that same month he married Princess Alice of Hesse.

The first surge of Russian industrialization was stirring restlessly. Discontent among workers and others, and internal struggles finally led to his abdication in 1917. A new government took over and arrested the former imperial family and deported them to Tobolsk. There they spent about a year in semiseclusion and uncomfortable circumstances. Nicholas II, now plain Nicholas Romanov, was executed on July 8, 1918 by order of the Bolsheviks. An announcement was made that the remainder of the royal family was executed also but their exact fate was really never known.

RUSSIAN ENAMEL (Fig. 1279–1291)

Around 1900, spoons, kovshes, bowls, tea sets, boxes of all kinds, vases, tea caddies, goblets, dresser sets and various other articles were made of gilded silver and decorated with enamel.

The enamel was sometimes set in depressions cut into the metal with raised

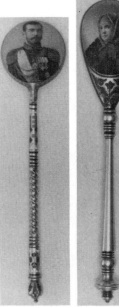

1277   1278

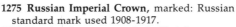

1275 **Russian Imperial Crown,** marked: Russian standard mark used 1908-1917.
1276 **Russian Lacquer,** marked: 78 A.L.
1277 **Nicholas II,** marked: Moscow assay mark, 84.
1278 **Russian Peasant Woman,** Moscow assay mark, 88.
1279 **Russian Enamel,** marked: Moscow assay mark, 88 AK.

1279

1283

1280

metal lines remaining between the depressions forming the outline of the design. The enamel was put in these depressions, fused and then polished. This is *champlevé* enamel.

On some pieces, delicate, ribbon-like strips, or cloisons, of metal were laid on the surface and fixed in the required designs. Enamel was placed in these, fused and then polished. This is *cloissonné* enamel.

Painted enamel work was also used, in which case, the enamel was laid over the entire surface on both sides and fused.

These techniques were often combined with *plique à jour*, a technique in which translucent enamel is enclosed within metal frames without a backing, giving a jewel-like or stained glass window effect.

Designs were sometimes geometric but more often were arabesques or scrolling foliage and flowers, either naturalistic or stylized. The multi-colored enamels were tones of blue, green, yellow, red, pink, purple and white and were opaque or translucent, according to the effect desired. Shaded enamels produced some of the most beautiful floral designs but are less often encountered.

NIELLO (Fig. 1292–1296, 1298)

Russian niello work, unlike the black of Thailand, is a darkish gray suggesting polished lead and is most often inlaid in silver.

Lines are cut into the metal with en-

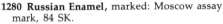

1280 **Russian Enamel,** marked: Moscow assay mark, 84 SK.
1281 **Russian Enamel,** marked: Moscow assay mark, 84.
1282 **Russian Enamel,** marked: Moscow assay mark GK.
1283 **Russian Enamel,** marked: Moscow assay mark 84.
1284 **Russian Shaded Enamel,** marked: Moscow assay mark 84 BA.

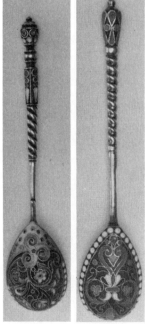

1281   1282

1284

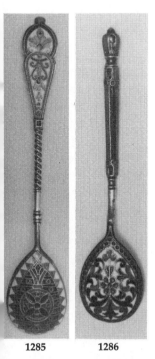

graver's tools. In cutting away the silver to take the niello, the sides of the channels are slightly undercut so that the niello composition stays in position like an inverted wedge. After cutting, the surface is covered with a granulated black composition of copper, silver, lead and sulphur with a little borax to act as a flux. The composition may vary but is usually lead two parts, silver one and copper one. The articles are placed in a furnace until the composition becomes liquid and runs into the lines of the design. After cooling, the surface of the metal is scraped and burnished, leaving the design in dark gray.

Niello work was done as early as the Roman Empire and has survived as one of the outstanding arts of the Middle and Far East. In Japan, bright-cut work sometimes highlights the niello. The art was revived in Italy in the fifteenth century and was also adopted by other European craftsmen.

Of all the European craftsmen who worked in niello, the Russians were perhaps the most skilled. The technique had been mastered there in the twelfth century but used only occasionally until much later. In the seventeenth century niello was fashionable, both on Mount Athos and in Persia, and as a result of the Czar Alexis' preference for Near Eastern metalwork, it also became popular in Moscow, where it remained in favor until the Revolution of 1917.

1285 1286

1289

1285 **Russian Enamel and Plique À Jour,**
    marked: Moscow assay mark 88 AK 1891.
1286 **Russian Enamel,** marked: Moscow assay
    mark 88 AS.
1287 **Russian Enamel,** marked: Moscow assay
    mark 84 AP 1889.
1288 **Russian Enamel,** marked: "Fleur-de-lis"
    88OS.
1289 **Russian Enamel,** marked: Moscow assay
    mark P.B. AA84 1898.
1290 **Russian Enamel,** marked: Moscow assay
    mark 84.
1291 **Russian Shaded Enamel,** marked: Moscow
    assay mark, 84.

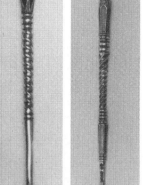

1287   1288

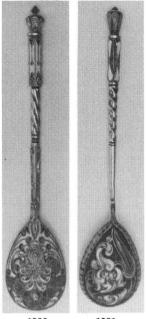

1290   1291

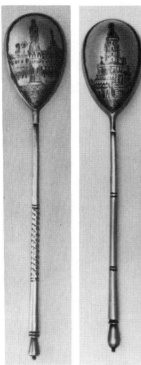

RUSSIAN NIELLO (Fig. 1292)

The building represented on this spoon is probably the Arsenal Tower which guards one corner of the Kremlin wall. It stands between the Historical Museum, on the left, and Alexandrovsky Park, to the right.

RUSSIAN NIELLO (Fig. 1295)

The building on this spoon may be Uspensky Cathedral, coronation church of the Czars.

RUSSIAN SILVER STANDARDS

Russian silver standards expressed as 84, 88 and 91, in each case means the number of zolotniks of pure silver in 96 zolotniks of silver alloy. In 1000 parts alloy in each case are 875, 916.6 and 947.9 parts of pure silver as compared with the English standard of .925. Therefore, the Russian 88 standard is below the English standard and the 91 is above it.

TURKISH CRESCENT AND STAR
(Fig. 1316–1323)

Several legends attempt to explain the origin of the crescent and star found on most of the many flags used in Turkey's long history and on many other Turkish articles. From early times the crescent was the symbol of Istanbul. A beneficent crescent moon revealed the attempts of Philip of Macedon, father of Alexander the Great, to undermine the city walls in 339 B.C., according to one account. Another tells that when Mohammed II conquered the city in

1292

1293

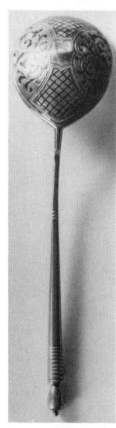

1294

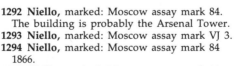

1292 **Niello,** marked: Moscow assay mark 84. The building is probably the Arsenal Tower.
1293 **Niello,** marked: Moscow assay mark VJ 3.
1294 **Niello,** marked: Moscow assay mark 84 1866.
1295 **Niello,** marked: Moscow assay mark 84 1895. The building is probably Uspensky Cathedral.
1296 **Niello,** marked: 1-CY "Hammer & sickle" 875.
1297 **Russia,** marked: 84 1888.

1295

1296

1297

1453, he added the city's crescent to his plain red flag. It was symbolic of good will to the conquered people.

The star (five-pointed in recent years), presents equal difficulties. One explanation is that it is Al Tarek, the morning star, mentioned in chapter eighty-six of the Koran. Another suggests that Richard the Lion-Hearted had a star and crescent badge in the Crusades and that the Turks added the star to their own crescent, possibly not realizing that it was the Star of Bethlehem. Still another explanation is that is represents Thrace, a part of Turkey which lies in Europe. The star was added to the Turkish flag about 1798.

DANCING DERVISH (Fig. 1324)

There are some hundred dervish orders in the East which practice some art which results in a state of trance or ecstasy said to release the soul from the body.

The Dancing Dervishes originated in Konya. The founder was Jelal-ed-din Mevlana (1207-1273), mystical poet of Persia. Passionately fond of music, he devised a devotional dance to the sound of flutes.

The ceremony is conducted in a dignified and solemn manner. Following prayers, a group of nine, eleven or thirteen dervishes is accompanied by eight musicians, playing old-fashioned instruments such as a tabor, dulcimer, and a one-stringed violin. The dancers wear long, high-waisted, pleated gowns

1298   1299

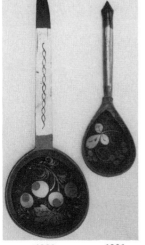
1300   1301

1302   1303

1304   1305

1298 **Niello,** marked: 84.
1299 **Russia,** marked: 84 1888.
1300 **Lacquer,** no mark. Carved wood base; lacquered and painted.
1301 **Lacquer,** no mark. Carved wood base; lacquered and painted.
1302 **Birchroot(?) and Enamel,** marked: 84 AP.
1303 **Niello,** marked: MOSCOW 1839.
1304 **Monkey,** marked: 3 "Hammer & sickle" 916 1.
1305 **Gilded Silver and Enamel,** marked: S .875.

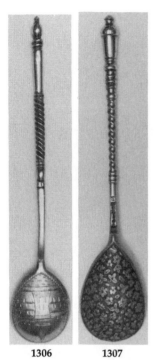

1306　　　1307

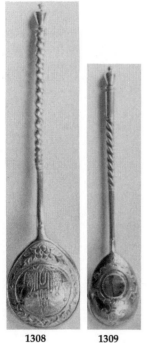

1308　　　1309

which fall to the ground and have tall, brown felt cones upon their heads. As each dancer begins to turn he stretches his right arm straight up with the palm held upwards to the roof, while his left arm is held stiffly down, the palm turned towards the earth. The head is inclined slightly to the right shoulder. The dance is symbolic of the revolution of the spheres, and the hands represent the reception of a blessing from above and its dispensation to the earth below.

TURKISH BRASS SPOONS
(Fig. 1325–1327)

These brass spoons reputedly are for eating yogurt.

Yogurt (yoghurt, also yoghourt) derives its name from the Turkish word *yogurt*. It is a fermented, slightly acid semifluid food made of skimmed cow's milk and milk solids to which cultures of two (*Lactobacillus acidophilus* and *Streptococcus thermophilus*) have been added. It is thought by many to possess extraordinary nutritive properties. In Turkey it is served as a sauce on cold foods, as a dessert, sweetened with honey or sugar, with garlic on fried zucchini, carrots, eggplant and other vegetables, in a borscht-type soup and anywhere sour cream might otherwise be used.

SIGNATURE OF SULEIMAN I
(Fig. 1328–1331)

The signature (Thugra) of Suleiman I the Magnificent, Sultan of Turkey, 1520–1566, is an example of the art of calligraphy or beautiful writing culti-

1306 **Russia,** marked: Moscow assay mark 1889 84.
1307 **Niello,** marked: Moscow assay mark 1891 84.
1308 **Russia,** no marks.
1309 **Russia,** marked: MAA 884.
1310 **Russia,** marks illegible.
1311 **Russia,** marked: BA(?) 84 1883.
1312 **Russian Enamel,** marked: AK 88.
1313 **Niello,** marked: A 84 1881.

1310　　　1311

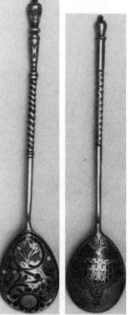

1312　　　1313

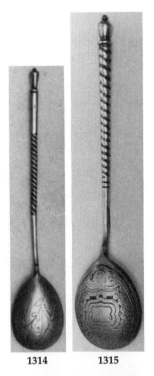

vated by the Mohammedans. According to tradition, this device originated in the fourteenth century when Sultan Murad, being unable to write his name on a treaty, dipped his open hand in ink and pressed it on the document. In the spaces of the figure his hand made, the scribes wrote his name, the title Khan, and the epithet "Ever Victorious." This signature is frequently found as a decorative device and is used on spoons and other silver where it is a quality mark.

1314 **Russia,** marked: MB 84.
1315 **Niello,** marked: AD 84 Moscow city mark.
1316-1319 **Turkish Crescent and Star,** no marks.
1320-1321 **Turkish Crescent and Star,** no marks.

1314   1315

1321

1316   1317   1318   1319   1320

265

1322

1330

1331

LEBANON (Fig. 1332–1333)

These spoons are handcrafted Djezzineware, practiced only in the ancient mountain village of Djezzine in Biblical Lebanon by native craftsmen using the same techniques as those used centuries ago and passed down from father to son.

Top quality stainless steel is used in knife blades and high quality white steel is used on all other pieces. Handles are

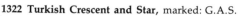

1322 Turkish Crescent and Star, marked: G.A.S.
1323 Turkish Crescent and Star, no marks.
1324 Dancing Dervish, no marks. Lacquer.
1325 Turkish Spoon, marked: TURKEY. Brass.
1326 Turkish Spoon, no marks. Brass.
1327 Turkish Spoon, marked: MADE IN TURKEY.
1328-1331 Signature of Suleiman I, Figure 1335 has Signature of Suleiman I used as a quality mark. The others are unmarked.

1323

1324

1325

1326

1327

1328

1329

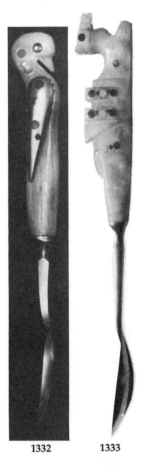

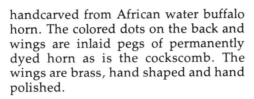

handcarved from African water buffalo horn. The colored dots on the back and wings are inlaid pegs of permanently dyed horn as is the cockscomb. The wings are brass, hand shaped and hand polished.

HAND OF FATIMA (1334–1336)

Fatima Bint Mohammed the Prophet, daughter of the prophet Mohammed by Khadija, his first wife, was born in Mecca. Her memory has been kept alive through the tragic history of her family and descendants, many of whom were massacred for political reasons in 680 at Karbala, Iraq. Her symbol, the "Hand of Fatima," is displayed frequently in religious processions.

BAGHDAD, IRAQ (Fig. 1337)

Baghdad, capital of Iraq, was founded in 752 by the Caliph Almanzor. It became the chief city of the Moslem world and a great center of culture and learning. This tradition has stimulated its development as the education center of modern Iraq.

SAUDI ARABIA COIN SPOONS (Fig. 1338–1339)

The coins used for the bowls of these spoons are silver, first minted in 1933, but later discontinued. Saudi Arabia has no silver currency at present. The coins are quarter rizals.

SYRIA (Fig. 1340)

Until the end of World War I the term "Syria" was applied rather loosely to the entire area later constituting the Repub-

1336   1337

1332-1333 **Lebanon,** no marks. Handles are made of African water buffalo horn; the wings on the bird are brass.
1334 **Hand of Fatima,** no marks.
1335 **Hand of Fatima,** marked: "Head of an African man."
1336 **Hand of Fatima,** marked: 800 5.
1337 **Bagdad, Iraq.**
1338-1339 **Saudi Arabia Coin Spoons,** no marks. The coins are quarter rizals.

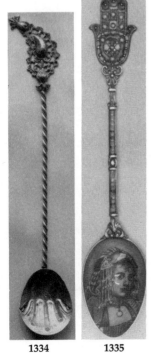

1332   1333

1334   1335

1338   1339

267

1340   1341

1343   1344

lic of Syria, Israel, the Hashemite King-dom of the Jordan and the Republic of Lebanon. In Roman and Ottoman days it extended from the Mediterranean to the Euphrates and from the Taurus Mountains to Sinai. Modern Syria is restricted to the U.A.R. region of the same name.

ARABIC WELCOME (Fig. 1341)

The inscription on the handle of the spoon means, "Have a good meal" and in the bowl is the word, "Welcome."

MOSQUE D'OMAR, JERUSALEM (Fig. 1342–1343)

The Mosque of Omar or *Kubbet es Lakhara* (The Dome of the Rock) is believed to have been erected by Omar, the second of the Moslem caliphs. The mosque is built over the rock which the Jews regard as the place upon which Abraham prepared to sacrifice his son Isaac, and which the Moslems believe was the scene of Mohammed's ascent to heaven.

MOSQUE-EL-AKSA, (Fig. 1395)

Just south of the Dome of the Rock, in Jerusalem, is the Mosque-el-Aksa (Aqsa or Aksah), one of the important points of historical and religious interests of the city. This, of course, is the Romanesque, churchlike structure built over the Stables of Solomon, to which God conveyed Mohammed from Mecca in one night.

JERUSALEM or CRUSADER'S CROSS (Fig. 1346–1349)

The Jerusalem or Crusader's Cross is usually found with four small crosses between the arms, all five crosses sym-

1342

1345

1340 **Syria,** marked: DAMAO.
1341 **Arabic Welcome,** no marks. "WELCOME" in the bowl; "HAVE A GOOD MEAL" on the handle.
1342 **Mosque D'Omar, Jerusalem,** marked: 800.
1343 **Mosque D'Omar, Jerusalem,** marked: GK 800.
1344 **Jerusalem,** no marks. Handmade c. 1942.
1345 **Mosque-El-Aksa,** no marks.

1346

1347

bolizing the five wounds of Jesus Christ. It was worn by the first ruler of Jerusalem, Godfrey de Bouillon, after the city's liberation from the Moslems.

The Holy Sepulchre, shown in the bowl of Fig. 1347, is the tomb in which Jesus' body was laid by the owner of the tomb, Joseph of Arimathea and by Nicodemus. The present buildings of the church of the Holy Sepulchre date from the capture of Jerusalem in 1099 by the Crusaders.

ISRAEL (1350–1356)

The Habima Theater in Tel-Aviv, featured on Fig. 1350, is the best-known of Israel's repertory theaters.

The Menorah, on Fig. 1351, is a seven-branched candelabrum which stands for perfection and is also a symbol for Old Testament worship. It has been a holy symbol of Judaism since the time of Moses and appears on the Israeli state seal and the president's flag.

Spoon Fig. 1352 commemorates Eilat, a southern city located on the Red Sea.

The Tower of David, featured on Fig. 1353 is actually a fourteenth-century group of towers erected on a massive structure at the bottom of a moat and forming a fine example of the ancient wall towers of Jerusalem.

JERUSALEM (Fig. 1355)

Through the ages this city has meant more to more people than any other human dwelling place. Stone Age men lived there and worshipped nature. Neolithic men lived there and battled each other for its possession and the struggle still continues. Jews, Christians and Moslems all call it the Holy City.

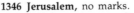

1346 **Jerusalem,** no marks.
1347-1348 **Jerusalem,** marked: 800.
1349 **Jerusalem,** no marks.
1350 **Habima Theater, Tel-Aviv,** no marks.
1351 **Israeli Coat of Arms,** no marks.

1348   1349

1350   1351

269

1356

NAZARETH (Fig. 1356)

The town of Nazareth in Israel is known especially as having been the home of Christ. It is not mentioned in the Old Testament but reference is made to it several times in the New Testament.

Among its points of interest are the Fountain of the Virgin, the church of the Orthodox Greeks, the workshop of St. Joseph and the *Mensa Christi* (table of Christ) where it is said that it is the rock upon which Christ took repast with his disciples.

MOROCCO (Fig. 1357–1358)

Morocco's name in French is *Maroc;* in Spanish, *Marruecos;* and in Arabic it is *El Maghreb El Aqsa,* which means literally "the Far West." This is a reminder that Morocco was the farthest westward extension of the Carthaginian Empire, under whose rule it first appeared in history.

The coin comprising the bowl of Fig. 1357 was coined during the reign of Mulai Abdul Aziz, 1894 to 1908.

OBELISK OF USERTSEN
(Fig. 1359–1360)

Usertsen I (Sen-usrit, also called Sesonchôsis) was the son of Amenemhat I, the founder of the XIIth Dynasty, which lasted about 200 years from about 2300 B.C. to 2100 B.C.

Amenemhat I and Usertsen I were both great builders of temples as was Usertsen's Son, Amenemhat II. One of the great temples founded by Amenemhat I was the temple dedicated to the Sun-god of Heliopolis. To the Hebrews, the city was known as "On"

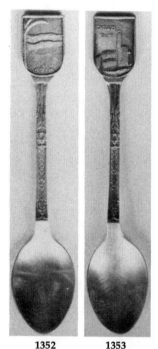

1352   1353

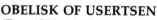

1352 **Eliat, Israel,** no marks.
1353 **Tower of David,** no marks.
1354 **Map of Israel,** no marks.
1355 **Jerusalem,** no marks.
1356 **Nazareth,** no marks.
1357 **Morocco Coin Spoon,** no marks. Coin from the reign of Mulai Abdul Aziz, 1894 to 1908.

1354   1355

1357

1358

1359   **1360**

or "Aven" and "Bêth Shemesh." After the erection of this magnificent temple, Usertsen set up two large granite obelisks, one on each side of the first gateway of the House of the Sun at Anu. Copper caps, in the shape of funnels, covered the tops of each to a depth of four feet six inches (1.3 m.) One of these obelisks fell, or was deliberately thrown down about 1160 A.D. The other, still standing, is a monolith of red granite about sixty-six feet (20 m.) high. Mud covers the pedestal, said to be of sandstone, and a portion of the obelisk, so that the exact height cannot be given. Down each of the four sides there is a single line of hieroglyphic text, all four reading the same.

The bowl of Fig. 1359 has the mosque of Mohammed Ali, first of the Kings of Egypt. This is the largest and most beautiful of all the mosques. Made of alabaster it is on the highest spot in Cairo. Mohammed Ali is buried there.

The Sphinx (Fig. 1360) and the Great Pyramids of Khufu and Khafre in Giza, and the considerably smaller one of their successor, Menkure, are the most famous group of such monuments. The Sphinx is hewn out of the living rock in the shape of a lion with the head of a king. It is thought to have originally been an ordinary rock shaped somewhat like a lion and that workmen, while building the tomb of Khafra noted the similarity and carved the likeness of their king.

The Great Pyramid ascribed to the Pharaoh Khufu, the second Pharaoh of the IVth Dynasty, is thought to have

---

1358 **Morocco Coin Spoon,** no marks.
1359 **Obelisk of Usertsen I at Heliopolis.**
   Mosque of Mohammed Ali in the bowl.
1360 **Obelisk of Usertsen I at Heliopolis.** The Great Pyramid of Khufu and the Sphinx are in the bowl. Engraved "Cairo Feb. 26th '96" on the back. Marked: 800.
1360a Translation of the hieroglyphs on the stem of the spoon.
1361 **Horus,** marked: 800.

The Horus

Ankh-mestu

King of the South and North

Kheperkara

Lord of the Vulture Crown and
   Lord of the Uraeus Crown
Ankh-mestu

Son of Rā

Usertsen (I)

Of the Souls of

Anu (Heliopolis)

beloved,

living forever.

The Golden Horus
The benevolent god

Kheperkara

[At the] time of [celebrating]
the Set Festival

he made [these obelisks that]

life might be given [to him]

for ever.

1360a

1361

1362

1363

been built between 4500 and 5000 years ago. It is the largest of the seventy pyramids of Egypt. Today, even with some of the top removed it stands about forty-five stories high. It is estimated to be composed of two and a half million blocks, each weighing two and a half to twelve tons.

HORUS (Fig. 1361)

Horus, posthumous son of Isis and Osiris, was worshipped throughout Egypt. He is represented on the spoon by the falcon head and the two eyes, the sun and the moon, with which he ruled as god of the sky.

Horus is the Latin form of the Greek name *Horos* and the Egyptian *Hor*. He was a solar god constantly identified with Apollo. Under the name Hor, which in Egyptian sounds like a word meaning "sky," Egyptians referred to the falcon overhead. They thought of the sky as a divine falcon whose two eyes were the sun and the moon.

Highly stylized and typically Egyptian versions of the Lotus appear in both the upper and lower sections of the spoon bowl. The Lotus was regarded by the Egyptians as a symbol of fertility and renewal of life. It was widely used in their decorative work. Even in ancient times, spoons and other utensils were decorated with Lotus flowers. Sacred to Osiris and Isis, the Lotus was symbolic of the recurring fertilization of the land by the River Nile, and, therefore, in a higher sense, of immortality.

The eyes in the center of the bowl are in the form of the Wedjat, "sound eye," of the god Horus. It is composed of the markings of a falcon's head added to the usual ancient Egyptian representation of a human eye. According to an ancient

1364

1365   1365 a

1362 **Sphinx,** marked: 800.
1363-1364 **Crux Ansata,** both marked: 800.
1365-1365a **Mummy Spoon,** marked 800. Figure 1365a shows the mummy case open and the gold figure inside.

1366

1367

1368

1369

myth, the eye of Horus, torn to pieces by the wicked god Sēth (Set), was miraculously restored, or "made sound" by the ibis god Thōt and was adopted as a symbol of "soundness" or "completion." The Wedjat was used extensively as an amulet.

ANKH OR CRUX ANSATA
(Fig. 1363–1364)

The symbol of the Crux Ansata was used in ancient Egypt as an attribute or sacred emblem symbolizing life. It was also called *ansate cross, handled cross* and *key of life*. It was the sacred symbol of Isis. It is carved in countless numbers on the monuments of Egypt, first as a word sign and later as a syllable. It was a popular shape for the design of a spoon even in ancient times. Modified and inverted, the Crux Ansata appeared as the Orb and Cross, symbol of royalty since the days of the Roman Empire and since the time of Constantine as the emblem of the Saviour.

EGYPTIAN MUMMY SPOONS
(Fig. 1365–1374)

The word "mummy" is believed to have been derived from an Arabic word meaning bitumen, or "bitumenized things." Ancient Egyptians had perfected the art of preserving bodies by bitumen, spices, gums, and natron (native sodium carbonate, $Na_2CO_3 \cdot 10 H_2O$). It is not definitely known whether the art came from Asiatic countries or originated in Egypt. It is known, however, that the second king of the first Dynasty, as early as 3366 B.C. wrote a book on anatomy, for the purpose of embalming, and that he experimented with drugs to dissolve the internal organs.

1366 **Mummy Spoon,** no marks.
1367 **Mummy Spoon,** marked: 800.
1368 **Mummy Spoon,** marked: 800 "Crescent & crown."
1369 **Mummy Spoon,** marked: (See drawing)

Preservation of the body was an essential part of the ancient Egyptian's religious concepts. They believed in the immortality and the duality of man. A vital life force was said to enter a man's body at birth and remain with him as his double. This "inner man" was called *Ka* and was roughly equivalent to what we term *conscience*. Man also possessed a Soul which would live in the hereafter much as it lived on earth. Sometime in the future Ka would return to take up residence in the body it had left behind so "Eternal Houses" or pyramids, were erected to preserve the body and store the treasures for use in the afterworld and again in this world when Ka should return.

MOSES (Fig. 1375–1376)

"Now there arose up a new king over Egypt . . . . And the king of Egypt spake to the Hebrew midwives . . . if it be a son, then ye shall kill him . . . . But the midwives feared God, and did not as the king of Egypt commanded them, but saved the men children alive . . . . And there went a man of the house of Levi, and took to wife a daughter of Levi. And the woman conceived, and bare a son: and when she saw him that he was a goodly child she hid him three months. And when she could not longer hide him, she took for him an ark of bulrushes, and daubed it with slime and with pitch, and put the child therein; and she laid it in the flags by the river's bank. And his sister stood afar off, to wit what would be done to him. And the daughter of Pharaoh came down to wash herself at the river; and her maidens

1370

1371

1373

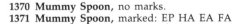

1370 **Mummy Spoon,** no marks.
1371 **Mummy Spoon,** marked: EP HA EA FA
A
(Atkins Brothers, Truro, Sheffield, England)
Silverplate.
1372 **Mummy Spoon,** marked: 800.
1373 **Mummy Spoon,** no marks.
1374-1374a **Mummy Spoon,** no marks. Figure
1374a shows the mummy case open.

1372

1374   1374 a

1375   1375 a

1376

walked along by the river's side; and when she saw the ark among the flags, she sent her maid to fetch it. And when she had opened it, she saw the child . . . . And she had compassion on him . . . And the child grew . . . . And she called his name Moses: and she said, Because I drew him out of the water . . . ." In this manner, is the birth of Moses recorded in Exodus II: 1-2.

The name "Moses" in Hebrew is *Mosheh* and is related etymologically to the Hebrew verb *mashah* meaning to draw. More recent thought tends to consider it as an adaptation of the Egyptian verb *msj,* to bring forth, which appears in the names Thutmose and Rameses.

Nineteenth-century historians tended to doubt the validity of the Biblical traditions concerning Moses. They merely affirmed his historical existence. More recent studies in the twentieth century however, give greater credence to the oral traditions connected with him.

It should be noted, however, that the basket story is a very old Semitic folk tale. Handed down through the centuries as oral tradition, it is also found on Neo-Babylonian tablets of the first millennium B.C. Cuneiform texts tell the story of King Sargon, founder of the Semitic dynasty of Akkad in 2360 B.C. as follows: "I am Sargon, the powerful king, the king of Akkad. My mother was a temple prostitute; I did not know any father. My mother conceived me and bore me in secret. She put me in a little box made of reeds, sealing its lid with pitch. She put me in the river . . . . The river carried me away and brought me to Akki the waterman. Akki the waterman adopted me and brought me up as his son . . . ."

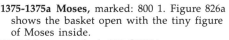

1375-1375a **Moses,** marked: 800 1. Figure 826a shows the basket open with the tiny figure of Moses inside.
1376 **Moses,** marked: 800 OTWA.
1377 **Nairobi,** no mark.
1378 **Lion of Judah,** no mark.
1379-1380 **Zanzibar Clove,** no marks on either.

1377

1378   1379

NAIROBI, KENYA (Fig. 1377)

Nairobi is the capital of Kenya Colony, British East Africa. The site of the city was chosen in 1899 as headquarters of the Uganda Railway which was then under construction. White settlement of the country's highlands early in the twentieth century brought about considerable commercial expansion in the area so that by 1907 Nairobi had replaced Mombasa as the capital. It is a favorite point of departure for many big-game safaris.

LION OF JUDAH, ETHIOPIA (Fig. 1378)

The figure on the spoon is the charge from the Ethiopian flag, and depicts the "Lion of Judah," one of the titles of the emperor of Ethiopia.

The last emperor, and bearer of the title was Haile Selassie First, who on November 2, 1930 was raised to occupy that position. He was the second son of Ras Makonnen and a direct descendant of the female side of King Haile Mailikot, founder of the Shoan Dynasty, which claims to belong to the Solomid family. (The Solomid family began with King Solomon and the Queen of Sheba.)

ZANZIBAR CLOVE, (Fig. 1379–1380)

The clove is one of the most important crops of Zanzibar. When Zanzibar became independent in 1963 she adopted a flag with a green disk on which were displayed two golden cloves. This flag was used until January 12, 1964 when Zanzibar merged with Tanganyika to become the Republic of Tanzania.

CICADE DA BEIRA, MOZAMBIQUE (Fig. 1381)

The city of Beira was founded in 1891 as the headquarters of the Companhia

1380

1381

1382

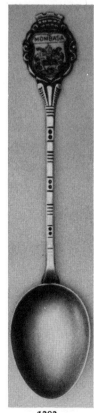

1383

1381 **Cidade Da Beira,** marked: INOX.
1382 **Mombasa,** no marks.
1383 **Mombasa,** marked: EPNS.

1384

1385

de Moçambique, the last of the chartered companies that operated in the Mozambique (Portuguese East Africa). With the surrender of all sovereign rights on July 19, 1942 all of Mozambique came under a single colonial administration. The present capital is Lourenço Marques.

MOMBASA, KENYA (Fig. 1382–1383)

Mombasa, the principal seaport of Kenya Colony, East Africa, is situated on an island of the same name. The native (Kiswahili) name for Mombasa is *Kisiwa Mvita*, Isle of War, a name often earned during its long and turbulent history.

In 1498 when Vasco de Gama visited Mombasa, Arabs were in possession. It was held by the Portuguese in the sixteenth and early seventeenth centuries. From 1824 to 1826 the town was under British protection and afterwards it was part of the sultanate of Zanzibar. In 1895 when the territories of the chartered company, the Imperial British East Africa Company, were taken over by the British government, Mombasa was made the capital of the East Africa Protectorate. Nairobi became the capital in 1907.

SOUTH AFRICA COAT-OF-ARMS (Fig. 1384–1385)

South Africa's coat-of-arms was granted in 1910. The four quarters of the shield represent the four provinces of the state: 1. The Cape of Good Hope is represented by a female figure holding an anchor; 2. Natal, by two wildebeeste; 3. Orange Free State by an orange tree; 4. Transvaal by a covered wagon. The crest is a red lion holding a bundle of rods and symbolizes the motto of the country and

1386

1387

1384 **South Africa Coat-Of-Arms**, marked: CANDIDA STER SILV.
1385 **South Africa Coat-Of-Arms**, marked: WJD Birmingham 1910-11.
1386 **Southern Rhodesia**, marked: EPNS.
1387 **Johannesburg**, no marks.

1388

1389

1390

had its origin in the coat-of-arms of the old Dutch States General. The motto is: *Ex Unitate Vires* (From unity comes strength). The supporters are a springbok and an oryx. There are Protea flowers, the national flower of South Africa, in the compartment.

SOUTHERN RHODESIA BADGE (Fig. 1386)

The former badge of Southern Rhodesia featured a golden pick symbolizing the mining industry and passant red lions between two thistles and was taken from the arms of the Rhodes family. This badge was granted by Royal Warrant in 1924.

On November 11, 1965 Southern Rhodesia became Rhodesia and in 1968 adopted a new flag with vertical stripes of green, white and green with the national arms in the center. The shield displays the same emblem and the supporters are sable antelopes.

JOHANNESBURG (Fig. 1387)

Johannesburg, in the Republic of South Africa, is the second largest city on the African continent. The city was founded, September 1886 soon after the discovery of the "Main Reef" of the Witwatersrand (Dutch, white water or ridge) of The Rand, the greatest gold-producing area in the world. Gold had been found in the area in 1853 by P. J. Marais but prospecting was forbidden for a time. In 1885 the brothers F. and H. Struben found the main Reef on the Langlaagte farm and in September of the following year Johannesburg was declared a public diggings. Johannesburg

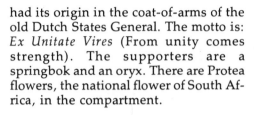

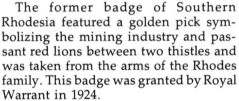

1391   1392

1393

1388 **Salisbury,** no marks.
1389 **Rhodesia,** no marks.
1390 **Johannesburg,** marked: S. AFRICA CANNA STERLING SILVER.
1391 **Zambia,** marked: SIMBA.
1392 **Port Elizabeth,** no marks.
1393 **Cape Town,** marked: STER SIL. CANDIDA.

1394

1395

was named for Johannes Rissik, surveyor-general then of Transvaal.

SALISBURY, RHODESIA (Fig. 1388)

Salisbury is the capital of Rhodesia, southeast Africa. The city grew up around Fort Salisbury founded there in 1890. It is an important market center for the surrounding area.

ZAMBIA (NORTHERN RHODESIA) (Fig. 1391)

Zambia was the name chosen for Northern Rhodesia on attainment of independence October 23, 1964.

PORT ELIZABETH, SOUTH AFRICA (Fig. 1392)

Port Elizabeth grew up on the site of Fort Frederick (1799) on a high plateau overlooking Algoa Bay in Cape province of the Republic of South Africa. Three thousand immigrants from Britain landed there in 1820 and the town was laid out on the orders of Sir Rufane Shaw Donkin, then acting governor, who named it in honor of his deceased wife.

CAPE TOWN, SOUTH AFRICA (Fig. 1393–1396)

Cape Town was established as a ship-victualing station by the Dutch pioneer Jan van Rieback. It was called Kapstad under Dutch rule and subsequently became the capital of Cape Colony. With the formation of the Union of South Africa in 1910, Cape Town was made the capital of the Dominion.

PRETORIA, SOUTH AFRICA (Fig. 1397–1398)

Pretoria, capital of the Republic of South Africa, laid out in 1855, was

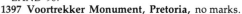

1394 **Cape Town,** no marks.
1395 **City of Cape Town,** marked: EXQUISITE PLATE.
1396 **Cape Town,** marked: IG MADE IN HOLLAND 90.
1397 **Voortrekker Monument, Pretoria,** no marks.

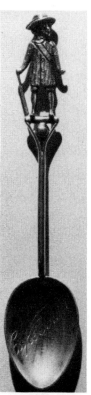

1396

1397

1401

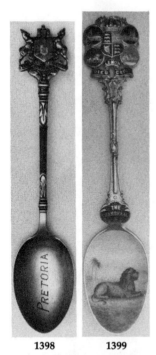

1398   1399

1400

founded by Marthinus Wessels Pretorius, the first president of the South African Republic, and named for his father, Andries Wilhelmus Jacobus Pretorius. It became the capital of that state when the seat of government was moved from Potchefstroom in 1860.

Exploitation of the gold fields of the Witwatersrand in the 1880s brought about development of the city.

The VOORTREKKER MONUMENT (Fig. 1397) was dedicated in 1949 and commemorates an epic migration known as the Great Trek (1836–38) which led to the settlement of South Africa's interior by the Boers.

TRANSVAAL PROVINCE (Fig. 1399)

Transvaal is one of the four provinces of the Republic of South Africa. The Transvaal was settled by Boers who were dissatisfied with conditions in the Cape Colony. The first small parties of these settlers crossed the Vaal River in 1836 and the first community of Potchefstroom was established in November 1838. Thousands followed and settled there. On January 17, 1852 the British government recognized the independence of the Transvaal but later unsettled conditions led to annexation. Independence was gained again on February 27, 1881 but annexation followed on September 1, 1900. Self-government was granted in 1906 and eventually the peaceful union of the four colonies into the Union of South Africa under the leadership of General Botha was concluded on May 31, 1910.

———————— •◦• ————————

1398 **Pretoria,** marked: WJD Birmingham 1909-10.
1399 **Transvaal Province,** marked: L & S Birmingham 1904-05.
1400 **Kruger National Park, South Africa,** marked: T. H. Marthinsen EPNS 40.
1401-1403 **Victoria Falls, South Africa,** all marked: VICTORIA FALLS.

1401

1402

1403

KRUGER NATIONAL PARK
(Fig. 1400)

The world's largest wildlife sanctuary is Kruger National Park, located in the northeast of the Transvaal Province. It is 200 miles long and 40 miles wide. There, thousands of animals live under natural conditions but protected by law from hunting. Though hunting is forbidden, the park is open to visitors from June 16 to October 15 each year.

The park began as the Sabi Game Reserve which was established in 1898 by President Stephanus Johannes Paulus Kruger, of the South African (Transvaal) Republic. The original park was greatly enlarged and in 1926 was renamed Kruger National Park.

VICTORIA FALLS (Fig. 1401–1403)

The native name *Mosi-oa-Runya,* "the smoke that thunders," is an apt one for the Victoria Falls, located between Northern and Southern Rhodesia on the Zambesi River. The falls are wider than Niagara Falls and more than twice the depth and fall from four main cataracts extending over a breadth of more than a mile. From a great rocky fissure, 400 feet deep, the Zambesi River plunges down the walls of hard basalt. There is only one narrow outlet through which the mile-wide waters have to force their way, dropping into the "boiling pot" so named because of the whirlpool turbulence. The roar of the falling waters can be heard from a great distance.

Victoria Falls was discovered by David Livingstone on November 17, 1855 who named them for Queen Victoria.

TAIWAN (Fig. 1404)

Taiwan (Formosa) is an island separated from the southeast coast of China

1404

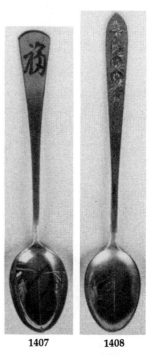

1407   1408

1405   1406

1409   1410

1404 **Taiwan,** marked: SILVER.
1405-1409 **Korea,** all marked: SILVER KOREA.
1410-1411 **Korea,** marked: SILVER KOREA.

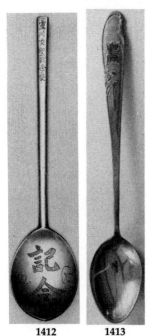

1411

1412   1413

by the Formosa strait. It was known to the Chinese as early as the beginning of the seventh century A.D. Chinese and Japanese pirates used the island as a base of operations. In 1590 the Portuguese named the island Formosa. Recurrent famines in the Fukien province of China in the first quarter of the seventeenth century encouraged emigration from there and a settlement was established by Chinese from the mainland.

In 1949 Chiang Kai-shek established his Nationalist government-in-exile in Taiwan.

KOREAN SPOONS (Fig. 1405–1415)

Korean spoons, made especially for foreign trade in the 1960s featured motifs of flowers, foliage and ideographs.

Figures 1411 and 1413 were sold at the 1964 New York World's Fair.

Figure 1412 is a mid-nineteenth-century Korean spoon with inscribed ideographs in the bowl meaning "Long (much) happiness."

The Korean dancer on the handle of Fig. 1415 is a *Keisaing* dancer, trained in Keijo. This Korean dance of the drums is a typical entertainment of that country.

HONG KONG (Fig. 1416)

Hong Kong is a British crown colony in southeast China. The capital city is Victoria.

On the handle of the spoon is a *junk*, a large, flat-bottomed vessel ranging from 100 to 1,000 tons, used by the Chinese and neighboring peoples of southeastern Asia for river and ocean navigation. It has a high poop, a short bowsprit placed on the starboard bow and often three pole masts. These masts are supported by two or three shrouds which at times are all carried on the windward

1414

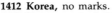

1412 **Korea,** no marks.
1413 **Korea,** marked: MADE IN KOREA.
1414 **Korea.**
1415 **Korea,** no marks.

1415

1416

1417

side. On the fore and main mast is a lug sail made of bamboo or cane matting.

PLUM BLOSSOM (Fig. 1417)

The plum blossoms early in spring having withstood winter's cold and hence, they are considered symbols of perseverence and patience. The plum blossom is one of three lucky symbols linked together (Shochikubi—literally pine-bamboo-plum.)

BAMBOO SUGAR SHELL (Fig. 1418)

Bamboo symbolizes devotion and unchangeableness. Throughout the Orient bamboo is one of the most useful plants. It is used as a building material, for kitchen utensils, for fencing, for furniture, for artistic crafts and bamboo sprouts, a real delicacy, are cooked in various ways.

GOOD LUCK SPOONS
(Fig. 1419–1421) (1426, 1428–1430)

Many spoons have been made for the tourist trade bearing Chinese characters which convey good luck, good health, long life and other similar sentiments.

JADE (Fig. 1421–1422)

Jade and jade carvings have long been associated with China because in no other country has it been worked with such skill. The Chinese have always regarded jade as the fairest and most desirable of stones.

Jade is remarkably tough, often too hard to be carved with steel. It varies in color from green to white.

Actually jade is a general term that includes two distinct minerals, jadeite and the more common nephrite.

1416 **Hong Kong,** no marks.
1417 **Plum Blossom,** marked: "Oriental characters."
1418 **Bamboo Sugar Scoop,** marked: "Chinese characters."
1419 **Teaspoon,** marked: TRADE YI-YI MARK.
1420 **Jade Spoon,** marked: CHINA SILVER.

1418

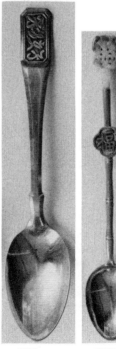

1419   1420

1421

1422

CHINESE DRAGON (Fig. 1423–1425)

The dragon, national symbol of China and badge of the imperial family, plays a large part in Chinese art. The Japanese and Chinese dragons are wingless although they are regarded as powers of the air. They are among the deified forces of nature in the Taoist religion and shrines of the dragon-kings, who dwell partly on land and partly in water.

PAGODA (Fig. 1427)

The five-storied pagoda (*Goju-no-To*) is found all over Japan. These Buddhist stupas or towers are erected for several purposes. Some are built as a part of a Buddhist cathedral to contain sacred ashes of the Buddha or Buddhist saint, or as a memorial tower. The pagoda is generally 320 Japanese feet high. It represents the five natural elements of ground, water, fire, sky and wind. Some stupas are only three stories high.

FUJIYAMA (Fig. 1431–1432)

Fujiyama (or Fujisan, both *san* and *yama* meaning "mountain"), as Mt. Fuji is called in Japan, stands all alone in a perfect cone shape. It is a dead volcano which must have erupted many times, judging from the geological conditions of the mountain and its surroundings. The latest eruption took place in 1707 when Mt. Hoei, a small mountain, standing on the southern side was formed. Fuji is called "The Matchless Mountain."

Tradition has it that Mt. Fuji arose in 285 B.C. simultaneously when Lake Biwa, the largest lake in Japan appeared during the reign of Emperor Korei the Fifth.

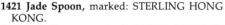

1421 **Jade Spoon,** marked: STERLING HONG KONG.
1422 **Jade Spoon,** marked: SILVER JUNGHUA CHINA.
1423 **Chinese Dragon,** "Hong Kong" engraved in bowl.
1424 **Chinese Dragon,** marked: (See drawing for mark.)

1423   side view

1424   side view

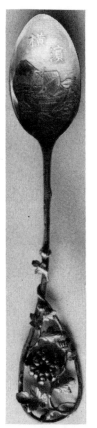

Mt. Fuji is almost always capped with snow and according to legend this is because Fujiyama turned away an ancestral *Kami* who sought overnight lodgings while Mt. Tsukuba made the *Kami* welcome. So, to this day, devotees may visit Mt. Tsukuba every day of the year and pay homage, while Mt. Fuji can be visited only rarely.

———————————————

1425 **Chinese Dragon**, marked: WH 90.
1426 **Long Life**, marked: "Chinese characters."
1427 **Pagoda**, marked: CHINA 90% SILVER LEE YEE HING.
1428 **Long Life**, marked: "Chinese characters."
1429 **Happiness-Long Life**, marked: "Chinese characters."
1430 **Happiness-Long Life**, no marks.
1431 **Fujiyama**, no marks.
1432 **Fujiyama** in the bowl.

1425

1432

1426   1427   1428   1429   1430   1431

1433

1434

BUDDHA (Fig. 1433)

The figure forming the bowl is the Daibutsu which is a Buddhist term meaning a statue of the Buddha. There are many of them in Japan. Usually, the term signifies two huge statues; one of

---

1433 **Daibutsu or Buddha.**
1434 **Daikoku.**
1435 **Chrysanthemum** (marked: See drawing for marks)
1436-1442 **Seven Gods of Happiness**
1436 **Fukurokuju,** god of wisdom and long life.
1437 **Daikoku,** a deity of the kitchen.
1438 **Ebisu,** patron of work.
1439 **Hotei,** lover of children and symbol of a happy life.
1440 **Bishamonten,** god of happiness and war.
1441 **Jurojin,** god of happiness and long life.
1442 **Benzaiten,** female deity of love. All are marked: TOKYO STERLING. The figures are porcelain.
1443 **Samisen,** marked: IW and "Chinese characters."

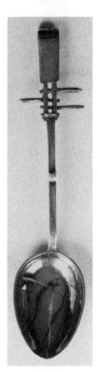

1443

1435

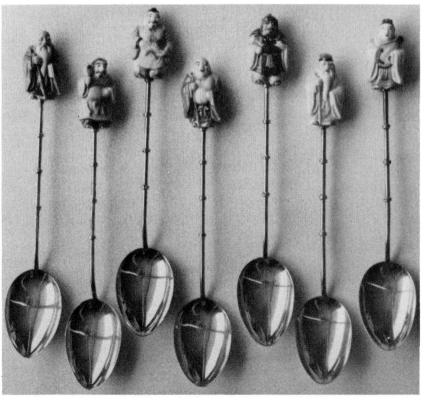

1436   1437   1438   1439   1440   1441   1442

1444

1445

these is at Nara, an ancient capital of Japan and the second at Kamakura, once a Shogunal capital. The Daibutsu at Kamakura was cast of bronze in 1252. Its total height is forty two and a half feet (fifteen meters). The boss in the center of the forehead contains thirty pounds of pure silver and the eyes are made of pure gold. (The boss represents a spot of white hair turning clockwise, a sign of wisdom.) The statue was originally erected with the object of enshrining a small statue of Amida or Amdabha in it. A tidal wave washed away the Daibutsu Hall of Kamakura in 1495 and the statue has since stood unsheltered.

The jinrikisha, forming the handle of the spoon, comes from three Japanese words meaning man, strength and carriage.

CHRYSANTHEMUM (Fig. 1435)

Chinese tradition says that once upon a time there lived a boy in China who lived upon the dews formed on chrysanthemum leaves and attained the age of seven hundred years. Therefore the chrysanthemum is considered a symbol of longevity in the Orient.

The Imperial crest of Japan is a sixteen-petaled chrysanthemum flower and the Emperor is the only person allowed to wear this crest.

SHICHI FUNKUJIN
(Fig. 1436–1442, 1434)

Shichi Fukujin, The Seven Gods of Happiness or Good Luck, are represented here. They are: *Fukurokuju*, literally, fortune-life-longevity, the god of wisdom and long life, with a very high skull. He is accompanied by a stork. *Daikoku* (literally, great-black) a deity of

---

1444 **Japanese Shrine,** marked: SILVER 950 JA-PAN.
1445 **Nikko.**
1446 **Nikko,** "Nikko" inscribed on back.
1447 **Yokohama,** marked: "Chinese characters." "Yokohama" inscribed on back.

1446

1447

287

1451

1448

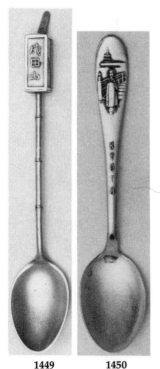

the kitchen, holds the hammer of wealth and a large sack of treasures on his back. He stands on two sacks of rice. *Ebisu*, the patron of work holds a line in his hands and a big fish on a line, symbolizing fisheries and industry. *Hotei*, a priest of the Sung dynasty in China holds a hand-screen and big sack. He is a lover of children and a symbol of a happy life. *Bishamonten* (Bishamon), god of happiness and war. He is represented as a soldier holding a small pagoda and a lance. *Jurojin* (literally, longevity-old man), god of happiness and long life, leans on a long staff and is accompanied by a stag. *Benzaiten* (Benten), the only female in the set is the deity of love. She is usually depicted riding a dragon, playing the *biwa* (lute), symbol of music and culture. Benzaiten's messenger is a snake.

SAMISEN (Fig. 1443)

The handle of this spoon represents the head of the three-stringed Japanese instrument resembling a banjo, often played for Japanese dancing. It accompanies *Ningyo* or marionette performers and is used by geisha.

NIKKO (Fig. 1445–1446)

Nikko (Sun's Brightness), is a mountainous district approximately one hundred miles north of Tokyo but the name is generally applied to the principal villages, Hachi-ishi and Irimachi. A Japanese proverb says, "Do not use the word magnificent till you have seen Nikko." It is noted for its superb wood carvings and paintings and for the most beautiful assemblage of shrines in all Japan. It is also noted for the glorious tints of its foliage in early November. Hence it has earned the description "double

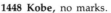

1448 **Kobe**, no marks.
1449 **Narita-San Temple**, marked: STERLING.
1450 **Kyoto.**
1451 **Geisha**, marked: STERLING SILVER 950.
1452 **Geisha**, marked: STERLING.

1452

1453

1458

glory—a glory of nature and a glory of art.''

YOKOHAMA (Fig. 1447)

It was here that Commodore Matthew Perry landed in 1854 and found a small fishing village of about fifty houses. A commercial treaty was later signed in which foreigners were granted permission to trade and settle in the area nearest the harbor and eventually "opened" the country to the western world.

————————•◦•————————

1453 Geisha, marked: STERLING 950.
1454-1456 Geisha.
1457 Geisha.
1458 Geisha, marked: HENTEN YOKOHAMA STERLING.

1454   **1455**   **1456**

1457

1459

1461

KOBE (Fig. 1448)

Kobe is one of Japan's great seaports. It is a modern city along the Osaka Bay shore and the lower slopes of a range of steep hills. There are several Christian churches there in addition to Shinto and Buddhist shrines. There is a noted Daibutsu, a bronze image of the Buddha, thirty-eight feet (11.5 m.) high.

NARITA-SAN TEMPLE (Fig. 1449)

The handle of this spoon is a fortune-telling box, a souvenir of Narita-San Temple of Tochigi Prefecture, Japan. Holding the spoon upside down and shaking it, different tabs appear, each telling a different "fortune."

KYOTO (Fig. 1450)

Kyoto is the ancient capital of Japan and the center of her civilization for more than 1,000 years. It is now part of the Osaka-Kobe industrial complex. The city was originally called Uda. It was chosen capital of Japan in 794, and it was laid out in 805 as Kyoto (Capital City). The Imperial palace was burned down in 960 and again in 1177. Kyoto endured much civil disturbance during the following four centuries but was restored to its former grandeur in the latter half of the sixteenth century. It has remained the classical capital of Japan although the government was moved to Tokyo in 1869.

GEISHA (Fig. 1451–1459)

Geisha (literally, accomplished person or artist) are an age-old tradition in Japan. The geisha studies as a *maiko* (apprentice) for several years, beginning after finishing school about the age of fifteen. Her main responsibilities are to dance, sing, play the samisen, be adept at the art of conversation, perform the tea ceremony and serve *sake* (rice wine)

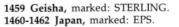

1459 **Geisha,** marked: STERLING.
1460-1462 **Japan,** marked: EPS.

1460

1462

1463

1464

with grace. There are all kinds of geisha. Whether or not they perform more personal services is left to their discretion. Youth and beauty are not prerequisites; the best geisha are usually middle-aged.

The hair of a geisha is arranged in an ornate coiffure, ornamented with flowers and tinkling bells. Her face and throat are whitened, leaving an expressionless appearance. Her ornate floor-length kimono with billowing sleeves is ornamented with a lustrous sash (*obi*) set in a large bow in back.

Geisha earn large salaries but most of their income is reinvested in their elaborate wardrobes. In recent years, fewer and fewer girls have entered the profession and it is rapidly disappearing.

IRAN (Fig. 1466)

Iran is situated on the strategically important land bridge linking Asia, Africa and Europe. Huge areas lack adequate rainfall and are wholly arid and barren. Nature's compensation lies in floating the country on a vast pool of oil—a major source of the country's income.

The few areas of Iran that receive plentiful rainfall are remarkably productive. It is believed that it was here that the peach, melon, cucumber, cherry, rose, wheat and poplar originated.

INDIA (Fig. 1467–1488)

The camel (Fig. 1467, 1470) used both for riding and as a draft animal, is well-suited to desert life. His padded feet keep him from sinking into the sand, he carries his own water reserve in his stomach and his nourishment in his hump, and his eyes are protected in sandstorms by their long lashes. The single hump (dromedary) camel can maintain a swinging trot at nine miles

---

1463-1465 **Japan,** all marked: TOSHIKANE JAPAN.

1466 **Iran,** no marks.

1465

1466

1467

1469

an hour for several hours and *can* cover a hundred miles in a day. The two-humped camel is slower but a better pack animal, being able to carry 500-1000 pounds twenty-five or thirty miles a day. The camel's adaptability to desert conditions have made it an important factor in colonizing vast areas of the Old World.

INDIAN ELEPHANT (Fig. 1467, 1472)

The Indian elephant for thousands of years has been the servant of man, bearing the Oriental warrior into battle and carrying his ammunition and equipment. In time of peace he has piled huge blocks of stone and logs.

The device below the elephant (Fig. 1467) is from the British royal standard—the three golden lions represent England, its red lion rampant standing for Scotland and the golden harp for Ireland.

THREE WISE MONKEYS (Fig. 1471)

The Three Wise Monkeys are also known as the Three Mystic Apes. They are in inheritance from Oriental tradition and culture, their message always has been to warn all humanity against the three principal temptations of gossip or speaking untruths, of looking for corruption or being lead into wickedness by the persuasion of a smooth talker.

INDIA'S STATE EMBLEM (Fig. 1473)

India's State Emblem was adopted at the formation of the Republic in 1950. It consists of one of the famous "lion" capitals from a column in the holy city of Sarnath, near Benares. It was at Sarnath that Buddha gave his first great sermon in the "Gazelle Park." The Emblem's de-

1467 **India,** marked: STERLING.
1468 **Bombay,** no marks. "BOMBAY" engraved on back.
1469 **India,** no marks. Tiger's eye stone on handle.
1470 **Camel,** marked: SILVER.

1468

1470

1471

1472   1473

1474

1475

sign was based on the capital of a column erected by the Apostle-Emperor Asoka (259–226 B.C.) and bears a representation of four lions. Beneath the lions is the *Chakra*, or Wheel of Life, representing Virtue, Motion and Natural Change.

CEREMONIAL SPOONS
(Fig. 1474–1482)

Spoons for ceremonial purposes have been made for many years by Hindu craftsmen. Some were made to use in temples for transferring oil from containers to lamps. Many of these spoons bear grotesque figures and foliage, boldly modeled or chased. Some are set with colored stones.

Spoons Fig. 1474 and 1475 were purchased in India from Tibetans who said they were selling personal possessions to raise money to return to Tibet. The spoons are said to be for temple use with a lamp with two reservoirs. Oil is dipped with a spoon from one to another, a wick is placed in the oil and lit with a candle which burns in a center holder. The flame and smoke waft prayers to heaven. The spoons are also said to be "gun metal"—old cannons were being melted down in Tibet after World War II and made into various objects.

Identical spoons were located with bowl of matching design. Four spoons and the bowl were said to have been used in Tibet for serving yak butter.

SNAKES AND SCORPIONS
(Fig. 1468, 1483–1488)

While older snake and scorpion spoons have had ceremonial significance, later specimens were made for the

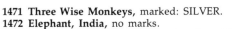

1471 **Three Wise Monkeys,** marked: SILVER.
1472 **Elephant, India,** no marks.
1473 **India's State Emblem,** no marks. Set with rose jade stone.
1474 **Tibet(?),** no marks. Set with red stone.
1475 **Tibet(?),** no marks. Set with blue stone.

souvenir trade. Other, more elaborate versions than those shown here, have representations of a Hindu deity embossed in the bowls.

CEYLON (SRI LANKA)
Fig. 1489–1498)

The device on the handle of Fig. 1491 is from an earlier flag of Ceylon and depicted the British Blue Ensign with a badge in the fly depicting an elephant in front of a Buddhist temple. After achieving a more liberal constitution in 1946, the island chose the Lion flag of the former kings of Kandy as its emblem. The national flag added vertical bars of green and saffron in the hoist in 1950.

1476 **India,** no marks. Bronze.
1477-1478 Ceremonial or Sacrificial Spoons, no marks. Brass.
1479-1482 Ceremonial or Sacrificial Spoons, no marks. Brass.
1483 Scorpion, no marks.

1476

1483

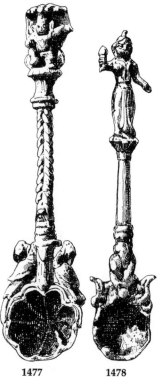

1477   1478   1479   1480   1481   1482

1484

1490

Columbo, Ceylon's capital, was settled in 1517 by the Portuguese who named it in honor of Christopher Columbus.

In the northern and eastern provinces elephants (Fig. 1492, 1494) are numerous although their numbers have been

1484 **Lizard,** no marks.
1485-1487 **Scorpions,** no marks.
1488 **Snake,** no marks.
1489 **Honey Spoon, Ceylon,** marked: VVV.
1490 **Ceylon,** marked: 800. "Oct. 1929" on back.

1486

1488

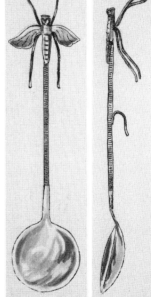

1489

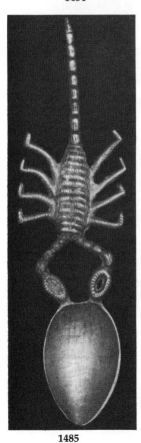

1485

1487

1491

greatly reduced by hunters. There was a time when wild elephants were rounded up, herded into stockades and tamed for use as draft animals. Although many are still used, the methods of capturing them have changed from that of the stockade to an even older, more ingenious and possibly more dangerous method. Like many professions on this island, the capturing of wild elephants is an hereditary one, confined to a class of people of Moorish descent.

———————————————————

1491 Mt. Lavinin, Ceylon, no marks. "Oct. 1929" on back.
1492-1493 Ceylon, no marks.
1494 Ceylon
1495-1498 Ceylon, no marks.

1498

1492

1493

1494

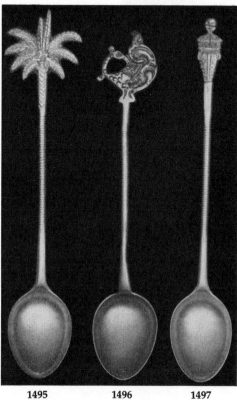

1495   1496   1497

1499

ئلستن

1500

NEPAL (Fig. 1499)

The immense Himalayan peaks that form Nepal's northern border with Chinese-controlled Tibet and the rugged mountain spurs and deep valleys that flow southward to its border with India dominate the land. Roads are rare, and most goods still travel on the backs of yaks, mules or men. Nepal is, however, emerging from its ancient isolation, admitting foreigners and aid funds, and taking hesitant steps to emerge from the poverty of an agricultural economy into the modern era.

SELANGOR (Fig. 1500)

One of the smaller units of the Federation of Malaya, Selangor is situated in the southern part of the Malay Peninsula. The state came under British rule in 1874 following acts of piracy which caused the British governor of the Straits Settlements to force a treaty on the local sultan. From 1896 to 1946 it was one of the Federated Malay States. From 1946 to February 1, 1948 it was part of the Malayan Union and then part of the Federation of Malaya thereafter. Capital of Selangor and of the Federation, Kuala Lumpur, is the center of a great rubber-producing region.

SINGAPORE (Fig. 1501–1502)

The coat-of-arms (Fig. 1502) for the Republic of Singapore was adopted in 1959. The emblem consists of a white crescent and five stars on a red field; the supporters are a lion and a tiger. The crescent and five stars represent a young nation in its ascent towards the five ideals; democracy, peace, progress, justice and equality. The lion represents Singapore "the City of Lions." The tiger sig-

1501

1502

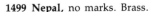

1499 **Nepal,** no marks. Brass.
1500 **Selangor,** marked: (See drawing for mark)
1501 **Singapore,** marked: SINGAPORE.
1502 **Singapore,** no marks.

nifies the country's former connection with Malaysia.

Below is the motto *"Majulah Singapura"* (Forward Singapore!)

PENANG (Fig. 1503–1504)

Penang on the Malay Peninsula is a

1503 Penang.

1504 Penang, marked: SILVER Birmingham 1938-39.

1505 Rangoon, marked: M & B Birmingham 1909-10. "Royal Lakes & Shwe Dagôn Pagoda" in bowl.

1506 Rangoon, marked: J·F Birmingham 1936-37.

1507 Java, no marks. "Java" in script on back.

1508 Wayang, no marks. Tortoise shell. The figure represents a character in a shadow puppet play.

1503

1508

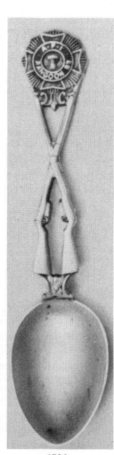

1504 **1505** **1506** **1507**

1509

settlement in the Federation of Malaya comprising the island of Penang and on the mainland two to ten miles distant, Province Welleslay. On August 11, 1786 the British flag was raised on the island which was then almost uninhabited. It was named the Prince of Wales Island and was used for some years as a penal colony.

RANGOON (Fig. 1505–1506)

Rangoon is the capital and the largest city and major port of the Union of Burma. It was probably founded about the sixth century but its modern history may be dated from 1753 when, after a victorious war over the Mons, Alaungpaya rebuilt the city and named it Yangon (the end of strife). The name was later corrupted to Rangoon.

JAVA (Fig. 1507–1509)

Java, island of Indonesia, is the fifth largest and most important of the islands of the Malay Archipelago.

The figures on the handles of Fig. 1508 and Fig. 1509 represent Javanese shadow puppets. In the oldest form of Javanese drama a man is hidden behind a screen. He operates various mechanical puppets or jumping jacks in front of a strong light, throwing their shadows on a white sheet.

Wayang plays are the supreme delight of the Javanese. Although Wild West movie thrillers from the United States are enjoyed, it is the old wayang plays which they know by heart that move the Javanese with unbounded appreciation. Performances may vary, ranging from marionettes with movable arms, throwing shadows on a screen, to the favorite *wayang orang,* in which human actors play the roles of mythical characters.

1511

1509 **Wayang,** marked: 800. "Java" inscribed on back.
1510 **Thailand,** marked: THAILAND.
1511 **Thailand,** marked: SIAM.
1512 **Thailand,** marked: HONG KONG.

1510

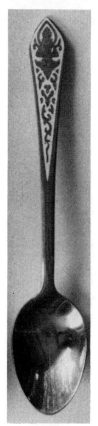

1513

1514

These plays are a series of postures, a "slow motion picture," with each turn of the hand and step having a meaning.

THAILAND (Fig. 1510–1514)

Thailand was called Siam until 1939 when the name was changed to Thailand. The earlier name was resumed in 1945 but on May 11, 1949, the name Thailand was once again proclaimed the official designation of the country.

In addition to representations of the Buddha, many mythological Hindu figures appear in Thai art.

VIETNAM (Fig. 1515)

The Vietnamese featured on the handle of this spoon is dressed in the national costume which consists of the flowing *ao dai,* with high collar and snug bodice. The skirt is split to the waist and swirls around the pajama-like *cuan* or pantaloons. This modern Vietnamese costume is a modification of the traditional dress by the artist Nguyen Cat Tuong and evolved about twenty-five years ago.

1513 Thailand, marked: "Elephant head" BAC.
1514 Thailand, no marks.
1515 Vietnam, marked: VIETNAM ARGENT.

1515

1516

1518

V
THE NEW WORLD

CANADA (Fig. 1516–1517)

Variations of Canada's coat of arms appear on spoons. The four quarters in the shield on this spoon represent the countries from which Canada was colonized—England, Scotland, Ireland and France. (Fig. 1517).

ROYAL VISIT (Fig. 1518)

(See IV, Fig. 840)

ROYAL CANADIAN AIR FORCE
(Fig. 1519)

On April 1, 1918, the many thousands of Canadians who served as pilots or observers in the British naval and military air services merged to form the Royal Air Force. Canadians formed approximately twenty-four percent of the air crews of the RAF at the time of the armistice. Authorization for the formation of the Canadian Air Force took place in 1918. Two squadrons, manned by Canadians who had served in the RAF were being organized in England when the war ended, but this embryo force was disbanded. The present Royal Canadian Air Force was formed April 1, 1924.

1516 **Canada,** marked: P. W. Ellis & Co. trademark, STERLING.
1517 **Canada,** marked: Roden Bros. Ltd. trademark, STERLING.
1518 **Royal Visit,** marked: WM. A. ROGERS, ONEIDA LTD.
1519 **Royal Canadian Air Force,** marked: R.

1517

1519

1520

1521

1522

1523

TORONTO, CANADA
(Fig. 1520–1521)

The site of Toronto, capital of Ontario, was first seen by a European in 1615, when the Huron Indians led French explorer, Etienne Brule, to their "meeting place." The land's westward location and friction between the Indians and eastern colonists delayed settlement until 1749, when French fur traders established Fort Rouille. Toronto began to boom in the latter part of the nineteenth century with increased lake travel and the coming of the railroad, and today is the largest English-speaking city in Canada.

ROYAL CANADIAN MOUNTED POLICE, OLD FORT HENRY, KINGSTON (Fig. 1522)

The famous red-coated national law enforcement department of Canada, the Royal Canadian Monted Police has been known by this name since 1920. Originally, they were called the Northwest Mounted Police. For ceremonies, the Mounted Police still wear their famed uniforms with wide-brimmed hats, breeches, high boots and spurs. However, their working uniform is a pill-box shaped hat, scarlet tunic, brown leather gloves, dark blue trousers with a broad yellow stripe, oxford shoes and side equipment. The color of the tunic has never changed. Scarlet was originally chosen because the Indians had come to consider this color as a symbol of justice.

Fort Frontenac was built by the French on the site of Kingston in 1673. The British burned it in 1758 and it was rebuilt in 1783 and renamed Kingston in

1520 **Toronto, Canada,** marked: STERLING REG 1906, Robert Hendery trademark.
1521 **Toronto, Canada,** marked: C & H STERLING 925.
1522 **Old Fort Henry, Kingston, Canada,** marked: STERLING, Birk's trademark.
1523 **Ottawa, Canada,** marked: 1908 STERLING RH.

1524

1525

1526

1527

honor of King George III of England. The city was incorporated in 1838.

OTTAWA, CANADA (Fig. 1523)

Ottawa, capital of Canada, was first explored by Samuel de Champlain. In 1615, he established a base camp here for future explorations from Quebec to Lake Huron and other points. For two hundred years, the Ottawa River remained the only means of travel for missionaries and fur traders. The first European settlement in the area was established in 1800. Its official name was By Town, in honor of Colonel John By, who directed the building of the Rideau Canal. Queen Victoria renamed it Ottawa in 1857.

PRINCE EDWARD ISLAND (Fig. 1524)

This island is Canada's smallest province and known as Canada's birthplace. place.

Foxes were first raised here for the commercial market and at one time a fine pair brought as much as $25,000. The provincial coat of arms features three oak saplings which stand for the three countries of Prince Edward Island. The oak tree symbolizes Canada and England, and a British lion stretches across the top of the shield. This coat of arms was adopted in 1905.

GLACE BAY, NOVA SCOTIA (Fig. 1525–1528)

The most important coal mining town in Canada, Glace Bay was incorporated in 1901. The mine known as Dominion No. 4, oldest producing mine in this province, started to operate in 1866.

1524 Prince Edward Island, marked: E. J. LTD. STERLING, Birmingham 1942-43.

1525 Nova Scotia. Maker: C & N, Birmingham 1942-43.

1526 Nova Scotia, marked: STERLING.

1527 Nova Scotia. Bowl is a 25¢ coin dated 1890.

1528

1529

NIAGARA FALLS, ONTARIO
(Fig. 1529–1530)

While there is wide variation from one season to another, it is reported that the average flow over the Horseshoe Falls is 114,000,000 gallons per minute, nineteen times greater than that over the American Falls. As its name implies, the crest of the Horseshoe Falls is shaped like a deep, irregular semicircle.

LACHINE RAPIDS, MONTREAL
(Fig. 1531–1533)

LaSalle set out from Lachine Rapids on his exploration in the latter part of the seventeenth century. The name was given by his men in ironic reference to LaSalle's search for China.

MONTREAL, QUEBEC
(Fig. 1534–1537, 1541)

Montreal, Canada's largest city, was first settled by the French and then by the English. Its turbulent growth under these two widely different regimes has produced a worldly, bilingual city, the second largest French-speaking city in the world. Jacques Cartier was the first European to explore the present site of Montreal when he visited the Indian settlement of Hochelaga in 1535. The settlement was known as Ville-Marie until about 1700.

NOTRE DAME DE MONTREAL
(Fig. 1538)

Among the more than three hundred and seventy-five religious institutions in Montreal, Notre-Dame, in Place'd'Arms, is the most magnificent. The first birchbark chapel was con-

---

1528 **Glace Bay, Nova Scotia,** marked: STERLING. (St. Joseph's Hospital in bowl).
1529 **Niagara Falls,** marked: P. W. Ellis & Co. trademark, STERLING.
1530 **Niagara Falls,** marked: Robert Hendrey trademark, STERLING REG. 1907.
1531 **Lachine Rapids, Montreal,** marked: STERLING R. MEMSLEY. 5¢ 1889 coin.

1530

1531

structed by early settlers in the fort of Ville-Marie. The present building, begun in 1824, succeeds two earlier ones built by the Sulpician Order in 1672 and 1757. Built of cut limestone in Gothic style, it is one of the largest and most impressive churches in North America. The church's stained glass windows illustrate the early history of Montreal, and the twin towers are called Tower of Perseverance and Tower of Temperance.

SIEUR DE MAISONNEUVE (Paul de Chamedey) (Fig. 1539–1540)

French colonial administrator, Sieur de Maisonneuve, was born at Neuville-sur-Vannes, France in 1612. Following a successful military career which began when he was only thirteen, Maisonneuve was selected by the Company of Notre-Dame de Montreal in 1641 to establish a new settlement in Canada. He arrived in Quebec August 20, 1641 accompanied by a small band of colonists, and on May 18, 1642 founded Ville-Marie (Montreal). Serving as governor for twenty-two years, Maisonneuve displayed great administrative ability.

SAINT LAWRENCE SEAWAY (Fig. 1542)

The United States and Canada began construction of the Saint Lawrence Seaway in 1954, and it officially opened in June, 1959. This seaway has opened the world's largest inland waterway to deep-sea navigation. It extends for one hundred and eighty-two miles from Montreal to the mouth of Lake Ontario.

1532 **Lachine Rapids, Montreal,** marked: RD 1903 STERLING.
1533 **Lachine Rapids, Montreal,** marked: STERLING, P. W. Ellis & Co. maple leaf trademark. "Corsican in Lachine Rapids" in bowl.
1534 **Montreal,** marked: STERLING.
1535 **Montreal,** marked: Roden Bros. Ltd. trademark.

1532

1533

1534

1535

THE GOLDEN DOG (Fig. 1543)

One of Quebec's oldest taverns displays the Dog Sign with the proverb, "I am a Dog gnawing the bone, while I am gnawing the bone I get my rest. Will come a day that hasn't come yet, when I shall bite he who will have bitten me."

1536 **Montreal,** marked: DMJ STERLING.
1537 **Montreal,** marked: P. W. Ellis & Co. trademark, STERLING.
1538 **Notre Dame de Montreal,** marked: STERLING.
1539 **Maisonneuve, Montreal,** marked: STERLING COCHENTHALER.
1540 **Maisonneuve Monument, Montreal,** marked: STERLING C3 RD.03.
1541 **Montreal.** No mark.
1542 **St. Lawrence Seaway,** marked: STERLING BMC○ MADE IN CANADA.

1536

1542

1537   1538   1539   1540   1541

1543

1544

QUEBEC (Fig. 1544)

The only walled city on the continent north of Mexico, Quebec is the capital of the Province of Quebec. It still retains its old French aspect and atmosphere. Known as the Indian town Stadacona, this site was visited by Jacques Cartier in 1535. Champlain established a trading post here in 1608 and gave the settlement its present name.

BARRIE, ONTARIO (Fig. 1545)

Situated fifty miles northwest of Toronto at the head of Kempenfeldt Bay, Barrie is the capital of Simcoe County.

The Canadian beaver on the handle of this spoon is a symbol of Canadian industriousness and well-being. Fortunes have been made in furs, and beaver hats long were fashionable in Europe as marks of status. For a time beaver skins were used as currency in Canada. Later, special beaver coins were minted, and today the animal appears on Canada's five-cent piece.

INGERSOLL, ONTARIO (Fig. 1546)

Ingersoll is located on the Thames River. The marketing center for a rich grain and fruit-producing section, it has an important trade in lumber, grain, cheese and general country produce. Furniture, condensed milk, automobile parts, paper and many other products are manufactured in Ingersoll.

PORT ARTHUR, ONTARIO
(Fig. 1547)

Port Arthur was originally a military outpost and became a town in 1884 after

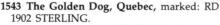

1543 The Golden Dog, Quebec, marked: RD 1902 STERLING.
1544 Quebec, marked: STERLING. (Lacrosse racket on handle).
1545 Barrie, Ontario, marked: P. W. Ellis & Co. trademark, STERLING.
1546 Ingersoll, Ontario, marked: Roden Bros. Ltd. trademark, STERLING.

1545

1546

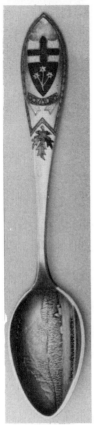

1547

1548

the railway reached it. It was incorporated as a city in 1907. It lies in the Thunder Bay District.

FORT WILLIAM, ONTARIO
(Fig. 1548)

Also in the Thunder Bay District, Fort William and Port Arthur are known as the Twin Cities of the Lakehead region. The first fort, Fort Camanistigoyan was built on this site in 1678 by French explorers. The Northwest Company began construction of a new fort in 1800. It was completed in 1803 and renamed Fort William for William McGillivray. From 1821 to 1881 it was one of the Hudson's Bay Company's chief trading centers.

PARLIAMENT BUILDINGS, VICTORIA, B.C. (Fig. 1550–1552)

The Parliament buildings in Victoria lie on the waterfront and overlook the inner harbor. Outlined by hundreds of electric lights, the buildings present an unforgettable spectacle at night.

VICTORIA, BRITISH COLUMBIA
(Fig. 1549, 1553)

Victoria had its beginnings when members of the Hudson's Bay Company founded Fort Victoria on Vancouver Island in 1843. Two years later the company made the new settlement its western headquarters because it feared, and correctly, that the proposed boundary between the United States and Canada would put their old headquarters, Fort Vancouver, in the United States. It is a favorite with tourists.

1547 **Thunder Cape, Port Arthur, Ontario,** marked: STERLING 3.

1548 **Fort William, Ontario,** marked: P. W. Ellis & Co. trademark, STERLING. (Old Hudson Bay Block House in bowl.)

1549 **Victoria and Vancouver,** marked: STERLING C3 RD.03. (Steamer Princess Victoria in bowl.)

1550 **Parliament Buildings, Victoria, B. C.,** marked: STERLING 925 Roden Bros. Ltd. trademark.

1549

1550

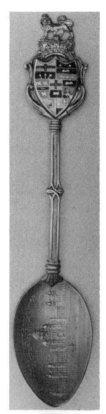

1551

1552

VANCOUVER, BRITISH COLUMBIA
(Fig. 1554–1555)

Vancouver, British Columbia's largest city and Canada's third largest, had its early beginnings in a sawmill in 1865. It was not until the arrival of the Canadian Pacific Railway in 1887 that it can be said to have become a city. The little mill town was known as Graville and in 1886 was incorporated as Vancouver. The entire city was destroyed by a disastrous forest fire on June 13, 1886, and rebuilding began immediately. From that time on, the city has been one of almost continuous growth.

BRITISH COLUMBIA PROVINCIAL COAT OF ARMS (Fig. 1556)

The coat of arms on the Phoenix, B.C. spoon is an adaptation of the provincial coat of arms. The crown and the Union Jack show the province's link with Great Britain. The setting sun is symbolic of British Columbia being the most Western province in Canada. This coat of arms was granted by royal warrant in 1906.

BRITISH COLUMBIA (Fig. 1557)

This province, the third largest, was named by Queen Victoria in 1858. It was admitted as a province into the Dominion of Canada on July 20, 1871. Its motto, *Splendor sine occasu* translated is "Splendor without waning."

FRASER RIVER, NEW WESTMINSTER, B.C. (Fig. 1558)

The principal river of British Columbia, Fraser River rises on the western

––––––––––– •◦• ◄ –––––––––––

1551 **Parliament Buildings, Victoria, B. C.,** marked: STERLING RED. 1906 RH.
1552 **Parliament Buildings, Victoria, B. C.,** marked: CHALLONER & MITCHELL, VICTORIA, B. C.
1553 **Victoria,** B. C., marked: CHALLONER & MITCHELL, VICTORIA, B. C.
1553 **Victoria,** B. C., marked: STERLING.
1554 **Vancouver,** B. C., MARKED: STERLING S.

1553

1554

1555

1557

slopes of Yellowhead Pass in the Rocky Mountains and then flows northwest between the Cariboo and Rocky Mountains. The river was discovered by Sir Alexander Mackenzie in 1793 and named after Simon Fraser, explorer and fur trader.

STANLEY PARK, VANCOUVER, B.C. (Fig. 1559)

Just five minutes from the heart of Vancouver is the entrance to world-famous Stanley Park. This 1,000-acre natural forest playground includes a children's zoo, golf course, cricket field, bathing beach, bowling green, rose garden and fifty miles of roads and bicycle trails. Also found here is the unique Theater Under the Stars where thousands gather on summer evenings to enjoy Broadway-type musical plays.

PENTICTON, BRITISH COLUMBIA (Fig. 1560)

Sandy-beached Penticton is in the heart of a rich fruit-growng district for which it is the commercial center. Its other industries include a lumber mill and large box factory.

CALGARY, ALBERTA, CANADA (Fig. 1561)

This city was founded in 1875 as a station of the Royal North West Mounted Police. It was incorporated as a town in 1884 and as a city in 1893. The Calgary Stampede, a famous rodeo, is an annual event in this city.

NORTH BATTLEFORD, SASKATCHEWAN (Fig. 1562)

North Battleford is situated at the

1555 Vancouver, B. C., marked: P. W. Ellis & Co. maple leaf trademark, STERLING. (Post Office in bowl).
1556 British Columbia Coat of Arms, marked: STERLING RD.03. (Phoenix in bowl).
1557 British Columbia, marked: STERLING.
1558 Fraser River Bridge, New Westminster, B. C., marked: P. W. Ellis & Co. trademark.

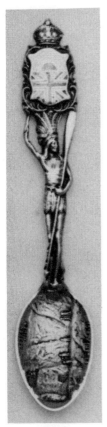

1556

1558

junction of the Battle and North Saskatchewan Rivers. It is the focal point of ten branch railroad lines and the distributing center for a mixed farming area.

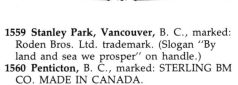

1559 **Stanley Park, Vancouver,** B. C., marked: Roden Bros. Ltd. trademark. (Slogan "By land and sea we prosper" on handle.)
1560 **Penticton,** B. C., marked: STERLING BM CO. MADE IN CANADA.
1561 **Calgary, Canada,** marked: STERLING, Robert Hendery trademark.
1562 **North Battleford, Saskatchewan,** marked: STERLING RD 03.
1563 **Saskatoon, Saskatchewan,** marked: BMC○. STERLING.
1564 **Portage La Prairie, Man.,** marked: P. W. Ellis & Co. trademark, STERLING.
1565 **Dauphin, Manitoba,** marked: STERLING.

1559

1565

1560

1561

1562

1563

1564

1566   side view

1567   side view

1568

SASKATOON, SASKATCHEWAN
(Fig. 1563)

The second largest city in Saskatchewan, Saskatoon is situated on the South Saskatchewan River. The site of this city was first surveyed in 1883. In 1901 it was incorporated as a village, in 1903 as a town and in 1906 as a city.

PORTAGE LA PRAIRIE, MANITOBA
(Fig. 1564)

Sieur de La Verendyre built a fort on this site in 1738 (Fort La Reine). A Hudson's Bay Post was established nearby in 1832. From earliest times these marked the point of departure on the Assiniboine River of the Indian portage over the prairie to Lake Manitoba— hence the name.

DAUPHIN, MANITOBA (Fig. 1565)

Dauphin had its beginning when the Canadian National Railways reached its site in 1896. The town was named after Fort Dauphin.

NORTHWEST COAST HORN SPOONS (Fig. 1566–1567)

Northwest Coast Indians of the Tlingit, Haida, Tsimshian and related tribes made beautifully carved spoons of horn. These were made in a wide range of sizes from a few inches to large ladles eighteen or more inches in length. These larger ladles were used at potlatches and held as much as two quarts or more.

The natural curve of tapering goat horns provided the graceful handles but the symmetrical bowls, made by deliberate effort, and the straightening of twisted sheep horns into more pleasing

---

1566 **Northwest Coast Horn Spoon.** No mark.
1567 **Northwest Coast Horn Spoon.** No mark.
1568 **Northwest Coast.** No mark. "Skagway Alaska" inscribed on back. Copper.
1569 **Northwest Coast.** No mark. "1891" engraved on back.
1570 **Northwest Coast.** No mark.

1569

1570

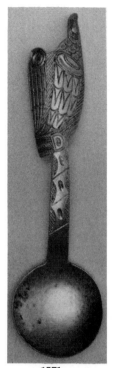

1571

1575   1576   1577

and manageable lines, indicate the artistic idea in the carver's mind.

By combining sheep and goat horn the most beautiful results were obtained, the black carved handle setting off the brownish yellow of the bowl. The figures carved on the handles were derived from totemic art in which the Indians excelled. The raven, the bear, the frog, the eagle, the whale and other animals were used. Though the faces of some animals so used were often treated somewhat like a human face, particularly the area around the eyes and nose, other features indicated an animal. In carvings representing the beaver, for instance, two large incisors serve to identify him. The beaver's tail is usually turned up in front of the body and is ornamented by cross-hatchings to represent the scales. The large incisors and the tail are sufficient to identify the beaver.

When the fad for souvenir spoon collecting spread, the Alaskan Indians learned to hammer out silver dollars into spoons. Many were made in imitation of fiddle pattern spoons, some enriched with etched or engraved totemic designs. (Fig. 1568–1577).

WALRUS IVORY SPOONS, ALASKA
(Fig. 1578–1580)

The small Eskimo carvings that are made now for the tourist trade have as their background hunting implements, carvings of people or animals used as toys or amulets, engraved pictures, fishing gear and other articles either essential to Alaskan Eskimo life or done for their pleasure.

1571 **Northwest Coast.** No mark.
1572 **Northwest Coast,** marked: SITKA.
1573 **Northwest Coast,** marked: SITKA.
1574 **Northwest Coast.** No mark.
1575 **Northwest Coast.** No mark.
1576 **Northwest Coast,** marked: SKAGWAY.
1577 **Northwest Coast,** marked: CMD '05.
1578 **Alaskan Ivory Spoon,** marked: 950 STERLING.

1572   1573   1574

1578

313

The tusks of the walrus supply the ivory used. Those of the bull walrus quite often grow to more than two feet long and those of the cows may be even longer, though more slender. The outer portion of the tusk is white but gradually turns yellow with age and exposure. It is plain in cross-section, lacking the fine intersecting lines that identify elephant ivory. The interior is darker and appears crystalline in structure. Being found only in walrus tusk, this core structure distinguishes it from any other kind of ivory. Modern carvers avoid showing the inner core.

An unknown group who lived on the western coast of Alaska more than a thousand years ago, before the Eskimo came, were the first to do fine work in walrus ivory. Most of these old carvings have become a handsome brownish tone from long burial. So-called "beach ivory" or that washed up by the sea is highly prized for ornaments or small carvings.

With the development of the tourist trade about 1850, Northwest Coast Indians began the production of cribbage boards and other items from walrus ivory. More recently, small totem poles and miniature animals have been made along the coast for sale to tourists. In the 1920s and 30s some of them were actually made in Japan from imported walrus tusks and shipped back across the Pacific to be sold as local North American work. These may often be spotted by the precision of the carving which is far above the usual artistic standards of the native craftsmen, though they lacked the primitive charm of the local ones.

ALASKA PURCHASE CENTENNIAL POTLATCH SPOON (Fig. 1581)

The Alaska Centennial Potlatch spoon is reminiscent of the past, carved in the tradition of a great people. This utensil is based on the Potlatch spoons of the ceremonial heritage of the Indian tribes of Southeast Alaska. Mr. Amos Wallace,

Tlingit of the Raven Clan, President of the Alaska Native Brotherhood and designer-carver unexcelled, designed the Raven Totem on the handle. Below is the seal of the Alaska Purchase Centennial. These three facets of this silver spoon symbolize the mixture of tradition and dynamics that represented Alaska in 1967.

The Alaska purchase Centennial Seal was created by Major Robert D. Vodicka. At the base—and beginning—of the characteristic totem design is a Russian church symbolizing Alaska's discovery and early ownership. Surmounting this is the American Eagle representing the purchase and ownership by the United States. Above this, the gold panner is a reminder of the fabulous gold strikes and of early industry. The stylized train represents the transportation of Alaska's first century, and crowning the totem is the star for Alaska, the 49th State. In the background of the design, but ever dominant, are Alaska's mountains against a sky and the eight-starred flag of "The Last Frontier."

The word "potlatch" is properly applied only to an institution which was the most remarkable custom of the northern coastal tribes and one about which all tribal life revolved. Defined briefly as a "concentrated effort on the part of a man or his kinship group to display wealth, to raise his rank, and to maintain the standard of his name." It was a supreme effort to outdo his rivals.

Potlatchs were given in celebration of the building of a house, birth or adoption of a son, a marriage, or other important social occasions.

Guests were invited from great distances. Feasting, dancing, speeches and other entertainment lasted for days.

Valuable gifts were distributed to all the guests by the host. These gifts could not be refused. The recipients were expected to return the gifts with interest, or in case of default, his heirs and relatives were liable for him. The host might

1579

1580

destroy his house or burn his canoes and his rivals would then be expected to sacrifice at least an equal amount. The presentation of gifts of greater value than could be returned by guests and the destruction of valuable property was the highest goal in life and often resulted in the pauperization of both host and guests.

DOCTOR G. W. LITTLE (Fig. 1582)

Dr. Little, a physician from Glen Falls, New York, was born in Vermont in 1836. He practiced medicine for fifty-three years, beginning in 1858 and concluding with his death in 1911. The following is Dr. Little's description of his own spoon:

The front represents my personality and tastes; the human skull, my profession and science of medicine; the hemispheres, travel in all lands; the parrot's head, natural history. My love for animals and birds and flowers is unprecedented. Bordering the portrait of the "doctor" are songbirds and orchids.—The collection of each has been a "fancy" over a quarter of a century. The shaft of the spoon is a golden pheasant—I have the second largest variety in the U. S.—The silver pill in the bowl, suggestive of the million dispensed to patients, many of whom call to mind the day when I manufactured my own pills without a sugar or chocolate coat, and the taking of one was regarded as formidable as an extraction of a tooth. The reverse side—46 years of practice among the rich and poor. The doctor in the old top sleigh in the sleet and storm hurrying to the bedside of the poor sufferer in the attic, with as much care and anxiety

1581

1579 **Alaskan Ivory Spoon.** No mark.
1580 **Alaskan Ivory Spoon.**
1581 **Alaskan Potlatch Spoon,** marked: STERLING.
1582 **Doctor G. W. Little,** marked: Watson Company trademark used 1879-1905, STERLING. Back of spoon inscribed, "DEDICATED TO MY PATIENTS WHO HAVE SURVIVED MY PRACTICE."

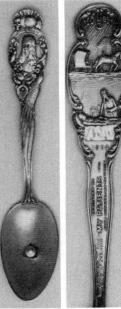

1582   **back**

1583

1584

as with the patient in the mansion across the way. The rest of the spoon speaks for itself.

SHOW ME. I AM FROM MISSOURI
(Fig. 1583)

The state of Missouri took its name from the Algonquin Indian word meaning "town of the great canoes." The nickname, the "Show Me State" is thought by most to have come from the speech made in Philadelphia in 1889 by Willard D. Vandiver. In this address he said, "I'm from Missouri, and you've got to show me."

UNITED STATES CAPITOL, WASHINGTON, D.C. (Fig. 1584)

The country's most familiar landmark, the United States Capitol is on Capitol Hill in a beautiful 131-acre park. Based on Dr. William Thornton's design with Benjamin Latrobe's revisions, it is 751 feet long, 350 feet wide and contains approximately 540 rooms. The nineteen and one-half foot high bronze statue of Freedom surmounts the Dome.

TAUNTON, MASSACHUSETTS
(Fig. 1585–1586)

Taunton was founded by Elizabeth Pole, and named in honor of Taunton, England. It was incorporated as a town in 1639 and as a city in 1864. Reed and Barton, silversmiths began there in 1824 as britannia makers.

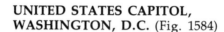

1583 **Show Me. I am From Missouri,** marked: Watson Company trademark used 1879-1905, STERLING.
1584 **U. S. Capitol, Washington, D.C.,** marked: Watson Company trademark used 1879-1905, STERLING.
1585 **Taunton, Mass. Tercentenary 1639-1939.** Maker: Reed & Barton, STERLING.
1586 **Taunton, Mass. Centennial City 1864-1964. Town 1639.** Maker: Reed & Barton, STERLING.
1587 **Adm. Raphael Semmes, Mobile, Alabama,** Maker: Whiting Mfg. Co., STERLING.

1585   **1586**

1587

316

ADMIRAL RAPHAEL SEMMES
(Fig. 1587)

Raphael Semmes, American naval officer, was born in Charles County, Maryland in 1809. He resigned from the U. S. Navy to enter the Confederate States navy in 1861 and commanded Confederate destroyers *Sumter* and *Alabama*. The *Alabama* became one of the most famous of commerce destroyers, sunk by the U. S. *Kearsarge* off Cherbourg Harbor, France. Subsequently, Admiral Semmes practiced law in Mobile, Alabama until his death in 1877.

PATRICK HENRY (Fig. 1588)

American Revolutionary leader, Patrick Henry (1736–1799) was born in Hanover County, Virginia. He was very active in Virginia politics, declining offers to be a U. S. senator. One of his most famous speeches contained the words, "Give me liberty, or give me death."

COUNTESS OF BATH (Bath, New York) (Fig. 1589)

This spoon commemorates Henrietta Laura Pulteney, "Countess of Bath," only child of the patron of the city, Sir William Pulteney. It was designed by a committee of Bath ladies as a souvenir for their centennial celebration held June 6–7, 1893. The portrait is based on an original painting now in the possession of the Bath Library Association.

LILLIAN RUSSELL (Fig. 1590)

Lillian Russell's real name was Helen

1590

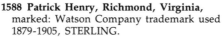

1588 **Patrick Henry, Richmond, Virginia,**
marked: Watson Company trademark used 1879-1905, STERLING.
1589 **Countess of Bath.** Maker: Gorham Corporation. Marked: STERLING M. P. SEDGWICK.
1590 **Lillian Russell, New York,** marked: STERLING Lebolt.
1591 **Jesse Welden, St. Albans, Vermont.** Maker: A. F. Towle & Son Co.

1588

1589

1591

317

1592

1593

Louise Leonard. This American operatic soprano was born in Clinton, Iowa in 1861. She sang in Tony Pastor's Bowery variety theater and rose to stardom in Edmond Audran's *The Great Mogul* (1881). She excelled in comic-opera roles. In 1899 Miss Russell joined the Weber and Fields burlesque company. She left the stage in 1912 and died ten years later.

JESSE WELDEN (Fig. 1591)

Connecticut Yankee, Jesse Welden was the first permanent citizen in the township of St. Albans, Vermont, "Maple Syrup Capital of the United States." He promoted local schooling, served as selectman, and left an endowment to the University of Vermont.

ARKANSAS TRAVELER (Fig. 1592)

The American folk tune, *Arkansas Traveler,* a favorite of old-time fiddlers, is supposedly of Arkansas origin. The lyrics tell about the fiddle-playing squatter traveling through Arkansas as a stranger.

MRS. LUCETTA S. CARTER, WICHITA, KANSAS (Fig. 1593)

Mrs. Lucetta Carter, often referred to as "Wichita's hired girl," spent almost forty years in service to Wichita and its people. Following the death of her elder son in 1881, she resolved to ease her own grief by working for others' joy. Mrs. Carter died July 4, 1919 and in the Maple Grove Cemetery is a ledger at her grave inscribed "A noble woman, God's

1592 **Arkansas Traveller.** Maker: Watson Company, STERLING.

1593 **Mrs. Lucetta Carter, Wichita Kansas,** marked: STERLING. C. M. Robbins 1900-1926 trademark.

1594 **Engine General, Chattanooga, Tennessee.** Maker: Shepard Mfg. Company, Inc., STERLING.

1595 **Albany, New York, State Capitol,** Maker: Shepard Mfg. Company, Inc., STERLING.

1594

1595

1596

1598

greatest gift to man. She devoted her life to the uplift of humanity. Love and Duty, her only creed."

ENGINE GENERAL (Fig. 1594)

In what has been described as the most daring exploit of the entire Civil War, a group of northern soldiers captured this wood-burning locomotive and sped north, stopping frequently to tear up tracks and burn bridges. The Engine General was on display in Chattanooga for seventy years but in 1970 the Supreme Court ruled that it belonged to the Georgia State Railroad and it was moved to Georgia following this decision.

ALBANY, NEW YORK (Fig. 1595)

The staunch, religious, courageous, industrious and somewhat taciturn character of the Hudson River Dutch colonists is represented in the sturdy fisherman on the handle. Fishing was an important industry in Albany's early days. One of the local names applied in the seventeenth and eighteenth centuries to the area that is now Albany was *de Fuyck*, referring to a fish net on a frame because of the contours of the shore.

ST. AUGUSTINE, FLORIDA COAT-OF-ARMS (Fig. 1596)

The device on this spoon represents the city of St. Augustine, Florida. It is described as the "Royal arms of Spain, erected over the sally port of the Castillo de San Marcos in 1756, symbolizing St. Augustine as an imperial seat of power in Florida. The shield bears the castles of

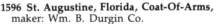

1596 **St. Augustine, Florida, Coat-Of-Arms,** maker: Wm. B. Durgin Co.
1597 **Brooklyn Bridge, New York,** marked: Watson Company trademark used 1879-1905, STERLING.
1598 **Brooklyn Bridge, New York,** marked: TIFFANY & CO. STERLING.
1599 **Needles, California,** marked: STERLING FRED HARVEY.

1597

1599

1600

1602

Castile and the lions of Leon in a collar of the Order of the Golden Fleece."

BROOKLYN BRIDGE, NEW YORK
(Fig. 1597–1598)

This bridge, suspended across the East River in New York City was designed by John Augustus Roebling. Begun in 1869 and completed fourteen years later, it opened May 24, 1883. At that time, the Brooklyn Bridge was the longest bridge in the world, holding this honor until 1903. When these spoons were made, the bridge had four lanes for motor traffic. A reconstruction, 1950–1954, added two traffic lanes and opened a new complex of approaches and exits at the Manhattan end of the bridge.

NEEDLES, CALIFORNIA (Fig. 1599)

One of the oldest towns on the Mojave Desert, Needles is a division point for the Santa Fe Railroad as well as a supply center for ranchers, hunters, fishermen and miners.

BLOOMINGTON, ILLINOIS
(Fig. 1600)

Originally Bloomington was known as Keg Grove, then became Blooming Grove in 1822. It gained its present name when McLean County received its charter in 1830. Bloomington's history is filled with American history. The Republican party was born here in 1856.

WALLA WALLA, WASHINGTON
(Fig. 1601)

First known as Steptoeville, Walla Walla derived its name from the Nez Perce Indian word meaning "little river."

1600 **Bloomington, Illinois,** marked: STER-LING.

1601 **Walla Walla, Washington,** maked: Mayer & Bros. crossed tools trademark, STERLING.

1602 **The Alamo, San Antonio, Texas,** marked: STERLING.

1603 **Pittsburgh, Pennsylvania.** Maker: Hall Bros. & Co. STERLING.

1601

1603

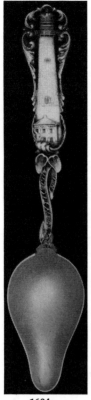

1604

1606

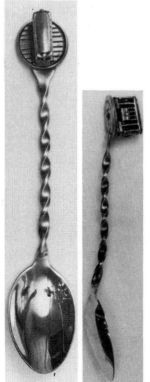

1605   side view

The Washington State Penitentiary (featured in the bowl) located within the city limits was established in 1887.

The Walla Walla Indians of North American Shahaptian language stock, were discovered by Lewis and Clark in 1805. Some sixteen hundred were inhabiting the Walla Walla River region and the junction of the Columbia and Snake rivers of Oregon and Washington.

THE ALAMO, SAN ANTONIO, TEXAS (Fig. 1602)

One of Texas' best known landmarks, "The Alamo" stands in the center of San Antonio. Built as part of a Catholic mission established by the Spanish missionary, Padre Olivares, it was erected circa 1718. The chapel and monastery were originally called *San Antonio de Valero*. Later the name was changed to *The Alamo*, the Spanish name for the cottonwood tree, many of which surround the mission building.

The famous battle cry, "Remember the Alamo" dates back to the War in 1836 when Texas was fighting for its independence. During the thirteen-day siege at this site (February 23–March 6) the brave Texans lost. Records show that every defender of this little mission, including Jim Bowie and Davy Crockett, were killed during this battle with the Mexican army.

The bluebonnet decorating the handle of this spoon is the flower of the Lone Star State.

PITTSBURGH, PENNSYLVANIA (Fig. 1603)

Pittsburgh, second largest city in the

1604 **Absecon Lighthouse, Atlantic City, New Jersey,** marked: STERLING 925/1000 silver.
1605 **Cable Car.** Maker: Bell Trading Post. STERLING.
1606 **Gulfport, Mississippi,** marked: STERLING.
1607 **Richfield Springs, New York.** Maker: Paye & Baker Mfg. Co. STERLING.

1607

state, is a river port situated at the junction of the Monongahela and Allegheny rivers, which unite at this point to form the Ohio River. An industrial center, Pittsburgh used to be known as the Smoky City because of the many soft coal-burning furnaces here. In addition to being located in the heart of the largest and most productive coal field on our continent, it is also near rich fields of natural gas and oil.

The first fort, little more than a stockade, was begun on the present site of the city in 1754 by a detachment of Virginia troops. The French seized the area and built Fort Duquesne in the same year. The British regained the area in 1758 and named it Pittsburgh, honoring William Pitt, First Earl of Chatham and Prime Minister of England. They built a temporary fort immediately and in 1759 replaced it with a strong permanent structure, Fort Pitt. By the next year a small trading post had grown up around the fort. In 1761 the fort was completed and in 1764 a redoubt was built. This redoubt, called the Blockhouse, is all that remains of Fort Pitt today.

ABSECON LIGHTHOUSE, ATLANTIC CITY, NEW JERSEY (Fig. 1604)

Built in 1854, Absecon lighthouse served the Atlantic coast for almost eighty years. The name Absecon (Absegami), is an Indian name "place of swans," applied to the island where Atlantic City stands.

After the tragic shipwreck of the *Powhatan* April 16, 1854, when 311 lives were lost, Dr. Jonathan Pitney, one of Atlantic City's founders, persuaded the federal government to put a beacon at Absecon Inlet. Built under the supervision of Lt. George Gordon Meade, its 167-foot tower was first illuminated January 15, 1857 and may be seen for more than twenty miles at sea.

Decommissioned in 1932, the old lighthouse became an historic site and museum in 1964.

CABLE CAR (Fig. 1605)

Andrew S. Hallidie invented the cable car in 1873 for use on San Francisco's steep hills. Since, they have been a landmark and tourist attraction of the city. Other American cities also adopted the cable car system, but around the turn of the century many abandoned it. Today, San Francisco, the first city to use these cars is the last to operate them.

More than 1,000 people gathered August 2, 1973 for a joyous kickoff of an eleven-day celebration honoring the century mark of San Francisco's legendary cable cars. A flatbed truck bearing the 100-year-old cable car, old No. 8, rolled down the Clay Street hill to re-enact the first ride in such a vehicle. It was at 5 a.m. on August 2nd, one hundred years before that Hallidie piloted his first cable car down the same route.

GULFPORT, MISSISSIPPI (Fig. 1606)

Gulfport was planned by the Gulf and Ship Island Compound as a railroad terminal for the Piney Woods section in 1887. However, it wasn't until 1892 that it was actually founded. Both a summer and winter resort area, Gulfport attracts large numbers of vacationists, tourists and conventioners.

SULPHUR SPRINGS, RICHFIELD, NEW YORK (Fig. 1607)

The old city of Richfield Springs lies almost in the center of the state. The original medicinal Spring, known to Indian tribes from time immemorial, was first discovered by the white man in 1754. This great spring flowed, unexploited until construction of the Great Western Turnpike, built late in the eighteenth century. In 1812 Dr. Horace Manley heard of its "magical properties" and the Indian lore concerning its cures, and he opened it to the public. Since then, a vast number of health seekers and tourists have made a mecca of Richfield Springs.

1608

1609

MOUNT HOOD, OREGON
(Fig. 1608)

Perpetually snow-capped Mount Hood is Oregon's highest peak, rising 11,245 feet above sea level. It was first sighted by British Lieutenant Broughton in 1792 and became a landmark for emigrants seeking the green lands west of the Cascade Range. Once an active volcano, it still sends out sulphurous fumes through vents in its upper slope. The first known climb above timberline was recorded in 1845. In 1887, seven men climbed to near the top and celebrated the Fourth of July by exploding a hundred pounds of red fire. Climbing Mount Hood has since become a popular pastime.

ASBURY PARK, NEW JERSEY
(Fig. 1609)

Longtime convention center and summer resort area, Asbury Park is situated on the shores of the Atlantic Ocean. New York businessman, James A. Bradley, developed Asbury Park as a summer resort in 1870. It was planned primarily for use by temperance advocates, thousands of whom attended Methodist camp meetings in Ocean Grove annually.

ROSWELL, NEW MEXICO (Fig. 1610)

Roswell is the center of a great farming and cattle-raising region. An early settler, Van C. Smith, named the city's post office for his father, Roswell, in 1871. It is the home of New Mexico's Military Institute and Walker Air Force Base.

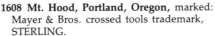

1608 Mt. Hood, Portland, Oregon, marked: Mayer & Bros. crossed tools trademark, STERLING.

1609 Asbury Park, New Jersey. Maker: Paye & Baker Mfg. Co. STERLING.

1610 Roswell, New Mexico, marked: Watson Company trademark used 1879-1905, STERLING.

1611 Willimantic, Connecticut, marked: STERLING.

1610

1611

1612

1613

WILLIMANTIC, CONNECTICUT
(Fig. 1611)

Often called "Thread City," Willimantic has been famed for cotton spinning since 1822. It is situated at the junction of the Willimantic and Natchaug rivers.

BRISTOL, CONNECTICUT
(Fig. 1612)

Bristol celebrated Old Home Week from August 30th through September 7, 1903. This spoon was just one of many souvenirs made to commemorate this "exciting" occasion in Bristol. It was designed by S. J. Large and manufactured by the American Silver Co. of Bristol. It sold for a quarter at the A. J. Muzzy & Co. store. The Old Pierce Homestead shown on the spoon handle no longer stands, but some parts of its paneling have been incorporated in a room in Bristol's American Clock and Watch Museum. The Congregational Church represented in the bowl is Bristol's first church. The old clock case was made by Eldridge Atkins early in the nineteenth century.

JACKSONVILLE, FLORIDA
(Fig. 1613)

Captain Jean Ribault and a band of French Huguenots landed at the St. Johns River mouth, near Mayport, and celebrated what is believed to be the first Protestant religious service in America in 1562. The town of Jacksonville, named for Andrew Jackson, provisional governor of Florida, was founded on the site of the English settlement of Cowford in 1822.

MAYFLOWER II (Fig. 1614–1622)

A set of spoons along with other

1615   1616

1612 **Bristol, Connecticut,** marked: "World Brand" trademark of the American Silver Co.
1613 **Jacksonville, Florida.** Maker: Shepard Mfg. Co. STERLING.
1615-1622 **Mayflower II,** all marked: HOLLAND STERLING VK.

1617   1618

1614 Contemporary advertisement for MAY-FLOWER II commemorative pieces.

Duplicates of the Precious Cargo in Shreve's Treasure Chest aboard Mayflower II

. . . Commemorative Spoons in Heavy Sterling Silver Wrought in Holland

Your choice of eight different handle figures in demi-tasse, tea and two serving sizes: Mayflower, Pilgrim Father, Pilgrim Mother, Pilgrim Daughter, Sailor Son, Soldier Son, Pilgrim Elder and Indian. Specify sizes and figures wanted.

Demi-tasse (4") $4.00 ea.   Serving (5¾") $13.50 ea.
Teaspoon (4½") $7.50 ea.   Serving (7") $22.50 ea.

Eight-piece demi-tasse set, cased, with the eight different figures, $37.50. (Not shown) Eight-piece service, seven 4½" and one 7" spoons, with the eight different figures, heirloom cased, $110.

For silver, add 50¢ for packing and shipping beyond our regular delivery area

Each spoon bears the
Royal Dutch Hall Mark
and Arms of City of
Plymouth, Massachusetts, 1620.

Mayflower Serving
or Dessert Spoon (5¾")

Shown actual size   Pilgrim Father Teaspoon (4½")

14 Kt. Gold Jewelry Made in England

Shown actual size

Shown actual size

Mayflower
$37.50*

Pilgrim
Father
$37.50*

Pilgrim
Mother
$37.50*

Pilgrim
Daughter
$37.50*

Sailor
Son
$37.50*

Soldier
Son
$37.50*

Pilgrim
Elder
$37.50*

Indian
$37.50*

Ship's
Bell
$27.50

Pilgrim
Hat
$15.

Charm
$125.

*in smaller size, $15.

Pendant
Earrings
$85. pr.

All prices
include
Federal tax

Clip Earrings
$55. pr.

Cuff Links
$170. pr.

Shreve
CRUMP & LOW COMPANY
BOYLSTON AT ARLINGTON STREET
BOSTON

1614

commemorative pieces were part of a chest of "Treasure" resembling that taken by the pilgrim fathers on the original *Mayflower*. This chest was aboard the *Mayflower II* when it set sail from New York in 1957. The spoons are duplicates of those in the chest.

MERIT SPOONS (Fig. 1623–1625)

Symbols featured on school spoons included the owl, symbol of wisdom; the lamp of learning; the books of knoweldge; the globe of the world; and the wreath of victory. Most were made with plain bowls in which representations of various schools were etched or engraved.

CHRISTMAS SPOONS
(Fig. 1626–1628)

The Christmas spoons pictured here are limited edition spoons made by Samuel Kirk & Son, Inc. and by the Gorham Corporation. The 1972 Kirk spoon, first annual Christmas spoon made by this company, is decorated with a snowflake in bas relief design (Fig. 1626). A different snowflake will adorn each Christmas spoon. Gorham made their first Christmas spoon in 1971 (Fig. 1627–1628).

SKYLINE SPOONS (Fig. 1629–1633)

One of the most famous towers in New York City, that of the Metropolitan Life Building on Madison Square tops the fifty-two story structure. The tower contains a huge clock with chimes (Fig. 1629).

The Chicago Public Library is famous for its marblework and mosaics and includes the Grand Army Memorial Hall featuring Civil War relics. This library was begun with books sent from England after the "Great Fire" (Fig. 1630).

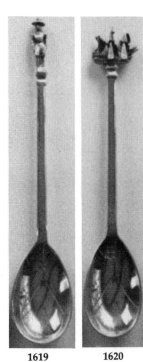

1619   1620

1621   1622

1623

1624

1623 **Merit.** Maker: R. Wallace & Sons Mfg. Co. STERLING.
1624 **Merit.** Maker: Rogers, Lunt & Bowlen Co. STERLING.

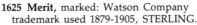

1625 Merit, marked: Watson Company trademark used 1879-1905, STERLING.

1626 Christmas, marked: KIRK STERLING CHRISTMAS 1972.

1627 Christmas, 1971, marked: Gorham trademark, GORHAM STERLING.

1628 Christmas, 1972, marked: Gorham trademark, GORHAM STERLING.

1629 New York City Skyline, marked: STERLING. (Metropolitan Life Building in bowl.)

1630 Chicago Skyline, marked: Watson Company pennant trademark, STERLING (Public Library in bowl.)

1631 Atlantic City Skyline, marked: Paye & Baker Co. trademark, STERLING. (Steel Pier in bowl.)

1632 New York City Skyline, marked: Paye & Baker Co. trademark, STERLING. (Public Library in bowl.)

1628

1625

1629

1630

1631

1632

1626   1627

327

1634

1635

The Steel Pier is Atlantic City's most elaborate pier. Over 2,000 feet long, it offers a variety of entertainment including the marine Ballroom and a carnival of water sports (Fig. 1631).

New York's public library, famed for the Lions on its impressive stairway was designed by Carrere and Hastings. It contains over four and one-half million volumes, and a geological collection said to be one of the most complete and finest in the world (Fig. 1632).

CHICAGO SKYLINE (Fig. 1633)

Chicago's U. S. Government Building was nine years being completed. On October 9, 1899 (Chicago Day) the cornerstone was laid by President McKinley; the building was not occupied until 1906. Henry Ives Cobb, architect, was well-known for his work around the turn of the century. However, this structure was never considered an architectural "gem," but it is remembered as being the only domed structure of consequence ever built in Chicago.

POSTAGE STAMP SPOONS
(Fig. 1634–1639)

Postage stamps were issued in a number of U. S. cities, notably New York, Baltimore, St. Louis, New Haven and Providence after their successful use in Great Britain. The United States introduced stamps in 1847 the five- and ten-

---

1633 Chicago Skyline, marked: Paye & Baker Co. trademark, STERLING. (Government Building in bowl.)
1634-1639 Postage Stamp. No marks.

1636

1637

1633

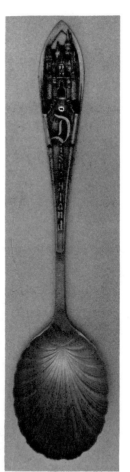

1640

1638

cent denominations bearing the faces of Franklin and Washington respectively. Prior to this, all postage was collected entirely in currency.

DISNEY (1901–1966) (Fig. 1640–1645)

Walt Disney, motion picture producer, was the creator of Mickey Mouse, Donald Duck and many other cartoon characters (Fig. 1642–1645). He made the first feature-length cartoon, *Snow White and the Seven Dwarfs,* and pioneered in mixing live action and animation, and also in the making of films such as Davy Crockett, especially for television. Disney is also given credit for developing nature films using animals as stars. Much of his work has gained worldwide popularity.

California's Disneyland has long been a famous out-door attraction for young and old alike (Fig. 1640). In 1970 a second Walt Disney Productions entertainment park opened, Walt Disney World, and has attracted millions of visitors (Fig. 1641).

MEXICO (Fig. 1646–1679)

The eagle featured on many Mexican spoons is a part of Mexico's state emblem adopted around 1821 and altered in detail in 1968. The arms originated with the Aztec legend in which they were directed to settle where they found an eagle on a nopal cactus growing out of a stylized rock in a lake and holding a snake in its beak (Fig. 1646–1648, 1653–1655, 1659–1664, 1668–1671, 1673–1674).

The old craft of filigree work was practiced in ancient Mesopotamia, Egypt, Etruria and classical Greece. This form of decoration, fine metal wire applied to a metal ground or *á jour,* that is, without a background as open lacework, is usually

1641

1639

1640 Disneyland, marked: STERLING "Circle-C" WALT DISNEY PRODUCTIONS.
1641 Walt Disney World, marked: STERLING "Circled-C" WALT DISNEY PRODUCTIONS.

executed in silver or gold because the precious metals lend themselves most readily to the forming of intricate patterns of curling wire, used singly or twisted together (Fig. 1651–1652, 1654, 1661, 1664–1665, 1667, 1676).

The *corrida de toros*, meaning literally

1642 **Mickey Mouse,** marked: "Circled-C" WALT DISNEY PROD. STAINLESS BY BONNY. JAPAN.
1643 **Minnie Mouse,** marked: "Circled-C" WALT DISNEY PROD. STAINLESS BY BONNY. JAPAN.
1644 **Pluto,** marked: "Circle-C" WALT DISNEY PROD. STAINLESS BY BONNY JAPAN.
1645 **Donald Duck,** marked: "Circled-C" WALT DISNEY PROD. STAINLESS BY BONNY. JAPAN.
1646 **Mexico.** No mark. 10 centavos 1892 coin.
1647 **Mexico.** No mark. 5 centavos, 1904 and 25 centavos 1875 coins.
1648 **Mexico,** marked: Shreve & Co. trademark.
1649 **Recuerdo De Mexico.**
1650 **Mexico.** No mark.
1651 **Mexican Filigree.**

1650   1651

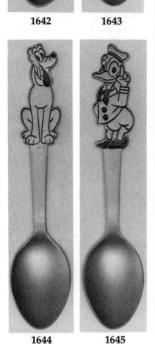

1642   1643

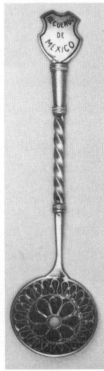

1644   1645   1646   1647   1648   1649

1660

the "running of the bull," is neither a fight nor a sport as we understand the meaning of those terms. It is a tradition played out in an artistic pageantry noted for its color. The richly dressed *matadores,* with embroidered silk capes swinging from their left shoulders, strut into the ring to begin the procession of performers (Fig. 1656).

------- •◦• -------

1652 **Mexican Filigree.**
1653 **Mexico.** 1887 coin bowl.
1654 **Mexican Filigree.**
1655 **Mexican Filigree,** silver gilt.
1656 **Matador, Corrido De Toros, Mexico.**
1657 **Castle of Chapultepec, Mexico** (President Porforio Diaz on handle).
1658 **Tampico, Mexico.**
1659 **Mexico.** 1890 coins on handle and bowl.
1660 **Mexico.** Two 1888 coins in bowl. Cut-out coin handle, date illegible.

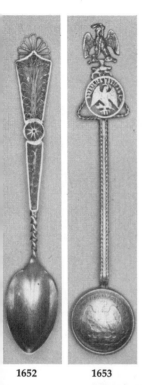

1652

1653

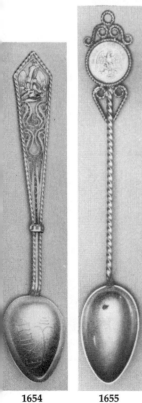

1654

1655

1656

1657

1658

1659

1661　　1662　　1663　　1664

1665　　　1666　　　1667　　　1668　　　1669　　　1670

1671

1672

The Cathedral in Mexico City is believed to be the largest church in Mexico. Built on the site of an earlier Christian church which was finished in 1525 and demolished in 1573, the present structure was begun the same year and completed in 1667. The exterior is a composite of Doric, Ionic and Corinthian architecture richly ornamented. The neoclassic style includes marble altars, statuary, wood carvings, silver railings and priceless paintings and tapestries (Fig. 1666, 1672, 1673).

Juárez, Mexico's largest city on the border with the United States lies on the Rio Grande, opposite El Paso, Texas. It was founded as El Paso de Norte in 1662 and renamed for President Benito Juárez in 1888. Its official name is Ciudad Juárez (Fig. 1667, 1674–1675).

The *Mission de Nuestra Señora de Guadalupe,* Juárez, was built by Father Garcia in 1659. Its four-foot thick adobe walls, hand-carved beams and altar and its tower bell are considered to be a marvel of workmanship (Fig. 1675).

Tijuana lies near the U. S.–Mexican border, sixteen miles south of San

1673

1674

1661 **Mexican Filigree.**

1662 **Mexico.** 1888 coin bowl, 1891 coin handle.

1663 **Mexico.** 1900 coin handle, "Mexico 1903" engraved in bowl.

1664 **Mexican Filigree.**

1665 **Mexican Filigree,** silver gilt.

1666 **Cathedral & Custom House, Mexico.** Maker: Watson Company, STERLING.

1667 **Juarez, Mexico Filigree.**

1668 **Tijuana, Mexico.** Maker: Shepard Mfg. Co., STERLING.

1669 **Church of Guadalupe,** marked: STERLING, L. D. ANDERSON JEWELRY COMPANY, READING, PA.

1670 **Mexico,** coins in bowl dated 1899 and 1872. Handle coin dated 1902.

1671 **Corrida De Toros, Mexico,** marked: Watson Co. trademark used 1910-1938.

1672 **Cathedral, City of Mexico,** marked: Paye & Baker Co. trademark.

1673 **Cathedral, Mexico.** No mark.

1674 **President Dias-Church of Guadalupe, Juarez, Mexico.** marked: Watson Company trademark used 1910-1938.

1675

1676

1677

1678

Diego, California. In 1900 it was a small village of just 242 people. Since 1940 a booming tourist trade has caused the city to grow rapidly (Fig. 1668).

The Mayan calendar consisted of two separate counts, one an approximate solar year and the other mainly ceremonial. The solar year, called the *tun*, consisted of 365 days. The ceremonial year, running concurrently with this so-called solar year, was only 260 days long. Although the Maya were unaware of the true significance of what they observed, they studied the cycles of the sun and moon and the planet Venus to measure the passage of time. They believed the earth was flat, and the sun and stars moved around it. They noted recurrent cycles so closely and were able to make remarkably accurate records of them. Scholars have interpreted that the cycles of the Maya calendar interlocked with each other like the meshing cogs of wheels of different sizes (Fig. 1677–1679).

GUATEMALA (Fig. 1680)

The Republic of Guatemala and El Salvador were conquered by Pedro de Alvarado from Mexico in 1523. Antiqua, the capital, was one of the most sumptuous of the New World, rivaling Lima, Peru and Mexico City in splendor and magnificence. After total destruction by earthquakes in 1773 the capital was moved to its present site, Guatemala City in 1776.

BRITISH HONDURAS (Fig. 1681)

The badge of British Honduras is a shield divided into three sections, displaying the Union Flag, a woodman's

1675 **Church of Guadalupe, Juarez, Mexico,** marked: 118.
1676 **Mexican Filigree,** marked: 800.
1677 **Mayan Calendar.**
1678 **Mayan Calendar,** marked: NECHO EN MEXICO DF 835 AR.

1679

1680

implements, and a sailing vessel, the last two representing the mahogany trade.

COSTA RICA (Fig. 1682–1684)

Costa Rica's state coat of arms was adopted in 1906 from an earlier design of 1948, and it was again altered in 1964. The shield depicts Costa Rica, with three volcanic mountain peaks, the Turriala, Irazú and Poas, between the Pacific and the Atlantic. The two ships indicate the State's mercantile interest and the stars represent the five original provinces.

PANAMA (Fig. 1685–1691)

The youngest republic in the Western Hemisphere, Panama was founded in 1903. Panamanians call their country the "Crossroads of the World," as it lies on the trade routes between South and North America and between the Pacific and Atlantic oceans.

GEORGE WASHINGTON GOETHALS (1858–1928)
(Fig. 1687, 1691)

Appointed by President Theodore Roosevelt as chief engineer on the Panama Canal Commission in 1907, after two civilian engineers had resigned, Goethals carried construction through to completion in 1914.

BERMUDA (Fig. 1692–1694)

Officially known as Somers Islands, Bermuda is a group of small islands in the western Atlantic Ocean, constituting a British colony (Fig. 192).

The word "onion" is derived from the

1679 **Mayan Calendar,** marked: STERLING.
1680 **Guatamala.** Center of bowl, 2 Reales (1894); cluster of 9 ¼ Real (1890) in bowl. Top of handle, dos Real (1867); middle, un Real (1862); bottom, ½ Real (1868).
1681 **British Honduras,** marked: STAINLESS CHROMIUM PLATE, SHEFFIELD, ENGLAND.
1682 **Costa Rica.** No mark. 25 centavos coin bowl.

1681

1682

Middle English *unyun*, from the French *oignon*, which came in turn from the Latin *unio* meaning onion. Ancient names for this plant indicate a widespread culture of onions from prehistoric times.

The Bermuda onion is believed to have originated in Italy or the Canary Islands. Considerable quantities of onions are grown here (Fig. 1693–1694).

1683 **Costa Rica.** No mark.
1684 **Costa Rica,** marked: 935 LE.
1685 **Hotel Tivoli, Panama,** marked: Chas. M. Robbins 1900-1926 trademark.
1686 **Hotel Tivoli, Panama,** marked: Chas. M. Robbins 1900-1926 trademark.
1687 **Panama Canal Builders,** silverplate.
1688 **Cathedral, Panama,** marked: STERLING. "1907" engraved on back. One centavo Republic de Panama postage stamp on handle.
1689 **Panama.**

1683

1689

1684   1685   1686   1687   1688

1690

1696

NASSAU (Fig. 1695)

The recorded history of Nassau, capital of the Bahamas, began in 1629 when King Charles I of England included the Bahamas in a grant to one of his favorite courtiers. A fort and city were constructed in 1695 and named Nassau in honor of William III who had been Prince of Orange-Nassau before being invited to rule England.

1690 Panama. No mark.
1691 George Washington Goethals, Panama. Maker: Rogers, Lunt & Bowlen, STERLING.
1692 Bermuda. Maker: BM Co. STERLING.
1693 Bermuda Onion, marked: combination trademark of the Gorham Corp. and P. W. Ellis & Co.
1694 Bermuda Onion, marked: t STERLING BERMUDA.
1695 Nassau, marked: Nickel silver.
1696 Havana, Cuba. marked: Watson Company 1910-1938 trademark. (Cathedral in bowl.)

1691

1692

1693

1694

1695

1697

1698

Nassau was besieged by pirates during the eighteenth century until George I sent out the ex-privateer, Captain Woodes Rogers as the first royal governor. Order was restored quickly by "Jolly Rogers" who hanged eight of the worst pirates in what are now the grounds of the British Colonial Hotel.

HAVANA, CUBA (Fig. 1696–1698)

Morro Castle has guarded Havana since the days of Sir Francis Drake. It was built by Spaniards in 1589–1597, taken by the British in 1762 and was bombarded by U. S. forces during the Spanish American War. It later served as a signal station and lighthouse. The 144-foot high lighthouse balcony affords one of Cuba's finest views (Fig. 1698).

Destruction of the United States Navy battleship, *Maine*, is considered the direct cause of the Spanish American War. The explosion, whose mystery has never been solved, took place in Havana Harbor at 9:40 P.M., February 15, 1898 (Fig. 1697).

PUERTO RICO (Fig. 1699)

Puerto Rico's seal of the commonwealth includes the lamb which symbolizes peace and brotherhood. In 1511 King Ferdinand of Spain granted this seal to Spanish settlers. The initials F and I stand for Ferdinand and Isabella and the symbols on the border are taken from the Spanish coat of arms.

VIRGIN ISLANDS (Fig. 1700–1701)

The Virgin Islands, lying east of Puerto Rico, form part of the chain of islands which extends between the Caribbean Sea and the Atlantic Ocean. These islands were purchased for $25

1699

1700

1697 **Havana, Cuba,** marked: STERLING. (Wreck of the Maine in bowl.)
1698 **Havana, Cuba.** No mark.
1699 **Puerto Rico,** marked: STERLING 3.
1700 **Virgin Islands,** marked: STERLING SILVER.

1701

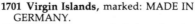

1702

1703

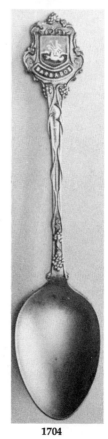

1704

million fron Denmark by the United States in 1916 and proclaimed a Possession January 25, 1917.

SAINT THOMAS (Fig. 1702)

Saint Thomas is one of the three main islands of the Virgin Islands. Charlotte Amalie on St. Thomas is the capital and chief port.

TRINIDAD, WEST INDIES (Fig. 1703)

Trinidad was first settled by Spain. Numerous immigrants arrived from the French Antilles in the late eighteenth century. It became British in 1802. However, the French and Spanish influences still reveal themselves in Trinidad.

BARBADOS (Fig. 1704)

The island of Barbados in the West Indies was a British colony from the 1620s until its independence in 1966. Its pleasant climate and sandy beaches have made it a popular vacation resort.

ARUBA (Fig. 1705)

Situated in the Netherlands Antilles, Aruba covers seventy square miles. It is a refining center for crude oil shipped from Venezuela

CURACAO (Fig. 1706–1709)

Largest island in Netherlands Antilles, Curacao was first settled by Spain in 1527. The Netherlands won the island along with Aruba and Bonaire from the Spanish in 1634 and have since retained possession except for a brief period during the Napoleonic Wars. Although the principal industry is oil refining, sisal, limes and oranges are the chief crops grown on the island and play an important part in its economy.

1701 **Virgin Islands,** marked: MADE IN GERMANY.
1702 **St. Thomas,** marked: (see drawing).
1703 **Columbia,** marked: 0900.
1704 **Bogota,** marked: 0900.

1705

1711

SAINT LUCIA (Fig. 1718)

Saint Lucia is the largest, most picturesque of the Windward Islands in the British West Indies. Its former badge was a black shield bearing a device in which two lengths of bamboo cane quartered two roses and two fleur-de-lis, representing the claim that the French once made to this island. The present badge, also incorporated into the blue flag, is a black triangle bordered with white with a yellow triangle at its base.

1705 **Aruba.** No mark.
1706 **Curacao,** marked: GOSEN STERLING.
1707 **Curacao,** marked: GERO 90.
1708 **St. Lucia.** No mark.
1709 **Jamica,** marked: STERLING RN.
1710 **Jamaica,** marked: STERLING 3.
1711 **Jamaica,** marked: MESKER EPNS.

1706

1707

1708

1709

1710

JAMAICA (Fig. 1709–1712)

Jamaica is the largest island of the British West Indies. Its coat of arms was granted in 1661. The shield, bearing the red Cross of St. George, is charged with five golden pineapples and is supported by two Arawak Indians. The motto found on the scroll, *Indus Uterque Serviet Uni*, declares that "Both Indies will serve one." This badge was reproduced on both the Blue Ensign and the Union Flag. When Jamaica became independent within the Commonwealth in 1962, it adopted a national flag bearing a gold cross. It is black in the hoist and fly and green at the top and bottom.

FORT-DE-FRANCE, MARTINIQUE, FRENCH WEST INDIES (Fig. 1713)

The official residence of the governor of this island is at Fort Royal, the city's former name. A statue of the Empress Josephine, wife of Napoleon Bonaparte, born in Martinique in 1763 stands in the public gardens. Fort-de-France was partially destroyed by an earthquake in 1839 and nearly totally consumed by fire in 1890.

GUADELOUPE, FRENCH WEST INDIES (Fig. 1714)

Guadeloupe was discovered by Columbus in 1493, on his second voyage, but the island was not settled until 1550 French settlers landed there in 1635. The British occupied Guadeloupe eight different times between 1664 and 1816 but since 1816, it has been French.

BOGOTÁ, COLUMBIA (Fig. 1715–1716)

The capital of Columbia, Bogotá was

1712

1713

1714

1715

1712 **Jamaica,** marked: STERLING.
1713 **Fort-De-France, Martinique, French West Indies,** marked: "Crescent & crown" G E SCHUTZ 800 KFK.
1714 **Guadeloupe, French West Indies,** marked: DC "turtle" 186.
1715 **Trinidad,** marked: STERLING.

founded in 1538 by Gonzalo Jiménez de Quesada. It was originally known as "Santa Fe de Bogotá."

BRAZIL (Fig. 1717–1720)

The fifth largest country in the world, Brazil was discovered for the Portuguese by Pedro Alvares Cabral in 1500. The original inhabitants were the Tupi-Guarani Indians, with the first settlement being established at Salvador de Bahía.

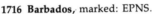

1716 **Barbados,** marked: EPNS.
1717 **Brazil.** 1913 coin, 1000 Reis.
1718 **Brazil.** 1938 coin, 5000 Reis.
1719 **Brazil.** 1907 coin, 2000 Reis.
1720 **Brazil.** 1930 coin, 2000 Reis.
1721 **Ecuador.** 1930 coin, Dos Sucres.
1722 **Ecuador.** 1944 coin.

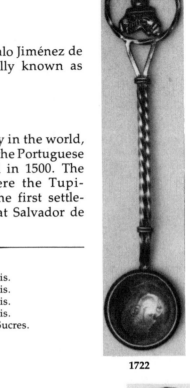

1722

1717

1718

1716

1719

1720

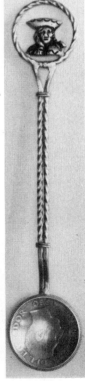

1721

ECUADOR (Fig. 1721–1726)

The name, Ecuador, means "Equator" and was given to the country by Simón Bolívar. Pack mules and llamas are still being used in the mountainous regions of this country.

BOLIVIA (Fig. 1727–1728)

The Bolivian coat of arms symbolizes its wealth by a llama, a tree, a wheat-sheaf and a horse.

1723 Ecuador. 1944 coin, Cinco Sucres, 0.720 silver.
1724 Ecuador, marked: ECUADOR.
1725 Ecuador. No mark.
1726 Ecuador, marked: ECUADOR.
1727 Bolivia, marked: L & S, Birmingham 1900-01.
1728 Bolivia, marked: 925 MML. 1901 coin.
1729 Peru, marked: RD No. 371236. L & S, Birmingham 1907-08.

1723

1729

| 1724 | 1725 | 1726 | 1727 | 1728 |

1730

1736

PERU (Fig. 1729–1737)

Peru's coat of arms was introduced in 1825. The quarters of the shield symbolize the country's fauna (llama, still being used in the mountainous areas), flora (cinchona tree) and minerals (cornucopia). In the background are four crossed Peruvian flags (Fig. 1729, 1737).

Cuzco, Peru is a joint product of Indian and Spanish cultural traditions—with the Indian contribution largely dominant. With reason, Cuzco is hailed

1730 Peru, marked: 900 "llama." 1907 coin.
1731 Peru. No mark.
1732 Cuzco. No mark.
1733 Lima, Peru. 1869 coin.
1734 Peru. 1916 1/2 Sol coin.
1735 Peru.
1736 Peru. No mark.

1731

1732

1733

1734

1735

as the "archaeological capital of South America" (Fig. 1732).

Lima, Peru was founded by Francisco Pizarro in 1535. He named it "the City of the Kings." Lima has retained its colonial atmosphere and is one of the most picturesque capitals of the New World (Fig. 1733).

CHILE (Fig. 1738–1745)

The world "Chile" is thought to be derived either from a Quechua Indian word for snow or the Aymará word *Chilli*

1737 **Peru,** marked: L & S, Birmingham 1915-16.
1738 **Chile,** marked: 900.
1739 **Chile,** marked: Plata 900. Peso.
1740 **Chile,** marked: MADE IN CHILE 900.
1741 **Chile,** marked: PLATA 900 CHILE.
1742 **Valparaiso, Chile.**
1743 **Valparaiso, Chile.**

1737

1743

1738

1739

1740

1741

1742

345

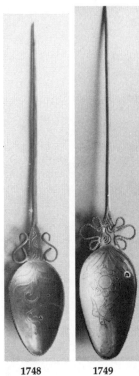

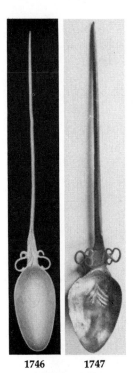

meaning "place where the earth ends." Its national flower, the copihue (*Lapageria rosea*) is a lovely red lily growing from one and one-half to three inches long (Fig. 1741).

Valparaiso, the most important seaport of Chile was founded by Juan de Saavedra, one of the Spanish conquerers of the Incas (Fig. 1742–1745).

Chile's coat of arms is based on the flag. It includes the motto "By right or might," an Andes deer and a condor (Fig. 1739).

1744-1750 Araucanian Topu (Tobu) Spoons. No marks.

1746   1747

1748   1749

1744

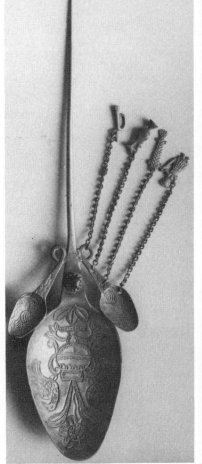

1745

1750

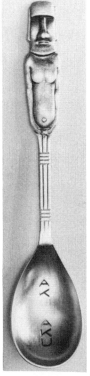

1752

ARAUCANIAN TOPU (TOBU) SPOONS (Fig. 1744–1750)

A large tribe of Araucanian Indians inhabited Chile from the Rio Choapa to the Gulf of Corcovado in the sixteenth century. Araucanian spoons show greater Spanish influence than their jewelry. They are used to hold their blankets around their shoulders and as hair ornaments.

EASTER ISLAND (Rapa Nui) (Fig. 1751–1752)

Easter Island is an isolated island dependency of Chile. *Isla de Pascua* is the Chilean name of this island which was discovered by Dutch navigator Jacob Roggeveen on Easter Sunday, 1722. It is famed for its prehistoric platforms, stone statues and other archaeological remains. Some of the statues stand more than thirty feet high and weigh up to fifty tons. These huge images were carved from volcanic ash blocks located in craters on the island by aborigines and were sometimes transported long distances. Archaeologists have related these stone constructions to other eastern Polynesian types of temple structure (marae), in which standing stones are back rests for gods and ancestors who are summoned to ceremonies. Easter Island has been in the news in recent years because of the work done there by the Danish anthropologist, Thor Heyerdahl.

ARGENTINA (Fig. 1753–1758)

Argentina's coat of arms is an ellipse divided into halves, the upper one being light blue and the lower one silver. In the center of the blue section is a Phrygian red liberty cap supported by a vertical lance held by two clasped hands, symbolizing unity of the nation. The ellipse is surmounted by a golden rising sun and surrounded by a wreath of in-

1751-1752 **Easter Island,** marked EIKS-P40.
1753 **Argentina.** 1882 coin, 20 Centavos.

1751

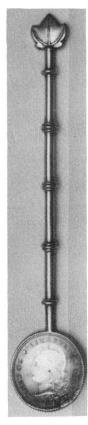

1753

tertwined laurel branches held together by a bow of blue ribbons.

The Bola or Bolas is a form of missile used by the Paraguay Indians, the Patagonians and other South American tribes for hunting, also by the cowboys (gauchos) of Argentina. This device consists of a thong or rope with a ball of

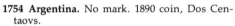

1754 **Argentina.** No mark. 1890 coin, Dos Centaovs.
1755 **Argentina,** marked: 900. 1882 coin, 20 Centavos.
1756 **Argentina,** marked: ARGENTINA 900.
1757 **Argentina.**
1758 **Buenos Aires, Argentina,** marked: 800.
1759 **Montevideo, Uruguay,** marked: 800 "Cresent & crown." "S. Guffin July 1, 1907" engraved on back.
1760 **Montevideo, Uruguay.** No mark.

1754

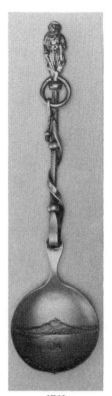

1760

1755   1756   1757   1758   1759

1761

1763

metal, stone or lump of clay attached to each end; or of three such balls united at a common center. The missile is swung round the head by one ball, then hurled at a running animal entangling its feet to bring it down. Small ivory Bolas are used by Alaskan Eskimos for catching birds (Fig. 1755).

MONTEVIDEO, URUGUAY
(Fig. 1759–1760)

Montevideo, capital and only large city in Uruguay, was founded in 1726 by colonists from Buenos Aires. It was named Montevideo, "I see the mountain" because of the Cerro, a cone-shaped hill on the mainland.

URUGUAY (Fig. 1761–1764)

The scales on the coat of arms of Uruguay represent equality before the law, the mountain signifies the strength of the country, the ox stands for richness and the horse for freedom.

1761 **Uruguay.**
1762 **Uruguay.** "Uruguay" on back.
1763 **Uruguay.**
1764 **Uruguay.** "Uruguay" on back.

1762

1764

1765

1766

VI
PEOPLE OF
THE WORLD

FRANZ JOSEPH I (1830–1916)
(Fig. 1765–1766)

Emperor of Austria and King of Hungary, Franz Joseph I came to the throne December 2, 1848, his reign lasting sixty-eight years. He married his cousin, Elizabeth of Bavaria in 1854, who was assassinated at Geneva in 1898. This was just one of the many tragedies in the personal life of Franz Joseph. He became the symbol of the empire, and his memory is still cherished.

FRANZ FERDINAND (1863–1914)
(Fig. 1767–1768)

Franz Ferdinand was Archduke of Austria. He was a nephew of, and after 1896, heir of Franz Joseph to the throne of Austria. Ferdinand was hopeful of carrying out extensive reforms in the monarchy. However, the emperor was embittered by the archduke's morganatic marriage to the Countess Sophie Chotek in 1900, and never permitted him to share in the government. Ferdinand and the archduchess were assassinated during a visit to Sarajevo, June 28, 1914.

KAISER WILHELM (1859–1941)
(Fig. 1769)

Son of Frederick III and Victoria, Princess Royal of Great Britain, Frederick

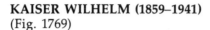

1765 **Franz Joseph.** Bowl is a 10 Kronen coin.
1766 **Franz Joseph,** marked: "Crescent & crown" 800. Maker's mark illegible.
1767 **Franz Ferdinand,** marked: "Crescent & crown" 800. Maker's mark not clear.
1768 **Franz Ferdinand.**

1767

1768

1769

1770

Wilhelm Victor Albert William II, commonly called Kaiser Wilhelm, was ex-German emperor and King of Prussia. He was one of the most powerful figures in Europe for a generation.

PRINCE WILHELM (1882–1951)
(Fig. 1770)

Crown prince of Germany and eldest son of William II, Prince Wilhelm was lieutenant general in World War I, supporting his father. After his father abdicated in 1918, he renounced the succession and followed William II to exile in Holland. Returning to Germany in 1923, he took up the Nazi cause. After World War II, Wilhelm fled to Austria, was captured by the French and allowed to return to Hechingen.

HINDENBURG (1847–1934)
(Fig. 1771–1772)

Paul Ludwig Hans Anton von Beneckendorff un von Hindenburg, German soldier and president at one time was one of the most powerful figures in Europe.

QUEEN LOUISE (1776–1810)
(Fig. 1773)

Auguste Wilhelmine Amalie Luise, daughter of Prince Charles of Mecklenburg-Strelitz. At nineteen she married the Crown Prince of Prussia, Frederich William. She was noted for her beauty and for her devotion to her family and country. To pay her country's war debts she sold her jewels except one strand of pearls which she is often pictured wearing.

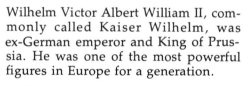

1769 **Kaiser Wilhelm,** marked: 3 "Crescent & crown" 800 SM.
1770 **Prince Wilhelm,** marked: 3 "Crescent & crown" 800 SM.
1771 **Von Hindenburg,** marked: 3 "Crescent & crown" 800 SM.
1772 **Von Hindenburg,** marked: M "Pine tree" in a circle.

1771

1772

1773

1775

MARIE ANTOINETTE (1755–1793)
(Fig. 1774–1775)

Joséphe Jeanne Marie Antoinette made enemies about the court because of youthful frivolities and extravagances. She was considered to be too much under the influence of her mother, Maria Theresa, and was spoken of contemptuously as "the Austrian woman." When led to the guillotine, Marie Antoinette heard her sentence with perfect calmness.

HUMBERT I (1844–1900) (Fig. 1776)

Humbert I (Ital. Umberto) was the eldest son of Victor Emmanauel II and Queen Marie Adelaide. Greatly respected by the Italians and known as "Humbert the Good," he was assassinated in 1900.

MARGHERITA DI SAVOIA
(1851–1926) (Fig. 1777)

Queen dowager of Italy, Margherita was the daughter of Ferdinand, Duke of Genoa. In 1868 she married Humbert, then crown prince of Italy, who ascended the throne of Italy in 1878. Her dignified performance and winning personality gained her wide popularity. After Humbert's assassination, their son, Victor Emmanuel III succeeded him as king.

AUGUSTUS II (1670–1733)
(Fig. 1778)

Called "Augustus the Strong," Augustus II was king from 1697–1704 and 1709–1733. Though a tyrant as a ruler, he was largely responsible for the architec-

---

1773 **Queen Louise,** marked: DEPOSÉ 800 "Crescent & crown" S & H interwined.
1774 **Marie Antoinette,** marked: IMPORTE "Pine tree" 800.
1775 **Marie Antoinette,** marked: "Crescent & crown."
1776 **Humbert I.** No mark.

1774

1776

1777

1778

1779

1780

tural beautification of his capital city, Dresden.

FREDERICK II, THE GREAT (1712–1786) (Fig. 1779–1780)

Frederick the Great, King of Prussia, wa the third son of Frederick William I of Prussia and Sophia Dorothea of Hanover. He married Elizabeth Christine, daughter of the Duke of Brunswick-Bevern. Frederick ascended to the throne May 31, 1740 following the death of his father. During his forty-six year reign, he consolidated his kingdom, raising Prussia to a commanding position in Germany, and one of respect in Europe.

WILHELMINA I (1880–1962) (Fig. 1781)

Daughter of King William III by his second wife, Emma of Waldeck, Wilhelmina became queen of the Netherlands upon her father's death. During her minority her mother ruled and soon after her eighteenth birthday, September 6, 1898, she was crowned. After her fiftieth anniversary on the throne, Wilhelmina abdicated and was succeeded by her daughter, Juliana.

WILLIAM COWPER (1731–1800) (Fig. 1782)

Well-known English poet, William Cowper's poems reflect the pleasures of English country life. In the bowl of the spoon is a gnarled oak tree from whose branches Cowper tried unsuccessfully three times to commit suicide.

BEAU BRUMMELL (1778–1837) (Fig. 1783)

George Bryan Brummell, known as Beau, the English dandy, was distin-

---

1777 **Margherita Di Savoia.** No mark.
1778 **Augustus II,** marked: (see drawing).
1779 **Frederick II, The Great.**
1780 **Frederick II, The Great.**

guished chiefly for that taste in dress which made him the autocrat in the world of fashion.

KITCHENER (1850–1916) (Fig. 1784)

Horatio Herbert Kitchener, 1st Earl Kitchener of Khartoum and of Broome, was a British military leader. He was lost at sea in the sinking of the cruiser *Hampshire*.

JOFFRE (1852–1931) (Fig. 1785)

French soldier, Joseph Jacques Césaire Joffre, is known as the hero of the Battle of the Marne of World War I. He later became supreme commander of the French armies. Subsequently he was blamed when the German attack on Verdun nearly succeeded. The French government relieved Joffre of his command, and he virtually retired with the rank of marshal of France.

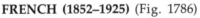

1781

1783

FRENCH (1852–1925) (Fig. 1786)

John Denton Pinkstone French, 1st Earl of Y'pres was in command of the British Expeditionary Force on the western front.

MARY STUART (1542–1587)
(Fig. 1787)

Mary, Queen of Scots, was the daughter of James V and Mary of Guise. She is shown here wearing the heart-shaped "attifet" headdress which she immortalized and which later became known as the widow's cap.

ROBERT TREAT (1622–1710)
(Fig. 1788)

Robert Treat was the founder of Newark, New Jersey. This spoon celebrates the 350th anniversary of Newark.

1781 Wilhelmina I, marked: (see drawing). "1896 6 Sept 1938" inscribed on back.
1782 William Cowper. Maker: MW. Sheffield 1899-1900.
1783 Beau Brummell.
1784 Horatio Kitchener. Maker: Caron Bros. S. Plate 3.

1782

1784

GEORGE WASHINGTON (1732–1799)
(Fig. 1789)

This spoon depicts George Washington attempting to conceal the stump of the chopped-down cherry tree, a myth by Parson Weems.

MARTIN LUTHER (1483–1546)
(Fig. 1790)

The Martin Luther monument fea-

1785 **Joseph Joffre.** Maker: Caron Bros. S. Plate 3.
1786 **French.** Maker: Caron Bros. S. Plate 3.
1787 **Mary, Queen of Scots.**
1788 **Robert Treat.**
1789 **George Washington.**
1790 **Martin Luther.**

1790

1785

1786   1787   1788   1789

1791

1793

tured on the handle and in the bowl of this spoon was erected in 1868 at a cost of $85,000. It stands in the old city of Worms in Hesse-Darmstadt. The Lutheran Church derives its name from Martin Luther, the German religious reformer.

SHAKESPEARE (1564–1616) (Fig. 1791–1795) (See also 716–III, 358, 359)

English poet and dramatist, William Shakespeare, joined a company of actors about 1594 to whom his first obligation was as an actor. However, his chief contribution was his plays. He provided, alone or in collaboration, thirty-eight between 1590–91 and 1612–13. Shakespeare retired from active service as leading playwright of the King's men in 1612 or 1613, and little is known of his later years.

LITTLE MISS MUFFET (Fig. 1796)

This nursery rhyme provides entertaining material for speculation. It has been suggested that Miss Muffet was Patience, daughter of the entomologist, Dr. Thomas Muffet (d. 1604, a man "whose admiration for spiders has never been surpassed." Since Dr. Muffet (Moffett or Moufet) was author of *The Silkworms and Their Flies* "lively described in verse," one can easily see how this rhyme can be attributed to him. But since only Dr. Muffet could describe this verse as "lively," and no record of this epigram has been found before 1805, any estimation must be cautious. It subsequently appears with material variations: "Little Mary Ester sat upon a tes-

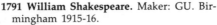

1791 **William Shakespeare.** Maker: GU. Birmingham 1915-16.
1792 **William Shakespeare.** Maker: GU. Birmingham 1892-93.
1793 **William Shakespeare.** marked: Birmingham 1918-19.
1794 **Shakespeare (Juliet Pattern).** Maker: A. F. Towle & Son Co., marked: **Sterling W. O. Amann.**

1792

1794

1795

1797

ter" in 1812, and "Little Miss Mopsey, Sat in the Shopsey" in 1842. It does have noticeable similarity to "Little Polly Flinders," "Little Poll Parrot," "Little General Monk," "Little Tommy Tacket," and "Little Jack Horner." The latter was current in 1720 and is probably earlier, as also the lampoon "Little General Monk." It has been inferred that this form of rhyme, a person sitting and waiting and something important arriving dates to pagan times. It is possible that this, along with many other rhymes, are parodies of earlier ones. A 1945–46 analysis of children's books showed that of all the nursery verses "Miss Muffet" appears most frequently, perhaps because the subject lends itself to illustration. The picture "Little Miss Muffet" was painted by Millais in 1884.

AMUNDSEN (1872–1928)
(Fig. 1797–1800)

Norwegian polar explorer, Roald Amundsen, navigated the Northwest Passage and fixed the position of the North Magnetic Pole (1903–06). He discovered the South Pole in December of 1911. Amundsen completed the Northeast Passage in 1920 and flew across the North Pole with Lincoln Ellsworth in 1926. He disappeared on a flight to rescue survivors of the Nobile expedition June 18, 1928.

VISCOUNT HORATIO NELSON
(1758–1806) (Fig. 1801–1802)

The Nelson column, a granite monument 184 feet 10 inches in height, rises in the center of Trafalgar Square in London. Dedicated to the memory of this famous British admiral, this monument

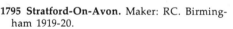

1795 **Stratford-On-Avon.** Maker: RC. Birmingham 1919-20.
1796 **Little Miss Muffet,** marked: R11 Birmingham 1970-71.
1797 **Roald Amundsen,** marked: HARALD NORDBY 830s.
1798 **Roald Amundsen.** No mark.

1796

1798

1799

1801

was erected from 1840 to 1843. It was designed by William Railton, and the statue of Nelson at its top was executed by E. H. Baily. Four bronze lions designed by Sir Edwin Landseer were added at the corners of the monument's base in 1868. The bronze head of the column was cast from gunmetal recovered from the British warship, *The Royal George*. Scenes from Nelson's famous sea battles are depicted on the base in bronze bas-reliefs.

JOAN OF ARC (JEANNE d' ARC 1412–1431) (Fig. 1803–1807)

The French heroine, Joan of Arc was sometimes known as "the Maid of Orleans." Born of an humble peasant family, she believed herself commissioned by heaven to liberate France. Convincing Charles VII of her divine authority, she was given command of a considerable force and by the victories she gained, enabled Charles to be crowned at Rheims. She was captured in 1430 by the Burgundians, delivered to the English and burned at the stake after a mock trial.

One of France's earliest standards displayed three gold toads on a blue field. However, in A.D. 496 King Clovis was inspired by a vision and converted them into three golden lilies, the heraldic *fleurs-de-lis*.

It is uncertain what flag Joan of Arc bore in her struggle against the English; however, it no doubt displayed religious emblems in addition to the fleurs-de-lis. (Fig. 1804, 1806–1807).

VAN DYKE (1599–1641) (Fig. 1808)

Flemish painter, Sir Anthony Van

1799 **Roald Amundsen.** No mark.
1800 **Ellsworth, Amundsen, Nobile.** No mark.
1801 **Viscount Horatio Nelson.** Maker: J.M.B. Chester 1905-06. Rd. 239765.
1802 **Viscount Horatio Nelson,** marked: London 1897-98, marks for foreign plate. (Also see drawing.)

1800

1802

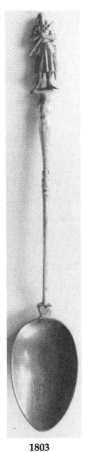

1803

1809

Dyke (Van Dyck) gained fame for the many portraits he painted of the English, Italian and Flemish society of his time. He also painted some mythological and many religious pictures. His best work is a happy mingling of the Flemish and Venetian schools which resulted in a rare form of art.

COLUMBUS (1446–1506) (Fig. 1809)

Genoese navigator, Christopher Columbus became a sailor at the age of

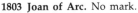

1803 **Joan of Arc.** No mark.
1804 **Joan of Arc.** Maker: LP. "PARIS 95" on back.
1805 **Joan of Arc.** French quality mark.
1806 **Joan of Arc.** French quality mark.
1807 **Joan of Arc.** marked: IMPORTE.
1808 **Van Dyck,** marked: S.
1809 **Columbus,** marked: STERLING.

1804

1805

1806

1807

1808

twenty-eight. He is best known for his 1492 voyage when he discovered the island of San Salvador. Not now credited with the discovery of the New World, he did make it generally known.

NAPOLÉON (1769–1821)
(Fig. 1810–1820)

Napoléon Bonaparte, French Emperor

1810 Napoleon. Maker HC. Quality mark for 950. "INVALIDES" in bowl.
1811 Napoleon. French quality mark. "INVALIDES" in bowl.
1812 Napoleon. French quality mark. "INVALIDES" in bowl.
1813 Napoleon. French quality mark. Maker: HC.
1814 Napoleon. marked: IMPORTE.
1815 Napoleon. No mark.
1816 Napoleon. No mark.

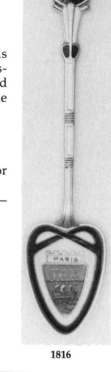

1816

1810

1811   1812   1813   1814   1815

and military genius whose overreaching ambition finally resulted in his defeat and exile.

Although the Invalides was founded in 1671 by Louis XIV to receive wounded soldiers, it contains the Musée l'Armée, the Church of Saint-Louis, and is best known for the tomb of Napoleon I beneath its dome.

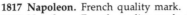

1817 Napoleon. French quality mark.
1818 Napoleon. French quality mark, GIC.
1819 Napoleon. Mark illegible.
1820 Napoleon.
1821 MacDonald, marked: P. W. Ellis & Co. maple leaf trademark.
1822 MacDonald, marked: STERLING.

1817

1822

1818   1819   1820   1821

MACDONALD (1851–1891)
(Fig. 1821–1822)

Sir John Alexander MacDonald was the first prime minister of the Dominion of Canada. He is often called the father of present day Canada because of his leading role in the establishment of the dominion in 1867. The MacDonald Memorial stands on Parliament Hill in Ottawa.

MOZART (1756–1791) (Fig. 1823)

Austrian composer, Wolfgang Amadeus Mozart, composed short pieces at the age of six. At seven he gave concerts in Paris and London. Mozart is distinguished for the universality of his genius.

1823

WAGNER (1813–1883) (Fig. 1824–1825)

The great German musical composer, Wilhelm Richard Wagner broke away from traditional music. He made his art a medium for the expression of ideas as well as emotions.

BEETHOVEN (1770–1827) (Fig. 1826)

Ludwig Van Beethoven, one of the greatest musical composers is known the world over for his symphonies and sonatas. A precocious genius for music, Beethoven commenced his education as a musician at four. About the age of thirty he was attacked with total deafness but continued composing music he could hear only within his mind.

1825

1823 Mozart. Maker: J·D, marked: 800 L?4.
1824 Wagner, marked: "Crescent & crown" 800.
1825 Wagner, marked: 800 SM.
1826 Beethoven, marked: 800 "Crescent & crown" KW.

1824

1826

BALBOA (1475–1517) (Fig. 1827–1828)

A Castilian noble, Vasco Núñez de Balboa, discovered the Pacific Ocean and took possession of the "Southern Sea" by marching into the water, and, in the names of the King and Queen of Castile, claiming "these seas and lands."

1827 **Balboa.** No mark.
1828 **Balboa.** Maker: T. H. Martinsen, EPNS. NORWAY.

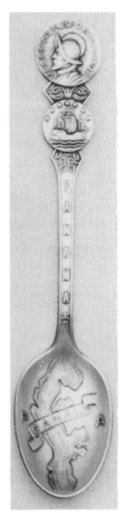

1827

1828

1829

1830

VII
THE PACIFIC
WORLD

P. & O. LINES (Fig. 1829–1832)

It all began in 1837 when two men, Willcox and Anderson, chartered an elderly paddle steamer, the quaint little *William Fawcett*, to trade with and carry the mails to the Iberian Peninsula and the Peninsular Steam Navigation Company was formed. Two years later the mail contract was extended to Egypt. In 1840 the name of the company was changed to Peninsular and Oriental when a Royal Charter was granted for the carriage of mails to India. Additional services were added in 1842 from Southampton to Alexandria, thence overland to Suez and from Suez via Ceylon to Calcutta; in 1844, service was extended to Penang, Singapore, Hong Kong and Shangai, and regular mail service to Australia.

At the outbreak of the Crimean War, eleven ships of the fleet were taken over by the Government but later, bigger, faster and more comfortable ships were built.

In 1914 the P & O Company acquired the British India Steam Navigation Company, Ltd., and in 1916 the New Zealand Shipping Company and the Federal Steam Navigation Company. The following year there were added the Hain and Nourse Companies, the Union

---

1829 S.S. Oriana, marked: SILVER.
1830 S.S. Orcades, marked: MN WE Birmingham 1956-57.
1831 S.S. Himalaya, marked: Angus & Cate, Sydney EPA1.
1832 S.S. Canberra, marked: MN WE Birmingham 1960-61.

1831

1832

1833

1835

1834

S. S. Company of New Zealand and after World War I, an interest was purchased in the Orient Line and the General Steam Navigation Company. During the grim years of World War II more than half the company ships were sunk—a total of 182 ships. New ships were built, bigger and more luxurious. New services were introduced, including one across the Pacific, pioneered by the Orient Line in 1954 and later operated jointly by the P & O and the Orient Line. These Sun Cruisers, the S. S. *Oriana* (1961); the S. S. *Canberra* (1961); the S. S. *Orcades* and the S. S. *Himalaya* are like great white clouds floating on the blue and silver Pacific. S. S. *Monterey* (Fig. 1833)

The S. S. *Monterey* was one of the Matson Line's luxury steamers.

The Matson Line began in 1882, with a single sailing vessel, on which Captain William Matson carried passengers and freight between Hawaii and San Francisco. By 1909 four ships flew his flag and by 1935 fifty vessels bore the big blue M on their stacks as they plied their way back and forth between Hawaii and the mainland.

The S. S. *Malolo* (Flying Fish), first of Matson's great luxury liners, was greeted with ceremony on her first arrival at Honolulu, November 21, 1927. She carried too much superstructure and was top heavy—and, the Hawaiians said she should never have been named the *Malolo* anyway because the name carried bad luck. She was rebuilt; much superstructure removed and she was rechristened S. S. *Matsonia*. Though she sailed the Pacific waters for many years thereafter, served as a troopship during World War II and was afterwards recon-

---

1833 **S.S. Monterey, Matson Line,** no marks. Silverplate.
1834 **Mango,** no marks.
1835 **Banana Leaf,** marked: STERLING.
1836 **Outrigger Canoe,** no marks.

1836

1837

1838

1839

verted for luxury passenger service, troops and luxury passengers alike can testify that she lived up to her nickname *Marolo*.

HAWAII (Fig. 1834–1844)

When the Polynesians from the Marquesas and Tahiti arrived in the Hawaiian Islands between 500 and 900 A.D. they did not find the lush subtropical fruits and flowers so highly publicized in travel folders. The climate and the fertile soil were there but the fruits and flowers were largely introductions. These early settlers brought with them their families and their household possessions, their pigs, dogs and chickens, and a variety of domesticated plants that included the hibiscus, wild ginger, taro, yams, ti, sugar cane, sweet potato, breadfruit, paper mulberry, bananas, gourds, bamboo and mountain apple. Because the climate was similar to the land they had left, the plants they brought with them thrived.

These Polynesians also brought with them the skill to make fishhooks and build outrigger canoes for fishing, for fish were a major source of food. Skilled fishermen were held in high esteem and their knowledge was handed down from one generation to another.

For more than a thousand years the Hawaiians lived a Stone Age life undisturbed. Their clothing was tapa cloth, made from the inner bark of various plants; their houses were of poles lashed together with coconut sennit and thatched with pili grass, pandanus, ti or sugar-cane leaves. Their most important cultivated food crop was taro, from

---

1837 **Fish,** no marks.
1838 **Bread Fruit,** no marks.
1839 **Banana Leaf,** marked: STERLING.
1840 **King Kamehameha,** marked: STERLING S.&S. S.F. CAL.

1840

1841

1842

which poi is made. This was supplemented by foods from the other plants they had brought with them and by many kinds of fish, some kinds of seaweed, shellfish and turtles.

Captain Cook's discovery of the islands in 1778 marked the beginning of a new era. The distinguished English navigator may not have been the first white man to see the islands he named for his patron, the Earl of Sandwich, but he was the first to make them known to the rest of the world.

A few years after Cook's voyages, Kamehameha I (called the Great) (Fig. 1840–1841) brought the islands under one rule. He is commemorated by a bronze statue in Honolulu that shows him wearing his famous feather cloak. In his left hand is a spear, while the right is extended in a gesture of aloha. The statue is actually a replica of the original which was lost off the Falkland Islands when the ship carrying it sank in a storm. After the replica was set up and unveiled by King Kalakaua on February 14, 1883, as a feature of his coronation celebration, the original statue was recovered and erected at Kohala, Hawaii, Kamehameha's birthplace.

The arrival of outsiders brought many changes to the islands. Among them was the change from *kahilis* (feather standards, symbols of royalty) to flags, and from feather cloaks and helmets to uniforms, royal orders and seals. Hawaii's coat of arms (Fig. 1840, 1843–1844) was based upon a design suggested by the College of Heraldry in London in 1850. The eight stripes represent the eight in-

1841 **King Kamehameha,** marked: STERLING.
1842 **Kalakaua Dime,** marked: H. F. WICHMAN STERLING.
1843 **Kalakaua Hapaha** (Quarter), marked: STERLING.
1844 **Hawaiian Statehood,** marked: EJTCo STERLING.

1843

1844

1845

1846

1847

habited islands. The triangular banner at the fess point was an ancient flag of Hawaiian chiefs. The white ball with which the second and third quarters are charged was an ancient emblem placed at the right and left of a door to indicate a place of refuge. The external ornaments consist of a crest, which is a crown, and two supporters: men clad in the ancient feather cloak and helmet, and one bearing a *kahili* and the other a spear. During Kalakaua's reign he changed the figures, Kameeiamoku and Kamanawa, counselors of Kamehameha I, to face out instead of in and he changed the background of an Hawaiian net to one of ermine. After the revolution of 1893, the Republic of Hawaii replaced the twins with Kamehameha on the left and the Goddess of Liberty on the right.

The motto below the coat of arms was uttered by Kamehameha III in 1843, and reads, *Ua mau ke ea o ka aina i ka pono,* (The life of the land is perpetuated in righteousness).

Hawaii's location at the "crossroads of the Pacific" meant that coins from many nations poured into the isalnds. By 1850, Hawaii was flooded with silver coins of many nations. In making remittances to the United States, where Hawaii did most of her buying and selling, loss by depreciation, and the expense of shipping coins and the insurance were a strain on island economy. In 1883, the Hawaiian government minted its own coins. These and the standard silver coins of the United States became the only legal tender.

Following annexation, an Act of Congress provided for the redemption of Hawaiian coins in United States' coins

---

1845 **Midway Island,** marked: SHREVE & CO.
1846 **Guam,** no marks. Twenty centimo coin, 1885.
1847 **Philippine Islands,** no mark.
1848 **Philippine Islands,** no mark.

1848

1849

at par value, and recoinage of the redeemed coins into United States' silver coins. After January 1, 1904, Kalakaua coins were no longer legal tender. Only a small portion showed up for redemption. Hundreds, perhaps thousands, of them were made into souvenirs (Fig. 1842–1843).

With very little change, the seal of the Territory of Hawaii became the seal of the State of Hawaii (Fig. 1844). On the handle, above the seal, is the hibiscus, State Flower of Hawaii; below the seal are coconut trees; a star and the figure "50" signifying that Hawaii is the 50th State of the Union. Below that is Aloha Tower, often called the "Statue of Liberty of the Pacific," for as the famous lady in New York's harbor is a symbol of hope to new citizens arriving from Europe, so does Aloha Tower carry this message to those arriving from Asia. On the reverse side is the date of admission, August 21, 1959 and the slogan, "The Aloha State."

MIDWAY ISLAND (Fig. 1845)

Midway Island is a coral atoll in the North Pacific. The atoll is made up of two coral islands, Sand Island and Eastern Island. The atoll was discovered in 1859 by N. C. Brooks, commander of the Hawaiian vessel *Gambia*, who found it uninhabited. Midway was known as Brooks for several years. It was annexed in 1867. In 1903 it became a responsibility of the United States Navy Department and a station site of the transpacific cable system. In 1935 it became a fueling stop for Pan American Airways on their flights between Honolulu and the

1851

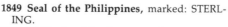

1849 **Seal of the Philippines,** marked: STERLING.
1850 **Philippine Islands,** no marks.
1851 **Philippine Islands,** no marks.
1852 **Philippine Islands,** marked: Watson Co. trademark used from 1879-1905.

1850

1852

1853

1855

Philippines. In 1941 Midway became a national defense area. The Battle of Midway, fought there from June 4 to June 6, 1942 was one of the decisive naval victories of the war.

Midway is home to thousands of Laysan albatross, known there as "Gooney birds" for their peculiarities. They nest on runways and collide with airplanes. Thousands have been relocated on other islands; runways have been relocated, but all to no avail. Gooney birds love people and they love airplanes and even though the Navy planes always win in a collision, the Gooney birds do not leave.

According to an old sailors' superstition, killing an albatross brings bad luck. Some of the superstitions concerning the bird are described in Samuel Taylor Coleridge's poem, *The Rime of the Ancient Mariner*.

GUAM (Fig. 1846)

Guam (Guahan) is the largest of the mid-Pacific Mariana Islands and lies more than fifteen hundred miles east of Manila. It is an unincorporated territory of the United States. Guam was discovered by Ferdinand Magellan on March 6, 1521 during his historic circumnavigation of the globe. The Mariana Islands were claimed by Spain in 1565. The Spanish sent missionaries there in 1668 but the native Chamorros fiercely resisted Spanish rule and customs, so that it was not until the end of the seventeenth century that they were finally subdued. Guam was taken by the United States naval forces during the Spanish American War and ceded to the United States by the Treaty of Paris, December 10, 1898.

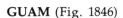

1853 **Carabao, Manila.**
1854 **Tahiti**
1855 **Tahiti,** marked: WV.
1856 **Nouméa, New Caledonia,** no marks.

1854

1856

1857

PHILIPPINE WARRIOR (Fig. 1847)

The Philippine warrior shown on the spoon is an Igorot (member of a Northern Luzon tribe) and wears a loin cloth, feather helmet, and carries a shield.

SEAL OF THE PHILIPPINES (Fig. 1849)

The Seal of the Philippine Islands was adopted in 1905. It was designed by Guillard Hunt, then Chief of the Manuscript Division, Library of Congress. The three cultures of the islands are symbolized. The three gold stars (mullets) are for the native peoples of the three major geographic regions—Luzon, the Visayas, and Mindanao. The castle of Castile and the sea lion of Aragon represent the Spanish period. The American eagle used as the crest represents the association of the Philippines with the United States.

CARABAO (Fig. 1852–1853)

The carabao is actually a small variety of water buffalo *(Buffalo bubalus)* that is found in the Philippines and is used by the natives for plowing, for drawing carts and for carrying burdens.

TAHITI (Fig. 1854–1855)

Tahiti (Otaheite) is the largest of the Society Islands in the South Pacific. Tahiti is mountainous and consists of two ancient volcanoes joined by a low, narrow neck of land, the Isthmus of Taravao. Because it is a "high island" as

1857 **Fiji Islands,** no marks.
1858 **Fiji Islands,** marked: EPNS.
1859 **Rarotonga, Cook Islands,** marked: SILVER.
1860 **Australian Aborigine,** no marks. "MELBOURNE, VICT. 1892" engraved in bowl. Australian coat-of-arms engraved on back of bowl.

1859

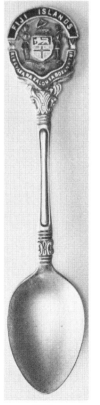

1858

1860

1861

1862

opposed to the low-lying atolls such as Midway, it supports lush tropical forests on the mountain slopes. Water is plentiful from the numerous streams that descend from the mountains. All the natural vegetation is luxuriant. Cultivation of crops such as coconuts (copra), taro, yams and vanilla is limited to the coastal plain.

Tahiti was discovered by a Spanish navigator, Queirós, in 1606. The first European to visit Tahiti was Samuel Wallis, who claimed the island for Great Britain in 1767. The French navigator, Louis Antoine de Bougainville, claimed Tahiti for France the following year. Tahiti became a French protectorate in 1842 or 1843 and a French colony in 1880. Tahitians are French citizens with full civil and political rights.

The natural beauty of Tahiti has long attracted artists and writers, some of whom have exaggerated their claims of the idyllic life there. These exaggerated claims have, in turn, attracted social outcasts and misfits whose presence brought about moral and physical degeneration to the native inhabitants. In recent years, the government has had to restrict this influx.

NOUMÉA (Fig. 1856)

Nouméa is the capital of New Caledonia, an island in the southwestern Pacific. The city was once known as Port de France. It became the capital of New Caledonia in 1854, a year after the island was annexed by France.

In 1768 while sailing southwards from the New Hebrides during his circumnavigation of the world, Louis Antoine de Bougainville saw indications of the

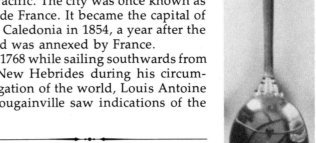

1861 **Goolay-Yali,** the pelican.
1862 **Gaya-Dari,** the platpus.
1863 **Bohra,** the kangaroo.
1864 **Dinewan,** the emu.

1863

1864

existence of a large island in the vicinity of New Caledonia but did not investigate it. So, credit for its discovery goes to Captain James Cook, the English explorer, who landed there September 4, 1774. Because the area around Balade, where he landed, bore some resemblance to the coast of Scotland, he named the island New Caledonia.

FIJI ISLANDS (Fig. 1857–1858)

The Fiji Islands consist of a group of two large islands and about 320 smaller islands scattered over an area of 7,036 square miles in the south Pacific. The islands were first seen by Europeans when sighted by Abel Janszoon Tasmas in 1643. In 1774 Captain James Cook visited there. Captain William Bligh of the *Bounty* sailed through the islands after being cast adrift by mutineers in 1789. "King" Thakombau ceded the islands to Great Britain in 1874 after offering them to the United States.

Fiji was granted a coat of arms in 1908. The main feature is an escutcheon bearing at the top on red, the British lion holding a coconut in its paws. Below is the red cross of St. George on a white background. The quarters thus formed bear specimens of sugar cane, coconut palms, a bunch of bananas and a dove carrying an olive branch. The shield is supported by two Polynesians wearing the *Tapa Sula* or Fijian kilt and standing on a scroll upon which is inscribed the motto, "*Rere Vaka na Kalou ka doka na Tui*" (Fear God and Honor the King). The crest is a native catamaran in full sail.

1865

1867

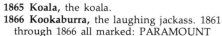

1865 **Koala,** the koala.
1866 **Kookaburra,** the laughing jackass. 1861 through 1866 all marked: PARAMOUNT EPNS. A.1.
1867 **Kangaroo,** no marks.
1868 **Parrot,** no marks.

1866

1868

1869

1871

RAROTONGA (Fig. 1859)

Rarotonga is the principal island of the group of fifteen small islands in the south-central Pacific known as the Cook Islands. A number of these islands were discovered 1773–1777 by Captain James Cook after whom they were named. The islands became a protectorate of Great Britain in 1888–1892 and in 1901 were annexed to the Dominion of New Zealand. In 1965 a new constitution gave the people of the islands control of their internal affairs.

This spoon in one of a series of twenty-seven, each representing a different island. The handle of each is set with a different shell; the one for Rarotonga being mother-of-pearl shell.

AUSTRALIAN ABORIGINE
(Fig. 1860)

Only in Australia and some remoter parts of Africa and South America there exists prehistoric peoples living in a Stone Age culture. A few years ago it was estimated that more than 40,000 of them remained on the continent of Australia. Australian anthropologists are making a frantic effort to record what amounts to a living museum of history before civilization makes inroads by disease and by bringing some of them into our culture.

The aborigines are thought to have arrived in Australia about 25,000 B.C. or perhaps earlier, at a time when there were land bridges between the Australian continent and New Guinea and the Asian mainland on the north. Their origins are uncertain though they may be related to certain primitive tribes of Ceylon, Malaya and Japan. The Austra-

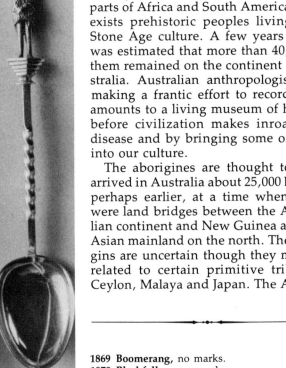

1872

1869 **Boomerang,** no marks.
1870 **Blackfellow,** no marks.
1871 **Emu,** no marks.
1872 **Swan,** no marks.

1870

lian aborigines are a nomadic hunting people who have no knowledge of seed-bearing plants and no animals except the dingo, a type of native dog. They scour the desert and eat everything edible: grubs, lizards, honey, ants, kangaroos, emus, grasses and seeds.

AUSTRALIAN WILDLIFE
(Fig. 1861–1866)

GOOLAY YALI
(Fig. 1861)

Goolay-Yali, the pelican (Fig. 1861) was seen capturing a fish in a net but no one in the tribe knew where he got it until one day children watched him twist and wriggle until to their amazement out popped the fishing net from his mouth. That is why pelicans always fish by dipping their long pouched bills into the water drawing them along like nets.

GAYA-DARI (Fig. 1862)

One day Biggoon, an immense water rat, captured a little duck and made her his wife. Once, while Biggoon slept, she escaped and swam back to her old home. When the laying season came and Duck hatched out her eggs, all her friends saw her two children and they were amazed. Instead of feathers they had fur, and four feet instead of two. When *they* had children they had fur and four feet too, and that is how the egg-laying, furry, four-footed Gaya-Dari or platypusses began.

BOHRA (Fig. 1863)

Once upon a time, Bohra, the kangaroo, walked on four legs like a dog. He was strolling about one night when he

1873

1875

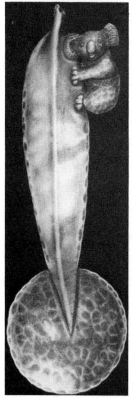

1874

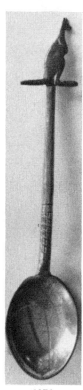

1876

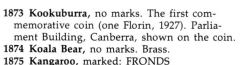

1873 **Kookuburra,** no marks. The first commemorative coin (one Florin, 1927). Parliament Building, Canberra, shown on the coin.
1874 **Koala Bear,** no marks. Brass.
1875 **Kangaroo,** marked: FRONDS
1876 **Kangaroo,** no marks.

375

1877

saw Blackfellows (aborigines) dancing their sacred corroboree around a bonfire. Bohra wanted to dance too and reared up on his hind legs and jumped around the ring in imitation. All of the Blackfellows were amused except the Medicine Man, who, in his fury said "Bohra should die; but as he has taught us a new dance, his life will be spared but from now on he and his tribe will hop on their hind legs, their forefeet shall be hands, and they shall balance on their tails."

DINEWAN (Fig. 1864)

"Before there was any sun," say the Blackfellows, "birds and beasts quarreled a lot. The Emu was King of the Birds and the gray Crane, with the red patch behind his head, was jealous. Once the Emu could fly high and once he saw the Cranes dancing and asked to be taught. The Queen of the Cranes said Dinewan, the Emu, could never dance with such long wings so he allowed the Cranes to cut them off. Then the Cranes unfolded their long wings, which they had hidden by folding them closely to their bodies, and flew away. Since that day, the Emu has been unable to fly."

KOALA (Fig. 1865)

Koala the native bear and Kangaroo were once good friends and proud of their long tails. They went to the river bed to dig water which was very scarce. It was hot so Koala suggested that Kangaroo dig first. He soon tired and asked his friend to take his turn. Koala pretended illness so Kangaroo did his share

1879

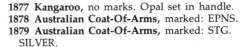

1877 **Kangaroo,** no marks. Opal set in handle.
1878 **Australian Coat-Of-Arms,** marked: EPNS.
1879 **Australian Coat-Of-Arms,** marked: STG.
  SILVER.
1880 **Australian Coat-Of-Arms,** marked: STG.
  SILVER.

1878

1880

1881

1883

of the work too. At last a trickle of water appeared and gradually filled the hole and immediately Koala rushed over and began to drink. As he bent over, his tail stuck up like a dry stick and Kangaroo, annoyed at Koala's cunning, cut off his tail with a boomerang (Fig. 1869). That is why the Koala has no tail and also why he is no longer friendly with Kangaroo.

KOOKABURRA (Fig. 1866)

When the vain and stupid Emu was tricked by the Cranes, one very interested spectator was Kookaburra, the Laughing Jackass. Up to this time Kookaburra had not spoken a word nor uttered a sound, but when he saw how easily the Emu had been tricked, he burst into a hearty laugh and has been laughing ever since.

AUSTRALIAN COAT OF ARMS (Fig. 1878)

Australia's coat of arms was granted in 1912. The six quarters, within an ermine border, contain the badges of the six states: 1. St. George's Cross, charged with a lion and four stars, for New South Wales; 2. the Southern Cross, under a Crown, for Victoria; 3. the Maltese Cross, for Queensland; 4. the bird (a species of shrike), for South Australia; 5. a black swan, for Western Australia; and 6. a lion, for Tasmania. The crest is the Commonwealth Star: found also in the Australian flag. The supporters are native animals, the kangaroo and emu.

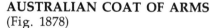

1881 **Melbourne, Australia,** marked: DUNKL-INGS STG. SIL.
1882 **Adelaide, Australia,** marked: EPNS.
1883 **Story Bridge, Brisbane, Australia,** marked: PENINSULA PLATE EPNS A1.
1884 **Harbour Bridge, Sydney, Australia,** marked: Birmingham 1949-50.

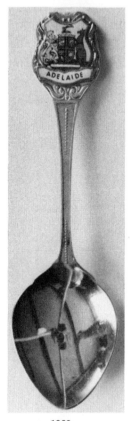

1882

1884

1885

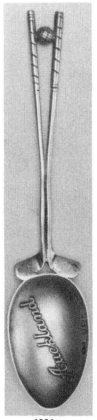

1886

MELBOURNE, AUSTRALIA
(Fig. 1881)

Melbourne is the capital of the State of Victoria. It was named after Lord Melbourne (William Lamb, 2nd Viscount Melbourne) who was prime minister of England at the time of the city's founding.

ADELAIDE, AUSTRALIA (Fig. 1882)

Adelaide is the capital of South Australia. The area was first settled in 1836 and in the following year was laid out for a city by Col. William Light. It was named for the queen consort of King William IV.

STORY BRIDGE (Fig. 1883)

The Story Bridge at Kangaroo Point over the Brisbane River, Queensland, Australia, was built between 1935 and 1940, with a cantilever span of 924 feet (281 m.) and is a government-owned toll bridge and the second longest span in Australia.

HARBOUR BRIDGE (Fig. 1884)

The Sydney Harbor is dominated by a single-span arch bridge which was opened in 1932 and links the northern and southern shores. The arch is 1,650 feet (502 m.) long.

AUCKLAND, NEW ZEALAND
(Fig. 1885–1886)

Auckland,   New   Zealand   was

1885 Auckland, New Zealand, marked: W. D. Birmingham 1949-50.
1886 Auckland, New Zealand, marked: W. D. Birmingham 1911-12.
1887 Christchurch, New Zealand, no marks. "August 2nd, 1903" engraved on the back. The handle is greenstone.
1888 New Zealand Greenstone, marked: STG SIL.

1887

1888

founded in 1840 by Captain William Hobson. The capital of New Zealand from 1841 to 1865, it is now the largest urban center and the leading port.

The Maori (Fig. 1885) man is wearing a feather cloak and carrying a *mere* club. The Maoris wore feather cloaks *(kahu huruhuru)* made of feathers from various birds. The most valuable cloaks were covered with red feathers from beneath the wings of the *kaka* parrot and from this red color, reserved for chieftains, it was named *kahu kura*. The short club has a flat blade somewhat spatulate in shape. The most valued of these were made of nephrite jade.

CHRISTCHURCH (Fig. 1887)

Christchurch, the capital of the province of Canterbury, on the east coast of the South Island of New Zealand, was founded by the Canterbury Association in 1850 under the leadership of John Robert Godley, who lead the Anglican pilgrims there from England.

City residents take great pride in their individual gardens as well as the innumerable public ones that make Christchurch "the garden city of New Zealand."

The city is well-known to American naval airmen because its Harewood Airport has been the staging base for the U. S. Navy's Operation Deep Freeze in the Antarctic.

NEW ZEALAND GREENSTONE
(Fig. 1887–1888)

Greenstone is the name given by *pakehas* (Europeans) in New Zealand to nephrite or jade. It is called jade by jewelers and *Pounamu* by the Maori who named it after one of their gods. Accord-

1891

1889

1890

1889-1893 Paua Shell, marked: STG SIL.

1892

1893

1895

ing to Maori tradition, either Nghue or Kupe, noted explorers from Hawaiki, discovered on the west coast of the South Island a large river, the Arahura, and found Pounamu, an offspring of Tangaroa (in Maori mythology, the God of the Ocean).

Greenstone is very tough in structure. This quality, in addition to its beauty, endeared it to the Maori who used it to make cutting and carving tools as it keeps a fine edge. It was also used to make the *mere* or fighting clubs and for articles of personal adornment such as ear pendants and the carved *tiki*. It is flecked with black spots and sometimes has white markings which imagination transforms into sea foam or clouds. The Maori have named many varieties or hues. One of them, named Tangiwai ("water of tears") is of almost transparent green. There is a romantic legend that a Maori warrior, in searching for his wife found her turned into greenstone, his tears being found in the stone to this day.

PAUA SHELL (Fig. 1889–1893)

The Paua shell (called abalone when found off the California coast) is one of the most beautiful shells in the world. Five species are found in New Zealand waters, of these, the largest, *Haliotis iris* ("the rainbow"), is used in the manufacture of shell jewelry and other souvenirs. The shell is thick and heavy; colors are opalescent greens and blues with occasional flashes of fiery red. They are difficult to find as they occur on rough beaches below spring tide level. The best ones are obtained from Stewart Island and the exposed southwest coast of the South Island.

1894 **Hei Tiki,** marked: C.J.N. & Co. REG^D· "KIA ORA" (Good Health) in the bowl.
1895 **Kiwi Bird,** marked: EPNS.
1896 **Kiwi Bird,** marked: EXQUISITE EPNS.

1894

1896

1897

1899

The brighter of the rosy shells were prized by the Maori of bygone days. They were specially chosen to give a fiery expression or a baleful glare to the eyes of carved wooden figures. These were known as *"Mura-aki"* ("blaze of fire").

The green variety was used for fishing lures and spinners.

The flesh of the animal is high in food value and was highly prized—almost a staple diet with the Maori. The Paua is often called "mutton fish" as the flesh when cooked tastes like mutton.

HEI TIKI (Fig. 1894–1896)

The Maori *hei tiki* or *tiki* is a breast ornament in the form of a human embryo. They are often made of nephrite and are the best-known of Maori ornaments. The origin of the term *tiki* goes back to the widely spread myth that the first male created by Tane (Polynesian god) was named Tiki. Consequently, when man carved the human form in wood, he called his creation *tiki*. The nephrite ornaments were termed *hei tiki*, *hei* meaning to tie around the neck.

According to another myth, the *hei tiki* was made in the form of the human embryo and was endowed with the magic power of promoting growth in the expectant woman. This myth was embellished with the idea that the first one was made for Hineteiwaiwa, the goddess of childbirth. The fact that early explorers saw men wearing the *tiki* would seem to indicate that this myth was a late development.

The tattooing on the face of the Maori in the bowl of the spoon (Fig. 1894) is a type that prevailed throughout

1898

1900

1897 **Kiwi Bird,** no marks.
1898 **New Zealand Kingfisher,** marked: EPNS.
1899 **New Zealand Tui,** marked: EPNS.
1900 **New Zealand Kiwi,** marked: EPNS.

1901

1902

Polynesia, except on Niue and some atolls. The art, apparently at its peak at the time of European contact, was markedly curvilinear, consisting of long, curved lines and spirals.

KIWI BIRD (Fig. 1887, 1891, 1892, 1895, 1897, 1900)

The Kiwis (*Apteryx*) are flightless birds restricted to New Zealand. They are about the size of a domestic chicken, have extremely stout legs and a long, curved bill much like a snipe. Their feathers are brownish-gray and are "incomplete" in structure, resembling and feeling like coarse hair. They have vestigial wings about two inches in length and hidden under the plumage.

Kiwis feed mainly on earthworms and have a keen sense of smell, apparently being able to sense the presence of worms underground.

An adult kiwi weighs about five or six pounds. One of the most remarkable features of the kiwi is its eggs. A female kiwi will lay an egg, about one-fourth as large as herself, and weighing a pound or more.

NEW ZEALAND KINGFISHER (Fig. 1898)

The New Zealand kingfisher is a bird of great beauty but according to medieval legend it was originally a plain gray bird. When it was first liberated from Noah's ark it flew towards the sun when its upper plumage became the color of the sky and its breast was scorched by the heat of the sun as it set.

TUI (Fig. 1899)

The Tui is one of the best songbirds of the New Zealand forests. Its song is

1903

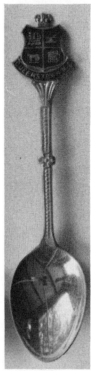

1904

1901 **New Zealand Fantail,** marked: EPNS.
1902 **Waitomo Caves, N. Z.,** marked: EPNS.
1903 **Wellington, N. Z., no marks.**
1904 **Queenstown, N. Z.,** marked: EPNS.

1905

1906

loud, varied, musical and pleasant. It mimics other birds as well, making unbirdlike sounds such as the squeaking of a pig, a boy's whistling or the barking of a dog.

FANTAILS (Fig. 1901)

The fantails of New Zealand are of several species belonging to the genus *Rhipidura*. They are flycatchers and often fly with their fan-like tails widespread.

WAITOMO CAVES (1902)

The Waitomo Caves, near Auckland, New Zealand, are the home of an unusual carnivorous glowworm *(Botelophela luminosa)*. Myriads of these tiny creatures with their lamps lit, cover the roof of the cavern and are reflected in the placid river that flows through the underground tunnel. Visitors in boats float along in absolute silence to gaze on this almost unbelievable spectacle. The slightest noise would cause them to extinguish their tiny lights, but the fantastic greenish-blue light silences even the most garrulous.

WELLINGTON, N. Z. (Fig. 1903)

The city of Wellington, capital city of New Zealand, began with the settlement of *Britannia* which was established at Petone in 1840 by 2,000 emigrants from the United Kingdom. From this grew the city of Wellington, named for Arthur Wellesley Wellington (1769–1852), Britain's well-known "Iron Duke."

QUEENSTOWN, N. Z. (Fig. 1904)

Queenstown is on the South Island of New Zealand at Lake Wakatipu, a favo-

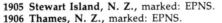

1905 **Stewart Island, N. Z.,** marked: EPNS.
1906 **Thames, N. Z.,** marked: EPNS.
1907 **Stratford, N. Z.,** no marks.
1908 **Crowned Pigeon, New Guinea,** marked: "CROWN"

1907

1908

1909

rite holiday center. The lake has long fascinated and puzzled scientists because its level inexplicably rises and falls three inches every five minutes.

STEWART ISLAND, N. Z. (Fig. 1905)

Stewart Island lies about twenty miles south of South Island and is separated from it by Foveaux Strait. Its main town is Oban, formerly called Half-moon Bay.

THAMES, N. Z. (Fig. 1906)

Thames, New Zealand is a town on the firth of Waihou (formerly called Thames). It is fifty miles southeast of Auckland (North Island). It was once the center of gold mining but is now chiefly concerned with Hauraki and Piako plains dairy production.

STRATFORD, N. Z. (Fig. 1907)

Stratford, New Zealand is a small town on the western side of North Island, not far from Mt. Egmont National

---

1909 **Papua & New Guinea,** marked: (See drawing for marks)

Park. There, in the province of Taranaki, rises "New Zealand's Fujiyama," a perfect isolated cone, Mt. Egmont, an extinct volcano. The majestic grandeur of the mountain is accentuated by the beauty of the rich farmlands surrounding it.

CROWNED PIGEON, NEW GUINEA (Fig. 1908)

Goura victoria beccarii, the Crowned Pigeon, is closely identified with New Guinea as are the birds-of-paradise. They were both hunted extensively for their beautiful, lacy plumage. They are protected now by law but the natives continue to hunt them for their delicious white flesh and may be on their way to extinction. Difficult to raise in captivity, only one man, former Zoo Director of Honolulu, Paul L. Breese, succeeded in breeding them.

PAPUA & NEW GUINEA (Fig. 1909)

Politically, the island of New Guinea is divided between the Netherlands or Dutch New Guinea (a colony of the Netherlands occupying the western half) and the Territory of Papua (a possession of Australia) and the Territory of New Guinea (a United Nations Trust Territory administered by Australia, occupying the eastern section). Since July 1, 1949 the Territories of Papua and New Guinea have been joined administratively.

The native peoples of the area fall into three broad types. In the higher mountain ranges they are of a short, Negroid type. The so-called "true Papuan" is a taller Negroid type with hair in small curls. There is also a lighter-colored Melanesian type with hair less curly and living in coastal areas. The one represented here is from the central highlands which boasts the most splendidly arrayed men in all the Pacific. They wear headdresses decorated with plumes of the Greater Bird of Paradise. The bows and arrows are still part of their essential food-hunting equipment.

VIII PAGES FROM CATALOGS

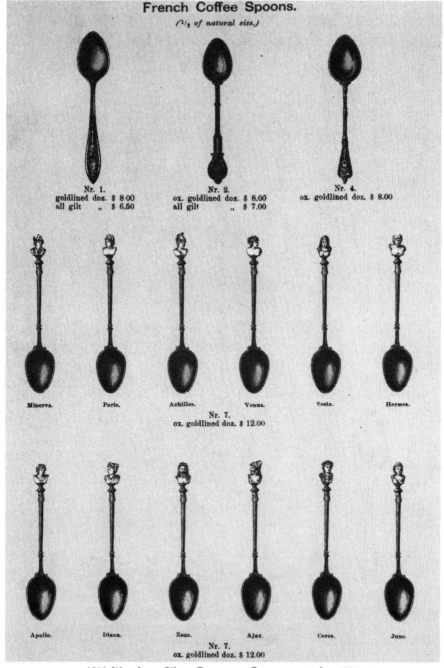

French Coffee Spoons.
(¹/₂ of natural size.)

Nr. 1.
goldlined doz. $ 8.00
all gilt „ $ 6.50

Nr. 2.
ox. goldlined doz. $ 8.00
all gilt „ $ 7.00

Nr. 4.
ox. goldlined doz. $ 8.00

Minerva. Paris. Achilles. Venus. Vesta. Hermes.

Nr. 7.
ox. goldlined doz. $ 12.00

Apollo. Diana. Zeus. Ajax. Ceres. Juno

Nr. 7.
ox. goldlined doz. $ 12.00

1910 Wurzburg Silver Company, Germany, catalog 1891.

ELECTRO-PLATED NICKEL SILVER.

MARMALADE SPOONS, GILT BOWLS. EACH.

Morocco Case, Velvet Lined, to hold 2 Spoons, 4/0.

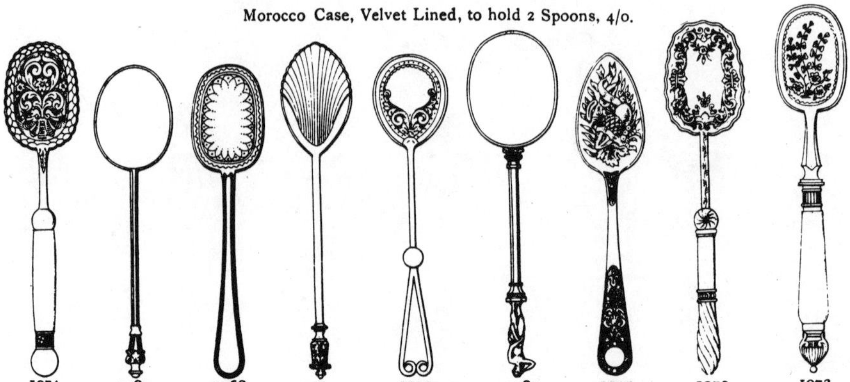

1074 Ivory Centre Plated Cap 6/6 — 1083 Plated 2/6 — 1068 Plated 2/6 — 1057 Plated 3/0 — 1070 Plated 3/9 — 1080 Plated 5/6 — 1045 Plated 2/6 — 1073 Ivory 6/6 — 1072 Ivory Centre Plated Cap 5/6

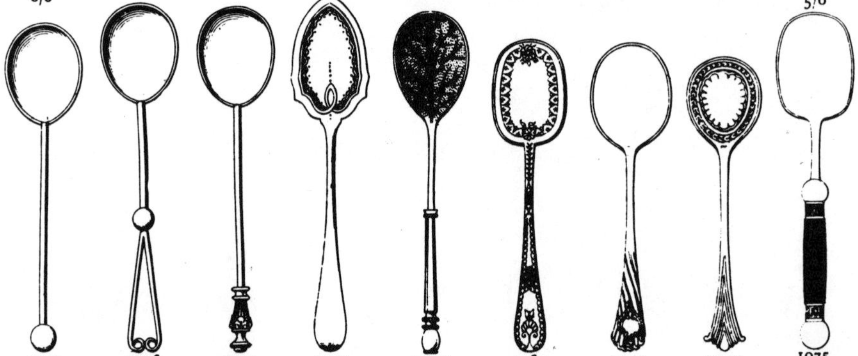

1043 2/6 — 1046 3/0 — 1047 3/0 — 1051 Bowl not Gilt 1/6 — 1052 3/3 — 1064 Plated 3/0 — 1090 2/6 — 1079 Plated 2/6 — 1075 Ebony Plated Cap 3/0

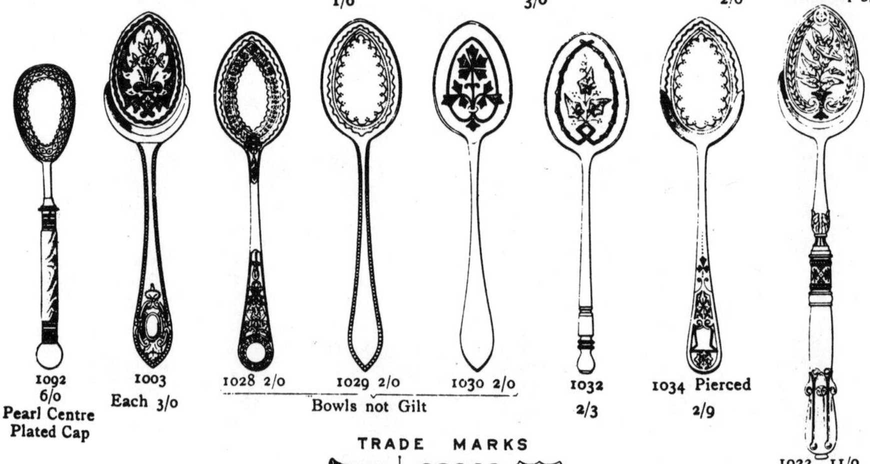

1092 6/0 Pearl Centre Plated Cap — 1003 Each 3/0 — 1028 2/0, 1029 2/0, 1030 2/0 Bowls not Gilt — 1032 2/3 — 1034 Pierced 2/9 — 1022 11/0 Ivory Handle

Prices in Silver on application.

TRADE MARKS

DIXON

Drawn ⅓ scale.

1911 James Dixon & Sons, Sheffield, England, catalog, no date.

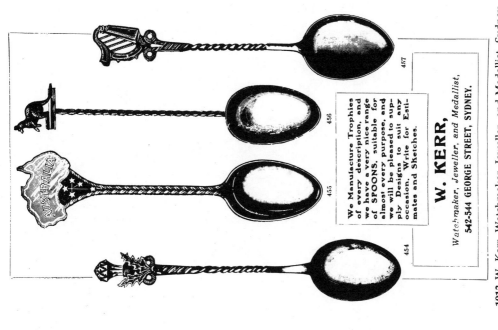

457

456

455

454

1913 W. Kerr, Watchmaker, Jeweller, and Medallist, Sydney, Australia, catalog, c. 1905.

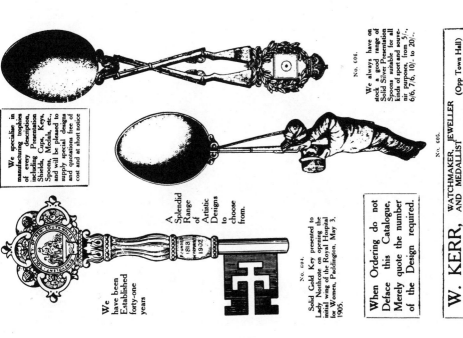

1912 W. Kerr, Watchmaker, Jeweller, and Medallist, Sydney, Australia, catalog, c. 1905.

1914 Joseph Mayer & Bros., Seattle, Washington, no date (E. J. Towle Company since c. 1945).

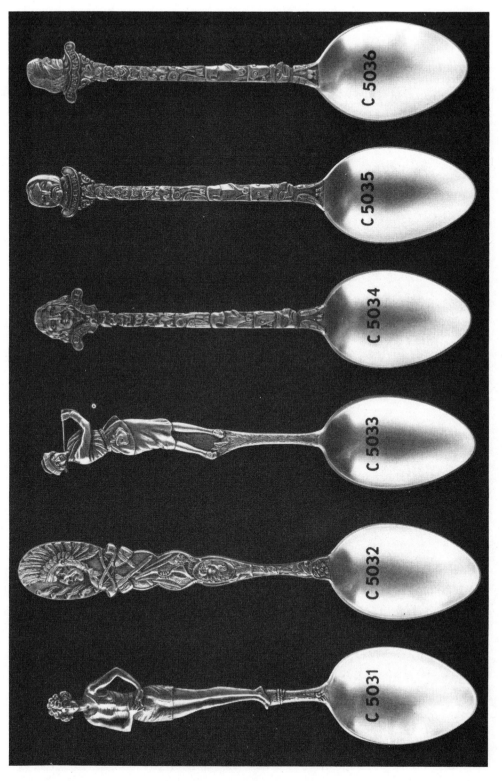

1915 Joseph Mayer & Bros., Seattle, Washington, no date (E. J. Towle Company since c. 1945).

389

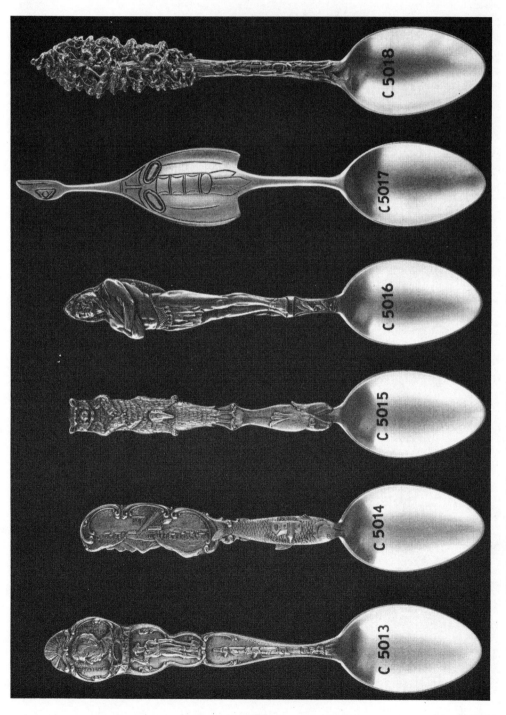

C 5018

C 5017

C 5016

C 5015

C 5014

C 5013

1916 Joseph Mayer & Bros., Seattle, Washington, no date (E. J. Towle Company since c. 1945).

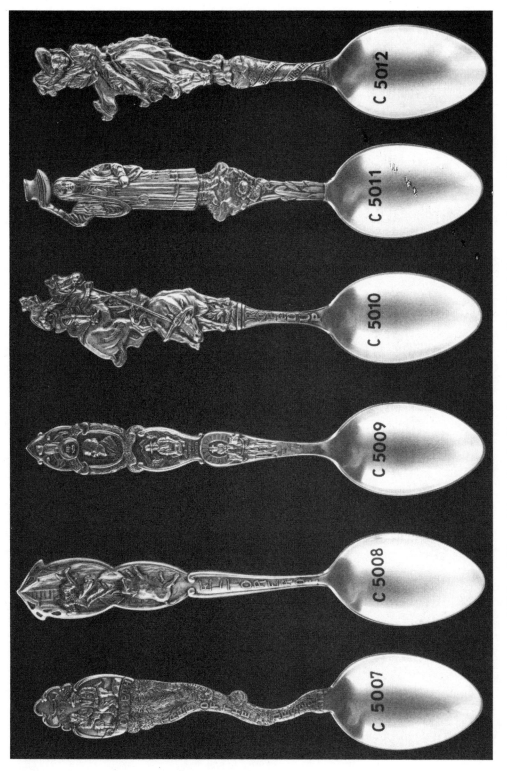

1917 Joseph Mayer & Bros., Seattle, Washington, no date (E. J. Towle Company since c. 1945).

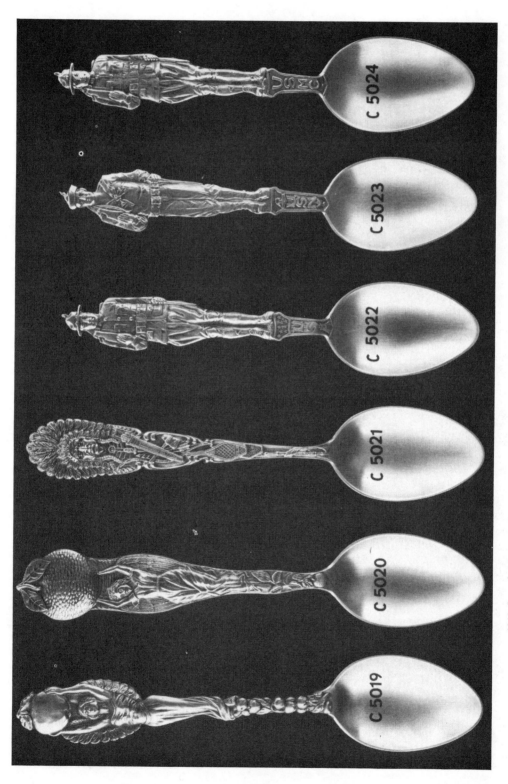

1918 Joseph Mayer & Bros., Seattle, Washington, no date (E. J. Towle Company since c. 1945).

1919 Joseph Mayer & Bros., Seattle, Washington, no date (E. J. Towle Company since c. 1945).

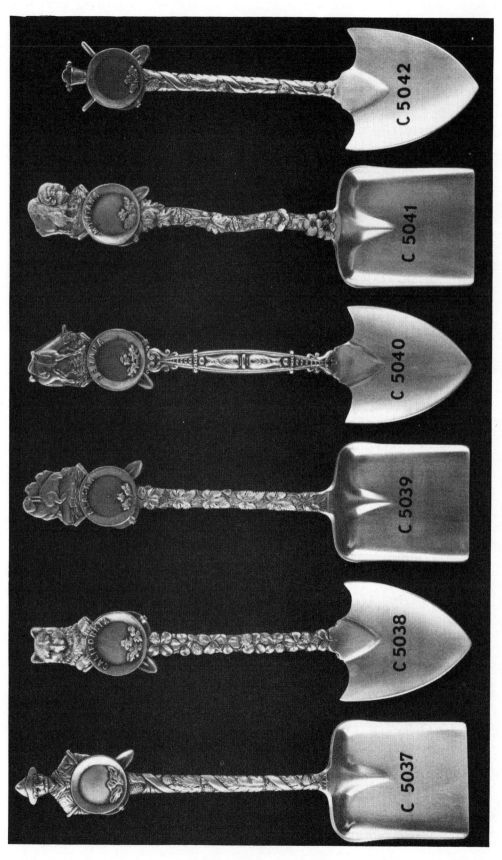

C 5042

C 5041

C 5040

C 5039

C 5038

C 5037

1920 Joseph Mayer & Bros., Seattle, Washington, no date (E. J. Towle Company since c. 1945).

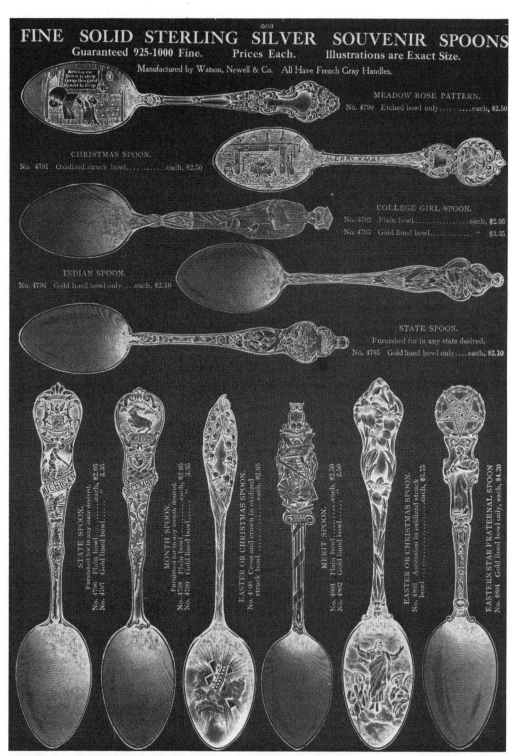

FINE SOLID STERLING SILVER SOUVENIR SPOONS

Guaranteed 925-1000 Fine.   Prices Each.   Illustrations are Exact Size.

Manufactured by Watson, Newell & Co.   All Have French Gray Handles.

MEADOW ROSE PATTERN.
No. 4790   Etched bowl only........each, $2.50

CHRISTMAS SPOON.
No. 4791   Oxidized struck bowl..........each, $2.50

COLLEGE GIRL SPOON.
No. 4792   Plain bowl.............each, $2.95
No. 4793   Gold lined bowl..........   " $3.35

INDIAN SPOON.
No. 4794   Gold lined bowl only....each, $2.10

STATE SPOON.
Furnished for in any state desired.
No. 4795   Gold lined bowl only....each, $2.10

STATE SPOON.
Furnished for in any state desired.
No. 4796   Plain bowl.......each, $2.95
No. 4797   Gold lined bowl......   "   3.35

MONTH SPOON.
Furnished for in any month desired.
No. 4798   Plain bowl.........each, $2.95
No. 4799   Gold lined bowl.......   "   3.35

EASTER OR CHRISTMAS SPOON.
No. 4800   Cross and crown in oxidized struck bowl.......each, $2.95

MERIT SPOON.
No. 4801   Plain bowl.......each, $2.50
No. 4802   Gold lined bowl......   "   2.90

EASTER OR CHRISTMAS SPOON.
No. 4803   Ascension in oxidized struck bowl.......each, $3.75

EASTERN STAR FRATERNAL SPOON
No. 4804   Gold lined bowl only, each, $4.50

1921 Illustrated Wholesale Catalogue and Price List of the Fort Dearborn Watch and Clock Co., catalog, c. 1915-16.

BIBLIOGRAPHY

A

Adam, Leonard, *Primitive Art*. Melbourne,-London,-Baltimore: Penguin Books, third edition, 1954.

The Age of the Renaissance, ed. by Denys Hay. New York: McGraw-Hill Book Company, 1967.

"All She Asked For Was a Sun Dial . . . ," *The Wichita Eagle and Beacon*. July 10, 1966.

The American Jeweler. June 1897.

Andren, Erik, *Swedish Silver*. New York: M. Barrows & Co., Inc., 1950.

Antiques Magazine. New York: 1922-present.

Austin, Oliver L. Jr., *Song Birds of the World*. New York: Golden Press, 1961.

Austria and the Bavarian Alps, Michelin Green Guide. London: The Dickens Press, 1969.

B

Baedeker, Karl, *Benelux*. Stuttgart, Germany: Baedaeker's Autoguides, 1958.

Baedeker's Touring Guides, *Scandinavia*. New York: George Allen & Urwin Ltd., 1963.

Bailey, Major C. T. P., *Knives and Forks*. London and Boston: The Medici Society, 1927.

Barraclough, E. M. C., *Flags of the World*. London: Frederick Warne & Co., Ltd., 1969.

Berczeller, Richard, *Time Was*. New York: The Viking Press, 1966.

Berlitz, Charles, *Mysteries from Forgotten Worlds*. New York: Doubleday & Co., 1972.

Bible, The Holy. King James Version.

Bingham, Madeleine. *Scotland Under Mary Stuart*. New York: St. Martin's Press, Inc., 1971.

Blue Guide to England, ed. by Stuart Rossiter. London: Ernest Benn Ltd., 1972.

Boaz, Franz. *Primitive Art*. Irvington-on-Hudson, New York: Capitol Publishing Co., Inc., 1951.

Boesen, Gudmund and Chr. A. Bøje, *Old Danish Silver*. Copenhagen: Hassing Publisher, MCMXLIX.

Bonechi, Edoardo, *Practical Guide to Venice*. Venice, Italy: Bonechi, 1967.

Bonechi, Edoardo, *Rome*. Florence, Italy: Bonechi, no date.

Bramsen, Bo, *Danske Guld Og Sølv Smedemaerker*. København: Politikens Forlag, 1954.

Brinton, Crane; Christopher, John B.; and Wolff, Robert Lee, *A History of Civilization, Prehistory to 1715*. Englewood Cliffs: New Jersey: Prentice-Hall, Inc., fourth edition, 1971.

Britain, The Shell Guide (Geoffrey Boumphrey, ed.) New York: E. P. Dutton & Co., Inc., 1969.

Broholm, H. C. and William P. Larsen and Godtfred Skjerne, *The Lures of the Bronze Age, an archaeological, technical and musicological investigation*. Copenhagen: Glydendalske Boghandel—Nordisk Forlag, 1949.

Brunner, Herbert, *Old Table Silver*. New York: Taplinger Publishing Co., 1964.

Budge, E. A. Wallis, *Cleopatra's Needles and Other Egyptian Obelisks*. London: The Religious Tract Society, 1926.

Bulfinch's Mythology. New York: Thos. Y. Crowell Co.

Bulley, Eleanor, *Life of Edward VII*. London: Wells Gardner, Darton & Co., MDCCCCI.

C

Caldwell, John C., *Let's Visit Mexico*. New York: The John Day Company, 1965.

Cammann, Schuyler. "Carvings in Walrus Ivory," in *University Museum Bulletin*, The University Museum, Univ. of Pennsylvania, Philadelphia, Vol. 18, No. 3, September 1954.

Carré, Louis, *A Guide to Old French Plate*. London: Chapman & Hall, 1931.

Carton, Jacques, *Paris*. Paris France: B. Arthaud, no date.

Catalog of the Collection of Spoons made by Mrs. S. P. Avery, 1867-1890. New York: Metropolitan Mus. of Art, 1898.

Chamber's Encyclopaedia. Oxford, England: Pergamon Press, 1967 edition.

Cities of Destiny, ed. by Arnold Toynbee. New York: McGraw-Hill Book Company, 1967.

Clark, Sydney A. *All the Best in Belgium and Luxembourg*. New York: Dodd, Mead & Company, 1963.

Clark, Sydney A. *All the Best in Britain*. New York: Dodd, Mead & Company, 1969.

A Collection of Early English Spoons of the 15th, 16th & 17th Centuries formed by The Reverend Thomas Staniforth. London: Messrs. Crichton bros., 1898.

"Collection of Peasants' Forks, Spoons and Knives from the Tyrol," *Bulletin of the Pennsylvania Museum*, Oct. 1913, No. 44.

The Collector's Weekly. Kermit, Texas: Dec. 15, 1970.

Collier's Encyclopedia. New York: P. F. Collier & Son Corporation, 1960 edition.

The Columbia Lippincott Gazetteer of the World, Leon E. Seltzer, ed. New York: Columbia University Press, 1961.

Complete Reference Guide to Germany and Its Islands. Pan American Airways, Inc., 1966.

Compton's Pictured Encyclopedia. Chicago: F. E. Compton & Company, 1960 edition.

Contini, Mila, *Fashion from Ancient Egypt to the Present Day.* New York: The Odessey Press, 1965.

Culican, William, *The Medes and the Persians.* New York: Frederick A. Praeger, 1965.

D

Delieb, Eric, *Investing in Silver.* New York: Clarkson N. Potter, Inc., 1967.

Dublin. Dublin Ireland: Mount Salus Press, no date.

E

Edinburgh. Edinburgh: Edinburgh Corp., 1970.

Edinburgh Castle. Edinburgh: Her Majesty's Stationery Office, 1960.

Egypt the Eternal. San Jose, California: The Rosiacrucian Press Ltd., 1955.

Encyclopedia Americana. New York: Americana Corp., 1969 edition.

Encyclopedia International. New York: Grolier Inc., 1970 edition.

Encyclopedia of Painting, ed. by Bernard S. Myers. New York: Crown Publishers, Inc., 1955.

England, The Shell Guide (John Hadfield, ed.) New York: American Heritage Press, 1970.

Etnografiska Museet, Arstryck for 1957 och 1958. Gothenburg, Sweden: Ethnographical Museum, 1960.

Europa Touring. Bern, Switzerland: Hallwag Bern, 1970.

Evans, F. E., *Discovering Civic Heraldry.* Tring, Herts., England: Shire Publications, 1968.

Evans, I. O., *Flags of the World.* New York: Bantam Books, 1970.

The Evening Star, Washington, D.C.: Nov. 10, 1970.

F

Fales, Martha Gandy, *American Silver in the Henry Francis du Pont Winterthur Museum.* Winterthur: 1958.

Feher, Joseph. *Hawaii: A Pictorial History.* Honolulu, Hawaii: Bishop Museum Press, 1969.

Ferguson, George, *Signs and Symbols in Christian Art.* New York: Oxford University Press, 1954.

Fine English and Continental Silver, Catalog. Parke-Bernet, Nov. 23, 1971.

Florentine Masterpieces. Florence, Italy: Gino Innocenti & Figli, no date.

Fodor, Eugene, *Belgium and Luxembourg 1963,* Fodor's Modern Guides. New York: David McKay Company, Inc., 1963.

Fodor, Eugene, *Europe.* New York: David McKay Company, Inc., 1972.

Fodor, Eugene, *France.* New York: David McKay Company, Inc., 1972.

Fodor, Eugene, *Holland 1969.* New York: David McKay Company, Inc., 1969.

Fodor's Modern Guides, *Belgium and Luxembourg 1962,* Eugene Fodor, Editor; Betty Glauert, Asst. Ed. New York: David McKay Company, Inc.

Folklore, Myths and Legends of Britain. London: The Reader's Digest Assoc. Ltd., 1973.

Forbes, H. A. Crosby; Kernan, John Devereaux and Wilkins, Ruth S. *Chinese Export Silver 1785 to 1885.* Milton, Massachusetts: Museum of the American China Trade, 1975.

Fraser, Antonia, *Mary Queen of Scots.* New York: Delacorte Press, 1969.

Fredericks, J. W. *Dutch Silver.* The Hague: Martinus Nijhoff, 1958.

Frei, Hans, *Lac Des Quatre Cantons.* Paris, France: Bibliotheque Des Arts, 1966.

G

Gans, M. H. and Th. M. Duyvené de Wit-Klinkhamer, *Dutch Silver.* London: Faber and Faber, 1961.

Gask, Norman *Old Silver Spoons of England.* London: Herbert Jenkins Ltd., MCMXXVI.

Germany (West Germany and Berlin), Michelin Green Guide, London: The Dickens Press, 1971.

Gibbon, Monk, *Austria.* London: B. T. Batsford, Ltd., 1962.

Gibbon, Monk, *Western Germany.* London: B. T. Batsford, Ltd., 1955.

Gold and Silver Treasures of Ancient Italy. Greenwich, Conn. and Milan, Italy: New York Graphic Society, 1963.

Gorsline, Douglas, *What People Wore.* New York: The Viking Press, 1951.

Gouker, Loice, *Dictionary of Church Terms and Symbols.* Norwalk, Conn.: C. R. Gibson Co., 1954.

Grant, Sir Francis J. *A Manual of Heraldry.* Edinburgh: John Grant, reprinted 1962.

Graves, Charles, *The Rich Man's Guide to Europe.* Englewood Cliffs, New Jersey: Prentice-Hall, Inc., 1966.

Great Cities of the World. Maplewood, New Jersey: C. S. Hammond & Co., 1958.

Groshskopf, Bernice, *The Treasure of Sutton Hoo.* New York: Atheneum, 1970.

H

Hagen, Anders, *Norway.* New York: Frederick A. Praeger, 1967.

Hamilton, Edith, *Mythology.* Boston: Little Brown & Co., 1942.

Hansen, Henny Harald, *Costume and Styles.* New York: E. P. Dutton & Co., Inc., 1956.

Hare, Richard, *The Arts and Artists of Russia.* London: Mechuen & Co., Ltd., 1965.

Harton, The Very Rev. F. P., Late Dean of Wells, *Wells Cathedral.* London: Pitkin Pictorials, Ltd., 1969.

Hazlitt, W. Carew, *Faiths and Folklore of the British Isles.* Vol. 1. New York: Benjamin Blom, 1965.

Hiroa, Te Rangi (Sir Peter Buck), *The Coming of the Maori.* Wellington, New Zealand: Whitcombe & Tombs Ltd., 1952.

The History of the Spoon, Knife & Fork. Taunton, Mass: Reed & Barton and Dominick & Haff, 1930.

Holland, Margaret, *English Provincial Silver.* New York: Arco Publishing Co., Inc., 1971.

Holmes, Martin, *The Crown Jewels at the Tower of London.* London: Her Majesty's Stationery Office, 1968.

Horizon Book of Lost Worlds, ed. Marshall B. Davidson; narrative, Leonard Cottrell. New York: American Heritage Publishing Co., Inc., 1962.

Hürliamann, Martin, *Germany.* New York: The Viking Press, 1961.

Hürliamann, Martin. *Vienna.* New York: The Viking Press, 1970.

I

Illustrated Guide to Britain. London: Drive Pub. Ltd. for the Automobile Assoc., 1972.

Inverarity, Robert Bruce. *Art of the Northwest Coast Indians.* Berkeley and Los Angeles: University of California Press, 1950.

"The Iron Maiden of Nürnberg," *Country Life.* July 22, 1965.

"The Iron Virgin's Kiss," *The Illustrated American,* April 9, 1892.

Italy, Michelin Green Guide. London: The Dickens Press, 1969.

J

Jackson, Sir Charles James, *English Goldsmiths and Their Marks.* London: Macmillan & Co., Ltd., 1921.

Jackson, Sir Charles James, *An Illustrated History of English Plate,* Vol. II. London: B. T. Batsford, 1911.

Jackson, C. J., Esq. "The Spoon and its history; its form, material, and development, more particularly in England" *Archaeologia.* Second Series, Vol. III, Feb. 13, 1890. London: Society of Antiquaries of London.

Jenkins, Elizabeth, *Elizabeth and Leicester.* New York: Coward-McCann, Inc., 1962.

Jones, E. Alfred, "Old Portugese Silver Spoons," *Burlington Magazine.* Dec. 1919.

K

Keller, Werner. *The Bible as History.* Translated by William Neil. New York: William Morrow and Company, 1956.

Kent, William, ed. *An Encyclopaedia of London.* New York: The Macmillan Company, 1951.

Keyes, Frances Parkinson, *All Flags Flying,* Reminiscences of Frances Parkinson Keyes. New York: McGraw-Hill Book Company, 1972.

Killanın, Lord and Michael V. Duignan, *The Shell Guide to Ireland.* London: Ebury Press in association with George Rainbird, 1967.

Kimbrough, Emily, *Pleasure by the Busload.* New York: Harper & Brothers, 1961.

Kitzinger, Ernst, "The Spoons," (Sutton Hoo Ship-Burial), *Antiquity.* Vol. IV, No. 53 March 1940.

Klindt-Jensen, Ole, *Vikingarnas värld.* Stockholm: Bokförlaget Forum AB, 1967.

L

"Lapp Collection," *Annual Reports for 1957 and 1958 and Attached Papers,"* Ethnographical Museum, Gothenburg, Sweden.

Larousse Encyclopedia of Mythology. New York: Prometheus Press, 1959.

Laughlin, Clara E., *So You're Going to Germany & Austria.* Boston and New York: Houghton Mifflin Co., 1930.

Lobsenz, Norman, *The First Book of West Germany.* New York: Franklin Watts, Inc., 1959.

Lockley, R. M., *Wales.* London: B. T. Batsford, Ltd., 1966.

London. A Holiday Magazine Travel Guide. New York: Random House, 1960.

Lottman, Herbert, *Detours from the Grand Tour.* Englewood Cliffs N.J.: Prentice-Hall, Inc., 1970.

Lucas-Dubreton, J., *Daily Life in Florence in the Time of the Medici.* New York: The Macmillan Company, 1961.

M

Martin, Lawrence & Sylvia, *Europe: The Grand Tour.* New York: McGraw-Hill Book Company, 1967.

Milestones of History, ed. S. G. F. Brandon. New York: W. W. Norton & Co., Inc., 1971.

Morton, H. V., *H. V. Morton's England.* New York: A Giniger Book pub. in association with Dodd, Mead & Co., 1969.

Morton, H. V. *In Search of London.* New York: Dodd Mead & Co., 1951.

Morton, H. V. *In the Steps of St. Paul.* New York: Dodd, Mead & Co., 1936.

N

Neubert, Karel and Mills, A. R., *Portrait of Moscow.* London: Paul Hamlyn, 1965.

New Century Book of Facts, ed. by Carroll D. Wright. Wheeling, West Virginia: The Continental Publishing Company, 1930.

New Zealand Paua Shell (pamphlet). Auckland: Mastercrafts Ltd., no date.

Nicholson, Nigel and Ian Graham, *Great Houses of the Western World.* New York: G. P. Putnam's Sons, 1968.

O

Oakes, George W., *Turn Left at the Pub.* New York: Van Rees Press. 1968.

Oakes, George W., *Turn Right at the Fountain.* New York: Holt, Rinehart and Winston, 1971.

Okie, Howard, Pitcher, *Old Silver and Old Sheffield Plate.* New York and Garden City: Doubleday & Co., Inc., 1955.

Olson, Harvey S., *Aboard and Abroad,* Olson's Complete Travel Guide to Europe. Philadelphia and New York: J. B. Lippincott Co., 1968.

Orlando Sentinel. Orlando, Florida: May 31, 1964.

The Oxford Dictionary of Nursery Rhymes, ed. by Iona and Peter Opie. Oxford: Clarendon Press, 1951.

P

Phillips, C. W., "The Sutton Hoo Ship-Burial," *Antiquity.* Vol. XIV, No. 83, March 1940.

Pinto, Edward H., *Treen or Small Woodenware Throughout the Ages.* London: B. T. Batsford Ltd., 1949.

Post, W. Ellwood, *Saints, Signs and Symbols.* New York: Morehouse-Barlow Co., 1962.

Price, F. G. Hilton, *Old Base Metal Spoons.* London: B. T. Batsford, 1908.

Pucci, Eugenio, *All Rome.* Florence, Italy: Ponechi Editore, 1968.

Q

Quennell, Marjorie & C. H. B., *A History of Everyday Things in England.* Vol. I, 1066 to 1499. London: B. T. Batsford, Ltd., 1819, fourth edition, 1966.

R

Rare Early English Silver Spoons, including a complete set of Apostle spoons with the Master spoon. New York: American Art Association, Anderson Galleries Inc., 1936.

Raymond, Ellsworth and Martin, John Stuart, *A Picture History of Eastern Europe.* New York: Crown Publishers Inc., 1971.

Rees, Goronwy, *The Rhine.* New York: G. P. Putnam's Sons, 1967.

The Republican-Courier. Findlay, Ohio: July 21, 1962.

Rest, Friederich, *Our Christian Symbols.* Philadelphia: The Christian Education Press, 1954.

Ross, Frances A., *The Land and People of Canada.* Philadelphia and New York: J. P. Lippincott Co., 1954.

Rotkin Chas. E., *Europe: An Aerial Close-Up.* Philadelphia and New York: J. P. Lippincott Co., 1962.

Ruland, Wilhelm, *The Finest Legends of the Rhine.* Köln-Ehrenfeld, Germany: Velag von Hoursch and Bechstedt, 1930.

Rupert, Charles G., *Apostle Spoons.* London: Oxford University Press, 1929.

S

Sakai, Atsuharu, *Japan in a Nutshell, Religion, Culture, Popular Practices.* Vol. I. Yokohama: Yamagata Printing Co., 1949.

Scidmore, Eliza Ruhamah, "Some American Spoons," (American Northwest Coast Indian) *The Jewelers' Circular & Horological Review,* Sept. 27, 1893.

The Scottish Clans and Their Tartans. Edinburgh: Johnston & Bacon, Ltd., 41st edition, 1968.

Sharman, J. S., "English Apostle Spoons and their Symbols," *Connoisseur.* Vol. LII, p. 138.

Silver (Formerly Silver-Rama,) ed. Beulah D. Hodgson. Vancouver, Washington: 1968—present.

Simpson, Colin, *The Viking Circle*. New York: Fielding Publications & William Morrow & Co., 1968.

Sitwell, H. D. W., *The Crown Jewels and Other Regalia in the Tower of London*. London: The Dropmore Press, 1953.

Smith, Robert C. "Liberty Displaying the Arts and Sciences" in *Winterthur Portfolio II*. Winterthur, Delaware: Henry Francis Du Pont Winterthur Museum, 1965.

Sølver, Aage, *Danske Guldsmede og Deres Arbejder Gennem 500 Aar*. København: Larsen & Larsen Forlag, 1929.

Souvenirs with a Story (pamphlet). Melbourne and Sydney: K. G. Luke Ltd., no date.

The Spoon from Earliest Times. Meriden, Connecticut: The International Silver Company, 1915.

Stieler, Karl, H. Wachenhusen, and F. W. Häcklander, *The Rhine, From Its Source to the Sea*. Philadelphia: Lippincott, 1878.

The Story of New Zealand Jade (Greenstone), (pamphlet). Auckland: Mastercrafts Ltd., no date.

The Strand Magazine (The International News Company, N.Y.) Vol. 12, No. 72, Jan. 1897.

Streeter, Edward, *Along the Ridge, From Northwestern Spain to Southern Yugoslavia*. New York: Harper & Row, 1964.

Stutzenberger, Albert, *The American Story in Spoons*. Springdale Spring, Kentucky: A Bookmaster Book, 1953.

Sutton, Felix and Hull, John, *The Illustrated Book About Europe*. New York: Grosset & Dunlap, 1962.

Switzerland. Michelin Green Guide. London: The Dickens Press, 1969.

"Symbol of the Nation," by Galo B. Ocampo, *Blue Book of the First Year of the Republic*. Manila: Bureau of Printing, 1947.

T

Taylor's Ency. of Gardening, ed. Norman Taylor. Boston: Houghton Mifflin Company, 1961.

Times Atlas of the World. Boston: Houghton Mifflin, 1967.

"Treasure of Traprain Law" by Donna H. Felger *Spinning Wheel*. Hanover, Pennsylvania: Everybodys Press, September 1971.

Treasures of Britain. London: Drive Publications Ltd. for the Automobile Assoc., 1968.

Tryckare, Tre. *The Vikings*. Gothenburg, Sweden: Tre Tryckare Cagner & Co., 1966.

V

Voet, Door Elias Jr., *Nederlandse Goud-en Zilvermerken*. The Hague: 'S-Gravenhage Martinus Nijhoff, 1966.

Von Hagen, Victor W., *The Roads That Led to Rome*. Cleveland and New York: World Publishing Company, 1967.

W

Waldo, Myra, *Myra Waldo's Travel and Motoring Guide to Europe*. New York: The Macmillan Company, 1968.

Walsh, Wm. S., *Heroes and Heroines of Fiction*. Philadelphia and London: J. B. Lippincott Co., 1914; republished by Gale research Co., Detroit, 1966.

Ward, Gordon, "The Silver Spoons from Sutton Hoo," *Antiquity*. Vol. XXVI, No. 101, March 1952.

Warwick Castle. Leamington Spa: English Counties Periodicals Ltd., no date.

Watts, May Theilgaard, *Reading the Landscape of Europe*. New York: Harper & Row, 1971.

Webster's Biographical Dictionary. Philippines: G. & C. Merriam Co., 1951.

Wechsberg, Joseph, *Vienna, My Vienna*. New York: The Macmillan Company, 1968.

Westman, Habakkuk O., "The Spoon: Primitive, Egyptian, Roman, Mediaeval & Modern" in *The Transactions of the Society of Literary and Scientific Chiffoniers*. New York: 1844.

Weston, Christine *Ceylon*. New York: Charles Scribner's Sons, 1960.

"When Forks and Knives Were Made for Show," *The Illustrated American*, Oct. 27, 1894.

Whittemore, Carroll E. *Symbols of the Church*. Boston: Whittemore Associates, Inc., 1959.

Wilcox, R. Turner, *The Mode in Hats and Headdresses*. New York: Charles Scribner's Sons, 1945.

Wright, Reginald W. M., *Pictorial History of Bath Abbey*. London: Pitkin Pictorials, Ltd., 1967.

Wright, R. W. M. and G. Lester, *Pictorial History of Bath*. London: Pitkin Pictorials, Ltd., 1968.

Wyler, Seymour B., *The Book of Old Silver*. New York: Crown Publishers, 1937.

Y

Yarwood, Doreen, *English Costume*. London: B. T. Batsford, Ltd., 1967.

INDEX BY SUBJECT

Aachen, Germany, 218, 219
Aberdeen, Scotland, 141, 142-143
Absecon Lighthouse, 321, 322
Adam and Eve, 65
Adelaide, Australia, 377, 378
After-dinner coffee spoons, 15
Aix-les-Bains, France, 187-188
Albany, New York, 318, 319
Alaska, 313-315
Alaska Purchase Centennial Potlatch
  Spoon, 314-315
Alençon, France, 186
Ålesund, Norway, 106
Alexandra, Queen, 162
Alamo, The, 320, 321
Alphenhorn, 193, 194
Alsatian Wolf Dog, 77
Amalfi, Italy, 255
Amsterdam, the Netherlands, 171,
  174-175
Amundsen, Roald, 357, 358
Andersen, Hans Christian, 120-121
Andorra, 235-236
Angel Gabriel, 63
Angels, 10
Ankh or Crux Ansata, 272, 273
Anointing Spoon, 151, 152-153
Antwerp, Belgium, 177
Apostle spoons, 10, 11, 27-66
Apostle Spoons, American, 54ff
Apostles, St. Jude, St. Thomas, St.
  James the Greater, St. Philip, St.
  Paul, St. Matthew, St. John, St.
  Bartholomew, St. Andrew, St.
  Peter, St. Matthias, St. Simon
  Zelotes, St. James the Less,
  Master, 29
Apostle spoons, baptismal gifts, 27
Apostle spoons, Continental, 54, 55
Apostle spoons, dating of, 54
Apostle spoons, earliest written
  record, 30
Apostle spoons, English, 54
Apostle spoons, introduced, 27
Apostles spoons, nimbus, 33ff
Apostle spoons, seated figures, 35
Apostle spoons, sets of thirteen, 32
Apostle spoons, symbols on, 36ff,
  41ff
Apostles, symbols, the Master, 36ff
Apostles, symbols, St. Peter, St.
  Andrew, 45
Apostles, symbols, St. James the
  Elder, 46
Apostles, symbols, St. John, 47
Apostles, symbols, St. Philip, 48
Apostles, symbols, St.
  Bartholomew, St. Thomas, 49
Apostles, symbols, St. Matthew, St.
  James the Less, 50
Apostles, symbols, St. Jude, St.
  Simon Zelotes, 51
Apostles, symbols, Judas Iscariot,
  St. Matthias, St. Paul, St.
  Barnabas, 52
Arabic Welcome, 268
Araucanian topu, 346, 347
Argentina, 347-348
Arkansas Traveler, 318
Aruba, Netherlands Antilles, 339,
  340
Asbury Park, New Jersey, 323
Athens, Greece, 255-256
Auckland, New Zealand, 378-379
Australian aborigine, 371, 374-375

Bad Flinsberg, Poland, 238, 239
Bad Pyrmont, Germany, 219
Bad Tölz, Germany, 219, 221
Baghdad, Iraq, 267
Balboa, Vasco Núñez de, 363
Ball Knops, 11
Baluster top, 11
Bamboo sugar shell, 283
Barbados, West Indies, 339, 340
Barcelona, Spain, 234, 235
Bardell, Mrs., 69, 71
Barmen, Germany, 218, 219
Barrie, Ontario, 307
Basle, Switzerland, 191, 193, 194-195
Basket-of-flowers, 14
Bath Abbey, 135, 136-137
Bath, Countess of, 317
Bath, England, 135, 136
Bath, New York, 317
Beaded design, 16
Becket, Thomas À, 137, 140
Beethoven, Ludwig Van, 362
Belfast, Northern Ireland, 147
Belgium's Independence, 178, 180
Bergen, Norway, 105-106
Berlin, Germany, 199, 200-202
Berne, Switzerland, 192, 193-194
Bermuda, 335-336, 337
Bermuda Onion, 337
Bernburg, East Germany, 225
Berwick-Upon-Tweed, 133, 136
Brazil, 342
Bristol, Connecticut, 324
British, Columbia, 308, 309, 310
British Lion, 72
Brooklyn Bridge, 319, 320
Biarritz, France, 185, 186
Biberach, Germany, 218-219
Bishop Absalon, 117
Blackfellow, 374
Blackgang Smuggler, 78-79
Blandiver, Jack, 73
Blarney Castle, 149, 150-151
Bloomington, Illinois, 320
Bogotá, Colombia, 341
Bohra, 372, 375-376
Bologna, Italy, 244, 245
Bolzano, Italy, 243-244
Bombay, India, 292
Bonbon spoons, 83-86
Bone spoons, 3, 5, 6
Bone spoons, Pre-Columbian, 5
Boomerang, 374
Bordeaux, France, 185-186
Bournemouth, England, 135, 138
Bowls: round, egg-shaped,
  fig-shaped, pointed ovals, 3
Braemar, Scotland, 141, 142
Brandy burning spoon, 91
Brass spoons, 6
Bratwurstglöcklein, 208, 209
Bremen, Germany, 202-203, 204
Breslau, Poland, 238, 240
Brest, France, 183, 184
Brighton, England, 128-129
Brisbane, Australia, 377, 378
Britannia, 123-124, 127
British Exhibitions, 139, 140-141
British Lion, 71
British Museum, 2
Bronze spoons, 3
Bruce, Robert, 71, 72
Brummell, Beau, 353-354
Brussels, Belgium, 176-179
Budapest, Hungary, 237, 238-239

Buddha, 286-287
Buenos Aires, Argentina, 348
Burns, Robert, 71, 72
Byzantine, 6

Cable car, 321, 322
Cadiz, Spain, 233, 234
Caddy spoons, 18, 67-83
Caddy Spoons, filigree, cast, 70
Caddy spoons, first hallmarked, 68
Caddy spoons, medicine spoons as,
  68
Caddy spoons, acanthus, Chinese
  mandarin, eagle's wing,
  grapevine, hand, ivy, jockey cap,
  leaf, oak, 68, 69
Calgary, Canada, 310, 311
Camel, 292
Canada, 301-312
Cannes, France, 189-190
Canterbury, England, 137, 140
Cape Town, South Africa, 278, 279
Capri, Italy, 255-256
Carabao, 370, 371
Cardiff, Wales, 141, 142
Cartagena, Spain, 233, 234
Carter, Mrs. Lucetta S., 318
Casting out the Devil, 65, 66
Cat & Fiddle, 75, 76
Castle of Chapultepec, Mexico, 331
Cathedral, Mexico City, 333
Cathedral of Notre Dame,
  Lausanne, Switzerland, 195-196
Cathedral, Panama, 336
Cavalier, 20
Celtic Cross, 150, 152
Ceremonial spoons, 3, 21, 22,
  293-294
Ceylon, 294-296
Chambéry, France, 185, 186
Chamonix, France, 185
Chamonix hoof spoon, 20
Charles II, 156
Charles, Prince of Wales, 165, 166
Chaumont, France, 183, 184
Cheddar, England, 137, 138
Cheltenham, England, 128, 130
Cherub heads, 11
Cherubim heads, 10
Cheshire Cat, 129
Chester, England, 129, 130
Chichester, England, 128, 129
Chién D'or, Quebec, Canada, 78
Chile, 345-346
Chinese dragon, 284, 285
Chips of wood as spoons, 2
Christchurch, New Zealand, 378,
  379
Christian, 3
Christian X, 112
Christiania, Norway, 104, 105
Christmas spoons, 326, 327
Chrysanthemum, 286, 287
Cicade Da Beira, Mozambique,
  276-277
Circular stems, 11
Coats of arms; Aberdeen, Scotland,
  141, 142-143
Coats of arms; Aix-les-Bains,
  France, 187
Coats of arms; Alençon, France, 186
Coats of arms; Amalfi, Italy, 255
Coats of arms; Amsterdam, 171
Coats of arms; Andorra, 235

Coats of arms, Anne of Brittany, 183, 184

Coats of arms; Antwerp, Belgium, 177

Coats of arms; Argentina, 347-348

Coats of arms; Arkansas, 318

Coats of arms; Austria, 226

Coats of arms; Australia, 376, 377

Coats of arms; Bad Flinsberg, Poland, 238, 239

Coats of arms; Bad Pyrmont, Germany, 218, 219

Coats of arms; Barcelona, Spain, 235

Coats of arms; Basle, Switzerland, 191, 192-193

Coats of arms; Bath Abbey, Bath, England, 135, 136-137

Coats of arms; Bath, England, 135, 136

Coats of arms; Belfast, Northern Ireland, 147, 148

Coats of arms; Berlin, Germany, 199, 200, 201

Coats of arms; Bernberg, East Germany, 225

Coats of arms; Biarritz, France, 186

Coats of arms; Bolzano, Italy, 243, 244, 245

Coats of arms; Bordeaux, France, 186

Coats of arms; Bournemouth, 135, 138

Coats of arms; Braemar, Scotland, 141, 142

Coats of arms; Bremen, Germany, 202, 203, 204

Coats of arms; Breslau, Poland, 238, 240

Coats of arms; Brest, France, 183, 184

Coats of arms; Brighton, England, 128

Coats of Arms, British Columbia Provincial, 309, 310

Coats of arms; Budapest, Hungary, 237, 238-239

Coats of arms; Canada, 301-311

Coats of arms; Cannes, France, 189-190

Coats of arms; Canterbury, England, 137, 140

Coats of arms; Capri, Italy, 255-256

Coats of arms; Cardiff, Wales, 141, 142

Coats of arms; Carlsbad, Czechoslovakia, 236-237

Coats of arms; Cidade Da Beira, Mozambique, 276

Coats of arms; Chambery, France, 186

Coats of arms; Cheddar, England, 137, 138

Coats of arms; Cheltenham, England, 128, 130

Coats of arms; Chester, England, 129, 130

Coats of arms; Chichester, England, 128, 129

Coats of arms; Claude of France, 183, 184

Coats of arms; Colmar, France, 182, 183

Coats of arms; Cologne Cathedral, 204-205

Coats of arms; Denmark, 116, 117

Coats of arms; Dinant, Belgium, 178, 180

Coats of arms; Dresden, East Germany, 223-224

Coats of arms; Dublin, Ireland, 150, 151, 152

Coats of arms; Dunkerque, France, 184, 185

Coats of arms; Edinburgh, Scotland, 77, 144, 145-146

Coats of arms; Erfurt, East Germany, 224-225

Coats of arms; Fiji Islands, 371, 373

Coats of arms; Finland, 123

Coats of arms; Fiumi, Yugoslavia, 237, 238

Coats of arms; Florence, Italy, 248, 249-252

Coats of arms; Crest of Francois I, 183, 184

Coats-of-arms, Frankfurt, Germany, 215

Coats of arms; Friedrichshafen, Germany, 214

Coats of arms; Galway, Ireland, 149-150

Coats of arms; Geneva, Switzerland, 192-193

Coats of arms; Genoa, Italy, 244

Coats of arms; Gibraltar, 236

Coats of arms; German, 201

Coats of arms; Glasgow, Scotland, 143, 144-145

Coats of arms; Glastonbury Abbey, 137, 138-139

Coats of arms; Great Britain, 126

Coats of arms; Hague, The, 169, 170

Coats of arms; Hamburg, Germany, 215, 216-217

Coats of arms; Hanover, Germany, 214-215

Coats of arms; Hatfield House, 129, 131-132

Coats of arms; Hawaii, 366, 367

Coats of arms; Heidelberg, Germany, 209, 210-211

Coats of arms; Helgoland, Germany, 220, 221-222

Coats of arms; Honiton, England, 137, 138

Coats of arms; India, 292-293

Coats of arms; Innsbruck, Austria, 227, 229

Coats of arms; Israel, 269

Coats of arms; Killarney, Ireland, 149

Coats of arms; Las Palmas, Spain, 235

Coats of arms; Leipzig, East Germany, 224, 225

Coats of arms; Liverpool, England, 129, 131

Coats of arms; London, England, 77, 126, 127

Coats of arms; Lucerne, Switzerland, 191, 192-193, 195

Coats of arms; Lyon, France, 187

Coats of arms; Madrid, 233

Coats of arms; Malta, 139, 141

Coats of arms; Menton, 189, 190

Coats of arms; Milan, Italy, 242-243

Coats of arms; Missouri, 316

Coats of arms; Mombasa, 276, 277

Coats of arms; Montreux, Switzerland, 195

Coats of arms; Munich, Germany, 210, 211

Coats of arms; Nancy, France, 187

Coats of arms; Nantes, France, 184, 185

Coats of arms; Naples, Italy, 250, 251, 252-253

Coats of arms; Netherlands, 168

Coats of arms; New York, 317

Coats of arms; Newcastle-Upon-Tyne, England, 133, 135

Coats of arms; Neuchâtel, Switzerland, 191, 192-193

Coats of arms; Nice, France, 187, 188-189

Coats of arms; Normandie, France, 184, 185

Coats of arms; Norway, 84, 103, 104

Coats of arms; Nuremberg, Germany, 206, 208

Coats of arms; Oban, Scotland, 143-144

Coats of arms; Osnabrück Germany, 213-214

Coats of arms; Ostende, Belgium, 177, 178

Coats of arms; Oxford, England, 75, 76

Coats of arms; Paris, France, 179

Coats of arms; Penang, 298-299

Coats of arms; Pisa, Italy, 244, 245-246

Coats of arms; Port Glasgow, Scotland, 77

Coats of arms; Portugal, 229, 230

Coats of arms; Pottsdam, East Germany, 225

Coats of arms; Rangoon, Burma, 298, 299

Coats of arms; Riva, Italy, 244-245

Coats of arms; Rome, Italy, 241

Coats of arms; Rothenburg, Germany, 212, 213

Coats of arms; Rotterdam, 175

Coats of arms; Rouen, France, 186

Coats of arms; Southern Rhodesia, 82

Coats of arms Saffron Walden, England, 129, 131

Coats of arms; St. Gallen, Switzerland, 192-193

Coats of arms; St. Mary's Abbey, York, England, 133, 135

Coats of arms; San Sebastian, Spain, 235

Coats of arms; Schaffhausen, Switzerland, 191, 192-193

Coats of arms; Siena, Italy, 254

Coats of arms; Singapore, 297-298

Coats of arms; South Africa, 277-278, 280

Coats of arms; Southern Rhodesia, 82, 277, 278

Coats of arms; Spain, 233

Coats of arms; Strasbourg, France, 182, 183-184

Coats of arms; Stuttgart, Germany, 218

Coats of arms; Swansea, Wales, 141, 142

Coats of arms; Sweden, 109, 111

Coats of arms; Tennessee, 318, 319

Coats of arms; Thurgau, Switzerland, 191, 192-193

Coats of arms; Transvaal, 280

Coats of arms; Uruguay, 349

Coats of arms; Vatican City, 241, 242

Coats of arms; Vaud, Switzerland, 191, 192-193

Coats of arms; Venice, Italy, 245, 246, 247-248

Coats of arms; Verdun, France, 183, 184
Coats of arms; Warsaw, Poland, 237, 238
Coats of arms; Waterloo, Belgium, 178, 180
Coats of arms; Weston-Super-Mare, England, 75, 76
Coats of arms; Wiesbaden, Germany, 219-220
Coats of arms; Wildbad, Germany, 217
Coats of arms; Yarmouth, England, 74, 75-76
Coats of arms; York, England, 133, 134
Coats of arms; Zurich, Switzerland, 195
Coffin-end, 14
Coin spoons; Argentina, 347, 348
Coin spoons; Austria, 229, 230
Coin spoons; Bavarian Taler, 219, 221
Coin spoons; Belgium, 178
Coin spoons; Bolivia, 343
Coin spoons; Brazil, 342
Coin spoons; Canada, 304
Coin Spoons; Costa Rica, 335
Coin spoons; Guatamala, 334, 335
Coin spoons; Ecuador, 342, 343
Coin spoons; Guam, 368, 370
Coin spoons; Hawaii, 366, 367
Coin spoons; Majorca, 323, 233
Coin spoons; Mexico, 90, 330, 331, 332
Coin spoons; Morocco, 270, 271
Coins spoons; Nova Scotia, 303
Coin spoons; Peru, 343, 344
Coin spoons; Portugal, 232
Coin spoons; Saudi Arabia, 267
Colmar, France, 182, 183
Cologne Cathedral, 203, 204-205, 206
Cologne, Germany, 203-205
Columbus, Christopher, 359-360
Copeland spoon, 10
Copenhagen, Denmark, 116, 117-120
Copper spoons, 3
Corinium Spoon, 2
Cornish pixie, 81
Coronation Chair, 153
Costa Rica, 335, 336
Coventry Cathedral, 131, 133-134
Cowper, William, 353, 354
Crescent & Star, Turkey, 262-263, 265, 266
Cross Cercelée, 81
Cross of Nails, 131, 133-134
Crowned Pigéon, New Guinéa, 383, 384
Crucifixion, 65
Crystal spoons, 24
Curacao, Netherlands Antilles, 339, 340
Cuzco, Peru, 344

Dancing dervish, Turkey, 263, 266
Dartmoor pixie, 80
Dauphin, Manitoba, 311, 312
Delft, the Netherlands, 175-176
Delphi, Greece, 256, 258
Denmark, 7, 112-121
Dessau, East German, 225, 226
Dessert spoon, 15
Dias, President, 333
Dickens, Charles, 69, 71
Die-embossed shell, 14
Dinant, Belgium, 178, 180

Dinewan, 372, 376
Disney, 329, 330
Disney World, 329
Donald Duck, 330
Double-die embossed, 16
Double-drop, 12
Dolphin handle, 2, 4
Dorothy, 80
Dorchester, England, 135, 137-138
Drake, Sir Francis, 69, 71-72
Dresden, East Germany, 222-223
Dublin, Ireland, 150, 151, 152
Dunkerque, France, 184, 185
Dutch parrot, 173, 176
Dutch shoes, 173, 175
Dutch spoons, 82
Dutch windmills, 170-173
Dybbøl Mølle, 113-114

Ear cleaning spoons, 92
Easter Island, 347
Edinburgh, Scotland, 76, 77, 144, 145-147
Edward VII, 158, 159, 161, 162
Edward VIII, 163, 164
Egg-shape, 11
Egyptian mummy, 272, 273-274
Egyptian spoons, 1, 3
18th century people, 166-167
Eilat, Israel, 269-270
Elizabeth II, 72, 73, 165-166
Emu, 374
Enamel, 24, 26
Engine General, 318, 319
English, 5
Engraved design, 16
Erfurt, East Germany, 224-225
Estoril, Portugal, 231
Evangelists, symbols of Matthew, Mark, Luke, John, 60ff
Exmoor Pixie, 80

Fairy tales, Hans Christian Andersen, 119, 120, 121
Falstaff, 69, 70
Fancy-back, 11, 12, 13
Fat Boy, 69, 71
Fiddleback, 15
Fig-shape, 11
Fiji Islands, 371, 373
Filigree, 26
"Finless" fiddleback, 14
Fiume, Yugoslavia, 237, 238
Flat handle, 11
Flags; British Empire, 124
Flags; Denmark, 111
Flags; Norway, 104, 107
Flags; Sweden, 109
Flags; Switzerland, 190, 193, 194
Flags; Union flag, 127
Flint spoons, 3
Florence, Italy, 248, 249, 250-252
Folding spoon, 5
Fork and spoon combinations, 17
Forks, 16
Fort William, Ontario, 308
Frankfurt, Germany, 215-216
Fraser River, 309-310
Franz Ferdinand, 350
Franz Joseph I, 350
Frederick II, 353
Frederick VIII, 114, 115, 116
Frederick IX, 114-115, 116
Freiburg, Germany, 214, 215
Friedrichshafen, Germany, 214
Fujiyama, Mt., 284-285

Galway, Ireland, 149-150
Gaya-Dari, 372, 375
Geneva, Switzerland, 192, 193, 194
George V, 153, 161-163, 164
George VI, 71, 72, 73, 155, 164
Genoa, Italy, 244
Geisha, 290-291
German Milkmaid, 220, 221
German Wager Cup Miniature, 208, 209
Germany, 8
Ghent, Belgium, 177-178
Giant's Causeway, 147, 148-149
Gibraltar, 236-237
Glace Bay, Nova Scotia, 303-304
Glasgow, Scotland, 143, 144-145
Glass, 6
Glastonbury Abbey, 138-140
Goethals, George Washington, 335, 337
Gold spoons, 6
Golden Dog, The, 306, 307
Good Luck spoons, 283, 284, 285
Goolay-Yali, 372, 375
Gooseman Fountain, 207, 208
Göteborg, Sweden, 109, 110
Granada, Spain, 234-235
Greek, 3
Greenland, 124
Guadeloupe, French West Indies, 341, 342
Guadalupe, Church of, Juarez, 333, 334
Guam, 368, 370
Guatamala, 334, 335
Gudbrandsal, Norway, 107, 108
Gudvangen, Norway, 107-108
Gulfport, Mississippi, 321, 322

Haakon VII, 104, 105
Hague, The, the Netherlands, 168-171, 174
Hallmarks, English, 7
Hamburg, Germany, 215, 216-217
Hand of Fatima, 267
Hanover, Germany, 214-215
Harp, 150, 151
Hatfield House, 129, 131-132
Havana, Cuba, 337, 338
Hawaii, 366-369
Hei Tiki, 380, 381
Heidelberg, Germany, 209, 210-211
Heilag, Olav, 102, 103
Helgoland, Germany, 220, 221, 222
Helsinki, Finland, 123
Helvetia, Switzerland, 192
Henry I, 154, 155
Henry VIII, 154-155
Henry, Patrick, 317
Hexagonal stems, 11
Hindenburg, 351
Honey Spoon, 295
Hong Kong, 282-283
Honiton, England, 137, 138
Horn Spoons, Northwest Coast, 312
Horn, Pre-Columbian, 312-313
Horn spoons, 3, 5, 6, 23, 24, 82
Horn of Ulphus, 80-81
Horse's hoof spoon, 20
Horus, 271, 272-273
Hotel Tivoli, Panama, 336
House of Parliament, 75, 76, 124-125, 127
Humbert I, 352

Iceland, 123
Infant feeding spoons, 95-98
India, 291-293, 294

Indian Elephant, 292, 293
Ingersoll, Ontario, 307
Innsbruck, Austria, 227, 229-230
Interlaken, Switzerland, 195, 196
Iona, Scotland, 147, 148
Iran, 5, 291
Iron Maiden of Nuremberg, 205-208
Iron spoons, 3
Island of Rhodes, 257, 258
Ivory handles, 23
Ivory, Pre-Columbian, 5
Ivory Spoons, Alaska, 3, 6, 24, 313-314, 315

Jacksonville, Florida, 324
Jade spoon, 283, 284
Jamaica, British West Indies, 340, 341
James II, 156
Japan, 291
Japanese, Shrine, 287
Java, 298, 299-300
Jenny Jones, Wales, 74, 75
Jerusalem, 268-269
Jeweled spoons, 23, 24
Joan of Arc, 358, 359
Joffre, Joseph J., 354, 355
Johannesburg, South African, 277, 278-279
Johnson, Dr. Samuel, 127-128
Juarez, Mexico, 333

Kaahumanu's spoons, 19
Kaiser Wilhelm, 350-351
Kalmar Union, 109, 110
Kamehameha I, 366-369
Kamehameha IV's silver, 19
Kangaroo, 373, 376
Karlsbad, Czechoslovakia, 236, 237
Karlstad, Sweden, 111
"Keel and disk", 3
Kendal, England, 75, 76
Killarney, Ireland, 149
Kirkaldy, Fife, Scotland, 147, 148
Kitchener, Horatio H., 354
Kiwi, 380, 381, 382
Knops; acorn, 3, 7
Knops; baluster, 8
Knops; diamond point, 4, 7
Knops; cherub-head, 7
Knops; dove, 8
Knops; eagle, 8
Knops; falcon, 8
Knops; fluted ball, 9
Knops; fruitlet, 8
Knops; ivory figure, 4
Knops; lion séjant, 6, 8, 10, 11
Knops; maiden head, 4, 7
Knops; owl, 6, 8
Knops; pine cone, 5, 6, 9
Knops; puritan, 8
Knops; ribbed ball, 9
Knops; scallop shell, 9
Knops; seal top, 6, 8, 9
Knops; slip-end, 5, 8
Knops; strawberry, 5
Knops; spear point, 9
Knops; trifid, 9
Knops; writhen, 6, 8
Knossos, Greece, 256-257
Koala, 373, 376-377
Kobe, Japan, 288, 290
Kookaburra, 373, 377
Korean spoons, 281, 282
Kronborg, Denmark, 113, 114
Kruger National Park, South Africa, 280, 281
Kyoto, Japan, 290

Lachine Rapids, Montreal, 304
Ladies of Plas Newydd, 74-75
Lady Godiva, 131, 132-133
Lapland, 124, 125, 126
Las Palmas, 235
Latten, 3, 9, 11
Lausanne, Switzerland, 193, 195-196
Leaf design, 77
Lebanon, 266-267
Legend of the Cock, 232-233
Leipzig, East Germany, 224-225
Leningrad, Russia, 257, 258
Liechtenstein, 198, 199
Liège, Belgium, 176
Lincoln Imp, 79, 80, 133, 134
Lion of Judah, 275, 276
Lisbon, 230-231
Little, Doctor G. W., 315-316
Little Mermaid, 118, 119
Little Miss Muffett, 356-357
Liverpool, England, 129, 131
Lizard, 295
Llangollan, Wales, 74-75
London, England, 77, 121-122, 125-128
Lourdes, France, 186, 187
Louise, Queen, 351, 352
Low Countries, 8
Lucerne, Switzerland, 191, 196, 197-198
Ludwig II, 217-218
Lurer, 112-113
Lute player, 166
Luther, Martin, 355
Luxembourg, 178, 180
Lyon, France, 187

MacDonald, Sir John Alexander, 361, 362
Madrid, Spain, 233
Maisonneuve, Sieur de, 305, 306
Majorca, 232, 233
Malmo, Denmark, 116
Malta, 139, 141-142
Margherita, 352, 353
Margrethe II, 113, 114, 115
Marie Antoinette, 352
Marienbad, Czechoslovakia, 236
Marrow spoons, 17, 18
Martinique, French West Indies, 341
Mary, Mary, Quite Contrary, 79
Mary, Queen, 162, 163
Mary, Queen of Scots, 71, 72, 354, 355
Master-draught of Burgermeister Nusch, 213
Matador, Mexico, 331
Mayan calendar, 334, 335
Mayflower II, 324, 325-326
Medicine spoons, 95-101
Melbourne, Australia, 377, 378
Menton, France, 189, 190
Merit spoons, 326
Mexican filigree spoons, 330-334
Mexican spoons, 329-334
Mexico, El Chanel, Colima, 3
Mickey Mouse, 330
Middle Ages, 6, 15
Mid-rib, 13
Midway Islands, 368, 369-370
Milan, Italy, 242-243
Minnie Mouse, 330
Mobile, Alabama, 316, 317
Mombasa, 276-277
Monaco, 189, 191-192
Monkey spoons, 86-89
Montevideo, Uruguay, 348, 349
Montreal, Canada, 304, 305, 306

Montreux, Switzerland, 195, 196
Moscow, Russia, 257, 258
Moses, 274-275
Mosiac, 26
Mote spoons, 16, 17, 18
Mt. Hood, Oregon, 323
Mt. Lavinin, Ceylon, 296
Mozart, Wolfgang Amadeus, 362
Muddler, 91
Munich, Germany, 210, 211
Musicians, 221
Musicians of Bremen, 203, 205
Musicians; German, 220
Mustache spoons, 92-95
"My Broom", 20

Nabob, 78, 79
Nairobi, 275
Nancy, France, 187
Nantes, France, 184-185
Naples, Italy, 251, 252-253
Napoléon, 360-361
Narita-San Temple, 290
Narvik, Norway, 106-107
Nassau, 337-338
National Statue of the Niederwald, 202, 203
Nazareth, 270
Needles, California, 319, 320
Nelson, Horatio, 357, 358
Nepal, 297
Netherlands, The, 167-177
Neuchâtel, Switzerland, 191
Neuschwanstein Castle, 217-218
New Zealand Fantail, 382, 383
New Zealand Greenstone, 378, 379-380
New Zealand Kingfisher, 381, 382
New Zealand Tui, 381, 382-383
Newcastle-Upon-Tyne, 133, 135-136
Niagara Falls, Ontario, 304
Nice, France, 187, 188-189
Nicholas II (Russia), 259
Niello, 260-262
Nikko, Japan, 287, 288-289
Noah, 64, 65
Norge, Norway, 105, 106
Normandie, France, 184, 185
Norsk Christmas spoon, 108, 109
North Battleford, Canada, 310-311
Norway, 78
Norway at the Fair, 107
Northwest Coast Horn spoons, 312-313
Northwest Coast Indian, 5
Notre Dame de Montreal, 304-305, 306
Nouméa, New Caledonia, 370, 372-373
Nova Scotia, 303
Nuremberg Castle, 210
Nuremberg, Germany, 206-208
Nuremberg, Iron Maiden of, 206-208

Oban, Scotland, 143-144
Obelisk of Usertsen, 270-272
Oberammergau, Germany, 211-212
Olav V, 105
"Old English" pattern, 13, 14
Old Fort Henry, Kingston, 302-303
Olympic Games, Berlin, 202
Onslow, 13
Oscar II, 110, 111
Olso, Norway, 108-109
Osnabrück, Germany, 213-214
Ostende, Belgium, 177-178
Ottawa, Canada, 302, 303
Owl, 20, 79
Oxford, England, 75, 76

Pagoda, 284, 285
Paisley, Scotland, 143
Palermo, Italy, 253-254
Panama, 335, 336, 337
Pap & Caudle spoons, 94-95
Papua & New Guinea, 384
Paris Exhibition, 1900, 181-182
Paris, France, 179-182
Parrot, 373
Paua shell, 379, 380-381
Penang, 298-299
Penticton, British Columbia, 310, 311
Perkeo, 209, 210
Pewter spoons, 3, 6, 9
Philippine Islands, 368, 369, 371
Philippine wooden spoon, 22
Pipe cleaning spoon, 91
Pisa, Italy, 244, 245-247
Pittsburgh, Pennsylvania, 320, 321-322
Pixies, 79, 81
Pixie Puck, 81
Plique-à-jour, 24, 25, 26
Plum Blossom, 283
Pluto, 330
Plymouth, England, 135, 138
Pompeii, Italy, 253
Porcelain, 24
Porringer spoon, 15
Port Arthur, Ontario, 307-308
Port Elizabeth, South Africa, 278, 279
Port Glasgow, Scotland, 76-77
Portage La Prairie, Manitoba, 311, 312
Postage stamp spoons, Austria, 227
Postage stamp spoons; Panama, 336
Postage stamp spoons, Switzerland, 196
Postage stamp spoons; United States, 328-329
Pottery, Pre-Columbian, 5
Pottery spoon, 3
Pottsdam, East Germany, 224, 225
Prague, Czechoslovakia, 237-238
Pre-Columbian, 5
Pretoria, South Africa, 279-280
Prince Edward Island, Canada, 303
Pudsey spoon, 6
Puerto Rico, 338

Quebec, Canada, 307
Queenstown, N.Z., 382, 383-384

Raleigh, Sir Walter, 71, 72
Rangoon, 298, 299
Rarotonga, Cook Islands, 371, 374
Rat-tail, 12
Red Cross, Denmark, 113, 114
Richfield Springs, New York, 321-322
Richard I, 154, 155
Riva, Italy, 244-245
Rock crystal spoons, 3, 6
Rolex spoons, 199
Roman silver, 4
Roman spoons, 1, 3, 5, 6, 15
Rome, Italy, 238, 239, 240-241
Rose of Hildebrand, 26
Roswell, New Mexico, 323
Rothenburg, Germany, 212-213
Rotterdam, the Netherlands, 171, 176
Rouen, France, 185, 186
Royal Canadian Air Force, 301
Royal Canadian Mounted Police, 302-303
Royal Visit, 164, 301
Runic inscriptions, 102, 104
Russell, Lillian, 317-318
Russian enamel, 259-260
Russian lacquer, 258-259

Russian silver standards, 262
Russian spoons, 257-262

Sachs, Hans, 208, 209-210
Saffron Walden, England, 129, 131
St. Albans, Vermont, 317, 318
St. Andrews, City of, England, 75, 76
St. Augustine, 61, 63
St. Augustine, Florida, 319-320
St. Blaise, 63
St. Gallen, Switzerland, 192
St. George and the Dragon, 122-123
St. Lawrence Seaway, 305, 306
St. Lucia, British West Indies, 340-341
St. Malo, France, 183, 184
St. Mary's Abbey, 133
St. Michael, 66
St. Nicholas, 61, 63
St. Olav, 62, 63, 108
St. Paul's Cathedral, London, 126-127
St. Stephen's Cathedral, Vienna, 225-226
Saints, 10
Salisbury, Rhodesia, 278, 279
Salt spoons, 18, 89-91
Salzburg, Austria, 227-229
Samisen, 286, 288
San Remo, Italy, 244
San Sebastián, Spain, 235
Saskatoon, Saskatchewan, 311, 312
Schaffhausen, Switzerland, 191
Scheveningen, the Netherlands, 170
Schweiz, Switzerland, 193, 194
Scorpions, 293-295
Scotland, 4
Scottish Highlander, 141, 142
Scottish Thistle, 145, 146-147
Seal-top, 10, 11
Selangor, 297
Semmes, Adm. Raphael, 316, 317
Serpentine, 6
Seven gods of happiness, 286, 287-288
Seville, Spain, 234, 235
Shakespeare, William, 68, 70, 356
Shamrock, 150, 151
Sheaf-of-wheat design, 14
Shell design, 14
Shell, Pre-Columbian, 5
Shells as spoons, 1
Ships; Canberra, 364-366
Ships; Corsican, 305
Ships; Dutch, 173
Ships; Himalaya, 364-366
Ships; Imperator, 221, 222
Ships; Kaiser Wilhelm II, 222-223
Ships; Kronprinzessin Cecilie, 222, 223
Ships; Lucania, 222-223
Ships; Mayflower, 324-326
Ships; Monterey, 364-366
Ships; Orcades, 364-366
Ships; Oriana, 364-366
Ships; Viking, 102, 106, 109
Show Me. I Am From Missouri!, 316
Siena, Italy, 254
Silver spoons, 2, 6
Singapore, 297-298
Skyline spoons, 326, 327, 328
Slate spoons, 3
Snakes, 292, 293-295
Snuff spoons, 18, 91-93
Sorrento, Italy, 254
Southern Rhodesia, 82
Sphinx, 271, 272
Spitzbergen, Norway, 107
Stalheim, Norway, 106
Stanley Park, 310, 311
State Emblem, India, 292, 293

Stems, beaded border, 14
Stems, bright-cut, 14
Stems, feather-edge, 14
Stems, fiddle, 14
Stems, flat, 12
Stems, four-sided, 11
Stewart Island, N.Z., 383, 384
Stirling Castle, Stirling, Scotland, 146, 148
Stockholm, Sweden, 110-111
Stone, Pre-Columbian, 5
Strasbourg, France, 182, 183-184
Stratford, New Zealand, 383, 384
Stratford-Upon-Avon, 68, 70, 131, 132
Stuttgart, Germany, 218
Sugar masher, 91
Suleiman I, signature of, 264-265, 266
Suomi (Finland), 122, 123
Sutton Hoo, 2
Sutton Hoo, ship burial, 4
Sverige, 109, 110
Swan, 374
Swansea, Wales, 141, 142
Swiss cantons, 191, 192-193
Swiss chalet, 193
Switzerland, 190-198
Sydney, Australia, 377, 378
Syria, 267-268

Tablespoon, 15
Tahiti, 370, 371-372
Taiwan, 281-282
Tampico, Mexico, 331
Taunton, Massachusetts, 316
Teaspoons, 15
Tel-Aviv, 269
Tell, William, 197, 198-199
Thailand, 299-300
Thames, New Zealand, 383, 384
Thistle, 79
Thread design, 14
Three Wise Monkeys, 292, 293
Thurgau, Switzerland, 191
Thyra, 116
Tibet, 293
Tijuana, Mexico, 333
Tinned iron, 6
Tobacco leaf, Rhodesia, 79
Toledo, Spain, 234, 235
Toronto, Canada, 78, 302
Tower of London, 125-126
Transvaal Province, 280
Traprain Law, 1, 2, 4
Treat, Robert, 354, 355
Treen, 22, 23
Trifid-end, 10, 12, 13
Trinidad, West Indies, 339, 340
Triskelion, 256
Trondheim fisherman, 107, 108
Trondheim, Norway, 104-105
Trusty Servant, 129, 130
Tudor Rose, 155
Turkish spoons, 262-266

Uganda, 82-83
U.S. Capitol, Wash., D.C., 316

Valais, Switzerland, 193, 195
Valparaiso, Chile, 345, 346
Van Dyke, Anthony, 358-359
Vancouver, British Columbia, 309-310
Vasco Da Gama, 231, 232
Vatican City, Italy, 241-242
Vaud, Switzerland, 191
Venice, Italy, 245, 246, 247-250
Verdun, France, 183, 184
Victoria, British Columbia, 308, 309
Victoria Falls, South Africa, 280, 281

Victoria, Queen, 157, 158, 159-160
Victorian spoons, 19, 21
Victory Column, 201
Vienna, Austria, 225-228
Vietnam, 300
Vikings, 102-103
Virgin Islands, 338-339
Virgin Mary, 61, 62
Vision of Eustachius, 63, 64

Wagner, Wilhelm Richard, 362
Waitomo Caves, N.Z., 382, 383
Walla Walla, Washington, 320-321
Walrus ivory spoons, 313-314
Warsaw, Poland, 237, 239
Warwick, England, 131, 132
Warwick Castle, England, 78
Washington, George, 355

Waterloo, Belgium, 178, 180
Wayang, 298
Wavy end, 11, 13
Welden, Jesse, 317-318
Weller, Sam, 69, 71
Wellington, N.Z., 382, 383
Wells, Ancient Gate House, 72, 73
Wells Cathedral, 73-74
Welsh love spoons, 22, 23
Weston-Super-Mare, England, 75, 76
Whistle spoon, 18, 21
Wiesbaden, Germany, 219-220
Wildbad, Germany, 217
Wilhelm, Prince, 351
Wilhelmina I, 353, 354
William III, 156, 157
William and Mary, 156, 158
William Tell Chapel, 198

Willimantic, Connecticut, 323, 324
Winchester, England, 77-78
Windmills, Dutch, 170-173
Wood, chip of, 5
Wood, Pre-Columbian, 5
Wooden spoons, 3, 6, 24
Wookey, Witch of, 81-82

Yarmouth, England, 74, 75-76
Ye Olde Cheshire Cheese, 127-128
Yokohama, Japan, 287, 289
York, England, 134-135

Zanzibar Clove, 275
Zambia (Northern Rhodesia), 278, 279
Zurich, Switzerland, 195, 196-197